Drinking in the Rivers

Drinking in the Rivers

VOL I: THE MEMORABLE PUBS AND UNFORGETTABLE
CHARACTERS OF THE MURRAY AND EDWARD RIVERS

Colin Whelan

NEW
HOLLAND

CONTENTS

DEDICATION

Just two days before the manuscript deadline for this book, my mother,
Helen McDougall Whelan, died – peacefully and without pain.
More than any other person or factor, my mother was the instiller of my spirit and my passion.

This book is dedicated to her memory.

AUTHOR'S NOTE

On 31 December 2019, New Year's Eve, the Upper Murray was hit with the first of three horrendous waves of bushfires. For almost a month the people on the river east of Albury lived with choking smoke and fought continuous ember attacks to save their properties and stock.

I had already visited all the pubs in this area several times but felt compelled to return as soon as the roads were reopened. The devastation that I found toward the end of January was as mind-numbing as the resilience and the spirit of the people I met were inspiring.

Then, of course, in early 2020 COVID-19 changed the landscape. Forever. The entire country took the hits but few communities suffered more incomprehensible and arguably inappropriate restrictions and difficulties than the border communities, especially those along the Murray.

New Holland decided to delay this book's publication from August 2020, firstly until Christmas – when the pandemic would be a memory, right? – and then until August 2021.

Another run along the length of the majestic river, another visit to so many wonderful pubs, was in order.

No pub, and few publicans, licensees, managers or patrons were left unscarred. Thankfully only a very few of the marvellous old mates whom I'd encountered had passed away. Tributes to them are within the rewritten chapters. But COVID and legislative bastardry had killed off one pub – the Grand Central in Cobram – and so chapter 22 is the most heavily changed from the original.

But through all these challenges the resilience and the strength of the pubs' owners and the loyalty of their clientele won through. The fires of 2019–20 and COVID have, if anything, reaffirmed the centrality of pubs to communities, and the importance of communities to pubs. And these events also caused this book to grow from a recognition of these places to become a true celebration of them and the people on both sides of the bars within.

This project had been planned to read as a single trip along Australia's greatest river, but the return to the burn zone and the very necessary coverage of the immediate aftermath of the bushfires, plus the post-COVID lockdown updates, make some of the chapters a little jumpy. I hope the reader will understand and will forgive.

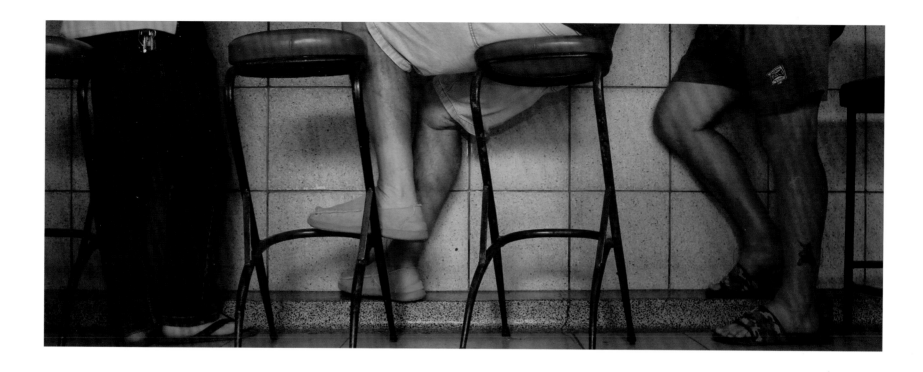

INTRODUCTION

Since time immemorial the rivers have been the arteries of Australia's red heart.

Defining 'a river' in a very different way to subsequent peoples – not differentiating between the flows and the banks but including the totality in their concept – the First Nation people of this continent used them as a food source and as a navigation aid.

When whites arrived and began venturing out from the coastal fringes, the rivers and the fantasy of a rich inland sea preoccupied most of the explorers from Mitchell to Leichhardt.

And as the nascent Australian literature and poetry developed, the words of the artists reflected the pre-eminent role that rivers played in the thinking of urban dwellers and those pushing into the interior.

Banjo Paterson exemplified this state of mind. His 'Man' didn't come from the Snowy Mountains, he was 'from Snowy River', just as Clancy wasn't from Condoblin, he was 'of the Overflow'. Banjo hadn't met him in Cowra or some town like that, he, 'met him down the Lachlan' and didn't imagine him gone a'droving around Tambo or Charters Towers – his mind saw him 'down the Cooper'.

The bush christening took place where 'churches were few and men of religion were scanty' – but that wasn't Isisford or Yaraka, it was 'On the outer Barcoo'.

And of course the 'matilda' wasn't waltzed at any town or roadside, it was unfurled as the billy boiled beside a 'billabong'.

When 'Banjo' took on the persona of a shearer, he defined where he'd shore in terms of rivers, boasting that he'd:

... coasted on the Barwon—low down the Darling, too,
I've been on the Murrumbidgee, and out on the Paroo;

Before finally explaining that:

so you can understand, my boys, just from this little rhyme,
I'm a Murrumbidgee shearer, and one of the good old time.

The rivers defined not just the landscape but also the people.

These flows were sustaining but also dividing: they facilitated exploration but also acted as obstacles to be overcome, to be crossed; they brought people together but they also became barriers.

And no river has played a more important role in the development of this nation than the Murray. For around 1850 kilometres it defines who is a Victorian and who is New South Welsh; but if it divided the colonies, this river, known to first nation people as the Milawa, also unified the new occupants.

The inter-colonial tariffs of the late-19th century brought about the construction of customs houses at all crossings of the Murray east of Renmark, and the outrage at the imposition of these taxes gave birth to the Federation Leagues, which originated along each side of its banks. They became the irresistible flood tide of sentiment which brought about the unification of the continent into a single country.

The Murray and the obstacle its waters constituted to travellers, especially drovers and bullock teams, represented a special money-making opportunity to a special mob of astute businessmen.

In 1846 the Bell brothers opened the first punt across the Murray at Wellington. It was rough, it was hand pulled, it was barely buoyant but it was beside the pub they'd built the previous year. In doing so, they became the foundation members of the 'Pub 'n' Punter' club. They were soon joined by a ragtag mob of opportunists, exploiters, mean-spirited hard-headed capitalists, and a few social altruists and canny businessmen.

From Tintaldra to Jingellic to Howlong to Wahgunyah, Corowa, Echuca, Moama and beyond they realised that travellers needed to cross the river, and those waiting to cross needed feeding, their thirsts quenched, and a comfortable bed to break their journeys.

They soon appreciated that drovers needed pens for their sheep and cattle and the bullockies needed spelling yards for their beasts. And so, cheek by jowl beside their punts they built pubs on large grounds with paddocks and yards out the back for the animals and rooms with not much more comfort inside for the workers.

The crossing places grew and as business flourished the publicans would inevitably fight losing battles against the applications for the second and then the third pub in the settlement.

Before the railways came, the rivers were the trade routes of much of the interior. For almost a century from the late 1800s daily newspapers would carry a column on the 'shipping news' which would give equal coverage to the ports on the coast and to those on the major rivers. As the port towns along the Murray and the Darling grew, so too did the pubs.

Governments which oversaw the killing of the riverboat trade by the introduction of the railways, were in turn followed by legislators who facilitated the death of those same railways. With the river trade gone, and rail tracks rusting all over the country, all that seems left for politicians to kill is the river itself.

The pubs – the hubs of the towns – felt, and still feel, each body blow to their communities, but these places which provide such social glue have faced their own challenges – some more than others.

In 1885 Alfred Deakin, who was to become our second (and fifth and seventh) prime minister, caught up with George and William Chaffey, a pair of brothers in California, and convinced George to come to Victoria. George duly arrived in Melbourne and headed up to the Murray, liked what he saw, called his brother to sell everything and join him down under.

In 1886, in what was probably the first instance of this country 'selling the farm' to foreigners, the brothers signed a deal for control of a quarter of a million acres of prime riverside land. In 1887 Victoria passed the *Chaffey Brothers Irrigation Works Act* granting them extraordinary rights and privileges.

The Chaffeys were irrigation pioneers and they undertook to develop an irrigation industry on the Murray around Mildura, and in a similar deal with the South Australians, they nabbed the same amount of land around Renmark and Berri.

But the brothers weren't just irrigators. They were also wowsers – strong temperance fanatics – and the deal included making the entire half a

million acres devoid of hotels. It was fine for the young of the colonies to work up thirsts in the scorching heat of summer. They just weren't permitted to quench it.

By 1893 the Chaffeys were insolvent, but over a century later the open wounds they inflicted on the pub culture along the river Murray are still unhealed and weeping.

These brothers grim weren't the last wowser threat to the health of pubs along the river. In 1916 early closing was forced upon the nation by the emboldened temperance movement. Slated as a necessary war measure to keep the soldiers sober, it remained a hobble – especially on working people – until 1955 in New South Wales, 1966 in Victoria and until 1967 in South Australia.

That so many memorable pubs along the Murray, and its anabranch the Edward, survived these challenges – so many hotels both rich in their own character and filled with other characters – is a testament to the core values of the bush and to the continuing role pubs have in their local communities.

Their stories today are inevitably intertwined with the river and with their yesterdays. Savouring the pubs, enjoying them and soaking them in, necessarily involves swimming deeply in their histories and refreshing in their waters.

I hope I've managed to do the places and the people justice. These are their stories, not mine. I hope they will entice, encourage, tempt and motivate you not just to visit and have a drink in the pubs, but also to, in a different sense, *drink in the river* and its people.

Because one thing can be guaranteed: when you push your money across the bar to the publican for a drink at a country hotel, both of you'll get just a fraction richer.

CHAPTER 1 – BENAMBRA

THE BEGINNING OF THE RIVER AND THE END OF NOT JUST THE WORLD

Myths – if you don't love 'em you're on the wrong river.

Ava Gardner came to Australia in 1959 to star as the local love interest of Gregory Peck's character in an adaptation of Nevil Shute's post-apocalyptic book, *On the Beach*. Two years earlier – having divorced husband number one actor Mickey Rooney due to his incessant adultery in 1943, and then divorcing jazz musician Artie Shaw in 1946 after just a year of being hitched – she'd divorced her third husband, a singer named Frank Sinatra.

The film also had a young up-and-comer by the name of Anthony Perkins (who went on to star as Norman Bates in Hitchcock's *Psycho*) playing an Australian Navy officer. His and Ava's Aussie accents are right up there on the credibility scale with Sean Connery's Russian (from Edinburgh) accent in *The Hunt for Red October*.

Anyway, so Ava knew a bit about apocalyptic endings, but she grew bored of Bleak City, and her dalliance with a local jazz singer wasn't all she craved so she called Ol' Blue Eyes. Sinatra was free and had cancelled a tour down here a few years earlier, so he organised some new gigs and headed to Melbourne.

Sinatra's concert at the old Festival Hall was recorded by Max Hull, but it was almost forty years until the record was released as *With the Red Norvo Quintet: Live in Australia, 1959*. It's described as 'one of the wildest performances he ever recorded'.

It was while she was waiting for her ex-husband, now gigolo for hire, Frank, to arrive in early 1959 that one of the truly great and enduring myths of (semi) recent Victorian history was born – the one that goes: 'Ava

Gardner said that Melbourne is an ideal place for a film about the end of the world.'

Well, er ... she didn't.

It was an invention by Neil Jillett, a hack for Sydney's *Sun Herald,* who inserted the line into his story on the making of the film as 'a joke' that he knew would be appreciated north of the Murray because Ava wasn't giving interviews and the best thing to do in such circumstances is follow that indispensable journalists' policy known as 'MSU' – Make Stuff Up.

Melbourne might have a history of hosting big-budget productions (like *The Castle*) but towns across Victoria have had their share of the limelight too – places like Muckleford, Craigburn, Little River and Dimboola.

And also on the list is Benambra – closest pub town to the western end of the Black-Allan Line, that straight bit of the border between the Port Phillip District and New South Wales, which stretches from the east coast at Cape Howe to the extreme headwaters of the Murray at Indi Springs. Population around forty, it's a village with its own connections to thespian arts – and it's not without its own odd myth or two.

I pull Super Ten, my motorbike, up across the road from the pub at the southern end of the village. I'm right outside Slim's Barbershop – its venetian blinds down and closed, four old tyres resting against the peeling paint and the wooden front door is bolted. No red and blue pole out front, and no price list in the window. You get the feeling that nothing much has happened here for yonks and I'm thinking the only locks around this barbershop are those on the doors.

Turns out that it's not so much that Slim's has been a long time closed: more like it's been closed forever.

In 2010 Aussie film director Patrick Hughes rode into Benambra with a posse of actors and a film crew to shoot what would be his breakthrough movie, *Red Hill*. In place of an insatiable Hollywood diva and make-'em-swoon leading man, the film starred Ryan Kwanten and Claire van der Boom. (She went on to star in stuff like *5 Flights Up* with Morgan Freeman and Diane Keaton, while in same year Kwanten would be the voice of the title character in *Blinky Bill the Movie*. Now that's what some call career path divergence!)

Anyway, *Red Hill* had a bloke named Christopher Davis, who played a barber named Slim, whose shop was set up right where I'm parked. No-one in the town can be bothered to remove the sign from the window of what actually, many years ago, was a tiny store selling 'lollies and ice cream and milkshakes'.

They must like the old signs in this place. Hanging over the entrance to the bar at the pub across the road is an old faded advertisement for Courage beer, which was launched in October 1968, struggled against the Carlton United juggernaut (in a time when the breweries owned most of the pubs) for just under a decade, and then was taken over by Tooheys, which closed all the brands in 1978. So that sign over the public bar entrance is around fifty years old and it's been irrelevant for over forty of them. That's half the lifetime of the pub in roughly its present shape.

In 1928 Margaret Canny, the publican, had been issued an order to rebuild the hotel by Licensing Inspector Ashton and she fronted the court that August. Mounted Constable Collins testified that the pub had been erected in 1880 and:

> *The walls ... were of hessian and paper, and there was sawdust in between which was full of bugs and fleas ... the galvanized iron roof ... had rotted and every room in the hotel let in water during wet weather. The foundation blocks were almost eaten away with white ants ... Thousands of bugs were nested in the saw dust, and they could not be got out. In the bedsteads ... there were nests of bugs and 'knits' [sic].*

Okay, who's itching just reading that? Coulda, shoulda shot a horror movie there.

In the background the leaders of Victoria's temperance movement were mobilising their followers in a campaign to outlaw all liquor in the state. Margaret Canny's case was adjourned for a month and when she returned to court she 'asked the Licensing Court to allow temporary improvements to be made. She explained that a modern building would be put up in 1930 if prohibition was not brought in.'

The court agreed and in December 1929 Premier Hogan announced that 'the referendum on prohibition would be taken on March 29th, 1930. Voting would be compulsory.'

For prohibition to be introduced, it had to be supported by at least 60 per cent of the vote. The Drys came nowhere close, managing just 43.3 per cent. The *Sydney Morning Herald* toasted the victory with a three-tier headline:

THE WETS
Sweep the Polls
VICTORIAN REFERENDUM

And the pubs – which were still shackled by six o'clock closing – were out of danger from total annihilation.

Margaret Canny had gambled on this result and had advertised for tenders for the building of her new brick hotel. She was forced to have it constructed down the road from the original place and, though it's been modified a few times since, as I head inside, it's pretty much as it was eighty years ago.

Chris is the only out-of-towner in the bar apart from me. He reckons he first came to Benambra about ten years ago, and by then he'd been fascinated by this area and the source of the Murray for, probably five years.

'I've had a few bad years. Four strokes and a triple by-pass and I could hardly walk. Walking became an aim for me. Just trying to take ten steps. And then fifteen and then twenty. I just tried to do a bit better each day. Then I got to do 300 metres, 150 out and 150 back and the next day my wife took out an AVO against me and had me kicked out of home. I had two kids with her – they're four and eight now. Anyway I went to live with my adult son from my first marriage and his place was a kilometre and a half from the shop so I set that as my goal and eventually could walk there and back.'

Chris hasn't been permitted to see his kids since the day he left.

'So I was living with my son and was getting the hang of walking again and I had no-one who cared how I was or where I was so I thought if I can't be with the people I want – my kids – I might as well be where I wanted.

THE WETS.

VICTORIAN REFERENDUM.

Polling throughout Victoria on Saturday resulted in a sweeping victory for the opponents of "no license."

The "yes" votes numbered 43.32 per cent. of the total, whereas 60 per cent. was required to carry the proposal.

Only in seven of the 65 State electorates, each of which was regarded as a licensing district for the purpose of the poll, were there majorities in favor of no license. These were:—

Boroondara, 55 per cent. of votes polled; Brighton, 50.1 per cent.; Gouldburn Valley 51 per cent., Kew,

FAR BACK HOTEL.

Tourists' Complaints.

According to evidence given before the Full Licensing Court yesterday the surroundings of the Benambra Hotel, Benambra, are not giving complete satisfaction to those venturous spirits who penetrate the country between Omeo and Tom Groggin's Crossing near the foot of Mount Kosciusko. An order had been served upon Mrs. Margaret Canny as owner and Mr. Arthur H. Tuckwell (licensee as agent pending probate) calling upon them to rebuild the premises. The matter came before the Full Licensing Court yesterday. Inspector Ashton appeared for the police, and Mr. J. P. Minogue appeared for Mrs. Canny and Tuckwell

Mounted-constable Colin Campbell, of the Benambra district, in evidence, said that the place was built 48 years ago.

So I packed some stuff and got my son to drive me to the train station and I headed to Omeo.'

And started walking.

His plan is to walk to Indi Springs and stand astride the Murray.

'And then down the Murray as far as Kerang and then down to Ararat' and after that he's not sure.

He walks in open scuffs – no socks – because 'I can't stand my feet being bound up', and pushes a small four-wheeled cart which 'helps me stay upright'.

No tent, no sleeping bag, no water-proof gear, no thermals. And no shoes.

'But every step's a victory for me. I keep falling over – you can see the scars – but I keep getting up … and just maybe each step gets me closer to the places I want to see. And to my kids.'

I wish him luck as we move outside. As I get some drone shots of the pub, Chris pushes his cart down the side to the room he'll be staying in for a couple of nights before he makes tracks north for a place he's long wanted to be in but in circumstances he wishes he wasn't.

Johnno behind the bar came up from Hayfield around the time the Slim's Barbershop opened for non-business, liked the town, saw the pub was for sale, and bought it.

You get the feeling early that he runs it on his terms: opens around 5.30 most days and closes when the last person goes home. When I ask about meals, the response makes me glad I'm not hungry. The food sounds decent but at this time of evening, he's not too keen to cook it. When I mention the tribulations of Margaret Canny in 1928–29 he tells me he has no clue about the history of the place.

There's a clump of locals – my estimate is they make up 10 per cent of the area's populace – discussing the day's events. Off on his own at a middle table there's a bloke who's fair tuckered – been pushing cattle along the road all day and not much in the mood for a chat.

Over in the group one fella talks of being an extra in *Red Hill*. He tells of how they just came into town, asked who was interested, didn't pay anyone but provided pretty decent grub. He was an extra in the town hall scene,

shot inside Benambra's hall, where they returned six months later for a community screening of the finished movie. Walking-Chris and I are the first visitors here for weeks.

'Quietest summer I've ever had,' says Johnno.

Of the three groups who come here, the fishermen have no reason because 'the fires and the rain have turned the rivers to mud and the fish have vanished', the hunters have nothing because 'all the deer have migrated to New South Wales' and the dirt bike riders haven't been able to get here because 'the main road in from Bruthen has been closed for half the summer'.

And the road north through the Nariel Valley isn't opening any time soon.

Back in 1929 the scrupulous Inspector Ashton stressed the importance of a quality hotel in Benambra: 'A road is being constructed to Wagga, which will reduce the road distance between Melbourne and Canberra by 150 miles. A new road to Lakes Entrance is also being made.'

And then, to give weight to his case to force the pub to rebuild he invented his own myth for the town: 'Benambra is going to be one of the most important tourist resorts in the Commonwealth.'

Well, that didn't quite turn out did it? The *Gippsland Times* of 14 February 1929 quoted Licensing Inspector Ashton as saying:

The people of Benambra are opposed to the present site, which in winter is a quagmire, making motor transport difficult. The present premises had formerly been a cheese factory, and refuse from the factory has worked into the soil, rendering it very unsatisfactory.

Yep, rancid cow juice and stinking mud, combined with the fleas, bugs and nits in the beds, aren't about to entice too many tourists, so I'm with him on that.

But despite Ava Gardner being falsely accused of claiming Melbourne was a fitting place for a film about the end of the world, the putrid lactose under the Benambra hotel would've given it a fair claim to being, well, at the end of the entire Milky Way.

And that'd be no myth at all.

CHAPTER 2 – CORRYONG

MORE MYTHS OF MEN, HOTELS, DOGS AND HORSES

Forget nailing the daily double, how's this for a trifecta?

On 28 December 1882 in Corryong's Court of Petty Sessions, Sarah King successfully got off a charge of throwing a glass of dirty water at a bloke named William Riley by claiming he'd made use of 'language unfit for ears polite', in fact more disgusting than the water.

Later that same day the Licensing Court granted Mrs King a licence for the Courthouse Hotel.

She wasn't done yet! Back at the Court of Petty Sessions, as her public notice in the Albury paper announced, she, 'did ... apply for and obtain(ed) ... an ORDER to PROTECT MY PROPERTY and EFFECTS from my husband ...'

So ... gets off a charge of assault, secures the licence for a pub and dumps her husband. Probably celebrated that day with a coldie or two.

She must've flourished from the outset. A traveller the following July wrote of 'Mrs King's Hotel, newly painted' but just over a year later the pub was on the market, being touted as 'the only licensed house in the rapidly rising township of Corryong'. Which is a little weird. Back in 1883, on the same day Sarah King was granted a renewal of her licence for the Courthouse, the same court granted a transfer, 'from Janet McVean to Thomas McVean for the Corryong Hotel' which had been trading since at least 1877. Maybe Thomas went bust or maybe we'll just stick another one in the 'myth' column.

Anyway, the advertisement for the Courthouse Hotel claimed the place had eleven rooms, but by the time it was resold in 1891, 'a portion of the building (was) quite new (with) six brick rooms ... being just finished'. This had increased the place to a total of twenty-four rooms, including a large billiard room. Sounds like it was flourishing but, er, maybe not.

Two weeks after placing this ad, the publican, John Hughes, was found head down at the bottom of the hotel's well. In the weeks prior he'd been showing 'evidence of mental aberration'.

It's not long after opening when I front up to this airy bar-room lit by the morning sun through its front windows. The early odds are on the unobtrusive screens at the back wall – a pool table, well-worn and with good space on each side awaits attention off to one side.

So far Murray (yep, same as the river) has only pulled beers for a couple of blokes this morning and Ernie's just finishing his first pot for the day whilst Grumblebum's lips are still to touch liquor.

Ernie was born just down the river a bit at Towong – reckons he can remember the old pub there but he'd be pushing it; maybe the building was still standing when he was young. The place was closed by the Licences Reduction Board in 1913 but talk of Towong stirs George up and it turns out that like Benambra, back up the road, this place has its touch of Tinseltown.

'We got a racecourse out there, beautiful old grandstand, actually I think we had two grandstands and for some reason one of them was owned by New South Wales and the other by Victoria, anyway we have this annual Cup Day meeting – it's called the Flemington of the bush, second biggest racecourse in Victoria, it's where they filmed the movie *Phar Lap*.

So anyway, sometime in the 1920s they had Towong Cup Day and Squizzy

Taylor turned up. He had a whole lot of thugs with him and they stirred up a makeshift fight in the bookies' ring and while they were fighting, Squizzy and some others went in and stole all the takings.'

Later I track down a newspaper from 1928 and its report reads:

Towong Race Club, Wagga [sic], had an exciting day on January 16. Two jockeys flogged each other during the race, and continued the fight in the saddling paddock. The racehorse Euda was so over-doped that blindness and paralysis set in. And the whole of the day's takings were stolen.

Apart from that it was just another day at the races. (A number of subsequent articles heap scepticism and scorn on the claim that the heist can be put down to Squizzy. Another one in the myth column!)

Meanwhile, Grumblebum's settled onto his usual 'strategic' perch at the end of the bar with a coffee he didn't need to order. His real name's George and he's been coming here pretty much every day for twenty years. Starts every morning with the same coffee from Murray and once this is out of the way, just like every morning, he'll have a middy of the good stuff and then maybe go for a tour to the shops.

He's both a punter and a drinker and his is the one stool in the entire bar which is near the beer taps 'so my drink's always fresh' and from where every single race screen on the back wall is visible.

I ask him what he prefers to invest in, horses or dogs.

'Whatever's running next,' is the quiet, smiled reply, 'whatever's running next'.

'My right eye doesn't work, it's only there for cosmetic reasons to make me look good, I lost that in a car accident, they tried to fix it for years but the retina had too much damage. But my other one's bionic, truly, and I can read all those screens over there without glasses or anything. I had a cataract taken out and an artificial lens put in. Now I can easily see all the money I lose!'

Out front of the hotel, right beside the door, I'd passed a blue electric buggy, and on its footrest is a small dog, peering out from an enveloping bed. I ask George if the buggy's his.

'Hell no,' he replies. 'I'm just the dog's designated driver.'

George adopted Ajax a year or so ago, 'and that donut he's sitting in is his security blanket and at home he'll move it around into the sunny spots. When I'm getting ready to leave home he'll go and grab that and carry it

out to the scooter. He decides if he's going to come. Sometimes I'll just take off and he'll let me go but when he wants to come out he'll just stand there with his cushion in his mouth waiting for me. I put a little hand warmer in there to keep him warm.'

Much less demanding than George's previous dog: 'Patch was a miniature foxy and if I didn't bring him out with me he'd get out somehow and he'd just go all over town looking for me. The first place he'd look would be the pub and then the next place would be the 'stupormarket' as we call it, across the road, and then he'd go around to every mate's place until he found me. Great dog was Patch.'

A couple of blokes have arrived and are sitting around the bend in the bar and one of 'em, with long hair cascading from under a peaked cap, and a massive mo that must make supping soup a real challenge chimes in.

'One day I was going out fishing with George and we were almost at the river and I got out to open a gate and Patch jumped out wanting to chase a hare and George just hit the gas and ran over his dog – put skid marks on him and all but it was real muddy so Patch pretty much got squashed into the mud, but he was pretty messed up, bleeding and all. And I said we'd better take him up to the vet but George said we should put the rods in first so we did and the dog pulled through. When we got back our baits had been taken but the fish'd gone. Wasn't a real successful day.'

Everyone's heard the story but again they all laugh and then this bloke who's unsurprisingly known as 'Sheepdog' adds to the Patch myth.

'We were fishing down at Cudgewa and the thing is, Patch knew when there was a fish on the line, he could sense it before we could feel it, and he'd run up to the rod and watch us pull in the fish and then when it was close he'd jump in and grab the fish and bring it in. But this one day I had a massive trout on the line and he jumped in and knocked the thing off the hook. George reckons he's watched footy all his life but never seen a better drop kick!

'But he was a bloody good dog, old Patch. Had his uses too! He really suffered from worms and so if we were ever short of bait we'd stand him in the water and the worms would, well they'd start coming out of his you know what, and we'd grab them and hook 'em up!'

Uproar in the room – Murray spills a beer he's serving to Hume down at the end of the bar, but then Sheepdog fesses up: 'Okay that bit's bullshit!'

Murray tops up Hume's beer and hands it over. Can't be short-changing a bloke who's been drinking here for over sixty years.

Born in the local hospital, Hume – known to everyone as 'Hummer' after a Humber car he owned for ages – was ten years old when the Black Friday fires devastated the town in January 1939. He's in his Corryong Men's Shed sweater with matching faded cap.

'I remember it hitting the town. It went from one side of the hills to the other and then just swirled back onto the town. All the family got in a truck thing and we went down to the creek and stayed under the bridge there for a day and a night and then two days later after we left, the bridge burnt down too. Will never forget it – the noise and the heat. No-one who was there then ever could. Our farm was pretty much all burnt out, so we all just had to start all over again.'

As he has his first for the day, Hume tells that he was a late starter to drinking.

'Our farm was a fair way out of town and we didn't have grog in the house and we didn't have a car either – we used to have to ride the horse to come in here and I wasn't sure about riding home after a few so I never really had the opportunity until I was twenty-five and went to a party at Cudgewa.'

Once he'd established he could manage a horse after a beer, Hume starting drinking here at the Courthouse Hotel, but it was very different back then.

'Right here where I'm sitting was where the hitching rail for the horses was, and beside that was their water troughs – they were only knocked down maybe thirty years ago. And where the dining room is now, that used to be shops and a haberdashery.'

I show him an aerial shot that I've just taken from across the road.

'Yeah, so the original pub that I started drinking at was that double-storeyed building at the back.'

The photo sparks interest and others are keen to check it out. It's that sort of pub – everyone's interested in its story. Sheepdog's first, 'Apparently the pub was downstairs and at the end they did all the court work upstairs, and the lock-ups were out the back.'

Chris who owns the fishing shop right across the road reckons his mother used to work in the old pub, 'I'm guessing in the thirties'. He remembers this new section and coming in with his parents, and points out where the old Ladies' Lounge used to be, 'with half a dozen chairs and the ladies would all get served through a little servery window, and the old entrance to the toilets was there in the middle of the back wall there.'

Between pours, Murray joins the talk and explains the slow gentrification of the pub.

'When the door was open you could see straight to the guys standing at the urinals and old George Turner, he closed it up, and so now we just have to walk a bit further but at least you can take a leak in peace without everyone at the bar seeing you every time the door opens.'

Not that it was by any means uncivilised – see, 'this was before women were allowed in the bar. There were barmaids serving and they'd seen it all but there were no delicate ladies drinking.'

Murray, who's been working here 'off and on' since the turn of the century tells me that he'll take me on a tour of the old pub whenever I'm ready and show me the old smokehouse and fridge out the back of it. All the fireplaces are heritage listed and all the floors are from local Murray pine.

That'd be great, but first people, I have to address the jockey-sized elephant in the room: Jack Riley (no relation, as far as I can tell of William, the bloke who copped the glass of filthy water from Sarah King in 1882).

Loud guffaws fill the room. Comments of 'Was waiting for that' and 'Here we go' are followed by a crowd-pleasing, 'So this book of yours is fiction, eh?'

No town that I know of in Australia has forged (what an appropriate term!) its identity on unproven myth, legend, hearsay and downright invention more than Corryong has done with a bloke called Jack Riley. You can't enter the town from any direction without being welcomed by a silhouette of a bloke on a horse with a whip. There's a statue you can't avoid in the middle of the main street. There's hardly a store without some representation of 'The Man'.

Banjo Paterson explicitly denied that any one person was the model for his Man from Snowy River but that hasn't stopped 'experts' and vested

SIX MORE PERISH IN FIRES

GRAVE FEARS FOR OTHERS

TERRIBLE TOLL OVER WIDE AREA

TOWNSHIPS WIPED OUT

WARRANDYTE DEVASTATED

BY OUR SPECIAL REPORTERS

Breaking out afresh over an area extending throughout the mountains and from one end of the State to the other, shocking bush fires have taken further terrible toll of life and property. At least six more people have been burned to death, many are missing, and hundreds of homes have been lost.

With a blistering wind that reached a velocity of 70 miles an hour at times, and a record temperature of 114 deg. in the city and as high interests from pushing aside the claims of up to half a dozen old stockmen as being the inspiration for 'The Man' in favour of their bloke.

Jack Riley, whom Norman Abjorensen in 1995 labelled, 'a dubious character, a tailor by trade, and a man who did time for horse stealing ... a skilled bushman ... but a braggart as well,' is nothing more than just one of the claimants.

In 1948 the Melbourne *Age* carried a feature titled, 'The Man from Snowy River, Reality or Myth?' The writer tells of a meeting at a pub in Jindabyne in which the credentials of Lachie Cochran, 'Hellfire' Jack Clarke, McEacharn of Bredbo, Jack Riley, Lowder of Yass, George Hedger and Jim Spencer amongst others were discussed. (I'm not sure how much research they did, or whether they had subeditors back then but Bredbo's claimant was Charlie McKeahnie, not 'McEacharn' and he remains, for mine, the strongest contender – if there indeed is one.)

One of those present was Thomas Macnamara who claimed his brother-in-law was:

the Man from Snowy River. His graphic detailed story of the tide leaves little doubt in our minds, and in a mood of conviction we return the article and leave for home by way of Kosciusko with the feeling that the riddle has been solved.

On the way they drop into Corryong and head up to the cemetery where the headstone of Jack Riley causes them 'bewilderment'. He continues:

Corryong Heresy Tombstones have an authority and finality which seem to discourage contradiction. Indeed it is something like heresy to question Riley's title in Corryong, where pictures of Riley inscribed 'The Man from Snowy River' are a common possession ...

What the stunned author didn't mention is that unlike all the surrounding headstones, in fact unlike pretty much every headstone in every cemetery in the country, Jack's year of birth is not chiselled into the marble. Neither is his place of birth. This just might be because Jack Riley wasn't even born in this town that's claimed him as a son, but in Castlebar, County Mayo, Ireland in 1841 and he didn't arrive in Australia until he was thirteen.

Not only is Riley's connection to the poem tenuous other than his undoubtedly meeting Paterson, his connection to the town is also flimsy and the blokes around the bar know it damn well.

Hume puts his empty 7 oz glass back on the bar. 'It's a bit of fiction. It brings people to the town which is a good thing and no-one gets hurt so it's a harmless bit of fun.'

Sheepdog looks up and reckons it's true – 'As true as the dog's worms!'

We're not going to top that so I head out the back. Murray's just hoeing into a delicious looking lunch and says to make myself at home and beware of snakes.

As I make my way out, George says he's had some tips in one of the later races. I don't know how he went but I hope he boxed three and, like Sarah King, won a decent trifecta.

After the fires I catch up with Hummer and ask how he is and how he got through the latest fires – eighty years after his first home was burnt.

'This was a panic job this time and everyone was told to get out and no-one considered staying and, yes, "panic" is the word I'd use.'

The family opened all the paddock gates and herded the cattle down to the Corryong Creek at the foot of the property. 'We learnt to do that in '39 and just like then we didn't lose a single animal, apart from a few chooks the first time.'

His family all moved into town on that afternoon of 31 December and the plan was for Hume to follow them, 'but I lost my licence to drive a while back and when I went to fire up the old Ford had a flat battery and it wouldn't start so I just stayed here with my dog.'

The flames, 'sort of went around past the house and dropped into the paddock below us and burnt about 80 hectares and the bulldozer came and cut strips through the paddocks and around the house.'

He never felt he was going to lose his home.

'I could see the fires going around it and I could tell this wasn't our time, and besides, I had a lot more help than we did in '39 when all we had was a bathtub of water and a couple of wet bags.'

His family returned the next day. With the feed paddocks burnt out the cattle were fed on willow branches from beside the creek. His neighbours had also driven their cattle to the safe point and when the danger had passed, the boxed herds were drafted apart in the yards beside Hume's place.

'It was a bit of an ordeal,' he tells me, 'not as bad as '39 but if we don't get another one for another eighty years, I'll be happy.'

CHAPTER 3 – CORRYONG TO TOOMA

THE LUSH, THE SCARRED AND THE RIVER OF MUD

I head north-east on what was for so long the Murray Valley Highway – a decent enough name I would've thought. I head north-east out from Corryong for a bit over 6 kilometres and then follow the sign right for Thredbo, and then a bit less to the fork onto Upper Murray Road for the 9-kilometre sweep down to the Indi Bridge, maybe the smallest fixed crossing on the entire river. Then it's just on 13 kilometres to the highest (as in most upstream) bridge over this, our greatest river. In 2011 a new bridge replaced the 1951 original timber-footed and steal-beamed crossing known as the Goldsworthy or Maguires Bridge and it's more utilitarian than aesthetic.

Beside the road in, with the river on my left, contented-looking cows graze in lush knee-height grasses at the very edge of a totally burnt-out hillside to my right. Below the bridge what appears more a mud colloid than a river flows gently. I climb down to it. My hand completely disappears just two inches below the surface and of course there's no evidence of life below. All the waterbirds, smart enough to know the fish have long gone, have also deserted the place.

On the far side, the foothills of the Victorian Alps are almost completely burnt to the farm lines at their feet. A scant green patch has escaped. Before the rains of last week the paddocks too were all black but the resilient grasses have turned verdant again. The scale of the destruction is beyond description. The brown of the mountains and the brown of the usually sparkling river reinforce once again just how brutal our land can be.

Then back to the B440, right, over the Murray on the Bringenbrong Bridge then a quick left and half an hour later I'm passing the Tooma Inn on my right. It's my digs for tonight but 5 kilometres up the road is a lookout I want to check out.

CHAPTER 4 – TOOMA

COULDA BEEN THE CAPITAL

I'm headed for the memorial to the *Southern Cloud* aircraft, our nation's first commercial air disaster. The plane disappeared in 1931 and the wreck lay undiscovered for twenty-seven years until a worker on the Snowy scheme accidentally put his foot through remains of the fuselage.

I've been here a good number of times and always stop to check out the snow level on the high alps but this time progress up the road is slower than usual. A bit more than a kilometre short of the lookout, there's a flashing sign warning of cattle on the road and then the telltale pressed pats spotting the asphalt. Then I'm dancing a slow slalom around a mob of mainly Murray Grey cattle wandering south who're obviously used to this routine and for whom time isn't a top priority.

They're being gently pushed by a woman on horseback and a bloke on a quad. This is Lionel and his daughter Charlotte from a property about 10 kilometres further north. Three weeks ago they hit the road with these 300 head out of their total mob of about 450. The cattle needed to be in the long paddock but the family was too busy fighting fires and protecting their homestead.

Lionel: 'The first firestorm hit us on the night of December 31st and came right up to the edge of the house but we all managed to beat it back. Then it came back on the fourth [of January] and took out the rest of the paddocks and a couple of out buildings. And then we copped it again a week later but we managed to save the house again.'

And then the rains came. As soon as the danger had passed, with not a blade of feed on his property, Lionel secured permission from the Local Land Services and the Snowy Council to graze about 3 kilometres of the road reserve.

Each morning they release the cattle from a holding yard back on the Merangle and ease them out and south on the Tooma Road. They have a set limit that they can't go past – that's been reserved for some of their neighbours in the same situation. Later in the morning Charlotte will ride through the cattle and with her two dogs, halt them at their 'border'. Then it'll be the slow return to the holding yard where there's water and no night traffic to baulk the beasts.

Charlotte: 'We take it very slow. It's not like droving where you have to do ten kays a day or three if you have a slow permit. They're pretty sore-footed, the poor things, but there's just no feed at home, nothing at all.'

They expect to be doing this for another month – until the rains have brought some greenness to the home paddocks.

Drovers on travelling stock routes, taking their animals from point to point, are charged a per-head-per-day fee and I ask Lionel whether the fees have been waived for farmers forced off their land by these fires.

'That,' he smiles, 'is a contentious issue. They'd like us to pay, but we'll just have to see.'

As we yarn an army vehicle crawls up the hill from Tooma, waiting for the cattle to clear a path, its crew finished for now with its assistance to such people as Lionel and Charlotte: real people in real need. We wave them through and wave our thanks and I leave them both and track north to the lookout.

Travel guides to many cities and towns are out of date before the (increasingly 'virtual') ink is dry but out here in the bush, things move more slowly and truths are more resilient.

Just a year before the *Southern Cloud* went down, the 1930s travel writer for *The Sydney Mail* visited this area:

Of the three roads into Tooma Valley, that from Tumbarumba is the best from the scenic point of view. Down the high, heavily-timbered ranges it swings, twisting and turning and giving magnificent glimpses of the green Upper Murray valleys and the white, snow-cloaked peaks of the Snowy Range. Between Greenwood and Maragle it twists sharply to the right … affording wonderful views of the fertile valley and the high, white peaks of Kosciusko.

Despite the fires, this scene has only become more beautiful in the last almost ninety years since those words were set in metal. In winter the far eastern horizon is defined by the cobalt sky meeting the white tips of the higher peaks of the Alps. Come spring, some of that white will find its liquid way into the Snowy River, the Tumut, the Murrumbidgee and the Murray. Some of those melted snowflakes will make it all the way to Goolwa and the very mouth of our greatest river system.

Then I swing around and again wend my way through the cattle, wave to Charlotte and Lionel and not long after I leave their southern limit I'm slowing down again, this time for a mob of Herefords being overseen by Alice and Tom from a place just across the valley.

Soon I'm passing the old schoolhouse, this time on my right, before turning left and parking Super Ten on the stark but totally user-unfriendly white stones out front of the Tooma Inn. There's no other car parked out front, just a white 4WD at the guest house next door. Overhead a jet's white trail bisects the sky, its low rumble audible in the stillness.

Inside, Kris is arranging a delivery on the phone but still manages a smile and motions me to sit down, she'll be with me in a sec. She asks about my day and just what I'm doing here. I give her the short version and she smiles, 'Yeah, I've never been able to picture those hills out there covered with high-rise units and bitumen roads. Can you get your head around this pub being surrounded by twenty-storey office blocks?'

I tell her about the jet trail. 'No, and I can't imagine one of them landing here every couple of minutes.'

Well, it coulda been very different here.

See, one Friday arvo in 1908 a bunch of either nineteen or twenty (depending on which paper you read) blokes arrived in Albury on the train from Melbourne. They were met by some locals, had a bit of chinwag and a few sherbets and then they all headed over to the Globe Hotel for the night. (We'll get back to the Globe down the track a bit.)

The next morning's goods train from Melbourne was carrying eight cars they'd arranged so they could have a joyride up the Murray River to Tooma and back. The local mayor thought he'd tag along in his own vehicle. And, well, things didn't go all that smoothly. Only the local bloke's car made it through and the *Border Morning Mail* headlined its subsequent story on the trip as:

A GAY OLD TIME
NINE CARS GO OUT
ONLY ONE RETURNS

These weren't ordinary tourists. They were a mob of federal politicians and they were on a mission.

The Commonwealth of Australia *Constitution Act 1900* was the blueprint for the federation of the six colonies and the creation of the Commonwealth of Australia. Its section 125 stated that:

The seat of Government of the Commonwealth shall be determined by the Parliament, and shall be within territory which shall have been granted to or acquired by the Commonwealth, and shall be vested in and belong to the Commonwealth, and shall be in the State of New South Wales, and be distant not less than one hundred miles from Sydney.

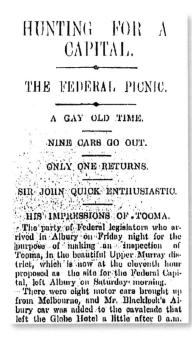

HUNTING FOR A CAPITAL.

THE FEDERAL PICNIC.

A GAY OLD TIME.

NINE CARS GO OUT.

ONLY ONE RETURNS.

SIR JOHN QUICK ENTHUSIASTIC.

HIS IMPRESSIONS OF TOOMA.

The party of Federal legislators who arrived in Albury on Friday night for the purpose of making an inspection of Tooma, in the beautiful Upper Murray district, which is now at the eleventh hour proposed as the site for the Federal Capital, left Albury on Saturday morning. There were eight motor cars brought up from Melbourne, and Mr. Blacklock's Albury car was added to the cavalcade that left the Globe Hotel a little after 9 a.m.

And while the pollies were working out just where in New South Wales this capital territory was to be, both houses of the new federal parliament met in Melbourne. The members, especially those from New South Wales ('the Mother State') and Victoria ('Australia Felix') wasted no time or energy in lobbying for their favourite places.

The Victorians pushed for a site with frontage to the Murray River. They argued that a federal capital totally within New South Wales would be prone to a blockade should things get nasty with the surrounding savages from Sydney. The New South Welsh wanted it closer and more convenient to Sydney and also not too distant from the coast as the Constitution also held that the capital must have a port (that's why Jervis Bay is still part of the ACT).

The original contenders list of over forty-five was fairly soon cut back to fifteen and then in 1902 the senators and house members began a series of visits to potential sites. By 1903 just nine remained in the running: Albury, Armidale, Bathurst, Bombala, Dalgety, Lake George, Lyndhurst, Orange and Tumut.

In October that year the House of Reps plumped for Tumut, but the Senate replaced this in the Bill with Bombala and the issue was deadlocked.

The next year both Houses agreed on Dalgety but the New South Wales government refused to hand over the land so again nothing happened. Federation was running real smooth eh! The whole thing was becoming a dilemma wrapped in a debacle all covered in a thick coating of short-sighted self-interest. Bucket lists were replaced by way-too-hard baskets.

It all stagnated deep in that basket for a few years but then some pollies with a bit of vision began a search for a site that might just suit everybody. And the popular new contender was this place: Tooma!

Which brings us back to the intrepid twenty in Albury. The leader of the expedition was Sir William Lyne, who could've been our first prime minister. Governor General Lord Hopetoun had invited Lyne to form the first Commonwealth government in 1900 but he couldn't muster enough compliant cattle to form a ministry. Instead he became Minister for Home Affairs and Deakin became head drover.

It was Lyne who was the driving force behind Tooma's candidacy. In 1907 he'd reaffirmed his longstanding love of the place, being quoted in the Sydney *Evening News* as saying he, 'regarded Tooma as absolutely the best site'.

And he sounds like the perfect bloke to lead a junket along the river.

When on the campaign trail in his local electorate Lyne was known to travel, 'with the boot of his buggy filled to the gunwales with liquid refreshment'.

They weren't talking cordial. He stayed true to form on this trip. When they all returned, *The Newsletter: an Australian Paper for Australian People* wryly advised:

The Federal Parliamentarians have returned from their trip to the proposed new capital site at Tooma. There is no road to the place but strangers can reach the spot by tracking the dead marines, now lying along the route.

Tooma made a damn fine impression on the visitors. Sir John Quick opened the sluice gates of compliments:

I had heard a great deal of Tooma before, but I must repeat that it has exceeded my most sanguine expectations. I am quite convinced that it is the best site that I have had any information about for a Federal Capital, and I intend to strongly advocate it in the House and use all my influence to support it ... I am profoundly impressed with the magnificence of the scenery, with the richness and fertility of the soil, with the presence of abundant water for all purposes including water power. Some of the richest country in Australia is in the area – a richness that I had never previously dreamt of.

Uniformly the press referred to the 'fact finding' junkets as 'picnics' and of course it all came to nought. Deals were done, backs were stabbed, promises were broken, and Canberra, where such traditions would long continue, got the gong as the new federal seat.

But if just three senators had voted differently Tooma, this place which now has a pub, a guest house and a part-time post office, but no longer any store or school, would've been our national capital. We mull this over as the locals begin to trickle in.

One of the first to front is Noel, whose grandfather David Maginnity bought the pub in 1910 and kept it for the rest of his life. When he died in 1943, his wife, Catherine took over and ran it until 1952, she then leased out the place until 1968.

Noel would ride her old bicycle up the hill to the one-room one-teacher school, but most kids had other transport.

'There was a pony paddock attached to the school and most of the kids would ride their ponies each day and just let them graze untethered in the paddock. One family from down at Possum Point had four children in the school and the oldest kid would drive the others each day in the family sulky.'

Roger from Coonara Station, a bit to the south of town, has joined us and chimes in, 'I always preferred to ride my horse than get a lift from mum. She was great friends with Noel and if she picked me up, they'd gasbag for an hour while I played in the dirt so I'd get home faster on my pony. Some of us had saddles, but most didn't. It was all just so normal to do that sort of thing.'

Noel doesn't have many memories of her publican grandfather, but she reckons he wasn't the best businessman. 'I heard a story the other day that he would rather take you out to the kitchen and get you a cup of tea than sell you a drink.'

She does recall growing up in the pub and for a short time around 1958 she and her brother ran the place.

'Dad had the licence but wasn't living here and in those days by law the licensee had to live on site. My brother and I were sharing a room down the end so we became the licensees. I was the cook. This was before they started the Snowy and we had the engineers who were working on the road staying here. I must've been able to cook because they ate it. I didn't have any complaints.'

Her grandfather's sister, Auntie Rose, lived in a small room at the eastern side of the pub. 'Her room had a small door into the post office next door. She ran the post office for years.'

And years! In 1949 even the far-off *Herald* in Melbourne recognised her. Under a heading, 'SWITCH-GIRL 92 TODAY', it wrote:

Miss Rosanna Maginnity, who is 92 today, has run the post office at Tooma in Tumbarumba Shire since 1911 claims to be the oldest switch-girl In Australia …

And it was obviously a time of both expansion for this wild town and the introduction of some pretty fancy technology. The Melbourne *Herald* went on:

A new switchboard has just been installed to cope with the nine subscribers and a trunk line. Miss Maginnity celebrated her birthday by going to church. Later the family will have a small party.

It may not've been the capital, but damn, it was obviously still party central!

In 1963 Noel stepped into her grand-aunt's (no doubt sensible) shoes and ran the post office for the next forty-four years. It's officially classified as a community postal agency. After her husband died in 2006, she moved it from beside the pub to a room in her own house up the hill, finally severing the long association between her family and the Tooma Inn.

But the pub's not the only connection Noel has with this 'coulda been capital' town. Forty-five years before David Maginnity took over the Tooma Inn, this tiny village was in the news for another capital reason. This time it was a capital offence.

Two local police, a sergeant and a trooper, were out on patrol in the hills to the north when they stumbled on bushranger Mad Dog Morgan. A few weeks earlier Morgan had shot and killed the overseer at nearby Round Hill station and he wasted no time in firing at this pair. His first volley felled the sergeant, and the trooper, one Constable Churchley, turned and fled, leaving his boss to die alone on the mountain.

In its coverage of the affair the *Gundagai Independent* chose its words delicately: 'Constable Churchley's part in the affray was anything but heroic'. He was later dismissed from the force, charged with cowardice.

The slain officer left a wife and four children. One of those sons, David, went on to buy the Tooma pub. That dead policeman was Noel's great-grandfather, also known as David Maginnity. Today, near the spot of the killing, on a side road from the main drag up to Tumbarumba, there's a monument, a plinth and a plaque, in honour of Noel's ancestor. There's nothing for Churchley.

Noel knows these stories well and as she's winding up, Jeff joins us.

There were thirty kids at Tooma Public School when Jeff was there in the late fifties but by the time he'd left town in 1979 to study interior design in Sydney, there were less than five and the school was in its final year. But Jeff maintained his connections with the town.

'In 2016 I came down for Easter for the gymkhana and everyone said, why don't you buy the store (next to the pub). A lady who'd converted it from the store to what it is today came from Thredbo in the late '80s but she struggled to make a go of it as a quality restaurant; it'd been closed for two years. I asked Rob if he had a key to the building and he told me that he thought the far window wasn't locked, and we climbed in. We came through to the kitchen and the light was on, so we turned it off and had a look all over the place. It was very impressive.

'On the way back to Sydney I processed all this and I rang the owner, I was asking questions about rates and water, all that sort of stuff. I was asking about the solar panels on the roof and she told me that she had to leave a light on all the time as a safety thing so I franticly rang Rob here and told him he had to break in and turn the light on before the solar all exploded!'

Long story short, Jeff and a partner from just outta town bought the place, extended the outside wall into where the old skillion post office had been to accommodate his new kitchen, and opened it as an exquisite boutique B & B.

And it's going quite nicely thank you! The area's beauty and its tranquillity draw visitors from every state and increasingly Europe and the USA. Just to the north is the Maragle State Forest where the deer hunting is so coveted Parks and Wildlife are forced to hold annual ballots for rights to shoot there. Jeff's not too sure about hunting and has a strict rule that no dead bodies are to be brought inside.

'We had a woman doctor come down for a week and she was upfront and told me she was coming down to hunt deer. I told her that was fine but I didn't want any body parts or blood on the premises. She could shoot all the deer she wanted but when she came through the door here, I wanted her in high heels and lipstick. She hadn't brought heels but she came back at night with her lippy on and no carcass crossed the threshold!'

As we've been yarning, a steady flow of folks from around has dropped in, ordered tea and a drink and drifted off again. It's Wednesday night and as the pub's closed on Mondays and Tuesdays this is the start of their visiting week. There's no gambling, no pokies and the television hasn't been switched on. Everyone just gets a drink, orders a feed and opens up a yarn with whoever's closest.

Kris, a qualified nurse and chef, and her partner Trevor, a painter and decorator, were in Mackay, North Queensland in late 2018 looking for a change of scene and change of pace.

'We somehow heard that Rob and Lindy, who'd had it since 2013, were quietly interested in selling this place, so we contacted them.'

A price was quoted, an offer made and agreement reached. Trevor and Kris went away for a week or so to think about it. And then came back and bought the freehold, opening the doors of their own pub for the first time on 7 May 2019.

It's a lot more work than they thought it'd be. Kris does all the meals, Trevor all the maintenance and they share the bar work. On weekends they call in extra staff, locals from surrounding farms. One of them is Charlotte – Lionel's daughter – the same Charlotte I've been talking with up the road with their cattle.

'We always planned to only employ locals when we needed help,' says Trevor, who's joined us after fixing a pipe out the back, 'and especially now after the fires it's important they have some money flowing back in.'

We head out front of the pub and Trevor points to the ridges to the south:

'On December 30 the fire came at us from over that hill where you can see the dirt road to Tintaldra. We thought it was going to miss us but it swirled around and looped over those hills to the east and doubled back around us to the north. That's when it hit Lionel's place. Then the wind changed again and it came at us one more time.'

The town's power went out that first night and stayed out until 27 January. The pub became the community's base. Donations of food and water, clothes, even chainsaws were all delivered to the front door then stored inside behind unlocked doors so locals could take what they needed. A team of Sikhs from Melbourne was permitted through the roadblocks and set up a BBQ for a couple of days.

'No-one around here will ever use that saying 'baptism of fire' the same way again.'

But this catastrophe also ripped open schisms in the community.

In 2020 the council constructed toilets in the park across from the pub and saw the value to the greater area in permitting free camping along the edge of the creek. It was an initiative embraced by the publicans but opposed by a group of locals who didn't want 'that sort of people' in the village.

The differences grew into a feud which spilled into battles over generators during the fires. A free government gennie was delivered to the community hall where it was little utilised whilst the pub, the hub of the rescue efforts was forced to pay full freight for one.

Later there'd be false claims of land ownership of the creek bank and of spurious arguments over the type of licence that covered the pub.

And, unfortunately, it led to a boycott of the pub by a number of residents. But Kris and Trevor have seen their absence offset by visitors from the wider surrounding area and travellers from further afield, who've heard on the mulga wire of their hospitality and their intentions.

'We'd of course love to be at one with everyone in the community,' Kris tells me, 'but we're not going to do that if it means not putting out the welcome mat to a large number of travellers who are here because they

choose to, not just because they were born here.'

The sun's fast disappearing and the light becomes interesting. I grab Super Ten and head out for a quick squirt on the dirt on the back road towards Tintaldra. I'm not let down. The ends of the day rarely disappoint and when I'm back the crowd's thinned.

There's no other town of forty people anywhere in this country that can offer the accommodation options that you have in Tooma. Jeff's Brigham House next door provides luxury, classy comfort; the Inn has traditional shared facility pub rooms that're comfortable and clean, and across the road the council's erected an amenities block and enabled free camping for budget travellers. (The pub offers free showers to diners and drinkers.)

Next to the purring generator that's a perfect foil for my tinnitus, I pass the night in perfect slumber in a double bed. In the morning, the kitchen's been left unlocked so I can boil the water for my first brew, which is taken back to bed, then I head out for some sunrise shots. Super Ten's black lambswool seat is frosted white. Smoke curls from Jeff's chimney, the grass in the riverside reserve crackles under my steps. It's brisk!

Overhead another plane is carving a jet trail across the sky and once again I try to envision what would've happened if those three senators had voted differently and Tooma was the capital of Australia. I try to imagine Charlotte driving her cattle past Parliament House and a hotel with its doors open so residents in need could help themselves.

But I can't.

CHAPTER 5 – TOOMA TO TINTALDRA

BEAUTY ON A BACK ROAD

I t's way too good a day to take the easy sealed route on Tooma Road so after crossing the three bridges I continue straight on the way I took at sunset last night. Pretty soon the bitumen ends and I'm standing on the pegs, riding tame gravel and descending Pipeclay Hill through stunning though scarred beauty.

Way, way back in 1910, during a better season when the rains had come and the fires had stayed away, a correspondent for the *Border Morning Mail* came up from Tintaldra on this same track. He enthused:

> *Pursuing our journey to the northward, up the Welaregang valley, the road rising through rich pasture land until, we reach the crest of the range on Pipeclay Hill, and we are on down country, reminding one strongly of the Salisbury Downs and Hampshire. Approaching Tooma we open up a view— unrivalled in its picturesqueness ... this sequestered vale, ribboned with creeks and lagoons and soil of the most undoubted richness, enchains the eye.*

The writer didn't quite get it right. The beauty of his old country was, and still is, based on the luxury of the lush. The beauty here is founded more on the strength of the harsh, the underlying hardness of the land and the elements. On the Salisbury Downs and in Hampshire life may be epitomised by a delicate rose. Out here the symbol is more the green sprouts of regrowth from a charred eucalypt.

And it's the 'undoubted richness' of this type of beauty-in-strength that enchains my eye.

CHAPTER 6 – TINTALDRA

DEAD HOUSES, INTERSTATE NAKEDNESS, CAPITALISM, AND NIGHTS THAT END AT MIDDAY

At the edge of the Tintaldra bridge, I pause, kick the side stand down and check out the river languidly flowing from my left to right. Somewhere there's a gurgle where the flows must be stepping over a rock or perhaps a larger log. Corellas screech and argue amongst themselves. A pair in the river gum to my right mine the bark with the overbite of their beaks, maybe excavating a burrow.

Across the Murray River, in another state, the nameplate of the Tintaldra pub is framed by the bridge.

White settlement of this area began in the 1840s with the taking up of the Tintaldra run. It was taken over in dirty circumstances by a bloke named Sydney Grandison Watson in 1858. Watson was a retired English naval officer with a pretty keen eye for business and a talent for stepping on those he deemed beneath him (which was pretty much everyone).

He developed and expanded his Tintaldra run until it covered more than 100,000 acres. He commissioned a German settler, Christian Vogel, to build and then operate a hand-hauled punt across the Murray and in 1864 commissioned someone, probably Vogel, to build a brick store to sell supplies to those using his punt.

Just exactly when the first pub was built is moot but in a legal trial in 1875 a witness, Rupert Byatt, deposed that he had known the pub, known as the 'Pet Lamb' since it was built twelve years prior (1863) by one Dobson who then sold the place to Watson.

I wasn't quite sure what happened next because in 1869 Watson commissioned Vogel to build a brick hotel across from his store and adjacent to his punt. But then I met Phillip in the bar of the 'Tin Pot' – the Tintaldra Hotel. He was adamant that the store had been built by Edwin Jephcott, an ancestor through his mother's side of the family, and he was also certain that, 'The Pet Lamb Hotel wasn't built here, it was built about 5 kilometres up the road, right at the end of the Tintaldra Riding where the Walwa Riding started. [A Riding was a defined local government division.] My older brother used to talk about having to open a huge wooden gate on the road at the boundary. The pub used to be near that gate, you can still see the footings of the chimney.'

I ask him how he knows.

'It's on my property.'

But I'm getting ahead of myself. Will get back to Phillip in a bit.

Christian Vogel was one of those annoying people who are good at pretty much everything. He wasn't just the town's punt operator and carpenter; he also moonlighted as the place's blacksmith and dentist. (What could go wrong?)

In 1870 Watson employed a bloke named David Waller to manage his new brick pub and a year later Waller took out a three-year lease over it, including the house, outhouses and the paddock behind.

Watson was now lording over a private fiefdom. He owned the pub, the store and the punt. He refused to allow a school to be built on his land, refused to have a town meeting hall and refused to have a second hotel.

When the lease expired, Watson refused Waller's request for an extension and Waller moved out. Watson and a couple of landed gentry mates inspected the place and didn't much like what they saw (bit like Trevor and Kris back at Tooma).

Among Sydney Grandison Watson's numerous less than endearing traits was his eagerness to lawyer up and go litigious! A couple of years earlier, after complying with a police request to pull down a fence that was partly over a government road, SGW tried to sue Waller for the cost. As ever-lovable Syd said later, 'I did not get a verdict.' So in 1875 Watson again took Waller to court, this time suing for alleged damage to the structure and the unlawful removal of a pile of stuff including, 'bolts, a buggy and cart, shed, a small room, a hut, flooring boards, a counter flap, sign-board, four iron quoits (and) three fruit trees'.

Amongst his list of claims, Watson was seeking recompense of the £10 that he'd paid the succeeding tenant, Mr Mildren, for the cost of 'repairing the dead-house' despite admitting in court that, 'the dead-house was not there when I let the place to Waller.'

This was seemingly the 'hut' which had been removed, as later in the case, the ubiquitous Christian Vogel had his day in court, testifying that he 'recollected ... about the dead-house. The dead-house was built of bark. I saw Waller taking it away.'

Mildren, the pub's new tenant swore that a new house had been placed 'over the site where the dead-house formerly stood.'

'The dead-house'? The what? Time for quick detour before we cross this bridge!

Since pubs first appeared in the colonies, they've had a connection with the freshly dead. Government Acts are printed in two columns, the body of the Act in a fat column near the spine and a thinner column closer to the page edge with a very brief synopsis of each neighbouring paragraph. Beside section twenty-four of the Victoria Licensing Act of 1839 which laid out, among other things, the responsibilities of publicans, the synopsis reads beautifully and simply:

Travellers and corpses
not to be refused,
under a penalty.

Truly! The relevant section states:

XXIV. ... if any licensed person being an innkeeper shall, without lawful excuse, refuse to receive and provide for a traveller and his horse, or a traveller without a horse ... or shall refuse to receive any corpse which may be brought to his public house for the purpose of a Coroner's Inquest being held thereon ... shall ... pay a penalty of not less than One Pound nor more than Twenty Pounds.

And the Victorians weren't on their Pat! The fourteenth Act of the New South Wales Parliament was concerned with, 'Publicans and other Persons engaged in the sale of Liquor'. Its section 86 held that:

Every holder of a publican's license shall at the request of any officer or constable of police receive into the house ... any dead body that may be brought to such house for the purpose of an inquest being held thereon ... And if he shall refuse to receive such dead body for the purpose aforesaid he shall be liable to a penalty not exceeding five pounds.

Inquests were held in bush pubs because their saloons and bars were often the largest rooms in the town and the cellars were among the coolest places to store the corpse. Officials were able to do their work then relax and stay all in the one building. Some publicans had special rooms constructed for the storage of the cadavers and not too far down the Murray, a bit south of the river at Rutherglen, there's a pub that still has its old mortuary building.

But the Tintaldra pub's 'dead-house' wasn't concerned with corpses and the judge in *Watson v Waller* wasn't across just exactly what it was. He sought a 'please explain'. Watson obliged: 'The dead-house is where they put in those who are dead drunk.'

The beak can't have been much of a pub guy because Waller wasn't being inventive or original in constructing a room for his 'lambed down' customers. The practice had been going on since the colony was too young to drink.

In his 1888 *The Chronicles of Early Melbourne 1835 to 1852*, Edmund Finn, writing under his nom de plume, 'Garryowen' opined that:

Another usage grew up with the old hotels ... i.e., the attaching of a littered room or dead-house, a secure, unwindowed, comfortably-strawed exterior apartment, into which the bodies of those who got dead drunk by day or night were stowed away, and suffered to rest in peace and sleep off the debauch ... The 'dead-house' in reality was a humane institution for the accommodation of 'casuals' helplessly intoxicated, who, instead of being tumbled out of doors, were 'bedded down' for the night.

He later claimed that he'd never seen either the inside or the outside of such a facility but it's certain to have existed.

In 1890 the *Australian Workman* newspaper asked, 'Is the House of Legislative Assembly a sort of 'Hotel Dead House,' to which Members of Parliament Retire to Get Sober?'

Before answering itself:

In some of the hotels round Sydney, an empty room is kept for the purpose of stowing away helpless drunken men until they get sober. The hall in which our legislators meet would appear to be a room of this character.

And it sure wasn't a short-lived trend. As late as 1925 Brisbane's *Daily Standard* quoted an AWU organiser who was inspecting staff digs up at Winton, Queensland:

I interviewed the local police sergeant about the accommodation for employees in some of the hotels here, which, to say the least, is rotten. The employees have what is termed the 'dead house' for quarters. This is the place where all the drunks or dead beats are put when they are ... 'fly blown.'

Vogel continued to operate the punt across the Murray until 1892 when the firm of JB and W Farquharson finished building the first Tintaldra bridge in December that year. They got the job done just a fortnight over schedule and the New South Wales supervising engineer of roads and bridges declared it a splendid job indeed!

And then the bridge just stood there. Unused. Nothing crossed it because nothing could. You see, the cronies at the Towong Council who'd led the unsuccessful campaign to have the crossing built on their doorstep at Towong and nearer to their own runs, hadn't even begun to have the approaches to the bridge built.

The *Argus* commented, 'The bridge will not be open for traffic for some time, as the Victorian approaches, which will be constructed by the Towong Shire Council, have not yet been commenced.'

By April when they'd finally got their act together and the bridge was accessible, the folks in New South Wales had lost interest and so the Towong Council stepped up, and no doubt taking more than a pannikin of credit, had their engineer, one Mr Dixie, declare it open.

With the approaches beyond reproach I fire up Super Ten for the squirt over the new version and the pub waits straight ahead.

Sydney Grandison Watson didn't live to see the bridge. He died in 1891 and the *Bendigo Advertiser* reported that he was reputed to be worth over £1,000,000 and was the 'wealthiest man in the North-eastern district.'

The first bridge was eventually replaced by the current structure in 1959 but the original bridge's columns remain in the river, rusting gloriously about the flows. (Towong had eventually got its own crossing in 1938.)

Now, I don't know about old Christian Vogel's dentistry or about his blacksmithing but when he turned his multitalented hands and mind to making stuff, it stayed made. The village is still defined by his pub on my right and the general store on the left.

I park outside the pub where there're signs of life inside, but the doors are all still bolted and then cross Main Street to the store with its kerbside welcome sign. This place, built by Vogel for Watson in 1864, isn't just still standing – some restored empty shell, cutely testifying in faded tones to a distant glowing past. Not even close! Nah! It crowns the east side of the street, freshly painted and glowing in the sun, proudly still open as a store, a museum, a cafe and a post office.

Inside, Betty Walton's been expecting me. I'd rung ahead to make sure she'd keep (at least) one of her scones for my morning tea and as I shed the riding gear and greet her, the kettle's already bubbling up behind the counter.

Out back, near where the pre-Federation customs house (the highest one ever built on the Murray) was, in the sun there's a great old gazebo from where you can watch the river, but we settle down around an inside table and I hoe into Betty's scones. And some of her homemade jam.

We start with some health news. Betty's had some serious panelbeating done in the couple of years since I was last here. A life in the sun's been exacting its cost: 'I'm very, very Irish. My skin should be in Ireland not here. My theory is that when the knife comes in, the cancer cells pack up their bags and move quickly to another spot, so I've had several treatments.'

I smear fresh cream and Betty's jam on a decapitated scone.

Mary Walton passed away on 20 May 2020. The grief and sense of
loss of her extended family – her children, grandchildren and great-
grandchildren was echoed by all in Tintaldra and all who ever knew
her. She will long be remembered and her contributions valued.
To appropriate the words of the song, her flame – which burnt until
the end – was snuffed out long before her legend ever will.

'I think they're under control – for the last two years I've been religiously putting on sunscreen.'

In the early 1970s Allan and Betty Walton were living in Cronulla, just south of Botany Bay with their six kids and both of their mothers.

'All I'd ever wanted to do was entertain, go on the stage but Mum said there was no money in that so I ended up in teachers' college and then started teaching.'

Al was driving a truck and he had a mate, Malcolm, who owned some dirt down on the Upper Murray and kept telling them how beautiful it was, how they had to come down and experience it.

The two grans passed away in 1973, releasing the anchors they had to 'the smoke' and, as Betty describes it, 'so I said to Al, let's go down and have a look at this place that Malcolm's always talking about. 'So next Easter we came down and I'd never seen anything so beautiful.' Her eyes widen and hands get active, trying to encapsulate her wonderment.

'We found the store and the house inside but we stayed with Malcolm just a bit down the Walwa Road and I said to Malcolm it's so beautiful out there, so different to Cronulla. And he said, that's because the wind isn't blowing all the time and there isn't any humidity and then he added that there's also no cockroaches. So I said, whacko, one, two, three things, for me, I'm sold!

'There was just a very run-down general store here and the post office was just up the street. In the old days it used to take them three days to get the mail from Melbourne. It was the longest horse delivery mail run in Victoria, three changes of horses.'

Their three oldest children had left home so in 1974 Allan and Betty and their three youngest transplanted. Betty took over the post office and Al got to work sprucing up the general store, but they were spending a big chunk of each day running between the two.

'I said to Al this is a waste of time, so we combined them here.' And that's the way it's stayed. There're still fifteen post boxes in the wall but that side of the business has slowed, telegrams and money orders gone the way of dead houses.

In the early '80s Betty returned to teaching in Corryong and Khancoban and when Al passed away in '85 everything was on her shoulders. They'd lost one son in a motor accident but the other five kids had all gravitated back to the Upper Murray and they all pitched in.

'It was bloody hard but we got through.'

Al died in 1985 and his grave is down at Corryong, in the same plot as Jack Riley's, and I ask Betty about her late husband's eternal neighbour.

She reckons it's prophetic that the store and Banjo Paterson were born in the same year. 'The story is that Jack Riley used to call in here on his way from Corryong to Tom Groggin and that Banjo himself came in a few times. He was fascinated with the horsemen in the high country.'

And for good reason. 'They used to ride like madmen in those days. When we first came down here a fellow working on one of the high stations made a bet with a bloke that he could get down here quicker on his horse than the bloke could in his car. And he won because he just came straight down the mountain and over all the fences and that's how they used to ride, completely without fear.'

But if the men of the mountains drew Banjo Paterson down here, it's the river that's always enchanted Betty and which holds her still, and when we get on to its health and wellbeing, this wonderful woman's spirit breaks out.

'The river is this town. "Taldra" means young man and "Tin" means by the water, so without the river there's no town. But we don't look after it and now they are talking about a carp virus which they don't understand and it'll be like the cane toad.'

By now she's really fired up!

'Please, NO! NO! NO! These experts in their horn-rimmed glasses don't know a bee from a bull's feet. What we need is fishing competitions! We need carpathons all up and down the river to get rid of them. We don't need another virus killing fish which are going to lie on the bottom of the rivers sucking up all the oxygen and killing everything else.'

My scones are history so I swig on the last remnants of my brew as Betty, soul now fully stoked switches her aim. 'The best thing we have going for us is the river and the worst thing is the council.' (The same Toowong Council that couldn't get its act together to build the bridge approaches.)

'There's a lot of intermarrying around here and they've had it very good for very long. I went to the council and told them we needed some public toilets for the tourists and they told me they didn't want tourists, they'd only frighten the cattle and leave gates open. They're all third or fourth generation graziers and are opposed to the growth of this town!'

Betty dials it back a bit and changes her focus.

'You know, I believe in two teachings of God. Jesus said to love God and one another, and he said we need to live life simply. My life is simple and it's simply wonderful – it's perfect. I love waking up in the morning and looking forward to the next day.'

The drive to entertain, snuffed by her mother so long ago when Betty was diverted into teaching, has never died. Before I go I buy a book of her poetry and she insists on reciting rote one of her pieces and then I'm treated to a couple of tunes on the pianola.

Betty sees me to the door. I say I'll see her again soon and finally walk the remaining paces to the pub. Off to my right a group of adventure motorcycle riders is setting up camp beside the river in a sort of no-man's-land.

Everyone knows that the Murray River is the border between New South Wales and Victoria and that the river itself is in New South Wales. It's just that no-one's really sure what exactly constitutes 'The Murray River'. If the river's low, does Victoria stretch a bit down to the contracted water's edge? When it's flooding, does New South Wales grow to the southern shore? Are the states elastic?

I'll get onto that a bit further downstream but, meanwhile, the bike riders are enjoying the uncertainty. The local council ain't keen on folks free camping beside the river but even they're not sure whether the bank is in their jurisdiction or across the border in the 'mother state', so campers are pretty much left in peace.

Every time I drop by the Tintaldra pub I'm convinced I have to write about it for one of my monthly columns but when I get back home and start hitting the keys there's always some detail I've missed and need to ring back to clarify. Each time, it's been a new voice at the other end. The pub's been sold, the manager's been sacked, things didn't work out. So I shelve it.

This time (yet) another new face welcomes me. The Tin Pot closed in acrimonious circumstances in November 2018 and stayed closed for a year before a bloke from the coast bought it in October 2019 and nominated Mark, a long-time mate with experience in pubs, as the licensee. But Mark had some fifty-year-old 'form', and the licensing people took a dim view and didn't make things easy.

Then any preoccupation they had with getting the beer taps running changed to taps of a way more important variety when the fires hit on 30 December.

'We just turned the pub into the town's central point. Over a week there were three main fire attacks and they each got to about fifty metres, on all sides except the river. We were the base for town.'

Two families who'd lost their homes were put up in the rooms earmarked for renovation and the kitchen kicked into overdrive, feeding anyone who turned up.

'The power went out but after four days someone donated a gennie and an electrician wired it all up so we were up and running again.' Mark pauses. 'Yeah the only day we really thought we might lose the place was January 4th. There was no certain way out and the dirty old river was starting to look a decent option.'

The rainfall at the end of January coincided with the end of their licence issues and the first round of drinks was on the house.

Our chat is interrupted by quick enquires: was that family's house saved? Was that person evacuated? Is that bloke back yet? From Mark's answers, a lot of it sounds good news.

The previous licensees, the ones who'd been driven to insolvency and who walked away in 2018, had been pushing for camping at the back of the pub but had been rebuffed at every turn by the local council – the same mob Betty reckons could benefit from an expansion of their gene pool, and whose forefathers' ineptitude, petulance and pettiness delayed the opening of the original Tintaldra Bridge.

Mark reckons the hurdles are too high right now and fixing the rooms is more a priority than the camping, besides there's always across beside the river.

And it's now that Phillip, all flailing windmill arms, mutton-chops sideburns and drooping moustache comes over.

'I heard you talking about the Towong Council,' and when he asks if I know what Towong (pronounced 'Toe wong') means I tell him that I don't.

'It means "piss off" "get lost". When the early explorers came through they thought it was the most idyllic spot they'd ever seen and tried to engage with the local Aborigines who kept waving their spears and shields and calling out "Towong Towong" and the idiot whites thought it was a welcome. But it wasn't it was them saying "get the hell out of here".'

Phillip's waiting for the meals he's ordered for himself, his wife Suzi and his sister. The kitchen's busy so he has a bit of time.

'The fire jumped the river 50 kilometres that way and then tore south at such a speed it was on top of people before they knew it. We'd look down Cudgewa Valley in those early days of it and it'd be like staring into Armageddon. We had a couple of days to work on our plan – which was to stay and fight – and then it came at us. We'd blocked the downpipes at the ground and filled all the gutters and pipes with water and kept the roof soaking. Sprayed so much water on the hay that we thought we might've ruined it but we didn't.'

'About two hours before it hit us on the fourth, two coppers came by. One was very emotional and wanted us out but we had great water pressure and were pretty confident. My daughter wanted to leave but wouldn't go without me so we all stayed.

'Then it just tore up the road just like I can remember it did in '52 when I was six. But in those days all we had was an old army blitz and six 44-gallon drums of water and damp bags to fight it. We were prepared this time but we still needed a bit of luck.'

He takes a swig of his spritzer. 'Yeah we were lucky alright.'

But there's another, a happier story that Phillip wants to share. It's about glorious achievement against extreme odds – about what he believes is a unique episode in the story of the Murray:

'My brother who's gone to God is an important part of the history of the river and this town, and this pub. Remember back in the '70s when streaking at the cricket was the thing to do? Well my brother, Keplar, had a drink or two here one afternoon and dropped his gear and streaked interstate. Right across the bridge and back in the nude. Took off to much fanfare and came back with all his pieces intact and out there for the world to see. Not too many people would've streaked in two states in the one day.'

I tell him he must feel proud and he tells me his dinner must be about ready.

With the total fire ban relaxed, the Trangia steams in the morning sun and once my coffee's made my thoughts wander to Keplar and his naked sprint. Then my mind races 1300 kilometres away, to Tibooburra and Cameron's Corner where the borders of three states intersect. Records are made to be broken, right? And I think I know just the bloke to do it!

Phillip's right where he said he'd be, fixing fences destroyed by felled trees. He takes me to a raised flat section above an eroded dry creek bed. This is where the two long nails, definitely handmade, likely by Christian Vogel, and a flat lock-facing were found. As he stands at what would seem to be the corner of the old building he regrets moving a heap of the old stones before realising their significance. The silhouette of the Pet Lamb, where subterranean footings must still stand solid, is marked by harder soil, the last place where the wild grasses will return with the rains.

It would've been a decent spot for a roadside inn – accessible to passing trade and with an open view across the valley to the hills, but S. G. Watson's choice to decamp to beside his river crossing and near his store was the decision of a wise capitalist.

Phillip's got something else I have to see but he has a fence to mend and I have a road to ride so we say our 'cyas'.

It's getting close to noon and he smiles as we shake hands and I tell him, 'The best nights in pubs don't end till midday.'

Postscript: It didn't work out for Mark. A combination of regulatory bastardry and unacceptable lease conditions that would've made Sydney Grandison Watson proud left him with few options, and so once the fires had died and the community was saved and served, having lost time, money, a dream and a long friendship, he walked away.

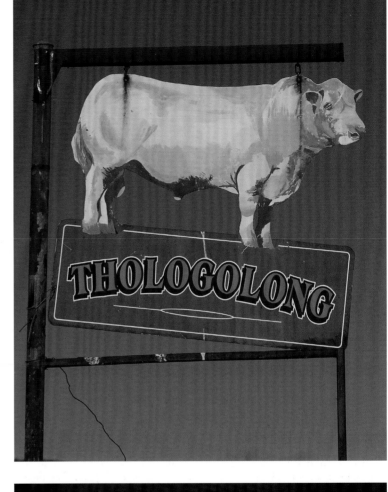

CHAPTER 7 – WALWA

SAVED BY THE BULL

Down the western side of the Walwa pub there's a narrow, sealed road heading north to the river and a gorgeous rest spot. I head down then to check the 'Old Man'.

It doesn't disappoint (does it ever?). Across the Murray's waters the trees bounce the early afternoon light back onto the waters as an eddy nearby gurgles and some ducks murmur about the danger I represent. Then it's back to the town, and into the lane behind the pub before parking Super Ten beside the sign warning to go no further.

Inside there's no other customer in the large front bar, just a woman sitting behind the counter. She looks up at me briefly, manages a quarter of smile, then it's back to her digital tablet.

I shed my riding gear at a distant wall-side table and head over. She looks up without getting up and after I tell her I have a booking for the night, finds the motivation to rouse herself, tell me it'll be forty dollars, takes my credit card, hands me the key, tells me where the room is and then is about to sit back down when I have the audacity to ask for a beer.

Now, she can get back to playing Candy Crush or whatever it is that's on her toy!

I take the pot (we're in Victoria remember!) back to my table. It's becoming a bit clearer why the bloke I'm wanting to talk with suggested we catch up back at his place rather than the local. This place is tired. Run by people who are obviously over it; people wanting to be rid of it. Beside me on the wall is an A4 sheet announcing the pub's for sale.

I finish the drink, grab my stuff and dump it in my room, rid the bike of superfluous equipment and then lift the leg over.

Walwa has a very special place in this country's history because it was here, well hereabouts, that Australia's sole contribution to the great cattle breeds was born. In 1898 two brothers, Peter and John Sutherland, bought Thologolong Station just up from where Walwa now is and worked sheep and black polled Angus. In 1902–03 a drought decimated their stock and they were forced to buy in cattle and the new beasts included an almost white roan cow. Somehow this cow was penned with Angus bulls and a 'mulberry' calf resulted. Peter Sutherland wanted to dispose of it but his wife, Ina, insisted it stay with them. Over the next twelve years the cow had a dozen more of these grey 'mulberries'.

Peter Sutherland died in 1929 and a woman by the name of Helen Player bought eight of the mulberries, which she systematically cross-bred and improved the strain.

Helen Player married Keith, the son of Peter and Ina Sutherland. Keith wasn't a great fan of the greys either but Helen persevered, attracted by the breed's quiet nature, its coat and its marbled meat. They registered the name 'Murray Greys' and, aided by other breeders like neighbour Mervyn Gadd, the breed began to take off. In 1967 three carcasses were shipped to the Smithfield Show in England, the most prestigious beef show on the planet. They finished first, second and third in the Commonwealth Carcass competition and their future looked assured.

In 2008 the Murray Grey, which had originated by accident at Walwa beside Australia's greatest river, was the largest represented breed at the 2008 Calgary Stampede Carcass Competition and that same year at Montana, a Murray Grey carcass hit, well, I guess the bullseye when for the first time in history the judges gave it perfect ten for marbling and added a nine for tenderness.

I leave the pub behind and point the bike into the afternoon sun. My GPS has the co-ords for a roadside monument and in a few minutes I'm pulling up at roadside plinth with an Aussie flag hanging limp behind. There's a plaque on the rock announcing this as 'The Birthplace of the

Murray Grey' and detailing a bit of the genesis of the breed. At the bottom is a quote:

This breed by accident was nature's which in turn is God's gift to our land Australia. These are our own cattle, our heritage, Australia's heritage in the beef cattle world and none can say agin this.

This is taken from the diary of Helen Sutherland and after taking it all it, I turn the bike around and head across the road to talk with Helen's son, and grandson of Peter and Ina, the current custodian of the birthplace of the Murray Grey. His name is also Peter Sutherland.

Peter and his partner, Gina, have seen me coming up the path and they both come out to welcome me. I can smell fresh baking aromas tempting me inside but Peter's had a good morning that he's wanting to share and something he's itching to show me before we go in.

'Back in 1954 when I was thirteen, we had this fox that was taking all our chickens and Dad tried to poison him and trap him but no luck. So one night I hid in the old toilet we had out the back and waited in the dark. Eventually I heard the chickens squawk and I jumped out with the old Harrington Richardson shotgun. And I got him! From about 60 yards running across the bridge!'

Well they've been having another vulpine visitor of late and early this morning Peter once again lay in ambush. He leads me out of the garden, round beside the shed, bends and picks up a not-yet-stiff dead fox.

'Here I am sixty-four years later and I can still hit one of these buggers from 50 yards! I got as much out of that as breeding a ribbon winner,' he laughs, 'and I used the same trusty Harrington to do it!' He dumps the carcass and we head inside where the perpetrators of the baking scents are front and centre on the table: a tray of big, country sultana scones.

Peter's a wiry little bloke with a focusing stare. He sits back with his brew and as he talks his hands, sinewy and worn from a life of work, cut through the air, pointing and accentuating.

It wasn't always certain that Peter Sutherland would follow his father and grandfather into cattle. When he was seventeen he did a wool-classing course and topped it.

'My teacher, he arranged for me to go to Sydney and get a job in the wool industry, but I just felt that the future was in cattle and not sheep. The Murray Grey was about at the time and my brother and I were both very interested in them so I never went. I did a lot of wool classing in New South Wales and locally here up until was twenty-five.'

But then he threw his lot in with the Murray Greys and has stayed with them ever since, and now as he looks for a quieter life, they have begun to slowly divest their stock. Finding buyers is not proving difficult.

'I had a bloke come from Bendigo wanting a bull and he drove up here and asked me how much I wanted and I said five thou for your pick of the paddock so he drove out to have a look and picked one and paid and took it.

'Next week he was back with a neighbour and a trailer and I didn't quite know what the neighbour wanted but they asked me, is it still five thou for the pick of the paddock and I said yes, so they gave be ten thou and took two.'

The heyday of the Murray Grey may have passed and Peter has no doubt where blame lies.

'There's been no other breed in the world that's declined like the Murray Grey and I put that down to administration: badly marketed, very badly marketed for twenty-five years. They had every opportunity to really push them but they had a bad marketing program and they took advice from the new breeders who thought they knew it all and didn't listen to the older breeders and when things didn't go so well they did nothing and let the industry fall apart. They moved the headquarters of the Murray Grey Association from Albury to Armidale.'

Gina offers me a second scone and chips in with her thoughts on the move from the spiritual home of the breed and the pork-barrelling politician behind it. Peter nods and agrees.

Clearly these feelings are part of their larger suspicion and contempt for much of city-based visionless bureaucracy. Peter says he'll tell me a story and he'll try to make it short:

Back in the '70s they had a hell of drought around Longreach and Roma. It was in a shocking mess and there was a Murray Grey breeder called Ray Buntine and he was the first to develop the semitrailers to take the cattle to the meat works. He was a marvellous man and he came down here in the '60s and took a semi full of Murray Greys, all females and two bulls. About five years later he was in the middle of the worst drought ever and he rang me and said this problem is immense, 'I have two small 'dozers pushing down the mulga to feed the stock. The calves are good but we just have to do something.'

So I rang around a found a truck that was taking a load of rams up to near Longreach and I went up there with him but even before we got there the truck driver said, 'This is hopeless, look at the land and look at the cattle here, we won't be able to even get 'em on the truck.'

About 50 miles out and we hit a small town and I rang Ray and he said, 'I'll meet you at the 7-mile peg, you can leave the truck there and I'll take you in and show you the cattle.'

The truck driver was a bit anxious and wanted to turn back but I kept him with me and Ray's son was pushing timber to the cattle and I said, 'Yeah the calves really do look okay.'

So I walked around the steers and we agreed on a deal for me to take all the steers, about forty-eight or fifty of them and we could fit 'em on the semi and I said, 'How are we going to yard 'em, it's 25 mile to the yards?'

And he said, 'I can make a yard?'

But I told him, 'the truck driver won't wait that long, he'll shoot me if I keep him waiting forty-eight hours!'

So he said to his young bloke, 'I'm taking these blokes to the homestead for some dinner, they must be starving, and you make a yard.'

So all the son did was push the timber that was already down, the branches and the trunks that the cattle wouldn't touch and made a yard.

When we got back we drove the truck through an opening in this circle of pushed logs and all the cattle just followed the truck in there and then Ray's son pushed some more trunks to close it behind them.

So I said, 'How're we going to load them onto the truck?'

He said Murray Greys are quite friendly and he guaranteed we could loan 'em. He went and got some old panels and we cut the steers out from the heifers. And he told the driver to back the truck up and he'd push some dirt up to make a funnel up and we loaded every beast, never left a steer behind.

We took them to a place north of Hay for agistment and it'd rained there and they had the best feed you've ever seen, clover this high. And I stayed away from them for about four or five months and I rang the bloke. 'Take 'em to Sydney for the fat stock show,' the bloke said, 'we've a lot of cattle here but yours are the best doing cattle on the place.'

So we sent them by road to Junee and then by train to Sydney for the show and when they arrived they were just magnificent.

Well we won fifty ribbons with them and they won the champion pens of nine, the hoop and the hook, which is very hard to do.

They jostle to assure me winning the ribbons wasn't the point of that story.

Now if Ray Buntine saved his cattle that way now, those idiots in power up in Brisbane would have him charged for pushing the mulga to feed his starving stock. They have these housing developments up there where it's okay to knock over every single tree because that makes it easier to build their houses cheaper and make more profits but if a grazier wants to save dying cattle, somehow he's a criminal.

But there's a more serious result of this sort of government policy. Gina takes over.

'We got really affected by the 2002–03 drought and we struggled to get water out of the river and there just wasn't enough in it for everyone. Animals were dying everywhere and every day. We know of seven suicides just in the Murray Grey community, you know farmers would go out to shoot cattle trapped in the mud of dried up dams and they'd just be overcome by the helplessness of it all and take their own lives instead.'

The three of us go quiet. They both sip their tea and I swig some coffee and collect scone crumbs.

Then Gina continues, 'The river was so dry that Peter rode old Shah across it from one side to the other and back without getting his stirrups wet.'

'Old Shah?' I ask, and Peter's face lights up, removed now from the gross stupidity and terrible costs of wrong decisions made many miles away.

'It was 1988 and I heard this bloke was going to put down one of his racehorses who'd done a fetlock and I said, no I'll take him, so they gave him to me and asked me what I was going to do with him.

'I said he's the best-looking horse I've ever seen, like a proper brumby and I said I was going to put him where the national park was, Mount Lawson State Park in those days. I said I'll just turn him out there for twelve months, plenty of feed, plenty of water and plenty of space to run around, no other horses.

'So I left him out for twelve months and we had an old war veteran who lived up there on the block and he used to hit the grog pretty badly. And we had a duck shooters' hut up there where we always kept a bridle and saddle to take a horse to muster with. So this one evening when it was dark this old bloke went into the park and caught the horse and saddled him up and rode him down here half tanked and fell off him over there under that tree. I had to cut the saddle off the horse because the old digger was trapped under him and I put the horse into the yard. Next morning I had a look at him and said this horse is no longer lame, the rider was in a bad way but the horse was okay. Next day I got on him and I used him for twenty-five years.

'See the secret is that he had one-eighth Clydesdale in him. Like the 'whalers' that stocked the Remount Units of the First World War. They were very tough animals. He was thirty-nine when he died, old Shah. Was a very sad day.'

We get up and head out the back of the house and Peter points up the slope. 'Shah died at the top of that hill and we buried him there. We've applied to have it registered as a cemetery so I can be buried right next to him when I go.'

In the paddock off to the side a Murray Grey cow eyes us and heads over when she sees Peter heading for the feed bucket. Her coat glistens in the lowering sun.

Gina remains with me and for the no doubt the umpteenth time in her life almost swoons. 'See how her coat is like someone's thrown a silken sheet over her? Just so beautiful.'

On that, there's no argument.

I say my thanks and take my leave. On the way back down the path I pass the old shed where the very first generations of Murray Greys were housed, a quick pause to photograph the signs at the front gate and I'm heading east back to the Walwa pub.

Across from the television, which seems never to be turned off or turned down, Candy Crush must be getting to an exciting stage, so I head straight to my basic but comfortable room.

In the morning I opt against the pub's offering of plastic white bread and a tiny slab of butter and head across the road. As I'm having a brew and pie in front of a raging fire at the wonderful Walwa General Store and Newsagency just up and across the main street from the pub, a bloke starts asking what I'm doing in town.

I tell him I'm headed down river with Jingellic my first port of call, and he makes himself comfortable in a seat beside.

'Two things you've gotta do, mate.' He gives me the name and a few scandal facts of a fella I 'must' see in Jingellic. 'And you've gotta head up to Lankeys Creek and see the ruins of the old shanty up there.'

I tell him it's great to be in a friendly place and pledge to honour his wisdom. Blokes like this know their stuff so I tell him I will, then I gear up and point Super Ten north-west. There's a bloke I've suddenly gotta see.

CHAPTER 8

FOLLOWING INSTRUCTIONS

A tricky right turn off the Murray River road and I'm on the new(ish) bridge crossing the Murray back into New South Wales and then off to the right is the Jingellic General Store with a couple of blokes in work gear heading out, mitts full of pastry and iced coffees.

Inside, Kylie's looking after the joint and I figure another brew's in order, and then I ask about the bloke I've just heard about back in Walwa.

'Ah, Rexy! You've not long missed him. Was down here to pick up his morning paper and sandwich but he's just walked back up to his house.'

She comes outside and points up the hill. 'That's his place, he'll probably be out on the verandah reading the paper in the sunshine like he always does.'

Then I ask for a few directions to Lankeys Creek and Kylie points north, gives a rough idea of the roads and turns and then finishes with the fatal words, 'You can't miss it.'

I'm running early so I take my time then thank Kylie and ride up to the place on the hill where, true to word, an old bloke is hunched on his verandah reading the paper – with a magnifying glass. Shirtless in the morning sun, Rex Beaver welcomes me like an old mate, as though I'm some prodigal son he's not seen for way too long, and invites me, instructs me, to take the weight off my feet.

I tell him why I'm hanging around and how I'd like to have a yarn with him down at the pub and he'd be only too happy. And could he drive down there, please?

He laughs – he obviously laughs a lot – and stabs a finger in my general direction, 'So you've heard about my machine have you?'

I tell him I have and wonder if we could do it in a couple of hours after I've been up to the road a bit and again he laughs, tells me it's all very easy and when I seek confirmation of the directions he duplicates Kylie's but adds, 'Just keep going and you'll see the place up on your left and maybe some camels but,' and here he adds the bit that always seems to be tagged onto instructions that men, especially men give in the bush, 'if you get to the railway cars on the right you've gone too far.'

Out here when you're getting directions there's always that 'if you get to the ... then you've gone too far' clause.

I leave Rex to his paper and his magnifying glass and head north on the Holbrook Road.

CHAPTER 9 – LANKEYS CREEK

A MAN'S NOT A CAMEL

This is a story not so much about a pub as the remnants of what was once a pub. Actually, better change that to the remnants what was once a wine shanty. In fact, best not to risk the ire of the probably pedantic ghost of its long-time owner and give it the full regal moniker on which she insisted.

Mrs Alexander, who ran the place between Holbrook and Jingellic for near half a century, would promptly admonish anyone who within her earshot demeaned her house by referring to it as a 'shanty'. Rather, it was the 'Lankeys Creek Wine Palace' and she would be ever so thankful if it were referred to as such! She was a stickler for proper behaviour and courtesy was Barbara Isabelle Alexander, and she had no truck with any lack of respect.

One summer afternoon at the end of December 1919, this woman, whose husband was absent, allegedly at the war, and who lived with her sister, had a visit from an old friend who was invited to stay for a cuppa. Things turned a bit heated when the visitor, Mrs Louise Hope, made some allegations against Barbara involving her intentions with Charlie Hope and called Barbara and her sister, 'liar(s) … low women, (whose) mode of living proves it.'

Charlie Hope was Louise's brother-in-law, and the owner of the Wine Palace (and village post mistress) was nothing if not sensitive, and so on the basis of a comment made in private, she sued her friend for slander in public. And for good measure her sister, Laura Gifford, filed as well. They each wanted £400 for damage to their reputations and the matter reached the District Court in Albury.

On the second day of the hearing one of the jurors decided he couldn't be bothered with the rubbish so he didn't turn up and the local cop told everyone he thought the plaintiffs both 'bore a high reputation' and that

the defendant also 'bore a good character'. His Honour smiled, struck out the case and Mrs Alexander, no doubt feeling vindicated and in need of a drink, returned to Lankeys Creek and her palace. The tongue-in-cheek report in the press was headlined: 'HIGH LIFE AT LANKEY'S CREEK'.

Meanwhile, I continue along the Holbrook Road, until I see the railway carriages that mean I've gone too far, swing around and then spot the less than palatial ruins up on my right. As I park Super Ten in the shade, there's a couple of blokes in the distance approaching on a quad bike and behind them a few camels.

From over the fence I check out the falling-down fibro wreck that is the shell of the old watering hole and as I do the two on the quad check out my bike and then come over.

'So you've been to Grong Grong eh?'

They've been reading the stickers on the bike's panniers and when I tell 'em yeah and it's a pretty decent pub, the same bloke lights up.

My brother Doug made that place famous, he's been written about in a book on pubs. It was all about how he played a hoax on the Sydney papers and bullshitted to them how Grong Grong was the home of neenish tarts. Did they tell you that story when you were there?

I walk back to Super Ten, open the top box and pull out a book.

'This one?'

'Yes, that's the book me brother's in!'

I point to the name of the author at the base of the cover. 'That's me. I wrote it. I'm Colin. How're ya goin?'

'Be buggered! It's a small world!'

We all shake hands, introduce ourselves and have a laugh. Turns out the other bloke's Peter and he owns the farm that the shanty ruins are on. He also owns the camels and would I like to meet one?

Now, no-one's too sure just when the Lankeys Creek wine saloon actually opened for the first time. In April 1897 the Wagga *Advertiser* advised that the licensing court to be held in Germanton on the thirtieth of that month was scheduled to hear an application for a colonial wine licence by James Gifford of Lankeys Creek.

That pretty much sounds to me like an application for a new licence. Problem is, the next month the same paper announced that at this hearing the court granted a renewal of a colonial wine licence to James Gifford of Lankeys Creek. Then a bit over twenty years later, in reporting the slander case brought by Mrs Alexander in 1919 which I mentioned above, the *Border Mail* reported testimony that the 'accommodation house and post office had been conducted by the family for 30 years' putting its birth at 1889.

So, let's just say late 19th century and from at least 1897 the place was in the name of Gifford, the maiden name of Mrs Barbara Alexander. Earlier she'd had the licence for the long-vanished Benambra Hotel down the road at Talgarno.

Back at Jingellic when I was getting directions here, I'd asked Rex Beaver about the shanty and he remembered his first drink here over a half century later in the early 1960s.

'Me and a mate, Chris Bowman, who used to make butter at Walwa, we got a lift to Holbrook, this is no bull, and we couldn't get a lift back here to Jingellic. So anyway, we had to walk from Holbrook to Lankeys Creek and we walked past Lankeys to old Sunshine Miller's place. Sunshine was a bloke I used to shear for and he said what're you guys doing and we told him we'd walked from Holbrook and he said bugger that, I'll give you a lift but first I'll take you up to the shanty for a drink. We'd never had a drink there, I was still probably only twenty-two, twenty-three.'

So the three of them headed up to Mrs Alexander's and Rex wasn't too impressed.

'I was a beer drinker then, didn't like wine but they only sold wine and it was pretty ordinary wine, very ordinary, but we drank it. I don't think we even had a choice. It was all just one wine but anyway we had one each and then Sunshine gave us a lift down to town.'

The bush really is a small place. I found a real goldmine when I was backgrounding this palace. Just up the road in Holbrook, a bloke named John Meredith was born in 1920. Inspired and encouraged by both his parents he developed a real love for Australian bush songs, poetry and music. In the 1950s he and a couple of mates formed a band which, after a couple of name changes, became The Bushwackers.

They were successful. Released in 1956 their 78rpm disc *The Drover's Dream* sold over 20,000 copies, which back then was unheard of. They can also be held responsible (accountable?) for introducing the lagerphone to Australian bush music!

But John Meredith's love of music wasn't limited to performance. Lugging cumbersome equipment all over the country, he recorded the music of, and conversations with, old timers with connections to the music for which he had unlimited passion.

His most priceless legacy is the Meredith Collection, now held in the National Library of Australia. Amongst its over 1000 unique and culturally valuable items is an audio yarn he recorded in 1989 with Jack 'Sunshine' Miller, the same bloke who gave Rex Beaver and his mate their first drink at Lankeys Creek.

In the interview Sunshine shone some light on the old Wine Palace of Mrs Alexander, going back to his memories of the very beginning. After Peter and his mate have gone and I've trod through the ruins, I sit on the old porch and switch on my phone and listen to my recording of John Meredith's yarn with Sunshine Miller.

The shanty's always been in the Alexanders' and the Giffords' name. Up to the beginning of WWI (it) was in Jim Gifford's name because in those days a woman couldn't hold a licence and Jim lived over the gap and Mrs Alexander was his sister. But then Jim Gifford went to war, Barbara married Alexander, a skin buyer from Corryong, and with the war forcing a change in ownership rules, she took over the licence.

According to Sunshine Miller, and just perhaps shedding an insight into Mrs Hope's allegations about Barbara Alexander's 'mode of living', she and Alexander 'parted pretty soon after [getting married].'

Her husband seemingly vanished without too much of a trace. In 1918 there was mention in the papers that' 'there was ... a round of cheers for Pte Alexander, who was home on leave [from the war]' at a function at the Lankeys Creek town hall but whether this was a son, the husband or some other relative is impossible to know.

But in 1942 Marie Isabelle Alexander married Ronald Keith Mott in Holbrook. Whilst the groom was described as the second son of Mr and Mrs T. Mott of Holbrook, the bride was described as the daughter of only Mrs B. Alexander of Lankeys Creek – no mention of her sire. Somewhere here there's that whiff of scandal!

Later there was mention of a son who'd married a lass from Spring Vale but again no mention of his father. This is the same father whom Mrs Alexander told the slander trial was serving in the war. And yet the only photograph from this time showing the farewell for young men headed to the front features three locals, including possibly Mrs Alexander's son, but no husband.

But enough of the suppositions of bastardry and loose living, let's get back to the pub. Sorry, Wine Palace! Irrespective of what type of wine you requested at the palace back then it all came out of the same cask and it was 'black port like treacle'. At some stage the authorities ordered Mrs Alexander to cease syphoning the wine out of the casks by sucking on a tube and then pouring it into the glasses.

The brew was known as 'block and tackle' because, according to Sunshine, 'if you had a drink of it and then walked around the block, you'd tackle the first bloke who crossed you.'

And he remembers her brown enamel mug with its inside as black as ink, 'because the wine had taken all the enamel off it, so what would it've done to your stomach?'

Jack Miller also recalled the endless fights at the Palace and how, 'just away from the house was what we called the chamber of horrors. That was where they put the drunks.'

In the interview, John Meredith, echoing Sydney Watson back at Tintaldra, here explains that such rooms were often called 'the deadhouse' and Miller agrees – 'that's right, the deadhouse of the chamber of horrors. She just called it the extra accommodation.'

High class, and slightly more sober visitors would sleep in two other rooms where Sunshine reckons 'they used to sleep up to eight in a double bed'. These were attached to the main building where the slab kitchen, 'had a window made out of old kerosene cases and that's where they used to serve the wine through. We used to call it the black hole of Calcutta.'

None of which seemed to trouble the clientele too much, and even after the local tin diggings closed, Mrs Alexander's place remained a goldmine. He reckons there were anything up to 100 men in the area, all of whom had nowhere else to go. 'They'd come in to the shanty to cash their cheques and they never used to get any change, they used to cut it out.'

The original Wine Palace burnt down in the epic Holbrook fires of January 1952, the Wagga *Daily Advertiser* reporting that, '... Mrs. Alexander's wine saloon and the Post Office were ... destroyed ... as well as the Lankey's Creek Hall and Presbyterian Church.'

But old Mrs Alexander was herself a real trooper and as soon as the embers had cooled, set up shop in what the press described as 'an old tine shed right opposite the ruined post-office.'

It took a few months longer for the insurance to cover the £5370 of damage to the palace (complete with the chamber of horrors) and for the place to be rebuilt. It staggered on for another decade or so but then the doors were finally closed for the last time and today the building is slowly imploding.

As we walk down to meet his camels, Peter explains that he bought the place in 1990 inspired in equal measure by the memories of times in these parts with his dad and a love of this part of the country. And he speaks with perspective. He's been all over Australia including travelling with camels in the Simpson and up through Boulia.

He used to harness them to a wagon and give rides along the Holbrook Road. 'But then the whole green slime started and they allowed the B-double trucks on the road to get the logs out so it became too dangerous,' and he had to keep them on his rolling farm. ('Green slime' is the local term for the pine plantations that infest so much of the scenery down here.)

The camels approach us. There're seven ladies plus a bull to look after them and Peter reckons so long as there's only one male in the joint, it'll all stay peaceful. He and his mate have to shove off but I'm free to roam over the ruin as long as I want, but before he scoots I ask him, why the camels?

His mate knows what's coming and laughs in anticipation. With logic that's hard to fault, half-turning to go, Peter explains, 'Well the place is closed, you can't get a drink and there's that saying about a man not being a camel. So I figured that if I can't get a drink I might as well get some fucking camels!'

After the fires I return to Lankeys Creek. The camels are all okay but the green slime has been uniformly cremated. For kilometre after kilometre on the road across from Tumbarumba there's hardly a patch of forest that's been spared.

I spot an echidna off to one side walking with the charming swagger they all have. It's digging for food in the burnt soil and not seeming to have much luck. A bit further on, at the very edge of the forest, a horse eyes me from just inside the burnt treeline. In the roadside culvert between us is some tempting green pick. It calls to me and I leave it to feed. The place is totally devastated.

CHAPTER 10 – JINGELLIC

WHERE A BEAVER LODGED FOR LIFE

As I'm coasting back down the hill on the return to Jingellic, I glance up at Rex's place and in the open carport a figure is whipping on the starter cord of an unseen engine which doesn't want to fire up. I watch the silhouette ripping the cord out in a motion similar to a cross-cut saw then rewinding it on the wheel and ripping it again without any engine coughing into life. If that's old Rex I feel guilty about my earlier request, then I coast down, knowing I've beaten my quarry to the pub.

Inside, Peter's manning the taps: five draughts and a cider plus a good range of wines in the fridge behind. The place has a wooden ceiling and as in so many country pubs, a wooden ceiling means money – notes of money stuck up there with drawing pins.

Here's how it's done: get a note and push a drawing pin though the centre of it. Place a 20 cent or 50 cent piece over the head of the pin and fold the note around the coin. Place it on the palm of your hand and keeping your hand horizontal throw the thing upwards as hard as you can. The weight of the coin should force the pin into the wood securing the note to the ceiling and the falling coin will unfold the note.

Easy eh? I'm an expert on the theory, total dunce on the practice!

It's getting near time for the annual harvest of the Jingellic pub's ceiling and Peter reckons the haul is usually around two grand, all of which goes to the Walwa bush nursing hub. I try to add to it, fail miserably, so just drop my fiver into the tip jar! Humiliated, I grab a quick beer and head out the front to what has to be one of the great beer gardens on the Murray River.

Off to the left are the remaining piles of the original Jingellic Bridge although sadly no sign of the old customs house visible in old photos of the crossing. Straight out front is just the best swimming hole in this part of the river and to the right, the pebbled elbow behind a couple of caravans.

No-one who's visited Jingellic doesn't love this place; doesn't list it among their favourite spots. I've had some of my most refreshing river swims here – just strip the boots, socks and jacket and dive in. And I've woken to some of my most exquisite riverside mornings.

My jar's soon droughted so I head back in, grab another from Peter and pretty soon Rex chugs into view.

Back up at his place he'd explained a few things. In 2018 Rex Beaver's glaucoma got more serious. This is why he now reads the daily rag with a magnifying glass. His mid-range and distance is not so badly affected – he reads the 'Canon eos' on my camera on the table and the brand on my bike without much problem but the government decided he could no longer drive. And since he lives just a bit beyond walking from the pub, this man without a bicycle and without a licence had a dilemma. But then he had a flash, called the local council and made them an offer: Would they be interested in having their roadside paths mowed regularly at no charge? Of course they were!

Well, Rex explained, he'd be more than happy to keep the place trimmed and tidy if they'd be sweet with him piloting his ride-on mower to the pub with the blades up on the days between shaves. The council was sweet with that too. As he puts it, 'Winner, winner chicken dinner!'

It was his reluctant mower that Rex was trying to start as I rolled down to the pub and it's the same red beast that sails past the pub's window and into a parking spot beside my bike.

You know those people you see in pubs, in groups, leading the discussion, causing the laughter, being the magnet, the glue, the source of endless and enduring good cheer? Well I know immediately that Rex is one of them. I splash out on a water for him and settle back for the fun.

Going to school, Rex Beaver had always been fascinated with Australia and in 1953 in an old cinema in his hometown of Leicester in the English

58

Midlands he watched *The Overlanders* with Chips Rafferty. The fifteen-year-old told his mum he wanted to go to this strange, foreign land and she said someone from down the street had gone and she'd have a chat with them and ask them about it.

'She found out and it was the Big Brotherhood movement that was involved and I had to go with Mum and Dad to London to have an interview and everything was right just like that and within five months I was on the *Himalaya*. I remember the date, it was the third of March, 1954.

'The rules were that they wouldn't let our parents see us off at the boat. We said our goodbyes at the railway station because they said it was too hard to say goodbye at the bloody boat and the neighbours saw me off.'

When the ship docked in Sydney a representative of the Big Brotherhood introduced Rex and a few other lads to a gentleman, 'who said he was taking us to a training farm out near Auburn on the Parramatta River to teach us how to milk cows. We were there for about a fortnight. Well it didn't take much for me to learn how to milk a cow. I had it worked out by the second day.'

When the two weeks were up, Rex was taken back to Auburn station with one ticket to Central railway and another to Albury.

'When I got to Albury this bloke walked up to me and said, "Are you Rex Beaver?" and I said, "Yeah," and he said he was George Palmer and he took me out to Dora Dora, well, Talmalmo, and the next morning told me to go have a look around. So I did and I went back to him and said, 'This is probably the most beautiful place I've ever seen.' I just instantly loved it.

'This farm was only about 50 yards from the river, it was magnificent and we only had about thirty cows that I had to milk each day. We got paid a tiny bit but at that stage it was really just an adventure.'

Rex was still only sixteen.

On the trip on the *Himalaya*, Rex'd made a few mates and one of them, Bill Shaw, had been sent to another farm not too far away and they palled up again. Despite loving the location and enjoying the work, Rex was lonely and looking for a bit of a change.

'Mr Palmer and his wife had no kids so I was pretty much on my own there and was missing young company. I went to another couple of farms and then a bloke named Eddie Coleman, he came up to me and my mate Bill Shaw from the ship and he said, "How'd you both like to come fencin' for us?" And I said, "Yeah!" I had no idea what fencing was but I learnt fast and loved it but my mate couldn't handle it.

'It was hard work. We'd axe down the stringybark and cross-cut saw them into shape, put a little point on 'em and make a bit of a hole with a crowbar and drive 'em in with this massive maul. Then we'd connect the ringlock wires and make the fences. Sheep fences. This bloke had bush leases and he had thousands, not a thousand but thousands of acres. And they went from the riverside a few thousand feet up and right over the ridge. I loved this. We were camping out in the bush at night, cooking our own food and then working like buggery all day.'

Once the fences were all done, Eddie Coleman had Rex muster his sheep and then the boss taught the ten-quid Pom to shear them. 'I thought I loved the other jobs but shearing was my calling; I really loved the shearing from the very start.'

Rex married in the early 1960s and welcomed children into his family in 1963, '65, '67, '69 and 1974 but in June 1979 his wife, newly converted to be a Jehovah's Witness, left him and took all five children. 'Well I hadn't made a family of beautiful kids so I could live alone so I started fighting and by October that year I had custody of them all. The youngest was five and the oldest was sixteen.'

They were all crammed into a place at Walwa and then in 1982 Rex's endless positivity and good humour came in trumps.

'I was shearing for a bloke over at Holbrook, and he said, "If you ever find a decent old shed that I can take down and reassemble where I need it, let me know." Anyway, a bit later I realised there's one up at Jingellic and it used to be an old super dump, about 100-foot long with a massive strong roof. So I rang him and said, "Reece there's a shed here for ya," and I gave him the details.

'Well a few weeks later he rings me and says, "I bought that shed but I'll tell ya what I'll do for ya. You help me take it apart and I'll give you the block of land it's on." So I helped him pull it down and he said, "Rex, you've shorn thousands of sheep for me sometimes in very tough times, and you never once complained." So he signed the place over to me and we all had a new home!

'He never got on with a lot of shearers and contractors, Reece, but I got on fine with him.'

Then one night the old house burnt down. Rex was asleep in bed but the kids were awake and they raced into his bedroom screaming and they all got out, 'but the place was destroyed and we were all homeless'. 'Lucky it was insured. This was in 1993 and the arson people came and checked it out and they found an electrical fault inside one of the walls caused it and we got this place out of it.'

In 2002, Rex bought 100 acres of the farm where he'd first tugged on cow teats more than half a century earlier. His land extends from the roadside up to past the top of the range. He doesn't run cattle and doesn't grow crops. It's just part of his home and from the top he can view the entire valley and the serpentine upper Murray.

Since the moment he arrived here, Rex's lived every single day as he says, with the certain belief that he's occupying a piece of heaven, that his life is blessed. Like Peter Sutherland, Rex wants to be buried on his plot up in the hills but he wants no eulogy saying he's in paradise, 'because I'll have just left it!'

And he's in no rush. 'If I could call god and have a word, I'd ask him to leave me here for another 190 years.'

I suggest he should also ask for a mower with electric start and he just laughs and tells me that a bit of toil's never hurt any man.

In early 2021 the council put up a new footbridge over the Jingellic Creek, midway between Rex's digs and the pub. In recognition of this bloke they named it 'Beaver's Bridge' and it sure chuffed Rex. 'It's bloody wonderful,' he beams. 'Can even handle the mower.'

After the fires of January 2020, I again sweep past the general store, past the showground which has maybe two dozen vans and a bundle of tents, and around to the Jingellic Pub. The place's been sold since last time – new owners from Albury – but Peter's a constant behind the bar.

'Welcome,' he wryly smiles and nods to the dark brown flow of the river out front, 'to the Upper Cadbury.'

The place is busy for a mid-week arvo but if most of the people at the bar aren't locals, they're not exactly tourists either. They're workers, contractors and volunteers down here to start rejuvenating the place and Chris, the bloke I plonk down next to, is one of the last type.

Probably in his mid-sixties, wearing a maroon polo with back printing indicating medical qualifications, he tells me about turning up here in October, planning to stay over Christmas (his folks live over in Albury) and then heading slowly down to Tasmania for a few months before winter set in.

He lives full-time on the road and his caravan is one of those I'd seen around at the showgrounds on the way in. He reckons it's a good life but it's one more thrust on him than chosen. Up until a bit over ten years ago, he was working in healthcare then, after a 27 ½ hour shift one day, he collapsed and spent almost nine weeks in rehab.

'When I arrived home there were cops at my place and they told me there'd been a court order taken out against me and I had thirty minutes to get my stuff and leave. I had no idea what was going on.'

As the police waited and watched, Chris said 'goodbye' to his two kids, then aged fourteen and nine, and moved what he could into his car. He hasn't seen his children since.

He started living rough out of his car and began to seriously consider suicide. He'd served as a medic in the army from 1979–85 and another stint in 1996–97. 'I'd been to too many funerals of my mates from the army and one day I just decided I could either keep going and join the dead or do a U-turn and help the living and I chose to help the living.'

He bought the caravan and a decent tug and started locating his old army mates, creating a data base of contacts and a support network. Now, when he hears of anyone in trouble, anyone with issues, he pulls up stumps and hits the road.

When the fires first came to Jingellic, Chris tried to get out on the road north but it was already too late and he was turned back.

'So I came back here to the pub and the police were telling us that we should all leave and right then this massive fireball went whoooosh over the ridge. This large group of blokes was staying to try to save the place and I thought that I might be able to be useful, so I stayed. We had a generator that was powering a pump getting water out of the river, and we were spraying everything, just keeping everything as soaked as we could.

'We kicked around a plan that if it all went very wrong we'd hide out in the coolroom and pour beer over ourselves while we drank expensive Scotch.'

That afternoon, New Year's Eve, Chris counted twenty-three fire trucks heading out of town and it was then that one of them lost his life to the fire.

The inferno reached the ridge about 80 metres from the pub but the team hosed down the ember attack and saved the hotel. For two weeks no-one left and no-one relaxed.

Many pubs have plaques honouring those who built them. As I leave Chris and his volunteer mates, the conviction grows within me that there must surely be a way of memorialising those who, in disastrous times like the fires of January 2020, have saved them.

62

TALMALMO'S QUAINT INN

The Dora Dora Hotel at Talmalmo in the Upper Murray district.

CHAPTER 11 – DORA DORA

GONE BUT NOT FORGOTTEN

After I got back from the bar with Rex Beaver's second tumbler of water at the Jingellic Hotel he told me about giving up the fags.

'I used to love smoking but in '82 I just gave it up one day and never thought about it again. I've got willpower to do things like that. Like drinking.'

Rex first gave up beer in 1974 and kept off it for nine years, 'just because'. Then he went dry again in the '90s when saving for his house and then he quit again in 2005 and has stayed with the H_2O ever since.

'Make no mistake, I've loved every mouthful of beer I've ever had and the next one will be sweet,' but right now he's doing just fine.

'I had my first drink at the Dora Dora hotel. I just went down there one Saturday and I decided it was time I had a drink so I went into the bar and old Alf Wright was there and he hadn't met me before. It was an ordinary 7-ounce beer and I had a sip and thought,' Rex smiles and pauses and his voice drops an octave, 'that's beautiful!'

Rex has good memories of the Dora Dora pub and of Alf and Emma who ran the place. Rex shore the few sheep they kept behind the pub and it was evident every memory he had was a fond one. 'In the pub he had a museum, everything from long bits of wool that hadn't been shorn for years, he had a joystick from a zero aeroplane and all sorts of stuff. But then Alf died in the late '80s and the pub closed a bit after that.'

Once Rex left, I headed inside and we found self-described 'chief bottle washer' Peter behind the bar. He's spent a lifetime working in pubs, from Tocumwal to Narromine, managing, owning, fixing up busted ones.

He pointed to the wall beside the bar: 'I remember sitting up against that wall when I was eight, maybe ten with my dad while we were supposed to be on a fishing trip.'

And as he grew up he continued to visit and, finally wearied by the pub life, in 2001 with his wife, bought a small riverside farm twenty minutes down the road. The place is called 'Dunpubbin'.

He asked me where I was headed and when I told him first west to Dora Dora he beamed and said how happy he was to've drunk at the old hotel.

The first time Peter ever went to Dora Dora with some local mates on their motorbikes it was on a fishing trip. The anglers club was across from the pub, and a bend of the Murray just a hundred metres away. They'd arrived early and had a bit of success and around 10.30ish Peter told his mates it might be time for a drink. 'Nah, the pub ain't open yet.'

'It's gotta be, it's after ten, it's gotta be open by now,' said the thirsty Peter.

'Nah, mate, trust me it's not open.'

So they kept cleaning their catches and half an hour later Peter again said, he'd go up and get some beers.

'Still not open.'

'Has to be open, it's almost a quarter to eleven.'

'Promise you, it's not open. You'll know when it's open.'

So, what Peter didn't know was that old Alf had a few rifles and shotties and amongst his collection was an old black powder flintlock long barrel. On weekends, when Alf was ready to open the doors and start serving drinks, he'd stuff the gunpowder into his antique rifle, head out the front of the pub and point the thing in the air.

As Peter sat around with no more fish to clean that first morning, BOOM!

'The sound was immense, the whole river valley echoed with this fucking explosion. I thought maybe the pub'd blown up. It was deafening!'

Peter's mate fixed on him and smiled, 'Pub's open.'

CHAPTER 12 – THE WYMAH FERRY

MOST CERTAIN PUNT I'LL HAVE TODAY

Abit over 30 kilometres of docile dirt road that kisses the Murray a few times from the northern side and I'm slowing down with a house on my left and a descent to the river straight ahead.

The house is the last remnant of the town of Wymah, which started out being named Wagra. Old Wagra was home to another of our original 'Pub 'n' Punters' and this bloke, one B. Vincent, seems to've been a way more decent human being than Sydney Grandison back at Tintaldra.

In 1877 *The Sydney Mail* published a yarn entitled, 'A Trip Through the Southern Districts' and the author enjoyed his time down on the Murray in general and at Wagra in particular:

From Dora Dora the road ascends gradually till we find ourselves approaching Wagra, which is mostly all selected; a good cutting on both sides of a mountain gap leads us pleasantly to the Victoria Inn, and in the host we met with an old schoolfellow who had received his education at the City of London School. Mr. B. Vincent is a man of considerable enterprise he holds some 1500 acres, keeps a good general store, and (opposite to his inn) has a blacksmith's shop.

His inn, for its completeness of detail and general excellence, took us completely by surprise. That there are but few hotels, even any, in our Australasian towns, which can set viands before the traveller in the recherche style to be met with at the Victoria Inn ... The bedrooms and the beds are worthy of special mention. The former are lofty and most excellently built, whilst the latter are all that the tired and weary traveller could possibly desire. Mr. Vincent, doubtless with a view to business, has

purchased and put a punt on the Murray in close proximity to the inn, and that his spirited enterprise will ultimately meet with its fitting reward we can but hope.

And Vinnie was no flash in the pan – a full decade later Charles Ager Atkin wrote about a 'trip to Mount Kosciusko' and enthused about his night at Vincent's Hotel, gushing that it was, 'one of the most comfortable in the Upper Murray. The hotels on the New South Wales side are much more comfortable than the Victorian ones.'

Another top pub that I'm (a century or so) too late for, but his other legacy, the punt, lives on. It's upper Murray's last remaining punt, an anachronism – just one of two interstate river ferries left in the country. The other is a good few days downstream.

The ferry's on the southern bank so I wait at the top of the drop, and pretty soon there's movement in the cables and the punt's on its way over. When the gates are opened and I get the signal, I roll Super Ten down bitumen, up the ramp and onto what has to be a pretty new punt. Last time I came through here, in the middle of the drought of 2008, the old ferry was beached on the southern side, up on chocks beside a river that wasn't much wider than it was long. Should've just left it straddling the stream and called it a bridge! Peter Sutherland would easily've ridden across without getting his stirrups wet!

This time there's a bit more water, not a whole lot more, and the punt is sparkling, well almost. It replaced the old one in 2013, and today Amanda's in charge and since there's no other bugger needs her services right now,

I tell her to just kick back while I get some photos and she can feed the wildlife.

Amanda lives with her partner in the house that I passed just up at the top of the rise. She was taught the ropes down on the Speewa ferry and moved up in 2017. She's currently mother goose to four white drakes who've paddled over to check their chances of falling food. She's been in contact with WIRES and the RSPCA about getting a gander for the boys but so far she's had no result (and no goslings!).

Old Mr Vincent must've done a decent job of the punt because sometime in the 1880s the government took it from him and the ticket prices were fixed by proclamation of the government. By 1903 fees were set at a penny for foot passengers over fourteen and half that for younger kids but those going to or from school travelled for nix. It was tuppence for every 'horse, mare, gelding, cow, ox, heifer, steer, camel, or dromedary' but only a halfpenny for 'any sheep, ewe, ram, lamb, piglet, goat, calf or foal'. No price was stated for geese!

The next year this tiny place with its punt, its pub and its blacksmith shop but bugger all little else, scored a cultural mention.

With the site of the national capital still not decided and Tooma still in with a chance, Banjo Paterson published 'A Nervous Governor General', a rollicking fun poem the last stanza of which went:

Does he think he'll be waked in the dead of the night
From Melbourne to go willy-nilly,
To live at the Federal Capital site
At Tumut or Wagra-go-billy?
Well, the Melbournites may let the Capital go
(Here we wink with one eye, please observe us!)
But not in a hurry! By no means! Oh, no!
He has not the least need to be nervous!

In October 1907 the Hume Shire, which was in charge of the service called for tenders to operate the ferry for calendar 1908 and announced that:

'(f)rom the 1st of December next, said Ferry will be free to all traffic between the hours of 6 a.m. and 11 p.m. (between the hours of 11 p.m. and 6 a.m. a toll to be fixed by the Council will be levied and retained by the successful tenderer).

The night rates didn't last long. Across the state, from Harwood on the Clarence to Tom Ugly's just south of Sydney and from The Spit at Mosman to Tilpa on the Darling, the nocturnal users cried foul long and loud.

In March 1908 the *Albury Banner and Wodonga Express* reported the end of a recurring headache:

At almost every meeting of the Hume Shire Council something has cropped up in connection with the Wagra Ferry, and the result has been that the work has come to be regarded as one of the 'worries' of the Shire. Consequently, when Councillor Shuter informed his colleagues at the last meeting that one of the fruits of the deputation to Sydney was an assurance from the Minister for Works that the Council would be relieved of all further anxiety on this particular score, the information appeared almost too good to be true ...

After June 30 next practically all the ferries will be, absolutely free, no charge being made in those midnight hours, during which the collector has retained his last hold.

Henceforth, after the date mentioned, ferry punts will be among the few Government services rendered absolutely free of charge to the beneficiary. As regards the shire ferries, the councils concerned have been informed that 'the department desires the local tolls abolished, and will bear the extra cost involved, after June 30.

The Wymah punt, like all other inland punts in New South Wales and on the Murray, has been free ever since. The operating hours at Wymah have changed from 7 am to 8 pm May through August and 6 am to 9 pm for the rest of the year. Amanda, though, has to be prepared for emergency call-outs outside these hours but as she explains, 'The emergency services try not to use us just in case the ferry breaks down midway across.'

Every fortnight with one of the other drivers in charge of the punt, she and her partner take the tinnie that's fastened to one side of the punt for a short testing run to ensure it's ready if needed. They must stay within eyeshot of the punt and a test run usually lasts as long as it takes to catch enough fish for dinner.

As we're chatting and the geese are realising they're not about to be fed again, a caravan turns up at the approach on the Victorian side so Amanda gets us moving for the short interstate trip south. It's near four in the afternoon and I'm her seventh passenger of the day including one hectic period when there were two cars on the ferry at once.

Then it's up the long gentle ramp, a left onto the Murray River road and five minutes later I'm turning sharp right and up the gravel to catch up with an old mate.

CHAPTER 13 - THE HOTEL GRANYA

BROKEN DREAMS AND SHATTERED LIVES AND REDEMPTION

The first time I rode the Murray River Road from the Bethanga Bridge, along the southern edge of Lake Hume, and then the upper reaches of our greatest river to Towong and then Corryong was just after the Sydney Olympics.

The country was in the vice grip of the millennial drought and yet the beauty of the river, regularly accompanying me on the left, was transfixing. It was early January and the tar was melting in places, but the Murray, in some places not much more than a creek, was nevertheless constantly entrancing.

We were rough camping with some mates not far out of Albury so one day I went for a solo squirt west for a swim under the Towong Bridge and then back via the Granya cutting. Back at camp my mates were cooking up the fish they'd caught, and around the fire someone asked if I'd dropped into the ex-Granya pub to the east of the punt. I hadn't seen any pub, ex or otherwise and Max, one of the happy campers, grabbed a smoking stick from the fire and drew me a dust map. I didn't make it that time – we were headed in another direction – but a coupla years later I went back

Instead of finding a sad testament to ex-pub, I found a live one – doing it tough for sure, but alive. I spent the arvo swapping tales with Mick the boss and promised both of us that I'd get myself back there again for a night.

And now, a couple more years later, I've finally made it, and if ever a pub's strong suit is also its difficulty – its seclusion and tranquillity make it perfect for a perch, but difficult to find – this is it. Heading east I miss it the first time even though I know what I'm looking for. Eventually I find it, turn up from the bitumen onto the gravel drive, past the old truck, park

Super Ten out front and head in. The place is open but empty; a bit of movement out the back. A few barks respond to my calling out and then 'Won't be a sec' echoes down the hall.

No problem! Gives me time to check out the place. There's a collection of signed Isle of Man TT posters on the walls and above them there's a clock with the island's famous three-legged emblem in the centre.

And there's some of the beautiful stained-glass window panels overhead as I make friends with the two little dogs who follow me out to a porch seat in the sun. Apart from the shuffling out back, there's no noise, just the peace of the breeze in the gums across the drive.

Then Mick turns up. There were a couple of riders in last night and he's just finished cleaning up the rooms. He's due for a smoko so he grabs a red to go with my white and brings them out into the afternoon sunshine.

Mick kinda sorta belongs to my 'Pub 'n' Punters' fraternity. For five years from 2009 Mick had the contract to operate the Wymah punt and its sibling down at Speewa. He and his then wife lived in the ferry master's cottage, where Amanda and her man now are just across in New South Wales, and they'd often eye the empty and slowly decaying old pub down the road. They both knew they couldn't just let it rot.

Like a lot of places, it was mining that caused the creation and sudden prosperity of Granya and in the late 1800s there were half a dozen pubs in the place. It must've been a wild town: in 1893 the publican at Granya's Central Hotel even applied for the required legal permission to conduct dances on Boxing Day! But the ore ran out fast, the miners deserted.

In 1909 the Licenses Reduction Board closed down the Granya Club

Hotel, paying the owners 150 quid in compensation. The place's other pub, the Granya Hotel, struggled on for another dozen years before surrendering its licence to the board in 1921. This time the owners got £225 and Granya was pub-less.

In 1927–28 the few remaining locals and surrounding farmers figured the beer drought needed fixing and pushed for a fix. The august *Construction and Local Government Journal* noted in January 1928 that, 'A license for a new hotel at Granya (Vic.) has been granted … provided that the building is completed before November 30 of this year.'

The new publican, J. Cecil Carey and his wife, had their concrete hotel up and running in time and they must've done a decent job, keeping it for seven years before off-loading it to an investor in 1935.

The Granya Hotel kept going until 1969, when the licence was changed to a licensed grocery but this went belly up eventually. It then became a youth refuge called Killara and a church-run drug and alcohol rehab centre, but in 2013 the funding stopped and the organisers pulled the pin and walked away. The beautiful building stood empty until Mick and his partner fronted.

They way Mick tells it they both had big dreams for the place. Problem was the dreams were different. He wanted a welcoming country pub, she wanted a niche country produce store/bistro and up-market B & B. Long story short: Mick now doesn't have a partner, but he does have a welcoming country pub.

It was all a hell of a gamble. They bought the premises without any certainty they'd get a liquor licence. 'We just hoped the powers-that-be could share our vision just a bit.'

Luckily they did, and six months after they'd bought it, the store/B & B opened in November 2014. The next year the store and the B & B (and the partner) went and it became a full-on pub. When I ask him how it's going, Mick smiles and says, 'It's still going. It's been tough but it's still going.'

The front bar is heated with an open fire and the furnace out the back heats the rear dining room and the five accommodation rooms which are separate to the main building and surround a small courtyard.

The bar prices are stupid low. You'll get change from a fiver for a stubby of lite and the two draughts, Carlton and VB, are also too cheap. You can get a feed there whenever the place is open. It's basic country pub food and it'll keep you satisfied.

It's a quiet midweek night, like way too many are at this place. A couple of locals drop by for an after-worker and then in the evening it's just me and Mick. We kick back and talk of his plans for a pool table and darts in the front bar and of good nights in the last month when larger groups of riders have overnighted.

The beautiful old Laverda that was parked out back last time I was here is gone. It belonged to Mick's brother-in-law who was doing some work in the pub but, 'Yeah, he's moved on. This place just can't support two people right now.'

The rights to the Wymah ferry are coming up for grabs again and Mick's put in a bid. Last time he had it he reckons he quadrupled the average monthly loads and he's hopeful.

'If I get it back, I'll be able to employ someone here and put any excess into doing up the place.' The thought quietens him and he drags deep on his durrie.

We talk about motorbikes and travelling and he speaks of his mate Doug, who's ridden a Triumph twice at the Isle of Man and who brings him the posters for the pub's walls, and he tells me of his attraction to the three-legged emblem. 'It's called the 'triskelion' and the motto is *quocunque jeceris stabit*. It means, 'whichever way you throw me, I'll land on my feet'. I like that. I reckon that applies to me.'

And then he adds, 'Well hopefully!'

In the morning, after a sun-drenched brew with dogs at my feet, I extract Super Ten from the shed and stroll around the pub's grounds, reciting the first new Latin I've learnt since high school in 1966: *quocunque jeceris stabit*. This pub's story is too rich and the prices paid too high for either Mick or the hotel to not fall on their feet.

Mick didn't score the ferry contract and toward the end of 2019 was forced to start thinking of his options. At the end of December the fires came to Granya. The roads were closed and the crucial business of the busiest part of the year evaporated with the heat of the flames. Mick was trapped with no cash flow and little capital in a pub that wasn't an attractive selling proposition. Then out of the blue he was thrown a lifeline. A bloke from down the river a bit was interested in buying him out. Mick didn't need too much thinking time.

The buyer's name was Garry. And if you want to find out about Garry it's probably an idea to stop here and flick forward to the chapter on Bethanga. Garry's the publican there and in the space of a year has completely turned that pub around, and like Australia back in the early post-war years, he did it on the sheep's back (and the goat's and the alpaca's and the chicken's …). So Garry's hit the jackpot at Bethanga through incorporating a petting zoo into his pub and reinforcing this with an upgrade of the food.

'We went after the families of Albury. People who have young kids but who want to spend an afternoon in a relaxed pub and have their children not be bored. 'The effect of the animals at Bethanga has exceeded any dreams we had. They draw the people to the place and then they find the quality of the food is top of the range but the prices aren't.'

The success at Bethanga inspired Garry and his partner to expand their ambitions and the big yards and existing structures at Granya suited their new plans.

Garry and his team of workies 'n' tradies used the COVID closures to rip out all the internal walls of the pub – give it an open, welcoming feel – and to replace and strengthen the perimeter fencing. They gave the two dwellings up the back a complete makeover and turned them into quality cottages with spa baths and other comforts.

Then they broke what let's call the 'beer garden' into a few paddocks and pens, and once all was in place the alpacas, the sheep, the Hereford cattle and the chickens were trucked in.

They were careful to keep the stained glass because it's important to this bloke that it retains its roadside pub character, just not like any other pub you're going to come across.

When I rock up Garry's on the rush. His son's getting married in the morning and there's a heap to do.

'Still a lot of ducks to line up?' I ask.

Garry smiles, 'Yeah, we're thinking of ducks a bit down the track.'

I leave him to his pre-nup duties and wander up the back, sit down on a log and pretty soon the animals come by to check out my intentions and food stocks. The alpha alpaca rates me worthy of a couple of spits as I get a few shots.

I ask one of the tradies about Mick and he and his son have scored digs on a farm just a bit up the river, and they've both got work. I think back to the triskelion and figure the pub's about to find some firm new footings and Mick's back on his feet too. Just wearing shoes that maybe fit him better this time.

CHAPTER 14 – GRANYA TO BETHANGA

ON A BACK ROAD TO A UNIQUE BRIDGE

An early morning brew and then Super Ten's ready for the trip back across the Wymah ferry, north to the T and then west onto the deserted Wymah Road. The fog's just lifting from the river valley providing tantalising views of mystery off to my left. Like some dancer of the seven veils, the morning swirls its coverings, and slowly and teasingly sheds them before the gaze of the rising sun.

I soak up the scenery and the pure exhilaration of a winding, climbing, descending back road – the stuff of bike riders' dreams. Over a small bridge then left at the T and suddenly I'm swinging south on the Hume for a short sprint and then it's left through Thurgoona, follow the signs and I'm soon at Trout Farm Road, across the Heywood Bridge, and pulling up just below the Hume Dam. Then it's back to the main road and with the Hume Reservoir now on my right I pull up at the reserve just short of the still shrouded Bethanga Bridge.

Walls are often things that need to be simply accepted, bridges are always things to be honoured. And of the forty crossings of the Murray, the Bethanga Bridge stands out as the only bridge spanning two states. Upstream from Renmark, every other bridge is in New South Wales, after that, they're all in South Aussie. This bridge, seemingly shy in the morning mist, stands alone in having its feet in both New South Wales and Victoria.

Construction of the Hume Dam was begun in 1919 and finished sixteen years later. The flooded portion of the Murray made it a bloody pain for geographers to establish the state borders, which it had been agreed would be on the Victorian bank. But the southern state wasn't about to lose its claim to the now-flooded land to the south river. So the border was drawn along where the pre-existing river flowed and that meant half the bridge through the waters was, uniquely, in Victoria. In return for retaining ownership of two flooded towns, Victoria had to foot half the cost of the bridge. Now I'm not an accountant but ...

Anyway the bridge was first mooted in 1927. A worldwide fishing trip for tenders netted just two and the successful tenderer for the steel spans in June 1928 was Vickers Ruwolt of Richmond, Melbourne for £71,890. The nine identical camel truss spans were all made in Melbourne, where the first one was assembled to check the bits fitted together and it was then completely taken apart again and carted to the site on the new railway.

Meanwhile the footings were being sunk in the riverbed. The flat-pack bridge bits were then assembled at the Victorian end and then slid across onto the footings. So the truss at the New South Wales end was the first one assembled and pushed the whole way across.

The whole thing was done in under three years and opened in 1930 with pretty much no ceremony. (The locals only had the energy for one damn opening – and maybe just the one ribbon – so they saved themselves for the dam opening five years later.)

Unlike the Sydney Harbour Bridge where the steel work was imported fully finished from England, every bit of this baby was Australian made, giving work to over 250 people.

Oh, and despite not a single one of the workers on this project (which was designed without a solitary calculator) wearing any hi-vis stuff; despite not a single backpacker standing with a mobile phone and a stop/go sign to make sure it was safe to cross; and despite there not being a single health

and safety officer to superintend the site, not a single life was lost during the entire job. Who'd a thunk?

But before the farmers, grateful for no longer having to use the old and small Ebden ferry, started thinking the Bethanga Bridge was a great bit of interstate cooperation, the northern neighbours had one last trick. Graziers from Granya, Talgarno and Bethanga jumped at the chance to drive their stock over the new bridge then, a bit over two miles later, back across where the Heywood Bridge now is just below the dam wall, and hence to the markets of Wodonga. Seems fair.

The ever-vigilant NSW Pastures Protection Board saw an opportunity, and imposed the need for travelling stock permits (with associated per-beast fees) on the farmers. It took a decade, over three times longer than it took actual workers to design, construct and deliver the bridge, for the politicians and the bureaucrats to tear down this artificial wall and frame a thirty-three word (works out at roughly a word a fortnight) regulation stating that:

No rate shall be charged when stock travel from another State through NSW to a destination in the first mentioned State when the total distance travelled does not exceed three miles.

When I arrive there's not a droving farmer nor any free-tripping animals to be seen. In fact six of the spans aren't visible either. A pair of crows checks the possibility of pecking out my eyes and, realising it's probably not going to happen, caw and rasp at me and continue their sad days.

The fog lifts quickly, the last veil being shed in just minutes, and the whole splendour of the crossing is revealed. Once across, I keep the water to my right, and then through some hills and the Kurrajong Gap Lookout and I'm rolling down Bridge Street to the Bethanga Hotel.

CHAPTER 15 – BETHANGA

THE FINE ARK OF BEING A GREAT PUBLICAN

It's not yet opening time but there're a pair of cars out front of the Bethanga pub when I rock up. My helmet's visor is misted up like a well-chilled schooner glass and the fog's just lifting as I head in.

A bloke and two women are having coffee and of course it's okay to come in, and come share the fire, and what brings me to these parts on a morning like this, and would I like a brew?

The bloke's Garry, the publican. In a grey sweatshirt, totally shapeless trackie pants, grandfather sandals and seven o'clock shadow, and with a double shot flat white in one hand, he doesn't so much look as though he's been up all night, more up all month.

One of the women is Bridget, Garry's partner, and the other is Rebecca, part-time employee here, long-time local, and officially, according to the boss, the pub's 'most annoying customer'.

I tell 'em what I'm doing. Garry takes a look at the camera and disappears with his caffeine. Bridget follows very soon after leaving me with Rebecca and my own fresh mug of heart-starter.

This place has changed hands since I was last here and Rebecca fills me in with how great the new team is and how the town is really getting behind what he's doing with the place.

Gaz and Bridg soon join us. He's had a shave, which he probably thinks makes him photogenic, and she's come carrying a freshly pressed shirt and jeans plus a pair of closed shoes. We leave the wardrobe on the pool table and start on this bloke's story.

Garry Paxton was born and grew up in Albury and after trying a few things, realised he had an affinity with pubs and hospitality and over the years had stints at places like Violet Town, Wodonga, Albury, Inverloch and Sale. A coupla years back he switched course a bit and, with his adult children, opened a coffee shop on the Gold Coast. It went well and then last year his kids told him he was too old to be a barista, 'and so I came back to Albury and was looking for a pub because they seem to be in my blood. I almost bought Tarrawingie but that didn't happen at the last moment and one of my mates is a hotel broker and he told me that he had a pub which was pretty broken but worth a look and they were only doing about a keg or a keg and a half a week.'

He'd tried to buy this same pub, 'five or six years ago but didn't. It's in a good area and apart from Rebecca living here all the locals are great and it's close to Albury so I thought it had potential.'

Rebecca ripostes, 'Actually, he met me and thought he had to live near me.'

It was like he was home. 'I played footy out here many years ago and I knew a few mates out here and I knew the Mitchells out here and they're a big family out in this district.'

I tell him we'll come back to the Mitchells in a bit.

Just on eight weeks after first checking out the place, Garry owned the Bethanga Hotel, opening it as his own on 1 February 2019. He knew that the town was too small to sustain the pub and that Albury-Wodonga, just 25 kilometres down river, had to be tapped for the place to start humming.

'We knew we had to offer good food at good prices. When I had Violet Town we had a top chef, a mature guy who was doing top food and had a great attitude. When we were in the process of buying this place, I heard that he was looking to move and I told him to hang on there for a bit and I would have something for him. Long story short, he's moved his family to a place over at Tallangatta and is our chef here now.'

But there's a pile of pubs around the place doing good food in pleasant surroundings and Garry knew he still needed a special hook for this place and he wanted to attract young families with young kids. 'About six, maybe seven years ago I had this idea and when we were checking out this place I was looking out from the deck at the back and realised this was the place to give it a go.'

The back yard of the pub was roughly grassed and sloped down to the creek and was used mostly for overflow parking on busy days. Garry fenced it all in and then subdivided it into smaller yards. Then he hit Google and Gumtree. See, Garry's idea was a pub with a petting zoo. Yep, he wanted a welcoming hotel with good food and good drinks for the adults and a whole bunch of farm animals out the back for the kids.

'Pretty soon I had myself a couple of sheep, a pair of alpacas, two Shetland ponies, and couple of mini goats which I've called Gordon and Ramsay because of their attitude, a dozen or so chooks, a pair of rabbits and I think that's it.'

He tamed them all up so that the alpacas don't spit and even the sheep sidle up to visitors. He bought in the various pellet feeds for each breed and opened for business.

How'd it go?

'Mate, it's exceeded even my most hopeful expectations! We're booked solid for three, four and five-year-old birthday parties. Groups of up to fifty or even seventy are rocking up. We give all the kids a bag of animal food and set 'em loose. We have to ration the time the rabbits are held as they stress a bit from all the attention but the looks on the kids' faces makes it all worthwhile.'

I show Garry a clipping from 1887 to show him just how far this place has come. Back then, on a crowded day at the Tallangatta Licensing Court, not one but two Bethanga publicans were hauled before the bench for allowing dancing on their premises. Chief nark, Constable John Elliot testified how shocked, scandalised and appalled he was when he, 'saw four couples dancing in a room off the bar.' Publican Smith defended that it was just a 'dance ... got up amongst his own children for their amusement,' but the beak was marching to another tune and fined him five quid with 18s 6d costs.

Next up was Williams Askew of the Bethanga Hotel who was charged with the same shocking offence of permitting bodily gyrations in his bar and copped the same fine but just 15s costs. We laugh and wonder how they'd have handled the advent of the jukebox.

Time to head out the back to check out the ark. Garry looks at the shirt and slacks on the pool table and asks if I know of anyone who's put on their best gear to go feed animals. Yeah nah. We head out as is.

Soon as we set foot out the back door I get a dose of the Old Macdonalds. The goats start yelling for some food, the alpacas run over and wait at their fence and the sheep jog up to the bottom of the stairs. The Shetland ponies have been agisted up with a mate at the edge of town and the rabbits stay in their hutch on the deck. Never seen a beer garden anything like this in my life!

They all get a morning snack and pat. I try without much success to work out the difference between Gordon and Ramsay and then we head back to normality on the deck. He asks me what else I'm interested in about this pub and I tell him about catching up with a lifetime resident named Max Mitchell.

He smiles and tells me there's a print on the wall inside I have to see, and then I mention that I'm also interested in the pub's connection with Ken Maynard, the cartoonist who invented the Ettamogah Pub and all its characters. But when I tell him about the original Ettamogah cartoon drawn on plaster and featuring this pub, in a frame, with another on paper featuring the Bethanga fire station that I checked out on the wall when I was here last time, Garry's got no idea what I'm talking about.

We head back into the bar and on the wall of the dining room he points to a brace of images within a frame of an ocean of kids in costumes and titled, 'A Fancy Dress Ball at Bethanga Hall in 1932'.

He points to a little bloke second from right in the front row. He's dressed as a Red Indian. 'That,' says Gaz, 'is Max Mitchell, or at least he says it is. His brother disputes that and reckons it's himself, John.'

We search around for the Ettamogah images but it seems they've become part of a tradition. Last time I was here the publican proudly showed me the cartoons and lamented how she was pretty certain that there were others by Maynard that showed the pub but that they'd somehow vanished just before she took over.

She thought she knew who took them and said she was always going to chase it up, but now she's moved on and the last remaining Ken Maynard cartoons have gone AWOL from the pub's walls. I'm just glad I got some images of them before they vanished. Maybe some weird bird with boots will drop them back sometime.

Max Mitchell, the kid in the Red Indian costume, has lived in Bethanga all his life on a property named 'Noel' at the top of the hill to the north of the pub.

'The spelling was originally Knowel after a horse my grandfather had. It was a beauty. It won six Open Sydney Hunts in '20 to '25 and three Melbourne Open Hunts. It was so successful he decided to name the property after it.

'He was very big in horses was Grandfather Mitchell but in 1938 when I was four, he was killed running brumbies up in Queensland. Dad went up in the old ute and brought his body back. I've still got the chassis of that old ute over in the garage.'

Max has a single memory of his grandfather: being held on top of his head when he was just two. 'I remember it scaring the life out of me!'

But if fear was a lasting memory, the legacy of his grandfather for Max was much different. Days after his grandfather was buried his will was read and the entire property had been left to this four-year-old.

War broke out and his father joined the fight, leaving the property to Max, his older brother and their mother and when he returned from the battles Max's dad met another woman, left them and settled in Shepparton. Max was sent to grammar school.

'I was captain of the form and wanted to be captain of the school but times got hard and Mum said we don't have the money to keep you at school. I was the only boy who ever cried I think when they were told they didn't have to go to school anymore.'

He hand-milked cows and then built a dairy and drove the milk bus for a few years. It wasn't easy work.

'It was just cans of milk. I had a tray-bodied truck and the cans held twelve-and-a-half gallons of milk. When they were full they were bloody heavy and I had to lift them from the ground up onto the tray. It was backbreaking. After a while I got a new truck and it had drop sides. They made everybody put stands in that were the same height and then I'd just pull up and drop the side of the truck and roll the milk cans onto the truck's tray.'

This gentle man smiles at the memories. 'That was a real progress.'

Max talks with his hands and most of his long slender fingers, though showing some signs of arthritic bumps, resemble more those of a piano player than a life of manual labour and farm work. The exception is the second finger on Max's left hand which, like so many fingers on so many rural hands, is missing its last joint.

'John my brother had a truck and he was loading some cattle and it had some metal strips along the side. One of the cows had its foot on top of the strip and I went to clear her but she stomped on the strip and it just sliced the end of my finger off. It was painful at the time but I got over it.'

But if a missing finger bit is far from unique out here, these hands have another very special claim to fame. When he was twenty-two, in recognition not just of his athletic abilities but also his character and sportsmanship, Max was chosen for the rare honour of carrying the 1956 Olympic torch through the town.

Forty-four years later, in recognition of his services to the community, Max Mitchell, by then aged sixty-six, was again invited to carry the Olympic torch through the town. His stint started on exactly the same spot as in '56 and he carried it to outside the school where his wife, Judy, taught.

'That was a bit special.'

Always self-effacing, Max says he's probably not unique, that there're probably others who've carried the torch for both Australian Olympiads but I certainly can't find record of any.

Now, I didn't know any of that stuff. I'd contacted Max for a very different reason, and her name was Helen Porter Mitchell. She was a distant relative of Max and she was born in Melbourne in 1861 but spent much of her younger years at Bethanga Park, the family property, much of which was flooded when the Hume Dam was built. A long-time neighbour of Max and Judy, Pat reckons she used to hear Helen Mitchell singing as she rode her up the Jarvis Creek Road to and from Bethanga Park. It no doubt sounded sweet if a bit raw.

Helen Mitchell was the oldest surviving daughter of David and Isabella Mitchell. Her father, a builder and contractor, was a giant of the fledgling Australia Felix. In 1857 he built the Menzies Hotel in William Street in Melbourne. In 1873 he built Scots' Church in Collins Street, and in 1888 he constructed and operated the colony's first mechanical milking device. Away from work he sang in the Scots' Church choir and at home played the violin and encouraged the musical talents of his daughter.

Helen Mitchell made her public singing debut in 1884 and two years later accompanied her father to London, where he'd been appointed commissioner to the Colonial and Indian Exhibition.

Along the way, in honour of her Melbourne home, Helen changed her surname to 'Melba' and then, this young woman who'd spent the afternoons of her youth singing on horseback as she rode around Bethanga, shortened her first name to 'Nellie'. And the rest, as they say, is history.

Max Mitchell refuses to push that he's related to this country's first international opera star. When I ask him, he diverts the talk to how the tops of the old Bethanga Park buildings are still visible when the drought shrinks the water in the dam. And he talks of his disappointment at how all the movies he's seen of the diva ignore her connection to the town of which he is so proud.

I tell him not to get up when I shape to leave. He's in need of two new knees but another medical issue has come up and he's had to postpone the operations. Judy sees me away.

As I cruise down the pass I try to get my head around a town with connections to one of this country's most outrageous cartoonists and with our first worldwide celebrity. Chuck in a pub where it's just possible that the thing acting the goat next to you on the back deck actually is a goat. Then to the mix I add a massive spoonful of people with extraordinary pasts and unique visions and once again I appreciate just how special the towns along this river really are.

CHAPTER 16 – ALBURY

SURVIVAL

John Roper, the bloke who founded Albury's Globe Hotel, was a survivor. Of sorts.

He'd arrived in Sydney from Norfolk, England, via a stint in New Zealand, in January 1843 and very soon became mates with a Prussian fella who'd arrived less than a year before.

Roper's new mate had been fascinated by the explorations in South America of his countryman Alexander von Humboldt, had studied in Berlin, Britain, France, Italy and Switzerland. He spun his globe and figured that with Latin America almost done, the next place that needed exploring was Terra Australis and also figured he was the man to do it. His name was Ludwig Leichhardt.

Leichhardt was obsessed with the guts of the continent, once writing, 'The interior, the heart of this dark continent is my goal, and I shall never relinquish the quest for it until I get there.'

So Roper buddied up with Ludwig and joined his first expedition from the Darling Downs to Port Essington (Darwin.) The party of ten left the Darling Downs on 1 October 1844 and pushed their way north-west. Roper had zero qualifications and not much more ability for a challenge like this. Ludwig obviously regretted inviting him along, telling his brother-in-law, he 'was an inexperienced and limited young man who seemed to consider it beneath his dignity to obey me'.

And John Gilbert, another member of the group described him as, 'Brash, no bushman and ... at all times foolhardy'. Roper got lost in the bush more than once and on 10 May 1845 he was kicked in the chest while trying to catch his horse by its tail.

John Gilbert didn't exactly live to regret those words. Six weeks after Roper was kicked in the chest, on the night of 28 June, the expedition party was attacked by Aboriginals.

The attackers tossed sticks on to the tent of Roper and fellow expeditioner Calvert to bring the occupants into the open, curious but not alarmed and therefore unarmed. Immediately, 'a terrific yell, that will ring in my ears for ever', was raised and the two men were set upon with spears and waddies. They were helpless on the ground within arms length of the attackers; both suffered multiple wounds ... Roper had five or six spear wounds: two or three in the scalp, one through his cheek into an eye socket, one through his left arm and one in his loins; he had taken a heavy blow on the shoulder.

Both Roper and Calvert – who 'had one spear through the left testicle into his groin, another 'at his knee', and whose nose, hands and elbow had been broken by waddi blows – survived and made it to Port Essington but John Gilbert was killed in the attack.

Roper moved to Albury, and didn't allow loss of the sight of his eye – barbed spears through the cheek and eye socket can do that – to put the brakes on his ambition or his rise in local society.

He became a clerk of petty sessions at the local court in 1847, was on the committee of the Albury Co-operative Storekeepers' Association, president of the local ag society and president of the Albury Jockey Club. And ten years after joining the petty sessions, having acquired land and influence, he was appointed to the bench of magistrates.

In 1859 he was a founding alderman on the local municipal council, and in 1860 commissioned the building of the Globe Hotel on the corner of Dean and Kiewa streets, installing a manager rather than working the bar himself.

It was a monster: designed and built by Daniel Driscoll it was a two-storeyed building containing eighteen rooms, kitchen, outhouse and stabling for fifteen horses. John Roper obviously reasoned that if you've survived an intense body-piercing session involving half a dozen spears, you could survive most things and do pretty much as you wished.

He followed that not just in professional and social life; he also wasn't intimidated by the barbs of social gossip when it came to his private affairs. 'In 1860 (a fellow magistrate) tried to get him struck off the roll of magistrates for "living in a state of undisguised and shameless adultery" with his housekeeper.'

The police magistrate, however, could see further than the keyhole and decided that their 'improper intimacy' had not affected Roper's social position and let him stay.

John Roper survived this attack on this boudoir and eventually became Mayor of Albury in 1862, but it's another glorious episode that year that truly put the Globe on the map of legendary watering holes. And like so many celebrated happenings, events, connections and characters along the river, separating the meat of the truth from the entrails of myth can prove to be self-serving and wasteful.

But what we do know is that back in these days when 'tinder' meant only the makings for a fire, two young local gentlemen had swiped right for the same young woman and neither was about douse his own flame willingly. So they agreed on a duel for her hand. A civilised duel – not with pistols, not with fists, and not with swords, but with champagne. As the Melbourne *Leader* explained in one version in May 1862:

On Wednesday evening there was some rather extensive shouting at the Globe Hotel, Albury, sufficient to recall the old times in these districts, when men used bottles of champagne for skittles, loaded rifles with small nuggets, or shod the horse of a successful electioneering candidate with shoes of gold. Two parties on the present occasion, whose names we do not desire to mention, called for 143 bottles of champagne, at £1 per bottle, and after treating everybody about the house, and drinking their fill themselves, demolished what was left. It appears the parties were rival claimants to the hand of a young lady, and were in a mood to settle the affair by a fistic tournament, when a friend proposed that the one who should fail to shout for the largest quantity of drink, should relinquish the suit in favor of the other. This was agreed to, and champagne was called for until one had paid for 70 bottles, and the other for 73. How many more would have been disposed of it would have been difficult to say, had not

the affair been terminated by one of the gentle swains falling asleep under the table.

Arthur Andrews, who wrote *The History of Albury* recalled it slightly differently:

Two suitors, competing for a 'lady's hand,' decided to settle matters, by the quantity of 'champagne' each could dispose of. Half-a-dozen choice spirits were called in, to see 'fair play,' and it is recorded that it was not till the 145th bottle was opened that one succumbed, and the other went off triumphantly, we presume, with 'the lady.' This wine was charged £1 per bottle.

Whether the two suitors drank all contents between themselves or shared with their 'choice spirits' of backers and just had a mouthful each from each bottle doesn't much matter. I sit in the Zed Bar in Dean Street at 11.30 am and raise a glass of bubbles to their class, their imagination and their place in the history of pubs along the river.

I sit with my drink in the near empty bar and survey this place, all that remains of the Globe Hotel apart from the Art Deco facade with the emblazoned name down on the corner where it originally stood. I've an hour or so to spare but I know there's as much chance of me encountering a local who's been drinking here for fifty years as there is of me drinking from 145 bottles and then winning a lady's hand. It has become a place with a personality but no soul.

Not six months after the day of the duelling magnums, John Roper – survivor – took a hit. His businesses had turned stagnant and in October he was declared bankrupt, thus becoming illegible for public office, and was forced to resign as mayor. This was a setback he couldn't survive.

The next year this tough old nut was having trouble with the socket of his crook eye, which was causing the nostril on that side to swell. Having a good old nose pick, he pulled out a 'splinter of the spear which had pierced him ... about two inches long by a quarter of an inch thick (which had been) imbedded between 17 and 18 years'.

That's five centimetres long by a bit over half a centimetre wide. Bloody lucky the termites hadn't moved into his shnoz! And it makes me wonder just how attentive his, er, housekeeper was!

Anyway, Roper retired to live at Merriwa and died, aged seventy-three in 1895. His entire estate of £708 was left to his 'improperly intimate' housekeeper, Lydia Witney.

I raise my glass to John Roper and to the champagne duellers, and my glass is dry. Outside Super Ten is ready and not far west, better pubs await. His hotel – described by Paul McGuire as 'one of Australia's favourite inns' – has been gutted, its character and its heritage sucked out, but John Roper's memory lives on in the river named in his honour that flows from the superb thermal springs at Mataranka in the Northern Territory to the Gulf at Limmen.

And that's survival in its own way too.

CHAPTER 17 - HOWLONG

NEVER LONG ENOUGH

(SPOILER ALERT: If you plan to visit Howlong with your partner, kids or a mate, don't let them read this story ... there's a bit you might want to keep as a surprise.)

About 22 kilometres west from Albury the Riverina Highway takes a right bend and then, just some 50 metres or so after passing the sign welcoming travellers to Howlong, I pull Super Ten to the side of the road under a big old gum.

To the south of the road, on my left just before the golf course, are the ruins of the grand old Howlong Mill, built in 1868–69. Opposite, across the highway is an understated and wonderfully maintained residence, its roof the shades of young eucalyptus leaves, and half a dozen duotone canvas blinds are pulled down to the ground for privacy.

First I head to the tall proud ruins of the old mill. This place was state of the art and really must've been something! A local paper enthused as it neared completion:

This mill, built by Mr. Edwards and Mr. Russom, on the main road from Howlong to Albury, and near the former township, is ... worked by a steam engine of 20-horse power, and has three pairs of stones. Several new principles have been introduced by the proprietors and the whole of the machinery was constructed to order by the Atlas Engineering Company, Melbourne. The building is 50 feet long by 30 feet wide, with four floors, and is very substantially erected of brick. There is a new arrangement in the cleaning department, by which the very fine flour, which is generally dissipated and lost, is entirely saved.

In 1872 the pucka *Australian Town and Country Journal* dispatched a correspondent to the mother colony's southern watery border. He reported that the engine had grown:

the Howlong Steam Mill, [is] a fine brick building four storeys high, and working three pairs of stones. A 30-horse-power engine, a capital silk-dresser, 24 feet long, smutting machinery, and exhaust fans on late principles of improvement and across the road was the Mill Hotel, kept by Mr. Easterby.

This is the eucalyptus and cream building across the road. It seems that the pub and the mill, like so many pubs and punts along the river, were legs of a single animal. In 1877 both were offered for sale in one line, but it seems like they were soon split.

The Mill Hotel changed hands every couple of years until a bloke named John R. Flegg took over in early 1915. He can't have been too happy with it because in April the following year he offloaded the licence to a bloke named Collier, and if the pub'd been causing him grief, he was about to enter a new dimension.

Before 1916 was out, Collier, the buyer, sicced his lawyers onto Flegg, the vendor, for some good old cooking of the books.

[Collier] claimed £300 damages from ... Flegg, on the grounds that plaintiff had been induced to purchase the lease and business of the Mill Hotel, Howlong, on the representation of defendant that the takings of the hotel were £14 per week, and, further, that defendant had given plaintiff a warranty that the takings of the said hotel would not be less than £14 per week for the remainder of the lease. The defence was that the representation was not made, and that if it was made it was false to defendant's mind, and, further, that no warranty was given.

The beak wasn't too impressed by Collier, and even less by Flegg who was ordered instead of the claimed £300, to cough up just £75 on which Collier had to pay tax and costs. It was pretty much a Pyrrhic victory and any spoils there were didn't last too long because in 1921 the Licensing Board poured through the Riverina. They held their beautifully named 'Deprivation Sittings' at Wagga Wagga, Albury, Corowa, Jerilderie and Deniliquin and ordered twenty-six licensees and owners to show cause why their premises should not be deprived of their licences.

The owners of the Mill Hotel were out of business. Fortunately the place didn't burn down, wasn't gutted, wasn't destroyed through wanton hand or careless neglect. Today at the edge of the highway and the edge of the town, with its shuttered blinds seemingly carrying an air of eyelids closed to the rush of the modern, it's a wonderful welcome to the town.

I pay my respects to this beautiful old pub and head into Howlong, past the golf course with, allegedly, the largest membership of any golf club in New South Wales, and then a low slung, anything-but-pretty squat brick pub is welcoming me. Not a single other vehicle is parked out the front of the place, its facade proclaiming its origin in 1858.

John Flegg, the 1915 book-cooker back at Howlong's Mill Hotel had a brother, Sydney Clifford Flegg. When I walk through the doors of the Howlong Hotel, Andrew the boss is behind the bar. He's the grandson of that same Sydney Flegg.

Andrew's been expecting me, actually he was expecting me an hour ago and he's called in the only other bloke who's in the bar and who he reckons knows pretty much all I'll need about the place.

I order a cleanser and head over to Keith, who's perched under the ubiquitous gambling screens: silver hair, matching goatee, old polo shirt, with old school tattoos on each forearm plus another on his left bicep. Keith reckons it's a pity that old Ron, who knew absolutely everything, 'and I'm talking everything,' about the town and its story is no longer with us but Keith's learnt a bit in the thirty years since he arrived here with his wife, refugees from Melbourne, so he'll do his best.

They had a caravan downstream at Mulwala which they'd visit each holidays but a permanent place there was out of their budget so they found a home here. They arrived in November and by March Keith was coaching a footy team, his wife was coaching a netball squad, and he was the advertising manager of *The Grapevine*, a monthly seventy-two page local volunteer-produced newspaper.

'If you're going to live in a place, you've got to get involved,' he enthuses, 'and from the start it was just fantastic. You fair dinkum get a sore arm most days from waving to people.'

He reckons they arrived in town on 9 November and had his first beer in this pub on 10 November. 'Didn't want to rush into it!'

A couple of medical issues have caused him to switch to the soft stuff lately, but while this is still his haunt, he's not really looking forward to achieving 'local' status.

'Only two ways in this town be a local,' pipes Andrew from behind the bar, 'be born here or to be long term in the cemetery.'

'All sorted,' chuckles Keith, 'already paid for my plot!'

We're summonsed over to the bar. One of the locals rescued this down at the local tip and brought it in, and Andrew reckons I might be interested. It's an old business card for the pub. One side has the address, the proprietor's name and the single digit phone number, simply '5'. At one end a V has been cut and the other side reveals why. It's meant to be used to sit on the rim of your glass to keep it being removed or, more likely, your space taken when you need to duck out to make room for more liquid. Almost genteel and so very civilised, but unlike the modern coaster over the top, it didn't keep the flies out of the fluid!

At the end of the bar, away from the bloody screens and gambling a very decent old hearth stands empty, waiting for the clarion chills of shorter days. The bricks are large and unevenly formed and many have strange indents. Pretty little doubt that they're thumb and finger marks and Andrew reckons they might be convict made, and he might just be right. Convicts more commonly used the broad arrow, hearts and diamonds to 'sign' their work whereas when free settlers (and their children) started manufacturing them, they'd use finger and thumb imprints to keep tally of their production. So you'd think that these are more likely from a later period.

Trouble is, there's one brick with a triangle diamond design cut into it and so the jury's out. Countering that is the problem that this pub has completely burnt down at least twice in its history and using the same convicts' bricks three times would seem, well, against the odds.

As ever, it doesn't much matter to me. They're worth the checking out and whatever the truth, when you visit, I dare you to not insert one of your digits to compare the size!

The connection Keith forged with this pub, the bottom pub in this two-pub town (and both on a very level street), on his second day in the joint, has endured ever since. He's been to the top pub once in the intervening thirty years, 'to try a special meal they were advertising at one time a few years back,' but otherwise this is his place.

It's not that the pubs don't get along, just that the customers are very much one or the other. 'We used to have a darts and pool comps between the two pubs but it got too unfriendly.'

I ask him about any wild times, ask if there's much romping going on nowadays. 'Ah,' says Keith, 'that's a word I've not heard for a while,' and I explain the choice.

Back in early 1865, the Howlong pub, a little hotel in a flyspeck town, hit the national papers big time. 'Love And Murder' screamed the headline over the tale of local scandal:

A sensational case comes this week from Howlong. On Saturday last, a man ... employed as groom at Boyle's Howlong Hotel, annoyed, it would seem, at some romping of his lady love (who is also a fellow servant at the Hotel) with some lads about the place, in a fit of jealousy got a revolver ... and rushed into a room where the young woman, Eliza Thomas, was at the time, and announced that he intended to shoot her.

Ah! Romping! But no stomping. Just shooting instead.

The young bloke wasn't, er, firing blanks, and his shot grazed the romperess's shoulder before he was disarmed. Gun-less now, he set plan B in motion and raced out to drink some poison he'd left in a cup outside. (This was a young man who'd thought things through!) But: 'This was dashed from his lips by Mr. Boyle, and steps taken to secure the love stricken youth.'

Almost wistfully the Albury paper dryly finished its piece: 'We don't often have to chronicle such an episode in colonial life,' before noting that, 'the matter has created quite a stir ... (especially) amongst the damsels of the district.'

The kid was found guilty but temporality insane (love can do that to you) but if that was his tragedy, a more serious one hit the pub itself later that same year when it went up in flames for the first time.

On Friday evening last, between seven and eight o'clock, a fire broke out in the premises of Mr Boyle, of the Howlong Hotel, which, in less than

an hour, destroyed the hotel and stores, scarcely anything comparatively worth notice having been saved.

Armer Boyle must've been a pretty popular fella because the report continued with coverage of a meeting in Albury where:

(s)everal propositions were discussed as to raising the means to enable Mr. Boyle to make a fresh start in the world, and if he can arrange with his several creditors, no doubt a tolerable sum will be raised to lighten the heavy calamity which has befallen him.

Boyle got the place going again and even created a half decent racetrack out the back which hosted regular rich-pickings meetings. The pub's complimentary stables are still standing – well remnants of 'em.

But then again in 1903 the pub felt the heat.

The Howlong Hotel was destroyed by fire on Tuesday morning. The hotel was a substantial brick building, the property of Mr. Geo. Waldron, Rutherglen, the licence being held by Mr. Eaton.

Since then the Howlong Hotel's not featured too much in the national press but it still rates regular mentions in the *Grapevine*, which still hits the stands in Howlong every month. Keith's no longer involved but spent a good few years double shifting as editor and local news reporter specialising in the social pages.

'On Saturday nights I'd just drive around the streets and if I saw more than half a dozen cars out the front of a place, I'd just pull up, go inside with my camera and notebook and get some photos and a story. There was always something going on!'

And if any romping was detected, he'd just drive on by!

With no reservation card for my beer glass, I drain it and start to get my stuff together. It's not long into the afternoon and already today I've experienced a beautifully maintained ex-pub and a history-imbued still-goer. But it's way too gambling-dominated for my tastes. Too crassly monopolised with form guides, racing screens, betting terminals and odds boards. It's been impossible to get shots of these two fine blokes without betting crap filling the background. Time to head up the road a bit to the 'top pub'.

The awning on the squat, unattractive, red-brick Howlong Hotel boasts that it was 'established 1858', but up the road, the charming facade of the Court House Hotel, lovingly maintained and bathed in tones redolent of the old Mill Hotel at the edge of town, elegantly carries its construction date of 1902. But this isn't the first edition of this pub.

It seems that the actual Court House and the eponymous pub opened their doors for criminals and customers, defendants and drinkers, nobblers and other nobblers at pretty much the same time, late in 1879.

The Howlong Court House held its first trials that year and from the start it was a boon for the town's pubs. The structure was an imposing and impressive building but the trouble was, the budget didn't stretch to more basic fundamentals like things to sit on.

> *The recently finished Court House at Howlong is a handsome and commodious structure. The accommodation is excellent but ... (l)ast Wednesday the Police Magistrate refused to hold the sittings within the Court House owing to the want of furniture, and [they] were therefore held at the ... Howlong Hotel.*

Seems the bench wasn't too impressed by their, er, bench.

But just why they went past the top pub isn't explained, because it's pretty certain that the Court House Hotel was up and cantering by then. Jon Howard (no, not *that* John Howard), had his licence for the Court House Hotel renewed in September 1879. The sequence is interesting but not crucial. Once erected and serving booze and giving shelter to many of those appearing in legal wrangles up the road it soon changed hands. Mr H (not 'J') Howard put it on the market in 1881, claiming it was 'doing a good paying trade' with its '8 rooms besides a billiard room' and a 'kitchen fitted with a baker's oven ... [and] very roomy stables.'

The original Court House Hotel met the same fate as its neighbour down the street, burning down in May 1901. The local paper quoted reports that it began next door at a Mr Foley's store and then 'destroyed' the hotel which 'was occupied by Mrs Camplin', who'd taken over the pub's licence from her husband when he carked it in 1892.

The pub didn't stay down for long. Catherine Camplin, who'd lost her livelihood in the fire, was obviously as popular as Armer Boyle had been at the bottom pub. Three months later the ruins went to auction and 'and after some spirited bidding the property finally fell to the bid of ... £925,

cash ... [and] (g)reat cheering resulted when it was known (that) ... Mrs Camplin' was the new owner.

At the start of September tenders were called for the erection of a new hotel (bricks supplied) and soon the phoenix beauty which is before me was beginning to rise. Just four months later the *Corowa Free Press* noted that:

> *The work of removing the old Court House Hotel has been completed, and work was started ... to excavate for the foundations, which are to be of concrete ... The plans show a most compact and roomy hotel all the rooms being far above the requirements of the Act.*

By June 1902 this same pub was hosting community meetings and auctions of local land. It'd become the hub of the town. I park Super Ten across the road.

In 1901 the Ovens Valley newspaper reported that, 'when finished, (the new Court-House Hotel) ... will be an ornament to the town.' And they weren't wrong. If the Howlong Hotel is a squat bulldog of a building, solid, utilitarian and bereft of ornament, this one's more an elegant old golden retriever, resplendent in the low western sun. There's a single ute parked out front and the pub's courtesy bus off to one side. I get some shots and head over.

Above the door is the obligatory sign of ownership and licence. It lists the licence number and the licensee's name as Peter John Knight, and at the bottom are the trading hours – all standard stuff. But slap in the middle is another line of large print: HOSTS PETER AND FAMILY.

Nice touch! Last time I saw a family listed as publicans was up at Prairie in Queensland where the three young daughters are named on the business cards.

The main bar has barrel tables, big barrel tables surrounded by high stools, and along the side of the front wall is an old-style wooden bench. There's not a single screaming betting board polluting the atmosphere, just a couple of muted screens silently showing afternoon soaps, and Leona behind the bar chatting with three blokes washing down the dust of the day. When I front, two of 'em are heading outside for a smoke and the other needs the toilet. They all leave their wallets on the bar when they head out. This is the country, and it'd be as insulting as it'd be unnecessary to take your stuff with you.

Off to the western side the sun pours in, swamping the old-style booths beside the parquet dance floor in an afternoon glow, and beside this in a small room is an exquisite blue-topped pool table, sadly no longer used for inter-pub championships. Around from that another alcove with eight pokies discretely, unobtrusively spinning false hope for a couple of travellers.

We're soon joined by a pair of women in clean fluoros who take their places at the bar and manage to drink and talk and pay without ever putting down their phones.

And then Publican Pete fronts with a clipboard, phone and beer manifest. He can work and talk. This is his first pub and he's the licensee. Worked part time for the owner for about six years and then came to an

agreement with him in 2016 when he'd decided he'd had enough. It's tough and it's competitive, what with the bottom pub and the golf club but the niche for this place is its honesty and its warm welcomes. And for me that's about the best niche a country pub can occupy.

I show them some clippings from old newspapers including the 1879 one when the magistrate bypassed this place to hold hearings at the bottom pub because he didn't like the seating. Laughter all around.

'He would've loved our special seat!'

'Surely the blow hole wasn't here back then!'

I manage a simple, 'Eh?'

Leona chirps in from behind the bar that 'It's not working' as I try to figure what the hell they're talking about.

They tell me to sit down on the bench along the front wall, no a bit to the left, no a bit more and then I'm in the right position. Peter's laughing, Leona's cacking herself and the two fluoros are giggling away. I'm told to look up at the security camera in the top right corner of the bar and I'm hit gently in the bum with, well probably what's best described as a dry bidet!

No-one knows when this thing was installed. No-one to take the credit or the blame but it works like this: beside the beer taps is a lever that's connected midway along a hose. At one end there's a bottle of compressed air. The other leads under the floor then up under the bench to a very hard to see hole in the bench with a diameter the size of a five-cent coin. Once the newbie is settled in the right spot, Leona or Peter or whoever else is working presses the lever and a blast of compressed air reverse farts into your bum.

'No-one doesn't spill their drink,' laughs Peter between calls to his suppliers, and everyone shares their stories of losing their virginity at the Howlong blow hole.

The compressor's not working today so I'm saved the initiation but I'll sure be ringing ahead next time I drop by with a mate who's there for the first time.

Like the bottom pub, the Court House no longer has accommodation. The rooms have been converted to owner's residence and storage rooms. And that's a pity. This is a truly friendly, 'leave-your-stuff-on-the-bar-why-don't-you-join-us-for-a-chat' pub and it'd surely be enjoyable to spend an evening in the front and the night at the back.

So I pack up my stuff and prepare for the twenty-minute squirt west to a place that played a crucial role in the history of this nation.

CHAPTER 18 – THE EMPIRE HOTEL, WAHGUNYAH

FAIRYLAND

A couple of klicks out of Wahgunyah I swing left off the Rutherglen Road into Victoria Street and understand why I've been feeling especially puckish for the last ten minutes. The headwinds have been blowing right over the Uncle Tobys muesli bar factory on the south-east edge of town. Once I'm upwind it's back to eucalyptus and roadkill.

The road swings north then a traffic light pauses me right outside the grand Old Empire Hotel as traffic flows south from across the bridge. I head over the John Foord Bridge, around the curves past the John Foord Oval and up the main street. The place is busy, parking scarce, but I find a spot for Super Ten adjacent to my pub in the middle of town, on the eastern side of the main street. It's one of the few that still has accommodation in Corowa.

When she's good and ready, done with organising the weekend ahead with a local farm boy, and checked there's nothing she needs to see right now on Facebook, a young woman glides over and in broad Irish brogue asks if I'm being served. Since she's the only one working and she's not currently serving me I don't quite understand the question but we get on to me having a room booked.

Obviously believing that making eye contact or small talk like enquiring how my day's been might turn her to a pillar of salt, she recites the cost, informs me even if I'm paying cash I need to have a credit card which she'll ring up 'for security', oh and she'll be needing to photograph my driver's licence as well. 'For security.' For a forty-buck room.

I ask her what security I have that my credit card number including CCV code and my licence details won't be misused or stored or shared and she blandly tells me that the people with access to my details can be trusted. 'As opposed to me?'

When she tells me it's so I don't do a runner, I respond that with three complete knee replacements it'd be difficult for me to manage a hobbler.

She now actually looks at me, and stares blankly. Off to the left the farm boy's getting restless.

I hand them all over (for security) and then – well there has to be a place in this historic town where pubs played such a pivotal role in our push for Federation which might have a handle on hospitality – so, yeah nah. I ask for my documents back and head out to the fresh air.

Turns out, no. I find nothing else in town, so I turn back to the bridge and to the pub I'd passed on the southern bank on the way in, park Super Ten around the side and two minutes later there's a face smiling across the bar and a couple of g'days from my side.

This is Kristi. With Brett her partner she runs this almost stately old pub and, oh, she looks at you when she talks and she wishes she had room but there's no longer any accommodation at the pub but if I have camping gear there's a top spot just across the road down by the river. And if I want to go down there and set up, it'll be safe to leave my tent and come back here for tea and can she do anything else?

Sounds a great solution so I head down to the river, weave past the sad for-sale motel and I'm at the free camp beside the river, switch off Super Ten, slip off the hat and *it's freakin' chaos!!!*

A million at least corellas are fighting for tree space while a family of kookaburras laugh and take the piss. But there's only one other camper in an area that'd take thirty, so I pick a water frontage spot, throw up the tent and say g'day to my neighbour.

He's going nowhere fast. The diff's buggered on his van and it'll be two lots of Centrelink before he's got the dosh to cover it. Meanwhile, I've been on the road for just under a week and it's washing day so I grab some rocks, load 'em into my riding pants and socks and chuck 'em into the river where the river's pretty much tuned to gentle rinse cycle.

Ask my neighbour to keep an eye, and what sorta beers he likes, and walk back up to the pub where a few utes and cars have filled the side car park. There's four at the bar, all pretty involved, and Robert's chiming in from a nearby table. I take in the flying pig adorned with a pair of 'Where the F#$* is Wahgunyah?' caps that're suspended from the ceiling. I settle for pulling up a pew beside Robert.

When he retired in 2008 and bought a block just on the edge of town, and had his home built, the town wasn't doing too flash. Woolies had opened across the river and that put the kybosh on the local shops, but the place is climbing off its knees and is in revival mode. Across the road the fish shop cafe's opened and selling 'the best hamburgers anywhere' and there's a barber as well.

'We might even be getting a little newsagent sort of general store. But this pub's the social centre of the town now. These owners, Kristi and her man Brett are a vast improvement over the previous ones. The ones who had it when I came back in 2008 sold it and a single lady took it over and it was too much for her and this couple have really rehabilitated it. A lot of people are coming back. The food is brilliant. There's a lot of people coming over here from Corowa. The beer's good and the people, well a lot of the old timers have passed away but the ones left, and the new ones are great.'

Then he adds, 'Pity Mick's not here, he's the one with the stories of the old days!'

It's my shout so I head up to the bar and show Kristi an old clipping of a review about this place in the 1860s. 'I put up at the Empire Hotel ... and found as landlord there M. Camile Reau ...' She stops me. That name rings a bell. She's pretty sure she has a picture of him and pulls down a framed photo from the wall. Sure enough, this woman knows her pub. It's a formal shot of Monsieur Reau 'publican', taken in 1861, just four years before the review was written.

Shirl and a Deano turn up in their fluoros. He tells a story about knocking a bloke through a window at a pub in Albury after being hit with a pool cue. There's no reason for any disbelief: it's obvious he's the sort of bloke you'd like in your corner – squat and solid, a keg with a head and a permanent smile on his mug.

We get talking about life choices and he pauses when I ask him a question.

'The best decision I ever made? Had to be when I was with the lady who became my wife and the mother of my wonderful kids and I made the decision not to be a gangster. I could've joined a gang and probably would've been dead by now but I chose to get a trade, get married and have kids. Yeah, that was the smartest thing I ever did. Well that and coming to this here. The people here are just amazing. But I haven't been here all that long to tell you any scandal about this place.'

Then he adds, 'What a pity old Mick's not here.'

I chow down on a very decent parmie, grab a couple of beers for my neighbour down by the river and walk to my digs. It's a clear night and again I marvel at how a million-star campsite leaves any five-star hotel in the moonshade.

When I get back my riding pants and socks have been hung to drip dry on a stump and Neighbour says I needn't have bothered with the tinnies but he's glad I did, every man needs his dinner!

Next morning my prayers for the death of the corellas haven't been answered so I have my brew on a river log as the mists lift off the river. A stick dangles in the fog at the end of a rope. Is there a single swimming hole on this river that doesn't have an iconic tyre or stick swing hanging from a tree?

There's no reason to hurry and it's just on ten by the time Super Ten is loaded up and we're ready to move. At the top of the road I pause to let an old codger on a mobility scooter cross and then watch him as he heads for the just opening Old Empire.

Back in October 1934 the *Corowa Free Press* ran a tribute to Mr R T. Savage, a retiring long-term resident and publican who'd bought his first hotel in Wahgunyah back in 1899, when there were 'six hotels in the town and a licensed bar at the railway refreshment rooms.'

The tributes blossomed for this bastion of the town who two years prior, with the Great Depression plunging unemployment rates to 32 per cent, had bucked the pessimism and made news by installing in his Empire Hotel a visionary 'all-electric refrigerator in the bar and dining-room (in which) no ice is used and ... the temperature is automatically controlled.'

He was lauded as a pillar of the town and his departure as a loss to the community but truth is, for the last decade he'd been at the pub on sufferance. After a fifteen year absence from the town, Savage had returned to Wahgunyah in 1917 to run his Empire Hotel after the expiration of a five-year lease to a Fred Lambert who'd kept it ticking over nicely for his tenure but then, as the Great War in Europe raged, things seem to've turned sour between owner and licensee.

In July 1917 Fred Lambert advertised all the pub's furniture and the fittings from all twenty-six rooms for sale by auction and a week later Savage advised that he was returning to take over the running of his own pub.

The Empire Hotel didn't just face challenges from the other pubs in town. At the height of the tuberculosis epidemic of 1919, the pub was quarantined for a period of seven days. I'd thought of writing something flippant about this being a unique excuse for not coming home – something like, 'Sorry luv but I'm at the pub and they've locked the doors and I'm trapped here for a week.' But then, just a few months more than 100 years later, the Covid-19 pandemic enveloped the world and once again the doors of Fairy's were bolted closed.

Like every pub across the country, the Old Empire, just as it was a century ago, was staring down an existential threat.

Back in 1925 Savage had had enough and found a buyer and the papers announced he'd sold the property and licence to a bloke from Mornington called Goodman. Seems this fella paid a £2000 deposit on the place, obviously after an inspection of the books. But, er seems that the er, elasticity of truth that our mate Flegg got caught stretching back at Howlong, may've just been part of a tradition in these parts. In January 1926 Goodman took Savage to court, suing him for the return of his deposit 'on the grounds of misrepresentation' of the pub's income and turnover.

Savage lost, so he kept at the pub he wanted to sell for another eight years as the pubs around him all closed down. By the time R. T. Savage pulled stumps at Wahgunyah's Empire Hotel he'd outlasted them all and his, 'Empire Hotel [wa]s the sole survivor' in this town, almost uniquely situated on the riverbank but elevated higher than any flood threat.

The year after Savage sold the Empire Hotel, 6 miles down the road at Rutherglen a couple with five young daughters decided to have another go at getting a son. They must've done something right in the waning days of summer 1936 because on 1 November the passing of one of their young girls was compensated by the arrival of twin boys, one fair, who'd forever be known as 'Snow' and the other more a chestnut who'd wear the moniker of 'Dark' for the rest of his life.

The twins grew up playing sport – footy and cricket – and trying to earn a bob. After school and at weekends they played for the Rutherglen team and would often come to Whagunyah to play on the park beside the river. Before school they'd be up at the crack.

Wahgunyah railway station with its licensed refreshment rooms was the end of the branch line running south through Rutherglen to Springhurst, where it connected with the main line to Melbourne. The early train each morning left the riverside before the day's newspapers could be delivered but the timing was better at its first stop. So Snow and Dark would carry bundles of the papers from the newsagents to the station and await the train. They had a captive market, guaranteed sales and a pocket full of money to start each day.

They came to like Wahgunyah and both took up butcher apprenticeships with a bloke over in Corowa. In 1953 they decided it was time for their first beer and figured it was safer to have it back across the river in Victoria at the Empire.

Meanwhile I've headed over the bridge to get some shots of Corowa and its hosting of the Federation conferences then cross back and, following a hunch, pull up outside the Empire.

As I walk in Kristi looks at me and points to the only bloke this side of the bar, the fella who was on the mobility scooter. 'Colin,' she laughs, 'this is Mick.'

Mick is the real name of 'Dark' and sixty-six years after his first beer in this pub, he's on his regular perch, recalling it to me.

'We were sixteen and a half and it was 1952 and my twin brother was here as well and this publican, George Jolly, yeah I think that was his name, and George said I know your faces and my brother said, yeah we're doing our apprenticeships up at the butchers and old George said, so what'll you have? And we had seven ounces, just the two each, and then we've just finished the second ones and in comes the local copper, Jack Reeves, his name was Jonathan Quentin Reeves. And he comes in and he says hello the Lee boys and he asked what are you two doing and we said we'd just come in to see Mr Jolly, so we got off.'

Mick later recalls how 'George Jolly' only stayed at the pub for two years before selling and moving down to run the pub in Springhurst. He was spot on with that but the bloke's name was Bill Perry, not that it matters.

But the cop was onto them and a bit later Mick was again having a pony when Officer Reeves again happened by.

'He asked me how old I was and I told him I was eighteen. He said, well that's strange, I've just been talking with your twin brother and he said he's seventeen so finish that and piss off!'

Dark and Snow both became butchers. Snow moved away and Mick and his wife eventually took over the Wahgunyah butchery, which was just across the road and down a bit. 'So the pub was always very handy, and Fairy's has been my local ever since.'

On the northern exterior wall of the pub, facing the traffic off the bridge and the old customs house, are two inscriptions. Along the edge of the balcony are the factual name and DOB: 'Old Empire Hotel est 1861'. On the brick body of the building in uneven old faux script is more intriguing, 'Fairy's Bistro'.

'Fairy,' says Mick, 'was Phyllis.'

'In the '60s the '70s and '80s Old Jack Parker ran the pub with his wife Phyllis. Old Jack used to go out with my sister before he met Phyllis and her parents had the dairy and she was the Dairy Girl.'

We've been joined by Robert who was born and grew up in Wahgunyah. He remembers Fairy very well.

'Jack didn't do near the work around the place that his wife did. She was a good hearted, a big-hearted woman. We were just kids and we didn't have much money but she used to look after us, mostly a free lemonade or cordial when we were young and it was hot. But she loved a drop herself. She'd often be on it from opening and by the afternoon she'd go up to bed and everyone would just serve themselves on the honour system – serve yourself and put the money in the till.'

They didn't allow Sunday trading back then but no-one's thirst observes the Sabbath, so Jack and Fairy decided to meet the demand. Mick explains:

'The front of the hotel was all closed up but around the back there was the most beautiful grape vine out there and it covered almost the whole back wall except for this little entrance to the back door. Fairy would spend Sundays serving illicit drinks to all who knew the system while Jack her husband would be keep cockatoo out the front.

'When he whistled the signal that the cops were arriving we'd all crush into room 13, the famous room 13, out there where the big fridge is now. Sometimes up to thirty of us squeezed in a single-bed bedroom, all trying not to laugh. The cops knew what was going on but they'd front up at half past eleven, twelve every Sunday, and sign the books and leave.'

Jack wasn't the best cockatoo in the flock and Mick 'got pinched three times. Didn't worry me. The publican would go to court and he'd pay the fines and then we'd all pay him.'

Robert chips in, 'Those two really looked after the people in this town

and from then on the locals have always called this place, Fairy's.'

Old Denis slides into his usual pew at the end of the bar against the wall. Over his shoulder, a bit across from the anticlockwise clock, there's a wooden sign with 'Three Wise Men' chiselled into it. It's obviously not left over from some nativity fresco so I ask him if he's one of the three.

'Only one that's left,' he smiles to himself with some secret memory. 'It's been there a while that sign. The other two've been looking at the wrong side of the grass for a few years now.'

I drink in that eloquence with my next mouthful and wonder about the pig suspended over the bar. Pat across the bar is the man for that story. He's a short bloke with restless fingers, constantly playing an imaginary keyboard on the bar as he speaks. Like Bobby Ford who's responsible for the porcine adornment, Pat was in the 7th Battalion RAR. Both of 'em went to Vietnam with the 7th, Pat in the first deployment in 1967 and 'Fordy' in the next, in 1971. Following its raising at Puckapunyal in September 1965 the battalion members had:

'... a gathering in the OR's mess and the next minute a huge fight broke out, the CO came in and there was mess everywhere and he just said, "You're nothing but a pack of fucking pigs!" From then on we were just known as the "pig battalion".'

Down the road a bit there's an R & R settlement for ex-diggers where many vets from the 7th come to clean out the cobwebs. The town of Wahgunyah welcomed them from the start and apparently Bobby Ford thought the only thing that'd make the boys feel more at home in the town and the pub was a flying pig.

Consider it done!

Pat knows the skin's real but he's not so sure about the innards. 'It's not money that's for sure but I'm buggered if I know what's inside. I just hope it never explodes in the heat one day!'

Ever since it was first built in 1861 for Frenchman, Camille Reau, this place has had aspirations of class. The advertisement advising of its opening boasted of it being all brick, and with facilities 'in such style as has never before been approached in the district' and with the cuisine department 'as usual under his own personal superintendence.' Even your horse could be assured of 'the best feed'.

Later adverts claimed this hotel to be the 'MOST COMMODIOUS out of Melbourne [with] good and careful grooms [and] a first-class billiard table'.

In 1865 he advertised a 'monster concert' by 'Senor Sipp ... kindly assisted by the Rutherglen, Wahgunyah and Beechworth Amateurs' and a decade later Herr Tomaque a 'talented conjuror [gave] one of his wonderful entertainments'.

Camille Reau eventually sold the pub in 1879 and retired to his various vineyards. When he died in 1912, a local obituary eulogised, that there were, 'few better pioneers ever ... in this district, and everyone who knew him respected him.'

Not every publican since has been top notch but it would seem that overwhelmingly they've been pretty fine and the current pair, Kristi and Brett, are magnets bringing the locals in, enticing the near locals to cross the river and ensuring that travellers like me'll never pass without dropping in.

It seems a long way from the characterless impersonal security-conscious dismissive place I first stopped at yesterday, but on the way north before turning west I pass that pub again and wish I could drag their staff back south to the Old Empire at Wahgunyah for a lesson about the essential ingredients in the ever-enticing dish that is a great country pub.

Postcript: The onset of COVID coincided with a bit of a drop in Mick's health and his family decided a care facility was the best option. He soon got tired of the clipped wings and one night tried the bolt. His efforts to vault the fence in the moonlight resulted in a broken ankle, rehab, and an acceptance of his situation. But his scooter has a long-range tank and he still makes it to Fairy's a couple of times a week.

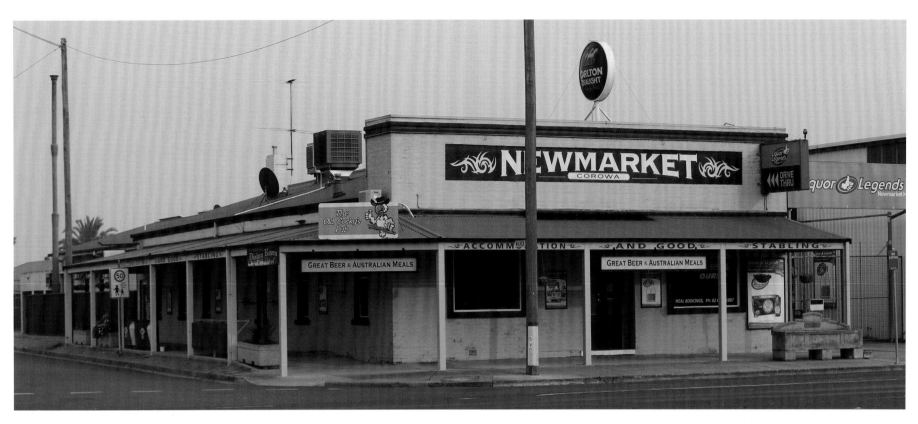

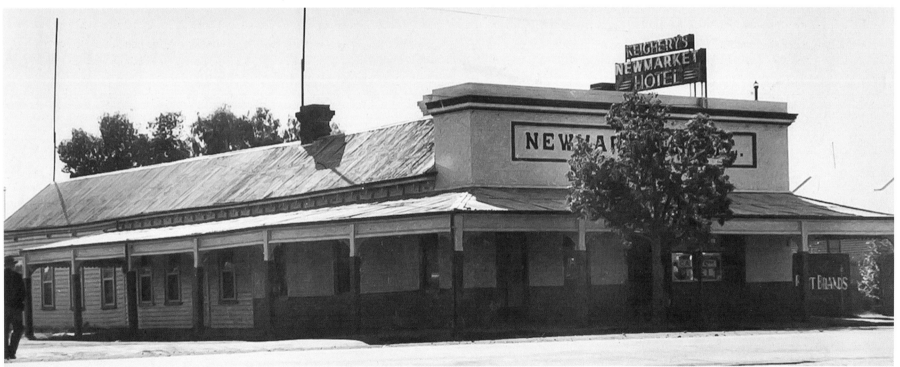

THE NEWMARKET HOTEL (AND A LOOK BACK AT THE GLOBE)

Not a problem at all for my stranded neighbour to keep an eye on my camp on the bank and my washing in the river so I head out, past the Old Empire and across the bridge into Corowa. In the water off to my right as I cross the bridge in Corowa, a couple of young kids are already enjoying the simple pleasure of the river and an inner tube.

Turns out I U-turned just a fraction early last night when I did the 180 at the big roundabout at the top of town. Just one block up on the left I would've found the squat Newmarket Hotel.

Joseph Redmayne opened the Newmarket Hotel in August 1888 hoping for 'a fair share of patronage' and offering 'stabling and paddocks'. The town's most distant pub from the river, at the edge of the settlement and on the main road to Albury, its position indicated the owner was targeting travellers and workers rather than the river merchants and visiting squatters.

And it seems he was onto something. He soon had a licensee running it on a two-year contract and just on a year after he built it this, 'brick [building] with 11 rooms, cellar, and underground tank' was on the market. In what the Albury paper described as a '"very satisfactory" auction sale', the pub was snapped up for £1350.

Eight weeks later Carlo Pola, the new owner, was advertising for tenders for 'the erection of a verandah'. And, I reckon the pub's not changed all that much since! Verandah's still there, wrapping the hotel, but there's a slightly newer addition out the front, on the right as I head from across the road where I've parked the bike. It's an old horse trough – probably been there since the '30s. And it's not just your ordinary horse trough. It's a Rolls Royce, or maybe the Hills Hoist of horse troughs – it's a Bills!

George Bills was born in Brighton, England in 1859 and migrated to Echuca in 1873. He married Annis who'd sailed from Sheffield. George started a business making the radical new inner-spring mattresses and made a packet. They had no kids and when George whose love of animals had seen him become a Life Governor of the RSPCA died, a trust fund of over £70,000 was set up in his memory to 'construct and erect and pay for horse troughs wherever they may be ... desirable for the relief of horses and other dumb animals either in Australasia, in the British Islands or in any other part of the world ...'

The old trough out front of the Newmarket Hotel, under the parapet which wonderfully reads, 'Accommodation and Good Stabling' has the uniform inscription of, 'DONATED BY ANNIS & GEORGE BILLS, AUSTRALIA'.

It's just on opening time and when Nicole who runs the place says that yes they do have accommodation free and a stable in the back yard for Super Ten, I tell her there's one less place available now. Then swing back to check out the town.

Most Australians have never heard of Corowa and yet pretty much every day, every single Aussie is directly affected by events here in the late 1800s. Many towns along the water encapsulate both the divisiveness and the unification qualities of the Murray River, but the story of this place stands above all others. And that spirit of conciliation, or cooperation, of just basic decency, extends back to the very start of white settlement here.

For every ounce of petty community-destroying short-sighted self-interest that Sydney Granderson Watson had evidenced back up-river at the birth of Tintaldra, John Foord, who pretty much created this settlement, had a pound of selfless, visionary, healing altruism. Foord's idea was that Wahgunyah (where he lived) and Corowa were just one big community with a big stream running up the middle, and as there was no way of getting around the water, citizens had to go across it.

In 1857 he did business with another of the Pub 'n' Punters, Henry Hopwood, down in Echuca and bought his punt for £550. Rather than employ anyone to run the conveyance at some crippling rental, Foord first engaged William Fleming and then George Ellis to run it and took half of their receipts for the next four years.

It was a good little earner for Foord but he soon realised that the makeshift old punt wasn't in the best interests of the settlements astride the Murray and so joined the campaign for a bridge crossing, even though it meant losing his local crossing monopoly.

Rather than wait for the feuding colonial governments to work out the finances for the permanent fixed crossing, Foord corralled a bunch of local businessmen together, raised the required ten thousand quid and got the thing built. The terms were such that he saw no return on his investment for seven years.

In 1859 Foord was granted several parcels of land in the town but when the Bishop of Sydney arrived in Corowa in 1861 and pledged to find the funds from Sydney and Melbourne to build a church, John Foord donated some of his newly acquired land for the building. He was that sort of bloke.

But (of course) the pettily jealous colonial governments of New South Wales and Victoria shared neither Foord's altruism nor his vision of peaceful unity across the river. You don't need to be a serial bankrupt New Yorker with ridiculous hair, tiny hands and a floating affinity with the truth to think that trade wars and tariffs are a great way to trump your partners and get along with your neighbours.

Both colonies began erecting customs posts at all Murray river crossings, and the repercussions were felt most keenly by those along each side of the river. Some of the repercussions were farcical:

Buggies purchased in Victoria for use in New South Wales are distinguished from buggies purchased for sale, and the puntman is invested with the duty of discriminating between them, and compelling the latter class to

travel to the nearest Custom House before they can be crossed over the river ...

The Corowa farmers cannot get their wheat ground at Wahgunyah mill, which is in sight of them, without being charged package duty on their bran and pollard coming back again ...

The Albury vineyards are going out of cultivation because Albury wine, which sells for three shillings a gallon, is charged three shillings a gallon duty before it can reach the Victorian market. Tobacco cultivation is abandoned because the raw leaf which yielded a good profit at nine pence a pound is charged a shilling a pound duty on going to Melbourne.

Federation Leagues were formed in towns all along the river and out into the backblocks – in Albury and Berrigan, in Cobram, Deniliquin and Echuca, Jerilderie, Moama, Mulwala, Rutherglen, Wodonga, Toucumwal, Yarrawonga and Blighty.

These Border federation leagues are a curious compost of settlers and the trading classes residing along the Murray with young Australian natives, a few graziers, and mostly all the vignerons. It is not surprising that they feel acutely in respect to the federation question, for many of them have property on both sides of the river.

The strongest and most vociferous Federation League was in Corowa and it was they who mobilised the other leagues, unified them and galvanised them into concerted action. In June 1893 the *Corowa Free Press* announced that, 'All branches of the Australian Federation League have ... agreed to the holding of a conference at Corowa on the 31st July and 1st August' and to which parliamentarians of all parties from both Sydney and Melbourne would be invited.

The assorted dignitaries, federalists, free traders and free loaders turned up en masse. The still beautifully maintained but (of course) no longer used railway station was hectic:

The special train from Melbourne brought up a large contingent, including the Premier, Mr. J. B. Patterson, the leader of the Opposition Sir Graham Berry, and at least 10 members of Parliament. The New South Wales Government and Parliament were strongly represented, there being four of the Ministry present.

I head south on Sanger Street, past the Hotel Australia, the Royal and the Corowa Hotel on my left and the Star on my right until just before Parliament Street there's a flat-faced red-ochre building abutting the corner to the west.

In 1893, disgorged from the trains back up at the top of the town, and from cars and gigs out front, the heavies and the hangers-on drifted to the agreed spot at 'the Globe Hotel, which was thronged with visitors, and federation was the one theme.'

And when 'the drag containing the Premier, Sir Graham Berry, and others drove up to the Globe Hotel those assembled on the balcony and in the street below gave three hearty cheers, which were acknowledged.'

Upstairs, 'William Lyne after all had been supplied with a glass of champagne, welcomed the Premier and other members of the Victorian Parliament to Corowa.'

The New South Wales delegation came by train on the newly opened branch line from Culcairn. The train, hard to believe, was late getting to the sparkling new Corowa station and they missed the morning session of the conference. The Gladys Berejiklian of the day explained that it was a simple teething problem with cutting-edge technology, that it was following world's best practice and anyway, morning sessions of 'these things' are mostly handshakes and posturing.

For most of 31 July and the horses' birthday the next day, the unification of the antipodean colonies was debated from every angle at the Oddfellows Hall.

Without doubt the advent of the customs posts at each Murray crossing was the tinder that fuelled the fires of discontent and again Corowa-Wahgunyah which saw itself as a single town split by the stream was front and centre:

the one point all the local speakers drew attention to was 'that gate,' and certainly they have cause of complaint. The Victorian Customs authorities have erected a huge gate across the Wahgunyah end of the bridge to protect the revenue, and this they close about eleven o'clock at night and then quietly go to bed. The result is that if a driver of a buggy, a horseman, a pedestrian or a drayman gets to that gate from either side of the river after the closing hour he has either to camp for the night or return to some hotel.

The major resolution to be passed over the two days read:

That in the opinion of this meeting the best interests, and the present and future prosperity of the Australian colonies will be promoted by their early and complete federation.

When the talking paused, well, like every conference and junket before or since, it was off to the pub. And on the first evening, when the talking stopped and the feed 'n' watering needed to begin, the pub of choice was again the Globe Hotel.

In the evening the cold collation on the magnificent balcony of the Globe was exceptional. I haven't sat down to many better in Melbourne or Sydney, or Adelaide.

And:

On Monday evening there was a large attendance at the Globe Hotel when a cold collation was served in a most excellent manner and hungry delegates and others succeeded in disposing of the many good things provided. There was no ceremony about the affair at all: just a pleasant little gathering whereat all enjoyed themselves.

And it's this old Globe Hotel which is on my right when I get to the end of Sanger Street. Unless it's on the left.

Last night over in Wahgunya the general thought was that the old Globe Hotel, what used to be the Globe Hotel, the one famous for its cold collation and for the place to stand to cheer a premier turning up in a horse and cart, was on the north-eastern corner of Sanger and Edward streets, behind the pepper trees, 'have a look at these photos'.

They pretty much had me convinced. The old shot of what is now Eastham house sure looks like what I'm after and what's now the Globe Hotel has no balcony, no scars of where one used to be, and not even a semblance of where any doors to access the now-vanished verandah might've been.

I ring the Corowa Museum and Leslie picks up.

'When did the Globe decamp across the road?'

'Er, it didn't.' Not to the best of her knowledge and though I've never met

Leslie, I get the immediate impression that her knowledge of this can't be scrawled on the back of a coaster.

'They demolished the balcony sometime in the sixties and cleaned the place up but it's always been in the same place.'

Leslie's word's good enough for me so I scout around the place, this now-closed pub which was at the very heart of the creation of this nation. It's big. Solid. Like some sort of foundation underpinning this end of the town and with a large yard behind.

Nicholas Chenhall a member of the Chiltern Mining Board and 'a prominent public man in the North-Eastern district of Victoria' and with an obvious interest in horses and the turf was announced as taking the place over in May 1878. Later that year he sublet the pub's stables and billiard room. The large rear yard was already being used for the holding area for mares waiting to be serviced by local stallions at rates around five guineas a time.

In 1882 his wife Mary Chenhall was listed as the publican and she was advertising that entries for local horse races should be made at the hotel and that there would be sweeps on the local events.

By the mid-1890s the spacious front rooms had become WOTSO co-working spaces of their time and it was here in 1889 that the auction for the Newmarket Hotel was held. This was a pub that, in a town of a dozen hotels, had stood out from the crowd and become the hub of the town. It was here that meetings of the fledgling Corowa Federation League were held and so, with its expansive bars and dining rooms and full-length balcony, it was the obvious choice for hosting the dignitaries in 1893. By then Mary Chenhall was well into widowhood and a leading citizen in her own right and when the conference rolled around in 1893 she did the town and her pub proud.

Across Parliament Street, the old Terminus Hotel also stands, closed for business but maintained and in great condition. Such a pity the guts of these two old pubs are no longer accessible, that the Globe no longer provides collations on the balcony and neither has drinks in the bar, but equally it's enriching that these places are fortunate enough to be in a community which treasures them and will look after them in their restful old age.

I take Super Ten back over the bridge, grab a couple of cans for my trapped camping mate and head back to my tent. Washing's all been drying on a fallen tree in the sun and just above the gurgling whirlpools of the river. Good to go.

I pack up my stuff and head north again and in less than ten I'm pulling into the yard behind the Newmarket Hotel. It's Monday afternoon and for the last thirty-five, maybe forty years that's meant the table in the middle of the bar is occupied with a bunch of gradually aging blokes who've spent the morning at the weekly Corowa sheep sales. Not all of them make it every week, and a couple have been rounded up to the greener pastures of the wide blue yonder but today there's Rolly (pretty much retired now) and his brother Sam (who's still having a crack), John (still with sales slips in his pocket), Rod (who used to be 'Bomber' but no longer, please), and there's Candles, with his face like a crushed brown paper bag.

John's been to the sales – sold a lot for Candles as well as some of his own, and the brothers were also up there to keep an eye on things.

For most of them, it's their only session of mid-week drinking and it's an essential part of their week. And for all of them, this is old school.

Rod grew up bleeding the red and black of Essendon and his fanaticism brought him the nickname of 'Bomber', but a few years back, independent, he reckons, of the peptide scandal, he made it known that moniker was to no longer be used. He points to a copy of the famous shot of Captain Blood, Jack Dyer, smacking down Tom Meehan in 1949 at Punt Road that's on the wall beside the bar.

'I grew up following football. When it was played like that. Real football! Played by men with real jobs during the week. Take your boots to work on Tuesdays and Thursdays and play serious on Saturday! They've gone from men like Captain Blood here to paying some bloke ten million for ten years when they know his body's only going to last for five if they're lucky. And they change the rules every five minutes so their mums won't worry about their darlings! When they gave away real play, I gave the game away. And 'Bomber' had to go.'

Back in the '60s, when he started coming to the river for his holidays, well before he fell for the place and sold his home in Canberra and bought a place just around the corner from the pub, Rod was in hospitality too. It was pretty basic, certainly wasn't five star, but there were few complaints. It was a joint down in Melbourne called, Pentridge. He started in '66, the year before Ronald Ryan became the last person hanged in Australia. Later he moved to Beechworth Prison and then to the national capital in 1977 to work in sport, where the clientele 'were probably not quite so tough'. He's been here long enough now to be considered a local and be an associate member of the Monday afternoon sheep meet.

The other blokes reckon Candles has the most sheep, most land and most money but I soon find out he might just have the most knowledge of the culture of the bush of any bloke I've happened across.

He's been drinking here, at this pub, all his life – remembers starting to pass his pocket money across the bar when he was sixteen, maybe seventeen.

'I was tall early so I could pass easily for eighteen even when I was maybe fifteen but then we went to Tasmania with the Young Farmers and this group of us went into a pub down there and ordered and we were used to bullshitting that we were eighteen so we trotted that out again and the publican said "well you should do your homework a bit better".'

They didn't realise the legal age down there was still twenty-one. 'So we all got turfed out except one fella who had just turned.'

'I used to play football for Wahgunyah and we'd drink out the back in Fairy's every Sunday morning in the mid-'70s and we'd get a keg from the pub and take it home. It was forty bucks for an eighteen and you had twenty blokes at two bucks each would cover the barrel. But if there were more, then that was money went to the club. Even at forty blokes, you'd still get half a gallon each.'

The crumpled brown bag face smiles. 'The last few glasses would be a bit warm but by that stage you wouldn't get too many complaints.'

He's interested in what I do and when I mention drovers, he brings up Harry Redford, expert drover and most famous cattle thief in the country's history. He knows the tale of the white bull and how Radford, selling his cattle as Harry Collins, got busted in South Australia, brought back to Queensland for a trial at Roma. And how the jury exonerated him to the disbelief of the presiding judge. He knows the full story about the Pub with No Beer controversy, about Gordon Parsons and Dan Sheahan, and he knows about Ned Buchanan and the opening up of the great droving tracks. Candles isn't on the land, he's of the land. He sure knows its story and a lot of its secrets.

His nickname was appropriated by his mates from Clayton 'Candles' Thompson, a South Australian AFL player who played fifty games over three seasons at Hawthorne in the 1950s, and whose long skinny legs inspired the name in both cases.

He cautions me to treat all his mates with respect as they're all 'OBEs' and I tell him I will, it's great that they've all been honoured, even if it's the old imperial system, as they all get onto the sheep side of things.

They're all glad they stayed with 'em when many pulled out a few years back. Prices are good despite buying in hay. Even feeding his 800 sheep four big bales every second day, John's happy with today's prices and won't be selling too many more before they're shorn in August. The biggest difference they've seen is the disappearance of the cocky farmer.

'Time was that every farmer who had a son would teach him to shear and that's how it'd work. If the kid was still at school, he'd get time off to shear his dad's mob and maybe the mob next door who'd help him. But now that's all gone and it's contractors who charge for this and for that, things like travelling fees, and so the romance and the family feel of it all has died out.'

My shout so I head to Mitzy at the bar. He's the husband of Nicole who's the official licensee and he's filling in after a day of being a sparky until Bree, the oldest of his five daughters and one of four who work in the pub, takes over in an hour.

He and Nic were looking for a pub in early 2018, almost got Fairy's over in Wahgunyah but missed out and the owner here, where Mitzy ('Dunno how it came about, had it since school') has been drinking all his life, heard about their interest and offered them a lease.

'We crunched numbers and then he offered us the freehold and we crunched some more numbers and we made a counteroffer for the lot and he accepted and we had ourselves a pub. Moved in in June 2018.'

With a decision to not have gambling, they've continued the character of the Newmarket as the town's workers' pub and the main sponsor of the town's three footy clubs. Which makes for a very blokey bar – something they're working to address. They're planning on taking out maybe half the accommodation rooms out the back, removing the internal walls, exposing the beams, removing the windows and creating a covered beer garden, exploiting a beefed-up kitchen and appealing to more family groups.

Nicole's fronted and joins us. Her caution that I may be confronted by the ghost of an ex-owner, Camplin, who died in a room out the back has me scurrying for my notes. I was sure he said his final 'goodbye' very differently.

Albert Camplin took over this hotel in 1897 after at least five years in a pub at Goonambil. He must've sold it at some stage and then bought it back but in 23 July 1907 the *Riverina Times* reported that as the host of the Newmarket, he'd been accidentally shot 'through the face' by his brother while out camping and had died two days previously (21 July).

Meanwhile, the *Corowa Chronicle* reported on 24 July 1907 that James Arthur Camplin had passed away peacefully in the hotel the previous Sunday (i.e. 21 July) from a long-standing illness.

Now that sounds like a pretty ordinary day. And if I died twice on the same day, one from illness and the other from being shot by my brother, I'd probably be tempted to haunt my old haunts.

No connection of the two deaths in any of the newspapers. No mistaking names and no identity confusion. Albert was mentioned as being forty-five, James a year younger. (It didn't turn the family off the pub though. That October the licence was transferred from James's estate to Jane Camplin, his widow.)

Nicole and I agree to scratch our scones and when I tell her I'll try to sort it out she says she's also on the trail of an old photo.

'My dad's favourite pub trick was doing a headstand on the bar and drinking a middy without spilling it. There's a photo of him doing it on the bar at the Southern Cross Hotel in Melbourne after Collingwood won the grand final that I've seen but the lady who had it has passed away.'

The woman's daughter's still in town so Nic will be chasing her up. And when she laments, 'It'd be a great photo to have in the bar,' and says her dad'll be in soon, I tell her I'm happy to take a new one for her.

She scoffs. 'He's way past that now!'

Damn. But being fifty years too late is less painful than missing by a day.

Rolly and his brother have left, John's about to head home and I pull aside the bloke with the face of John Gorton and ask quietly if they're all really OBEs.

'Bloody oath they're OBEs,' he swears, 'Over Bloody Eighty.'

With that, the candle's out and I'm off to bed.

CHAPTER 20

COROWA TO MULWALA

I head down Federation Avenue and then keep with it as it bends west and becomes Spring Drive, which briefly kisses the river and then curves with an arc of a billabong before Lake Mulwala is almost at the gear lever at my left foot.

I've been here when the lake's been very low but today the water's up and I pull up at the edge. There's an old wooden jetty to which some good soul has attached some stainless-steel steps.

A zephyr whispers the lake's surface into tiny ripples and far off there're

voices of a couple of fishermen with their outboard switched off. The day's heat doesn't yet demand a soak so I take some panoramic images, relax into the tranquillity of the waters, down a banana and remount.

Then it's just ten minutes until I'm stopping again to survey the mouth of the Mulwala Canal, the longest irrigation canal south of the equator. The then New South Wales Premier, Steven, turned the first ceremonial sod in April 1935 and it was finished in 1942.

A LUNATIC AND A SWINGING TIT

Jess ('I only get Jessica when I'm in trouble') has just checked me into the Royal Mail at Mulwala when she replies that it's 'the other place just up the road that's known as "the Swinger"'. And when I get a moment there're a couple of old images of the pub around the back she wants me to see – she's been trying to date them but with no luck so I get a drink and we get some clues and then crank up the laptop. The first one we narrow down to between 1891 and 1897 but the second, with a motorcyclist photobombing on the side we can only put between 1908 and 1925.

Jess is happy with that. She's a local, just about to turn nineteen and is more connected with her town, with her pub and with the history of the place than any other young bar person I've come across.

With the light lowering and the shadows becoming interesting, I sort a slate and head out to shoot the rest of the town.

This place is the head point of the Mulwala Canal, at just short of 2900 kilometres, the longest irrigation canal south of the equator. Construction began two years before the Royal Mail pub was built and it was done and dusted in 1942. It exits the lake just back east on the Corowa road. A mob of cormorants wait to pounce for their supper from a suspended wire. Once I'm done there, I head back to the Lake Mulwala Hotel.

Known far and wide as, 'the Swinging Tit' or simply 'the Swinger' in honour, allegedly of a barmaid of not so recent past who eschewed underwear, this place's main bar has all the personality of an X-ray. The rear beer garden is superb with unhindered views of the lake, if you don't mind a bit of smoke with the vista. And no, there's no photos around of the nickname's inspiration.

Over the bridge to neighbouring Yarrawonga and I'm eager to check the famous pressed tin ceilings of the Yarrawonga Hotel.

'Ah mate, nah. We got rid of those when we did the upgrade a few years ago.'

'Upgrade?' I settle for some shots of a gorgeous triptych glasswork depicting the lake and its flooded gums and get down to the weir.

Yarrawonga/Mulwala mark a real borderline for anyone following the Murray. The weir here is the highest one on the river without a lock. Launch your boat or canoe anywhere downstream from here and you can stay in it for the rest of the journey right to the ocean but arrive from upstream and you're going to have to drag it overland to get around. For captains and long-distance paddlers, for serious houseboat owners and travellers, this is the start of the achievable, the explorable Murray.

By the time I get back, the pub's filled up with tradies having an after-workie and if this isn't their first time here, and for pretty much all of them it isn't, Jess knows their drinks and their preferred perches.

One of them warns that, 'You have to be careful about Jess because if she sees you emptying your beer then she'll be at the taps getting your next one so if you're planning on cutting out you've gotta lay your glass down on the bar real quick.'

'Just make sure it's on its side and not upturned.'

Ray, partner of Leanne the licensee has turned up, tattooed and tanned. They took this place over four days before Christmas in 2018 and the first weeks:

'... were the hardest thing hour-wise that I've ever done. If we were awake we were working. Everything was broken down, the place was a brothel and we had to get the bar mats off the bar with a spatula they were so putrid. So we worked our guts out for weeks and some of the old staff were just standing around and I said to them, "If you can lean you can clean," and they said, 'That's not part of our award' so they didn't last long. And then we poached Jess from the "Tit" and we all started getting on our feet.'

His left ear looks like it's been too close to Mike Tyson. He chuckles. 'A lot of people ask me about the ear and I just put on my tough face and tell them, I'll tell you one day.'

But today he's happy to fess up.

'… It was cancer … they cut it off, shit it was hurting, just an aggressive cancer about 2005, I said to the doctor, cut the whole thing off. I don't take painkillers but they said, you're going to need these and they were right. Anyway a bit later we were out to dinner one night and Leanne told me, I think your ear smells. It had a dressing on it and we took the dressing off and shit it was rank. Those beer mats didn't even come close. And so we went to the hospital and within half an hour they were cutting more out of the ear and I told the doctor I'm not the best-looking bloke in the world so if there's even an inkling of cancer just cut the whole fucking thing off. But he said, that'd be enough for now.'

So now he gets it checked every three months and tells anyone with any suspicious scabs or marks to have 'the bloody thing looked at!'

He reckons the decision to hire Jess is on a par with getting that scab on his ear checked. When she heads off to study nursing she's assured of as many shifts at the pub as she can handle.

Things quieten down and I order a Caesar salad, which turns out to be the best one I've ever had, and chat to the young woman.

She talks of her pop moving off his long-held farm after the tornado ripped through in March 2013, destroying their fences, their homestead and many animals that Jess and the family had hand-reared. She was in town when the storm hit.

'We were called to come out to DC with as many chainsaws as we could round up, so we banged on all our neighbours' doors and piled into cars and headed out. We just started cutting all the trees across the road so we, and the ambulances could get through to the people and they could all get out. It was unbelievable carnage.'

But it also bonded the community. Everyone banded together and helped each other out and 'I think it did so much damage and destroyed so much but it really left a legacy of community spirit.'

I hadn't known Jess for long before she lied to me. After asking whether this or the other pub was the 'Swinger' and confirming it was the one up the road, I wondered what the nickname of this place was.

Jess looked sheepish and said it was just known as the 'Royal or the Mulwala'.

Now it's time for her confession that yes, I'm right, this one's known as the 'Finger Inn', but there's a simple and unexpected explanation.

She doesn't know just how long ago but, 'There was a barmaid here who, if you ordered a round of drinks, like three or four, she'd bring them to you with her fingers actually inside the glasses, inside the beer. So the place became known as the "Finger In" which, being a pub, understandably slid to "Inn".'

Now, just maybe that's believable and just maybe it goes back more than half a century. Just maybe it goes back to a lady, probably a widow, named Mrs Mary J. Mulqueeny. And even if it doesn't, Mary's story is still worth a run.

Mary didn't have the Mulwala Hotel for all that long. In January 1950 Mrs Ruby Gissing was charged, as licensee of the Mulwala Hotel, with having 'disposed of liquor during prohibited hours', and was fined £2, with 10/– court costs.

Ruby offloaded the place to our Mary the following September but then in July 1951, 'The renewal of the licence for the Mulwala Hotel, Mulwala, by Mrs. Mary. J. Mulqueeny was opposed by Sgt. J. T. Curran, District Licensing Inspector' who went on to testify that:

… on entering the bar (of the Mulwala Hotel) I saw a man named Jackson serving behind the bar. I said, 'I am Sgt. Curran: what is your name?' He replied 'Jackson.' I said 'Are you employed by the licensee?' and he said 'yes.' He was wearing a pair of shorts and shoes without shirt or underclothing. I said: 'Why are you not properly dressed when serving behind the bar?' He replied that it was very hot and he was trying to keep cool.

And you thought those 'No shirt no service' signs were a recent thing eh?

The officer continued:

I said: 'Does the licensee know you are dressed in this manner,' and he said 'yes' … The premises [are] not up to the standard. They had a very untidy appearance. Some skirting boards, etc. were white and eaten. The floors were not clean. The general appearance of the place was untidy. There was not the usual polish about.

Mr Doolan, the presiding magistrate said:

… the license would be refused. He did not consider Mrs Mulqueeny a fit

and proper person to hold a license. She was of intemperate habits and during the six months as licensee she had frequently been under the influence of liquor and drunk on a number of occasions.

And then he turned to address the publican herself:

You have allowed noise on premises in to the early hours of the morning. The hotel premises have been allowed to become untidy and continue to be untidy. You have failed to supervise the conduct of your barman Jackson. You yourself have become untidy in dress, due no doubt to your intemperate habits.

Now that just about convinces me that Mary might've been mad enough to serve you a round of beers with her fingers in, but this gets just a little weirder.

In July 1952 Walter Ward became the next host of the pub, but the licence wasn't directly transferred from Mary Mulqueeny. Seems that she may've taken the loss of her profession a bit hard, or maybe her habits became even more intemperate.

The *Corowa Free Press* reported the transfer thus: 'Walter Testrall Ward was granted a transfer of licence of the Mulwala Hotel, Mulwala.'

And the consignee? None other than 'the Deputy Master in Lunacy and Committee of Management re Mrs. Mulqueeny.'

Yep, Mary had been declared insane – a new one by me, but then again, if I'd been shouted a beer by every publican who's told me you have to be a lunatic to run a country pub, well, it would've been appreciated!

So yeah, the Mulwala Royal Mail Hotel, the illustrious 'Finger Inn' might just owe some sort of debt to Mary Mulqueeny.

I share that yarn with Jess and as we talk, Ray takes a phone call and excuses himself – someone's rung for the courtesy bus. It's not five minutes before he's back with two fellas, one in fluoros and another in civvies. As they walk in, Jess pours their drinks and when they take them, no money goes back across the bar.

John and Matt are contractors; been working up this way digging ditches for irrigators for over ten years. John's family's in Melbourne but he bought a place up here, travels up each Monday morning and back each Friday arvo. And every night they're in town, they have dinner here.

John, Matt's boss, has a weekly slate and so an entire visit here, being picked up and then dropped back later by Ray in the bus, involves no money exchange.

John: 'These people here are all family and when we come in it doesn't matter who's behind the bar, they know us and they know what we want. Paying by the week only enhances that feeling of being with family, being sorta guests in someone's home. And never having to wash dishes!'

John's been around, married to an Iraqi woman who grew up in Kuwait, he talks eloquently about places he's visited like Petra in Jordan and about the influence his father-in-law – who was shipped off by his family to boarding school in India for four years – has on his thinking. But he reckons that the Murray is the beating heart of Australia and can't think of its waters not being part of his life.

They order dinner and we try to sort out one of the really big issues of this world: why is it normal to have the same thing to drink every night when you'd never think of having the same thing to eat.

Jess laughs and looks at Matt who, when he's swallowed that mouthful tries to kybosh that theory: 'I have the same thing every night. Steak with vegetables.'

But Jess corrects him, 'Sometimes it's T-bone, sometimes Scotch, always medium and always with mushroom sauce on the side.'

The pub toughed out the lockdowns and then Lea and Ray spotted a new opportunity. They bought the languishing Ettamogah Pub, north of Albury and renamed it the 'Table Top'. Ray moved east to manage this new project whilst Lea stayed back to oversee the 'Finger'.

And Jess graduated, found work as a dental nurse and moved south. I'm sure she's still not getting 'Jessica' too often.

CHAPTER 22 – COBRAM

GRAND AND CENTRAL: MONGREL TALES

There's already a trio of blokes, glasses all partly drained, at the L-shaped front bar of the Grand Central Hotel in Cobram and yes, mate, just pull up a pew on the corner there if you like.

I do like, and ease down onto a stool as 'G'day, I'm Nikki, bit hot out there eh?' pours me a cold one. The two nearest pair of blokes could be brothers or distant school mates. Under his lamb-lined jacket, the nearer one's wearing a reddish polo with yellow piping and 'Hawks' embroidered under a gold logo.

'G'day, I'm Archie.'

On the stool next to him's a well-dressed sort of fella in a greenish possibly cashmere V-neck and very ready smile. This is Ralph.

At the far end, standing where you'd expect a stool is a goateed bloke who could be the son one of them has been trying to disown. He's wearing a brown and gold beanie, Hawks, that's not in its rookie season, pulled down to his eyebrows and a fluoro jacket that wouldn't be dirtier if he'd spent the day sleeping in a coal pit. His eyes fix on me from just under the cap and atop a face that's hard enough to chop wood on.

He's not a native of this place, but came up in his late teens to, 'play footy for Barooga and everyone had a nickname and they asked me what mine was and I said I don't have one. And they said everyone has to have a nickname, and I said well I don't and they said well we'll have to get you one. So I had a game and they saw how I played and they said, you played like a mongrel. Turned up for the game as "Dale" and went home as "Mongrel". Been that ever since.'

He reckons he's the only official 'Mongrel' around the place but that there's a few other random shadies in the town and he allows his eyes to smile just a bit when I tell him he's just the latest in a long historical connection between this pub and mongrels and mongrel acts.

Cobram already had a big pub when William Stewart opened the brand spanking doors of this hotel, slap in the guts of the town, on the corner of Punt Road and Terminus Street for the first time on Monday 8 September 1902.

Town interest in the progress of the Grand Central was such that four months before opening the *Cobram Courier* leaked a pen drawing and juicy details:

> *A public bar, 19 ft by 17 ft, occupies the ground floor corner of the building, while a second bar, 18 ft by 8 ft, is but a little distance off. On the ground floor are situated commercial, sample, first and second dining, and billiard rooms, kitchen ... There are 40 rooms in all in the building, the majority of them being capacious, lofty and well lighted, with every provision supplied for the prevention of fire.*

Once delivered, William Stewart and his forty-room creation didn't miss. The opening reviews were off the scale:

> *... the structure amply bears out its title the 'Grand Central.' It is grand in appearance, grand in architectural conception, and grand in practical construction whilst its central position, fair in the middle of the town, fully justifies the affix. It is a very aptly named house, for name and house are*

thoroughly in accord with each other ...

Downstairs, the rooms are more devoted to the study of the 'inner man,' likewise to the pleasure of patrons and the business of commercial men. There are two dining rooms —first and second.

Ah yes – the inner man. Not sure if that's the brain or the stomach. Maybe the soul.

Full disclosure: this seems to've been written on the Monday afternoon of the pub's opening. William Stewart obviously knew how to have grandiose pubs designed and built, but just as obviously he was a bloke who knew how to get people, important people – dare I say, 'influencers' – through his doors. 'The "Grand Central" was formally opened shortly after midday ... when the proprietor cordially invited every comer to partake of any beverage desired.'

And partake they did! Give a writer and everyone else in town an arvo of free booze and bonhomie and what're your chances of getting a bad review? Understandably, 'the house was well patronised throughout the day, and the visitors gave a good deal of attention to examining and admiring the various rooms but particularly the bar.'

Translation: most people didn't get past the bar.

Cobram's Grand Central Hotel was off and running. And of course as soon as any enterprise is showing signs of success the unrestrained mongrels of government start sniffing at the place's bum and peeing on its feet.

The year after he'd opened, still far from recouping his investment, the Licensing Court rejected the local council's valuation for the pub of £198 on which costs, taxes, rents and fees were pro rata based and banged it up to £235. (The Grand Central can't have affected its big brother Cobram Hotel too much as the same court rejected its £194 valuation and pushed it to £240.)

William Stewart beat back the wild dogs and in 1904 the *Cobram Courier* was again reporting on his success:

Mr W. Stewart, of the Grand Central hotel, has ... had to call in the carpenter to build extra stabling, in order to meet the demands made on his yard accommodation by the patrons of this popular hotel. The inside and outside appointments of the Grand Central, though always complete, are now more than ample to accommodate any rush that may take place.

But then in 1906 William Stewart, publican and public benefactor, went too far and again the mongrels barked:

The owner of the Grand Central hotel in Cobram has recently been compelled by the police to remove from under the verandah of his hotel seats placed there for the convenience of the public.

Yep! Inhale some fresh stuff and try to grasp that bit of pettiness. Old Bill, was made of sterner stuff than to lose sleep over yapping dogs so he offered them a longer leash: 'He now asks the Council's permission to construct seating accommodation round a large pepper tree on the footpath opposite the hotel.'

There is no greater love than a mongrel's for a tree! The council bureaucrats wrestled through this major issue and acted decisively, deciding that the, 'seat or seats should be the property of the Council, and ... Council would construct the seats if (Mr Stewart) bore the cost.'

And the world was suddenly a better place.

William Stewart had created an outstanding building and developed a thriving business. By 1909 he'd sold the licence and the new host, Leonard Gedye, and the wild dogs had a new bone.

Gedye soon found himself in court charged by Officer Matthew Leckie of Customs and Excise with the heinous crime of breaching copyright through selling homemade lemonade into bottles bearing the name of E. Rowlands, a major drink producer. The magistrate found no intent to deceive and dismissed the charge, pointedly indicating his thoughts on the instigating officer by awarding costs against him.

Now I'm not sure whether Mackie, his office and the E. Rowlands company all had distemper or rabies but they dragged Gedye to the Appeals Court. And again they were muzzled.

The good Officer Mackie was not a contented canine. Two weeks later the same bloke, like some Casterton cattle dog had rounded up Leonard Gedye into the local police court. This time it was more serious. With two other publicans – one each from Katamatite and Strathmerton, he'd been caught drawing beer through lead pipes. Now, *that* can leave a nasty taste. Finally, Mackie nailed it and the publicans were each hit with fines and costs. (Reflecting just how central pure beer is to this country, the headline on the *Argus*'s report of this case read, 'THE PEOPLE'S FOOD'.)

In 1941 as the war raged once again the local enforcers bit into the big pieces of meat and the publican was hit with a ten-shilling fine when two people were found in the bar after permitted hours.

With so many young men off fighting and the austerity on the home front, like many pubs, the Grand Central diversified. Opticians and oculists began advertising their attendance at the Grand Central Hotel where they would perform, 'scientific sight testing' and would have available, 'Oculine, the prefect eye food'.

Yeah, I don't know either.

Dr W. E. Thomas, a leading dentist who had 'the largest practice in Australia' and who offered a £10 payment 'if slightest pain' also started attending the hotel monthly.

That was pretty standard for the leading hotels in each country town but the Grand Central went one further. Every fourth Saturday for years starting in 1910, hopefully out the back but just maybe in the front bar, Mr L. L. Paterson, a veterinary surgeon would check out your sick animals. No, it's not recorded how many mongrels were brought it.

Then in 1949 a sting was on in the bush. A pack of police from the smoke was sweeping the country, slipping into rural pubs in the guise of travelling salesmen and prospective residents, avoiding the cockatoos out front and busting SP bookies. The Grand Central was a target. Ted Forrest, who'd taken over the pub in 1948 from a bloke named Whelan (which is probably interesting to me and my mum), was hauled into court. In November 1949, just in time for Christmas and at the onset of the thirst-inducing hot days of summer, the magistrate ordered the Grand Central licence be refused and the pub to close its doors for allowing gambling on the premises.

Hard to get a bigger mongrel act than timing a bust and court hearing so that a pub would be forced to close over the Christmas break.

Somehow Ted Forrest, a former squadron leader with the RAAF ensured that the pub kept plugging and in December the place hit the big time – and this is truly the big time – when a triple wedding at Cobram, including official photos taken inside the pub, scored a double-page spread in *The Australian Women's Weekly*.

By January Ted had worked out a permanent counter-canine/mongrel-management plan and transferred the licence to his wife, Betty Ambrosine Forrest, and the place was soon back doing what it'd long done.

Only, I'm guessing, with better cockatoos outside.

When I rock up there's no shady blokes keeping an eye out for suss blow-ins with unfamiliar dials or known faces, and no pepper tree across the road. And there's no seats across from the pub but somehow, at some time, someone's been permitted to position a bench right out front, unshaded by the verandah but probably very close to where the original offending chairs had been a century ago.

This is Nikki's first pub. After twenty years working for other people in hospitality she and partner Bernie started looking for a country hotel around 2014 and eventually settled on this one in her childhood home, and

not far from Bernie's family over in Numurkah.

She signed a thirty-year licence and'll feel she's achieved something if she reaches the five-year mark. Everything's in her name because Bernie's general duty policeman day job over at Shepparton precludes him, through conflict-of-interest issues, from having any involvement behind the bar.

Nikki pours me a lite and I take a pew at a corner of the L-shaped front bar. These blokes don't know me from Adam but that's irrelevant. I'm in town and I'm in their pub and I'm very welcome. After mentions of the weather and the dry and the heat and the zero chance of rain – one bloke swears that if it doesn't rain in town in the next week the council's going to drain two lanes of the swimming pool – I'm halfway down my middy and we're at the spot where I started this yarn. Back to why the bloke at the end's standing and why he's shed the name that, long ago, a mother who thought he was cute, had given him.

My attempt at opening conversation –'So you all Hawthorne fans?' – gets a death stare from Mongrel and a sideways is-this-bloke-for-real glance from the other two.

Haven't I heard of the Barooga Hawks? Barooga? Isn't that across the river? Isn't that on foreign ground? And I control the urge to ask them if they're a netball club.

Apparently like most of the Cobramites, Mongrel's been a Barooga follower ever since his first game, and the other pair are with him on that. 'It's a much friendlier club' and when the local derby's on, things can get heated in town but the rest of the time no-one gets too excited.

They ask me what I'm doing in town and when I tell them how so much of my life is a pub crawl of sorts one of the old blokes pipes up.

'I'm bloody envious. I had a mate with a very, very sick wife and we promised that when she passed, we'd get in his car and go visit every pub in the bush to cheer him up like.' There's a pause.

'But we never got around to it.'

'Change of plans?' I ask.

'Nah.'

That pause again.

'His wife recovered.'

When some semblance of decorum returns, the best I can add is, 'Great news for the wife.'

I ask where the toilets are and leave them leafing through a copy of my last book. When I get back Archie, who proudly tells me he's been kicked out of Young & Jacksons, has a problem.

'I've been trying to work out how you have so much time to travel and I said to Ralph I don't think he's a city bloke because he's been to all the country towns and now we're sure because you've just left all your money on the bar when you went to the toilet so I know you don't come from the bloody city, full stop.'

I tell him I won't drink in a bar where I can't leave all my stuff when I have to duck out, that's one of the reasons why not every pub on the river is in this book and Archie comes back with a memory.

'When I was a kid at the Bilby pub, it's closed now, but the publican would have enough and go to bed and all the cockies would stay there drinking, throwing their money on the bar and then they'd just lock the doors when the last one left and the publican would scoop up all the money off the bar in the morning. Good days.'

Archie was born up the river in Yarrawonga but, 'I was going broke so I went to work in Melbourne for fourteen years to make a bit of money.'

But you can't work all the time so he took up a hobby. 'I thought I'd have a go at having a drink in every pub in Melbourne,' which sounded like a doable thing for a young bloke, 'but then they kept building new ones and I couldn't keep up.'

He got himself a payout and came back to the river and settled in Cobram, got a job on the council

'Which means I didn't work much. Wasn't so much even appearance money coz we used to get paid even when we didn't appear. Thirteen of us in the gang, taking turns. Twelve blokes to watch the other one digging the hole. Next day it was different – twelve blokes taking turns to watch the other filling it in.'

But then he had to retire, exhausted.

'Leaning on a shovel for thirty-five hours a week could tire out the fittest bloke around. And I wasn't close to being that.'

But if work tired Archie out, it was play that got Ralph's heart racing. In 1957 this little nugget of a bloke won the B Grade section of the three-day Ensign Tour out of Benalla.

'I also came third in the A Grade and one of the other riders was Bruce Opperman, Hubert's younger brother. It was held on the long weekend in June and the local butcher just across the road here used to be my backup. He'd follow me and if I had a puncture, we'd fix it on the roadside and then get going again.'

They trained on a dirt track ringing the footy ground in Cobram and Ralph finally acquired an Australian built Hartley Max Rowley Special, the most lusted-after bike of its time.

After he gave racing away, Ralph used the ten speed, two front five rear bike as a commuter, 'Until I was in the pub here one day and someone stole it from out the front.' And that was the end of this riding days.

Just a pity there were no seats out front to chain it to!

And talking about bikes, it's about time to get on mine so I buy a round, say my thanks and tell the nameless one that I hope one day the obstacles'll be overcome and the impediments passed away and he too can crawl the pub trail.

And as I clear the town and the thought, 'Damn, never found out why Archie was punted from Young & Jacksons', hits me, a mangy dog, keeping low to the ground crosses the Murray Valley Highway maybe fifty metres ahead.

I slow and watch it disappear over the rail tracks to my left and realise I have an addition to my rules of the road: Unless a mongrel's wearing a beanie and has a beer in his hand, I'll steer clear.

Postcript: The Grand Central didn't survive COVID. In March 2021 I stop outside the Grand Central with its boarded-up windows, FOR SALE sign on the balcony and two street blackboards on which large 'Thanks for the

memories' script is surrounded by names of many of those mourning its demise.

Front and centre on one is 'Wormy', Ralph's son whom I ring to try to catch his dad.

'Just head over to Barooga, mate, Mum'll be dropping him off in half an hour.'

So I cross the river and there at the end of the bar, all three, Ralph, Archie and Mongrel, are in identical formation.

'It was like a death in the family,' says Ralph, 'came as a total shock.' And takes a sip from his seven.

Archie's a bit more animated. 'And it's not bloody fair when good people like Nikki who're having an honest crack have that happen to them.'

'Yep,' Mongrel mumbles, 'it was a loss to us and to the whole town.'

When I tell them that I pushed open the side door of the pub and came across Scott who was ripping up the floorboards out the back and who's planning on having the place reopened in a couple of months, they all reckon they'll be there on opening day if it happens.

I ask them why; this seems a good pub.

'Because that's our pub. Always has been. Always will be. Would take a very bad publican to drive us out. We're like barnacles.'

I ring Nikki who's moved down to Shepp.

'After the first lockdown we had a limit of fourteen and yet a large part of our community role was a meeting place for the older people of the town and some of them drink a single glass all afternoon. But I wasn't going to tell them they were taking up space. The council were …'

She pauses, looking for the right word.

'Mongrels?' I suggest.

'That'd be insulting Mongrel. They were arseholes, refused any rate reduction because they pointed to the other businesses – doctors and supermarkets – that weren't seeking any, ignoring that they were trading without restrictions. So we were paying them full freight. We were only seeking a reduction, not zero, but they refused. Meanwhile they were happy to see unregulated food vans serving right across the road from us.

We saw the writing on the wall and decided to shut the doors on Sunday August 2nd. Dan shut the state on Wednesday the 5th. We traded all day Sunday. It was emotional – even Mongrel teared up. Then we closed the doors and took a dozen or so locals out the back and sought their help in drinking the lines dry. And sure enough, they helped us to the end.'

"EUCHERED".

CHAPTER 23 – TOCUMWAL

EUCHRED ... A TOWN THAT CAME UP TRUMPS

One of my favourite pubs in the entire country is the Willawarrin Hotel, in the Macleay Valley, inland from Kempsey in New South Wales. It's the absolute embodiment of a village pub, fully committed to, and totally supported by, its local community. Gordon and Karen, who run it, are damn fine people who pretty much get along with everybody, and with each other, but there's one little issue that is a pebble in their boot.

In the front bar there's a probably fifty-year-old table with a top that started out as brown-and-white patterned laminex. It's not a thing of beauty. But its surface is no longer a uniform pattern but instead there's a rough wide whitish cross where the original laminate has been worn down. What's caused the erosion is a succession of thousands, tens of thousands, maybe hundreds of thousands of hands of cards being dealt on the table and being drawn back to each player's side.

Gordon and old-timers like Sherro reckon the game that's worn the table away is euchre: four handed, played in pairs, and Sherro's sure that 90 per cent of the 'damage' has been done by the same four blokes who played on the table most days for over thirty years.

If you're going to play cards in an Australian pub somehow it has to be euchre. Blokes who'd had a hard day out in the sun or underground, taking rubbish from customers or worse from overseers, blokes who'd not taken a trick all day would repair to the pub for a hand or two, knowing that sooner or later they'd be dealt a pair of red or black jacks or have a good enough hand to order up the dealer. And they'd come away knowing that if they'd won, it was down to skill but if they hadn't then they'd just been unlucky. Maybe tomorrow they'd reveal the six and five more often.

There always seemed to be a deck behind the bar and playing a few hands was an assumed freedom. And if it seemed to be a right that was natural, a lot of the credit has to be dealt to Tocumwal on the Murray. It was a pub here that trumped the opposition to cards in licensed premises and made it legal to play for bragging rights, if not for beers.

Euchre wasn't born here but damn it was quickly adopted. It originated in Germany – the jacks being called 'bowers' after the German 'bauer' meaning farmer – and spread to France then Devon and Cornwall in England before crossing the Atlantic to the American colonies where it was first mentioned in the 1820s. Euchre came to Australia about the same time and, like all card games was viewed as deviant by the gentry and an immoral waste of time by the religious classes. A bit like drinking.

In 1885 the Victorian government echoed others and passed a Licensing Act, which took the first legislative aim at playing cards in pubs. Section 86 read:

If any licensed victualler suffers or permits any person to play any unlawful game or sport in or upon his licensed premises or the appurtenances thereto ... he shall forfeit and pay for every such offence any sum not exceeding Twenty pounds.

You'd think it would've been helpful if the legislation had an attached schedule or list of just what constitute an 'unlawful game' but that would've made way too much sense. As over in the 'mother state' that was left to the discretion and the degree of wowsery of the various magistrates.

The very next year:

The licensee of the Zigzag Hotel was summoned by the licensing inspector for having allowed a game of euchre upon his licensed premises. There was no 'money or money's worth' on the game, but the inspector [Senior-sergeant Morrow] contended that cards was in itself an unlawful game, whether played for money or not. In support of this contention he quoted a ruling of the Full Court of Queen's Bench. [The Presiding Magistrate] dismissed the case, without, however, giving his reasons.

But later that same year:

Constable John Ritchie charged James Chalker with suffering gaming to be carried on in his licensed premises ... there was no secret made of the game; (it was) euchre ...

Despite there being no definition of an 'unlawful game' and despite there being no legal proscription of euchre:

[The Publican] was fined £5, including costs. His Worship also stated that card-playing in an hotel, being an unlawful game, was an offence whether the players played for stakes or pastime.

It looked like euchre was out. But then in August, still in the same year:

George Christian, a licensed victualler at Tungamah, [was charged with allowing] four persons to play a game of euchre in his hotel. There were no money stakes, but the two losers had to pay for drinks for themselves and the winner, the amount paid altogether being 2s. For this offence Christian was summoned by the police, and the Licensing Court fined him 60s and 30s costs.

Christian appealed to the Supreme Court who heard the case that December. 'His solicitor contended that the game of euchre ... was not an unlawful game within the meaning of section 86 of the *Licensing Act 1885*, but was a game of skill.'

Sir Bryan O'Loghlen was the barrister for the prosecution and while he conceded that 'There was no definition in the Licensing Act as to what was an unlawful game,' the government's position was that, 'Euchre was a gambling game, in which, although some skill was wanted, yet it was also a game of chance. If one player got all the best cards the others would have

no chance with him.'

He argued that the Act applied to every game of chance, to which one of the three judges responded, 'Even in cricket there is chance,' and so playing the gentlemen's game out the back of an hotel would be a breach.

The loquacious O'Loghlen quoted cases from Edward III and Henry VIII and in the end the Court split 2–1 in favour of the conviction. The dissenting Justice Hawkins 'said that every game of cards was not an unlawful game, but to make it unlawful it must be a game of chance. And it could not be suggested that euchre was purely a game of chance.'

But speaking for the other two, Justice Williams held that:

In this case the game was that of euchre. It was a game of chance, although no doubt partly also a game of skill. The competition under it was for drinks. It came, therefore, within the prohibition of section 5 of the Police Offences Act and was unlawful.

That's pretty much how it stayed until one quiet Monday night in 1908 when Senior-Sergeant MacHardy descended on the Terminus Hotel at Tocumwal and busted the publican, T. E. Campbell for playing euchre with three of his customers for drinks. In Goulburn Police Court the following January Campbell pleaded not guilty but his argument that it was just a friendly no-stakes game wasn't believed. He was convicted and fined £3 plus costs.

One of his customers, though wasn't going so easily.

Sydney Cottington was charged with playing a game of chance (euchre) on the same occasion. He pleaded not guilty, and was defended by Mr A.M. Betts. After hearing the evidence of Senior-Sergeant MacHardy, Mr Betts asked that the case be dismissed on two grounds that cards were not instruments of gaming in the meaning of section 4, sub-section 9, of the Police Offences Act.

It was, he said, an entirely new provision.

The second ground was that euchre was not a game of chance within the meaning of the Act, because skill came into it as much as chance.

(Presiding Magistrate) Mr Adrian said he recognised the seriousness of the question raised, and adjourned the Court for some time, (saying) he took it that if any skill was introduced into a game it was no longer a game of chance.

When the court was resumed, Magistrate Adrian ruled against Cottington's first argument but upheld the second, that euchre was not a game of chance. Euchre was now legal in all pubs.

Thanks to the doggedness of a card sharp at the Terminus Hotel in Tocumwal, groups of fellas in the public bars across the country and women in the ladies' lounges, customers, and hosts could play a few hands as they chewed the fat or peeled the spuds without fear they'd be arrested and charged or lose their licences.

Because of the sheer bloody-mindedness of a single player down on the Murray River, probably incensed at having his success at the game judicially considered mere chance, a group of fellas up at the Willawarrin were free to meet each day for years, to chat and yarn and laugh and while away endless afternoons in simple times of mateship.

This morning the front bar of the Terminus is pretty quiet. Not enough faces for a game of cards. Big Billy's in the corner demolishing a(nother) packet of chips while publican John is busy checking stock and thinking about his coming holiday in Bali. Both are wearing dark polo shirts with the emblem and logo of Brennan Racing Stables.

John's had the pub since 2012 and although card games are seldom played in the pub, John has a pretty decent racing and betting pedigree of his own. His grandfather was Albert Smith, acknowledged as Victoria's biggest bookmaker in the 1950s. When John's father became a bookie, Albert Smith presented him with the classic white bookie's bag that sits high on a shelf behind the bar, together with his odds board from the 1970s.

Also nestled up there is a collection of winning post shots, most of them featuring a gelding named Thetoppie taking out races like the Tocumwal Cup and the Tumut Cup.

'I didn't breed him but I bought him, owned him and trained him. Only horse ever to run in four Tumut Cups and get weighted in all four. Came first, second, third and fourth in four goes … should've won it twice. The year he came third the jockey came up to me after and said, I didn't do a great job, and I said I'm effing sure you didn't. Anyway we also won the Tocumwal Cup in 2013. Set a record time that still stands.

He's given the training away. The local track still holds its annual Easter meeting but he reckons it's too rough for morning workouts. But that sure doesn't mean he's lost any love for his horses and this bloke who has racing in his blood figures it's time to wear, if not his heart, then his racing colours on his sleeve.

'You're about a month too early,' he tells me in a variation of a song I hear too often. 'The main reason for heading to Bali is to get that shot of Thetoppie winning the Toc Cup tattooed on my forearm here. Just the horse in full stride, legs off the ground, not the post in the background.'

As I head out I wish him good luck with the tatt. On the way back to The Palms, I wonder what he'd do if he won the Melbourne Cup. I bet it would be memorable!

Raymond Jones was born in 1951 at Finley up the road a bit but went to primary school (which he saw to the end) and then high school (which he didn't) in Toc. His dad was a fettler on the railway, which was the lifeline of the town, and when he was fifteen, Ray:

'went to the sawmills. Jack Smithers owned it, Barry's father and I worked for them for years. Managed to keep all my fingers so I must've been okay. Then I got a job on the council doing relief work and then went back to the timber. I got onto doing firewood with Gus and Denis – cutting the wood into 18-inch and 2-foot lengths for Melbourne. There was a big demand for them 2-foot logs and it kept us busy.'

His older brother, who's 'no longer here' convinced Ray to have his first drink when he was almost legal age. It was full strength and he liked the taste and proved loyal, staying with the same drop 'for forty years until the doctor said I should drink less or switch to the light stuff.'

Ray saw the light and went with it. But in a town of four pubs, he's far more democratic in his venues, drinking 'at the whole bloody lot of them', although he reckons for a while now, the Tocumwal Hotel, known to everyone as The Palms, is his preferred crime scene.

Sharon, who runs the place with partner Don, is Ray's PA. ('Executive assistant' might be overstretching things a bit.)

In his almost seven decades on the planet, Ray's been out of the area, he reckons, maybe three times, all of them brief visits to Melbourne, and when he finally hung up his working boots and felt it time to apply for a pension, he had a problem. Never had a passport. Never had a licence. Never had a birth certificate.

So Sharon stepped up and established his identity and his right to benefits. She continues to do his paperwork, sort out his medical issues, his taxation liabilities and cut through the rest of the red tape that otherwise could bind this old bloke up.

'Ray's pretty much family,' she explains in a sweet sum-up. 'He's always a pleasure to have in the place and we've become his support network. It's the sort of thing country pubs do.'

Ray has no family, no kids or grandkids. When I ask if he ever married he laughs, tells me, 'almost, once,' but then deliberately detours the conversation back to his fettler father. Private space.

Sharon's partner Don has been working in the background but now most of it's done and he joins us. He's been to the Willawarrin pub and reckons he may've seen the euchre table. He and Sharon used to live up that way, at Macksville on the mid-north coast of New South Wales, and amongst his earliest pub memories are hitching a lift up to Taylors Arm in the back of the ute used for delivering the milk:

'... We had this bloke Chapman and he was a real big bloke and he'd get the two big full milk cans, one in each hand and just throw them up on the tray of the truck, ten gallons, never even wore boots, couldn't stand getting sawdust in his boots. Strongest bloke I ever met, I reckon. And then he'd sneak us into the pub and we'd have a couple of beers on the deck. No-one was going to argue with him.'

Don continues with stories from Taylors Arm, where the hotel is now officially known as The Pub with No Beer; tales of Gordon Parsons who co-wrote or wrote or adapted a poem (let's not get into that argument right now!), and ended up with the song, and how if he wasn't drinking and singing then he must've been asleep; how he always wore hobnail boots and hung out with a bloke with a terrible stutter and with blokes named Wally and Cecil.

They took out a ten-year lease on the The Palms in 2015 and have enjoyed their first foray into running a bush pub. The community's supported them and they've returned the joy. Sharon reckons she can count the dramas they've had on one hand which means they've totalled less than either five or four and a half, depending on which mitt you're using.

'I got it caught in the old freezer door. It used to be real stiff and it would take three goes and I couldn't do it this time even after three tries so I got real angry and on the fourth time I slammed the thing and my finger was in the way. It got crushed and I went to Albury and the doctor said it'd be disfigured for life. He wanted to put me on compo and I said bugger that I have to work in the morning. So I asked about the recovery period and he told me that it'd take about six months to recover if he left it on, and two weeks to heal if he cut it off.'

For Don it was a no-brainer. 'I told him to take it back to the first knuckle and they folded the extra skin back. Was back at work the next day.'

So is the total number of dramas five or four and a half?

Don smiles, 'Probably closer to just the two or three! We've had a few wild nights, had horses in the bar a coupla times but no-one's ever slept out in the donkey.'

Love that term: used to be that hot water was supplied to pubs from a boiler out in a back room that often doubled as the laundry behind the main building. The boiler was a large drum suspended over a log fire and the water'd be ladled into the copper for clothes washing or into buckets for filling the place's baths. The contraption was known as a 'donkey boiler' and 'donkey' slid to indicate the room that it was in.

With the fire and the hot water, this was the warmest room in the place and, like the 'dead house' back at Tintaldra, it was here that drunks and over-imbibers, too far gone to mount their horses, would be accommodated until they'd slept off last night's session and were ready for today's.

Sharon and Don have stuff to do, so we say our cyas and I head out past the palms.

Raymond Jones passed away in February 2021 from non-COVID causes. A wake was held up at the Terminus pub with maybe a couple of dozen people, but no family saw him off. Another character was gone from the river.

In the first lockdown, JB decided he needed to see his mum in Melbourne. When he left, his car was stuffed full with his gear and with his racing memorabilia – bookie's bag, winning post pics, the lot. He never returned. COVID had nobbled his business and no point throwing any more good money after bad, eh?

The landlord had an old mate Mark and his partner Andrea who'd sold the licence to JB about ten years earlier after running the pub for four years. Heard they were in town and asked if they'd help with the renos of the place.

When they'd moved on from this place a decade back, they'd sworn black and blue they wouldn't take on another pub but hey, help out a mate? Yeah okay. Until a new licensee is found.

So the Terminus, the beautiful building that it is, kicks on.

It ain't euchred just yet.

CHAPTER 24 – BARMAH

ONLY VICTORIAN PUB NORTH OF THE MURRAY

When James Maloney left Echuca in 1870 and brought his family to settle 80 kilometres upstream on the Murray at Barmah it was probably with a sense of shame and odium.

In the late 1860s James had been engaged or subcontracted by James McCullough to operate his crossing over the Campaspe at Echuca. McCullough wasn't certain he was receiving the agreed commission of fees and tolls and in 1869 he took Maloney to court in Echuca:

James Maloney was brought up on remand charged with having embezzled various sums of money amounting to 19s ... the property of James M'Culloch, of Echuca ... The evidence for the prosecution went to show that the above sums of money were paid ... by Edward Berryman to prisoner's wife, as tolls for crossing the Campaspe bridge, of which prosecutor was proprietor, and which sums had not been accounted for by the prisoner, who had been engaged to receive tolls for the proprietor.

Maloney utilised the time-proven I-never-done-it-but-if-I-did-it-wasn't-wrong-but-if-it-was-wrong-it's-not-my-fault defence:

The defence was that the prisoner had not been properly engaged as a hired servant, that he had not received the sums in question, and that on several occasions Mr M'Culloch had addressed orders to the prisoner's wife instead of to himself.

The sort of thing four-year-olds often try to use and seldom get away with.

But the magistrates were no experts in toddler training:

The Bench thought that the evidence was not sufficient to justify the committal of the prisoner, who was accordingly discharged.

McCullough was out of luck but Maloney was out of a job. The next week the *Riverine Herald* ran a public notice from Berryman advising that Maloney was no longer authorised to collect tolls on his behalf.

Maloney, may well've been chastened and shamed enough by the notoriety to decamp from the town, but he was obviously impressed by the business of owning river crossings.

This was a difficult time for punt operators. The rivalling colonies had begun levying tariffs and import duties and loading punt operators with legal responsibilities:

Mr. Henry Thorpe, who is owner of the Barmah punt, which is licensed by the Victorian Government, received notice from the New South Wales Customs Department to suspend the line of the punt till he had completed a bond of £200, and found two substantial sureties, that he would not allow dutiable goods to cross until an officer of the Customs had been communicated with, he is also to act as scavenger without pay.

The nearest Customs collector to Barmah is at Moama, a distance of twelve miles. It may be imagined, therefore, to what inconvenience any unfortunate might well be put who should happen to be detained at that inhospitable spot waiting the pleasure of Mr. Cordon.

Maloney hadn't borne such burdens on the intra-state crossing down on the Campaspe but the red tape didn't seem to daunt him. Not long after arriving in Barmah, he took over the licence to operate his new town's punt.

Then in June Maloney joined the gang of rouges, opportunists, astute businessmen, exploiters, altruists and visionaries – some whom we've met already – men like Sydney Grandison Watson back up at Tintaldra and John Foord at Wahgunyah/Corowa, and others who're still downstream like Henry Hopwood at Echuca and James Maiden at Moama. He applied for a beer licence for his house and became an affiliate member of the 'Pub 'n' Punters' Club.

James Maloney obviously reacted to an advert in the Riverland newspapers in May 1871 calling the attention of 'Men of small Capital in quest of a Safe Investment' to the availability to buy or let the Barmah Hotel 'replete with every convenience for carrying on a profitable trade.'

Two months later the Shire of Echuca posted its annual valuation notice for properties within its confines and amongst the listings was a 'hotel, Barmah' in the name of 'Maloney, James'.

Something may've happened with the licence because in 1874 he applied for a full licence for a house containing nine rooms and, 'to be known by the sign of the Bamah (sic) Hotel'.

He was now a fully-fledged member of the savvies, who controlled a crucial transport corridor and the adjacent accommodation for travellers and their stock. But the Barmah Punt, and the adjacent pub were unlike every other pub and punt along the entire stretch of the Murray, which forms the boundary between the Mother State and Australia Felix. One thing stood them apart from every other Murray River pub and Murray river punt.

Like the others the Barmah punt crossed the river north-south and the pub was adjacent the approach. But the difference was that the southern end of the punt was in New South Wales and the northern point was in Victoria. The Barmah Hotel was, and still is, the only Victorian pub where you can have a glass and then south for a dip in the Murray. It is the only Victorian pub on the north bank of the Murray.

The Maloney family weren't about to let their unique acquisitions fall into the hands of others. Once they secured the contract to the punt in 1870, the rights were never sold to any other private person, company or family. The Barmah punt stayed with the Maloneys for fifty-nine years until the New South Wales Department of Main Roads took it over in 1929.

It then operated as a government punt until it was closed down when the bridge was opened in 1966.

The Maloneys guarded their pub as they did their punt. In 1937 the Melbourne *Argus* recorded the transfer that saw the Barmah Hotel finally emancipated from the family:

> *The license of the Barmah Hotel at Barmah has been disposed of by Mr C M Maloney. Mr Maloney's grandfather settled in the district in 1868 and his son (the late ex Councillor W T Maloney was granted a licence for an hotel in 1882. Mr C M Maloney has, conducted the business since 1914.*

The dates on this stuff seem a bit elastic but they're all in the same ballpark as other sources.

New publican H. A. Day can't have had the same feel for the job as the members of the family who'd grown and nurtured the pub for over sixty-five years. His name hadn't been over the doors for two years when he sold the lease to Mabel Seeger.

She didn't make much of a fist of it either. Harry Day was soon back at the helm and in 1942 was mentioned, not too honourably, in dispatches:

> *It was announced by Sub-Inspector Kennedy at the annual sittings of the Licensing Court on Wednesday that it was intended to oppose the renewal of the licences of the hotel at Barmah ... Harry Alfred Day, licensee of the Barmah Hotel, Barmah (on the Murray) was warned by the Licensing Court that if caste natives were supplied with too much liquor either by glass or by bottle at his hotel, the Licensing Inspector might link him directly with this evil and then the licence would be in grave jeopardy. Day was strongly advised not to supply liquor in bottles to caste natives. The Court, however, granted the renewal of Day's licence for 12 months.*

When the old punt was retired in 1966 it was parked on the northern side of the river across from the pub, a tribute to the old days when things were slower, less hectic; a hands-on relic of a technology that'd reached its use-by. There it stayed, a magnet for those interested in the story of our waterways. But it was rotting and rusting away and Heritage Victoria and the local council allocated funds for its restoration.

Apparently not everyone was happy with the way the money was to be spent and in October 2017 some criminals ransacked and then set it alight. The firies got to it in time to prevent the old punt's total demise and when I rock up, the buzz of an angle grinder and the banging of a hammer drowns out the insects and corellas.

Adam's up from Echuca and is leading the project to get the remains back to a living piece of history. He and his helpers are working off two sets of plans – one from the Department of Main Roads when they switched it from a hand-crank car ferry to a motorised unit, and another set drawn up just before the fire.

This punt first saw service way down river at Euston in 1922 and was towed up here in 1929 when the DMR took over its running from the Maloneys, and Adam reckons it'll take a bit over two months to have it all shipshape.

'The firies stopped it burning pretty much perfectly,' explains Adam as he takes a quick break. 'All the boards and beams and rails that were burnt were going to be replaced anyway and so removing them's a bit easier.'

I quit disturbing his work and wander south to the old punt docking point which is now the town boat ramp beside the new bridge. Between the two there's a big old river gum – gotta be a couple of hundred years old – and across the flow, where the other old punt approach is now a simple dirt track heading into the water, more old gums stand beside younger brethren. Ah to talk with the thick trunks and ask them about their youth!

This place hit the national news in 1878 when the wires reported that:

A party of four troopers have been watching in the vicinity of the Barmah punt during the greater part of last week lest the Kelly party of desperadoes should attempt to cross into New South Wales at that point. The party consisted of two Echuca troopers, one from Moama, and one from Mathoura. They returned to their respective stations on Friday night, the expedition having been quite fruitless.

I wonder which trees they hid behind, to which ones they tied their horses.

Adam's too busy to join me across the road so I head north to the pub and go through the side entrance off, fittingly, Maloney Street, and into the back bar.

A couple of pairs of blank eyes follow me from the front bar as I make my way around the room, checking out the images on the walls: a great pic of the 1905 Redgummers footy team, a shot of the punt and a newer painting of it on the bank, almost a pile of bones, and a pile of seemingly re-enactment photos.

Then I stand at the bar. The drinkers across can see me but the bar staff has her back to me, in conversation with, I'm guessing, a local. I know that atmosphere. My mind turns back to those police of 1848 and their staking out of Ned Kelly. When they returned:

The troopers (gave) very disparaging accounts of the treatment they experienced at the hands of overseers of stations at which they called after being worn out by camp and sentinel duty.

Just down Maloney Street I find a cafe and a welcoming face, a decent brew and a steaming pie. Twenty minutes later I'm refreshed and recharged and smiling again at looking south in Victoria to the Murray River.

PURSUIT OF THE KELLYS. —A party of four troopers have been watching in the vicinity of the Barmah punt during the greater part of last week lest the Kelly party of desperadoes should attempt to cross into New South Wales at that point. The party consisted of two Echuca troopers, one from Moama, and one from Mathoura. They returned to their respective stations on Friday night, the expedition having been quite fruitless. The troopers give very disparaging accounts of the treatment they experienced at the hands of overseers of stations at which they called after being worn out by camp and sentinel duty. Trooper Nolan, of Echuca, leaves this morning by the first train for the Richmond depot, preparatory to being transferred to Benalla, to join in the search for the bushrangers.

CHAPTER 25 – PICNIC POINT

THE WATERS SPLIT

I swing west over the Barmah Bridge and then right on the Cobb Highway for a bit over 20 kilometres, say g'day to another big fish and the cop with the radar hiding behind the trees. Pat the cattle dog in the back of the ute, check out the bra fence and then turn back east for Picnic Point.

I've already sorted camping right beside the separation of the Murray into the Edward, the longest anabranch of our greatest river and one of the least well-know.

As I pitch the tent, a family of roos checks me out before surveying the fences around the Timbercutter cafe and bar's juicy lawn. The junction is an awkward one – the Edward forms a Devil's Elbow with the main stream, its waters forced to flow back on themselves at an acute angle.

The lights of the cafe illuminate the scene all night as the fish jump and the roos eventually knock down the protective fence and feast until dawn. From here the waters of the Edward flow almost directly north through the Murray Valley National Park. We'll meet them again at Deniliquin.

In the morning I head back to the Cobb Highway, swing south, and 40 kilometres later I'm at one of the real jewels of the Murray.

CHAPTER 26 – ECHUCA

'HAPPY AS ...'

It's just on ten in the morning and at the Star Hotel there's an expansive bloke running around like a blue arsed, carrying on half a dozen conversations at once, advising staff on special arrangements, taking calls on his mobile and shaking hands with some early starters. His name's Paul Jarman and he's got ten minutes to spare, 'if we're lucky'.

Paul was 'born into hospitality', probably, I'm guessing, about fifty-odd years ago. His father ran the pub down in Rochester but in his twenties Paul headed overseas, working in Paris and London before coming back to Echuca at the turn of the century to raise his kids.

A self-described 'river man', he's done the full length of the Murray in a tinny. It took him just over three years off and on and he managed a drink, he guesses, in '98 per cent of the pubs'. The trip convinced him of his connection to the river and the pubs convinced him of his desire to own one.

In 2009 along with another local couple, he and his wife bought the 'pretty run down' Star Hotel and in the decade since, including a major renovation of the front section facing the main street in 2013, the place has been fully made over. The work involved retaining the working-class character of the back section facing the river and the town's old port, a bar which had from the start been the haunt of wharfies and river boat crews – blokes who'd drink with dirty hands.

The Star first opened in 1867 and to deal with the heat it advertised that 'a large underground bar ... has been excavated'. This subterranean slop house was known from the start as 'The Shades'. It wasn't always a money-spinner. Just four years later its owner was declared insolvent with debts of £351/8/3 and assets of just £66/0/0. The press announcement of his bankruptcy gave the reason as 'Losses at the Star Hotel'.

It was taken over and the new publican made a better fist of it. To make the most of the quieter periods, he multitasked the accommodation rooms.

In 1877 the *Riverine Herald* ran an advert: 'Dr Butler, Military Surgeon and Master of Midwifery ... may be consulted at all hours at his private rooms at the Star Hotel, Wharf, Echuca.' I'll just leave the image of a bloke combining military surgery and midwifery and doing it in a pub with you and I'll move on!

But even this wasn't enough and in 1881 the empty Star Hotel was advertised for lease.

In 1897 the local option winds blew up the Murray to Echuca, where the overwhelmingly Protestant temperance zealots found some strange sympathisers – the publicans who were all struggling to make a quid in this town of three dozen pubs. A poll was conducted and as the *Bendigo Independent* observed in its coverage of the plebiscite:

> The lion and the lamb laid down together. The publican and the prohibitionist went peacefully to the poll together and cast in their respective ballots. Publican and prohibitionist alike voted for a reduction in the number of hotels.

Those opposing the forces, the bonifaces and the wowsers, had joined forces because by now the town had some forty pubs, equivalent to one hotel for every fourteen ratepayers. To keep them all going, the same paper raised its editorial glass to the:

> Echuca people ... [who] for many years [have] been in the habit of sorely but heroically punishing their stomachs throughout the day and over night and their unfortunate heads in the morning.

The good burghers voted to cut the pubs by about half but a seriously hardcore group of diehards (over 10 per cent – 47 out of 400) urged that all forty should remain.

Like, no doubt, the livers of the stalwart forty-seven, the Star Hotel didn't survive. It lost its licence and could no longer provide alcohol and liquor. Well, not legally at any rate. The wharfies weren't impressed. The place was right across from the docks and a thirsty worker is looking for drink not exercise.

The pub's cellar, so beautifully cool in the hot post knock-off arvos was pretty close to their ideal waterhole – close, discreet and cool. Only one thing was lacking to make the place perfect: the workers and the owners got down and dirty and built a tunnel under the street and then up to the fresh air. Now they had an escape route if the cops ever tried to raid the place, and the sly grog started flowing and 'The Shades' got truly shady. The underground hideaway bar has been fully restored not so much as a museum but as a tribute to the ingenuity born from thirst of those desperate to drink and those desperate to serve!

Paul has to go. The day's started and there's people queuing to speak with him. Anything else just call him, and he's off. I mooch around the place and decide it's five o'clock somewhere so time for a taste. Ah, decisions! The blackboard menu lists over three dozen. There're ales, porter, lagers, pilseners, stouts and ciders. There're craft beers from down the street and across the state. There's amber nectar from the Czech Republic, China, Ireland, Belgium and a cider from Sweden.

The seating is varied and comfortable. There's conspiratorial nooks and bar front stools and no matter your mood or your company, you're going to be comfortable. All off it's tastefully done and with an obvious sense of style and humour.

Out back, past the pizza oven is the far more old-school open area looking out to the wharf esplanade. This is history in good hands.

Once they had the Star sorted, Paul and his partners bought the Bridge Hotel at the down-river end of the Esplanade. They closed it for six months for a complete rejuvenation and in December 2016 opened what Paul describes as, 'a family slash traveller's historic hotel'.

This is the pub that Henry built. In the town that Henry built.

Henry Hopwood was one of a disparate group of opportunists and businessmen, scoundrels and altruists, rascals and exploiters who, in the middle to late 1800s adopted a novel business model. Paul describes Hopwood as an 'entrepreneurial rogue'. Find a spot where a popular stock route meets a major river and where the riverbanks facilitate crossing, build a pub on one side to feed and accommodate travellers and with yards for stock, and construct a punt to get the herds and the bullock drays across the water. Charge 'em when they go and charge 'em when they stop! These are the band of blokes I've dubbed, 'the Pub 'n' Punters'.

Ex-convict Henry's first gig in Echuca was at the boiling down works, and when this stinker went bust, he bought the property, consolidated the buildings and opened his New Road Inn. 'Echuca' allegedly means 'meeting of the waters' and it stands on the confluence of the Murray and the Campaspe. Henry first punted on a punt over the Campaspe but that was small beans to the traffic that was crossing the Murray a bit downstream at Maiden's Punt at Moama. So Henry built not just a punt, but a revolutionary pontoon bridge.

He ingratiated himself so successfully with the Victorian political establishment that in 1857 they passed, 'An Act for making and maintaining a Bridge over the Campaspe River at Echuca'. It allowed, 'Henry Hopwood … to take and demand for a limited period a moderate toll on all persons animals and vehicles passing over the said bridge.' For Hopwood it wasn't so much a government Act as a licence to print money. So he did – minting his own notes. Known as 'Hopwood's Shin Plasters', and redeemable at his river crossings, his store, his blacksmiths and at this hotel, Henry used them to pay his employees.

Through savage discounting, bullying and political greasing, Hopwood soon ground James Maiden into the grey dust and bought out his Murray punt. Now he owned both Murray crossings and the transit of the Campaspe.

In 1858 Hopwood commissioned the building of his all-brick Bridge Hotel at the southern side of his Murray crossing, at the downstream end to the wharf precinct. The following year the *Empire* newspaper waxed lyrical:

> *Hopwood's bridges were the foundation of Echuca's prosperity. His exceedingly fine hotel … is also worthy of commendation; it is a beautiful structure.*

Four years later a travelling evangelist, J. J. Westwood, dropped by to save some souls, spread his gospel and sing some hymns. By the time he left he'd composed a psalm to Henry Hopwood and his hotel: '(I) drove

over the pontoon bridge into Victoria. Paid 2/– toll and put up at the Bridge Hotel (Mr Hopwood's), the best kept hotel that I have seen out of Melbourne.'

This glorious place is still standing, and in the afternoon sun it's a seriously beautiful pub. As I try to get some external images, it's obvious the corellas share my enthusiasm for the place. Inside, just off from the front entrance, the only known photographic image of Henry Hopwood, publican and punter, stares down from behind an old-style gumball dispenser.

The Bridge Hotel's a perfect place for an end-of-day's-ride refreshing cold one either in the sun out front or in the spacious garden out the back. And if Henry's punt was a stepfather to this pub, today, thankfully the river punt's gone and the pub itself hasn't sold its soul to the scourge of punting of the other variety.

Unlike the Star which opened at eleven, the Bridge, with its cafe/bar and bistro has been open since eight and when I get there, it's in full swing and the kitchen whiffs underline my lack of breakfast and the proximity of lunchtime.

I grab a red and order the house speciality, a genuine Yoder smoked platter of spiced brisket, pulled pork, beef snags and wings with corn, wedges and a couple of sauces. This, people, was good! Eight hours to smoke, gone in thirty minutes!

Old Henry Hopwood may've been a top businessman but he was a way better dummy spitter. An advertisement in October 1858 announced that 'in conjunction with the Murray Pontoon Bridge and Punt, and the Echuca Bridge recently built' the pub was on the market 'by order of the Proprietor,

Mr Hopwood', who was, allegedly, 'retiring from Business.' Actually he was just having one of his toy-throwing tantrums.

The bluff wasn't called and Henry kept the place but in 1864, disenchanted by the loss of his ferry monopoly, and chastened by the realisation that he'd been greasing the wheels of the wrong colony, Hopwood leased the Bridge Hotel to a manager and pretty much only then retired from public life.

Hopwood died in 1869 and the pub, facing daily increasing competition from over three dozen other pubs, struggled on, but like the Star Hotel, the Bridge also eventually became victim of the wowser push.

In 1910 the Licenses Reduction Board met for almost a week in Echuca. Five pubs were notified they'd be closed immediately and then, '(o)f the existing 22 hotels in Echuca, 12 were called upon to show cause against forfeiture, viz.:—West End, Globe and Crossenvale, Bridge, Federal Club, Riverine, Tara's Hall, American, Shamrock, Victoria, Crown, Rodney, and Harp and Shamrock.'

The Bridge couldn't show sufficient and was closed.

It was reopened, renovated and then, under the leadership of Paul Jarman and his partners, restored and rejuvenated. Like a proud grandfather it seems to sit back in the glow and proudly survey its descendants and offspring. Few pubs along this river are absolute essentials. If this place'd been built ten years ago – if it didn't have its own century and a half of stories – it'd be a mandatory stop. But like its founder, this pub played its role in much of the extraordinary history of Echuca.

Sitting contentedly out front, happy as Larry, sipping on my fading red, feeling no pain, totally relaxed and watching the birds in Hopwood

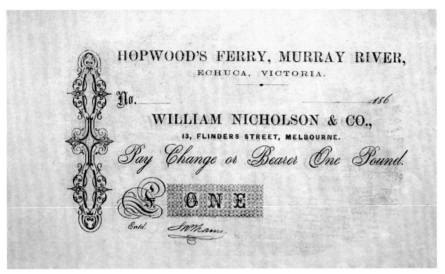

The Hicken and Foley Prize Fight.

(From our Intercolonial Exchanges.)

At twelve minutes to 7 o'clock, the men stepped into the ring, and after shaking hands in the ordinary manner, Hicken offered to bet Foley £100 more on the result, but the Sydney champion declined to take more than £10. The betting at this time among the spectators was 2 to 1 on Hicken, whose science was expected to defeat the acknowledged superior strength, enduring power, and youth of his opponent ; in fact, the anticipations generally expressed on all sides were that Hicken would blind his opponent in the first few rounds, but that if he did not, Foley must outlast the older man and win. The fight then commenced. Round 1: Hicken led, but was cleverly stopped. Foley then got heavily on to Hicken's nose, drawing first blood. Hicken missed a chance, but got on to the Sydney man's eye at the next attempt, following this with five sounding blows on Foley's ribs. There was then some very equal close fighting, and both went down. This was not only the first but the longest round, for it lasted twenty-two minutes. Round 2: Foley got on to Hicken's eye, and Hicken on to Foley's ribs. The Northerner tried the left, but found it no use. Both then sparred for an opening for some time, and Hicken at last again got on to Foley's ribs. They then closed, and both fell. Foley had by this time shown such good science and defence, and had damaged Hicken so much in the face, that £15 to £10 was offered on him at the close of the round, without takers. Round 3:

RECEPTION OF THE PUGILISTS.—The pugilistic trio—Foley, Mace, and Thompson—arrived early this morning from Melbourne, and were received on the wharf by a party of admirers. They were conveyed to Punch's Hotel, where champagne flowed freely and appropriate toasts were drunk. Reference was made to the manly actions of Mace and Thompson, who spared neither time nor money to secure a win for this colony, and to the satisfaction of all present, it was announced that a grand joint benefit would be given at the Victoria Theatre during the coming week. During to-day Punch's Hotel has been crowded; and, while Foley was complimented all round for his pluck and endurance, Mace was applauded for the fine British spirit he had displayed all through the affair; and Thompson, for liberality, received many thanks. It is not unlikely something will be done here for Hicken.—Evening News.

Gardens across the parking area, I try to envision the park filled with an angry mob about to ignite into what became known as the Echuca Bridge Riot of 1879.

In 1873 the push for a permanent bridge over the Murray really began to hit its straps and in response the governments of both New South Wales and Victoria fell back on the default blame game. First, they couldn't agree on the best site and then they couldn't agree on design and then they couldn't agree on payment. Finally, rather than disagree they simply decided to stop answering each other's letters.

The Government were again questioned respecting the construction of the Echuca bridge over the Murray — the present cost is stated to amount to £26,000. No reply has been received from Sydney to the last communication from here on this subject.

In 1874 Henry Parkes, Premier of New South Wales, visited Echuca and sidestepped questions about the construction of the crossing. The *Riverine Herald* wasn't hugely impressed:

(W)e must reluctantly pronounce much of [Premier Parkes's answers] to be unsatisfactory.

What was wanted was a definite and most distinct utterance as to the time at which, the bridge, should be commenced; and this was clearly evaded.

One of the factors in the mix was the private Denilquin to Moama railway that'd been approved by the New South Wales government and how, given the changes in gauge between the colonies, the trains were going to cross the river border.

Finally, in May 1875 the *Adelaide Observer* was able to report:

It appears that after many years of dispute the Governments of Victoria and New South Wales have agreed as to the kind of bridge to be erected over the Murray at Echuca. It is to be of iron, 35 feet wide, and capable of sustaining railway, and general traffic. The floor will be placed in pillars of brick, and steamers will be able to pass under it. The cost of the bridge and approaches will be defrayed by both Governments in equal proportions. The prospect of the bridge has quite enlivened the inhabitants of the district who urged Mr. Casey, when he was there soma few days ago, to settle a question of such importance to the trading community.

And then:

In November, 1875, the engineer-in-chief of railways in Melbourne, with the sanction of the government of New South Wales, let to Messrs. Walker and Halliday a contract for the erection of an iron bridge at a cost of £81,825.

Parkes had assured everybody who cared to listen, and that wasn't many, that the bridge'd be ready when the railway was completed. Of course it wasn't and it took four more years for the job to be done and for it to be finally opened: but only to the private trains on the private railway line across the publicly owned bridge.

The Echucaites who'd campaigned so long for this crossing and who'd paid for it, were denied access, forced to use (and pay for) the old punt, while the health and safety geniuses from both colonies renewed their bickering and turf wars.

But the locals weren't about to cop this for too long. On 3 March 1879, out front of the Bridge Hotel, where the car park and the beautiful parklands now stand, a rally was called:

An open-air indignation meeting was held this afternoon, in front of the Bridge hotel, in reference to the opening of the Murray Bridge. The Mayor who occupied the chair, read a letter from the Victorian Government and a telegram from the New South Wales Government, both of which were deemed unsatisfactory. A resolution was moved to open the gates by force, but the mayor declined it, and the proceedings ended somewhat abruptly. The crowd then, proceeded to both ends of the bridge, unlocked the gate at the Moama end, and forced the gate at the Echuca end, amidst tremendous shouts. Vehicles of all kinds then passed over, and traffic was carried on amid continued cheers The greatest indignation is expressed everywhere at the manner in which the people of Echuca and Moama have been trifled with, and the excitement has now culminated in a forcible opening of the bridge.

But for what would later be termed a 'riot' it was a damn orderly one:

A whole stream of horsemen cabs, buggies, spring carts, etc., now poured across the bridge amidst loud cheers from those assembled, and a sort of impromptu procession was formed, and for some time kept going to and fro.

When they were done they cleaned up, and, 'the gates were carefully pegged, so that they could not interfere with the railway traffic, and by six o'clock everything had resumed its wonted quietude,' and they adjourned to the Bridge Hotel to toast the liberation of 'their' bridge.

Busily taking notes in the crowd had been the foreman of the contractors who'd built the bridge and who'd had the sweetheart deal with the railway allowing it priority use of the crossing.

Mr. Vincent Lambert, the foreman of the bridge works in the employ of the contractors (Messrs. Walker and Halliday) was present all the time, but did not offer any resistance, contenting him self with taking the names of a few of the most prominent of those taking part in the proceedings.

The unimpressed Victorian government huffed and puffed:

Ministers were agreed that the forcible demonstration of Monday evening could not in any way be countenanced, and the Acting Chief Secretary was directed to communicate with the Government of New South Wales on this point, and also on the importance of obtaining the legal opening of the bridge without delay.

But the threats came to nothing and the locals stepped up to sort out any safety issues. The next day's dispatch read:

The new bridge over the Murray has been left open for general traffic all day, and it is generally believed that no endeavor will be made to prohibit the public from using it. Signalmen have been placed at each extremity of the bridge, and it is now recognised as a crossingplace, for officers of both the Victorian and New South Wales Custom service are stationed on the bridge. The gates are looked after by the signalmen. Trains crossing the bridge whistle continuously from where the ascent of the approach on the one side commences till they get nearly across, and see that the road is clear. This whistling is to warn people about to cross to wait till the train has gone over, as no horse could stand in such close proximity to an

approaching train as the animal would be forced to do if both were allowed on the bridge together. The pontoon bridge is entirely unused since the iron bridge was opened.

So the people of Echuca (and Moama) had indeed crossed that bridge when they came to it. Hopwood's fine old Bridge Hotel finally had a bridge which complemented it fittingly but the pub, the town and the river crossing were very soon the centre of a different and more infamous battle, and this time the gloves really were off!

The embers of the firestorm of the Bridge Riot of 1879 were still glowing when another massive stoush, the biggest brawl in Echuca's history, thrust the town back into the spotlight.

And if the Bridge Hotel played a big part as a backdrop to events leading to the storming of the river crossing, this time it was the Echuca Hotel, my digs for the night, that played its role in a confrontation which would gain headlines across the country and even overseas. This fight didn't just add to the history of the place; uniquely, it added to our country's vernacular.

On 12 March 1879 the *Geelong Advertiser*'s regular report from its Melbourne correspondent led with coverage of the aftermath of the bridge riot:

The Echuca Bridge business is not entirely at rest. As a portion of the forcible opening took place upon Victorian soil, an officer of the Law Department has proceeded to the district to ascertain if the proceedings were of a character sufficient to necessitate taking proceedings to punish the persons who committed a breach of the peace upon the occasion of the forcible opening of the bridge for traffic.

But the last paragraph of this same report was concerned elsewhere:

Now that the time for the pugilistic encounter between Foley, of Sydney, and Hicken, of Melbourne, draws near, the police are beginning to open their eyes.

To-day Foley and Hicken were brought before the City Police Court, and bound over to keep the peace for twelve months, in sureties of £500 each. They were also compelled to find sureties to the extent of £1000 for their good behavior. Messrs Mace and Thompson became guarantees for the latter. The fight was to have come off at the end of the present week,

but has been postponed until next week.

On the same day Adelaide's *Evening Journal* also covered the proposed but outlawed bare-knuckle boxing match between Larry Foley and Abe Hicken and followed it up with a note on another outlaw:

Foley and Hicken, the principals in the forthcoming prize fight, were to-day bound over to keep the peace for twelve months in £500 each ... The Kelly sympathisers were further remanded at the Beechworth Court to-day for another week.

Illegal, bare-knuckle boxing drew crowds and interest on a par with horse racing in the first seventy years of the 19th century and its champions were household names. There was none more famous than Sydney's Foley, and Hicken, his counterpart from Melbourne.

Larry Foley was still young when he declined an opportunity to join the priesthood and instead became a street thug in Sydney's Rocks, where his fists saw him rise to leadership of the 'Green' or Catholic Push. In March 1871 he settled a turf war with the rival Protestant gang by fighting their leader in an organised bare-knuckle bout. It went for seventy-one, yes, seventy-one rounds before the cops rocked up and stopped it, but Foley was the moral victor and the spoils were control of the Rocks.

He was adopted by 'The Fancy' and began fighting more legitimate bouts. In 1878 he was challenged by the Melbourne champion, Abe Hicken, to fight for what they'd call the Inter-colonial Championship, and Larry Foley's backers were only too happy to oblige. Purse was set at £500 each plus all you could win with the bookies. The fact that it was all illegal was a minor technicality and was considered a logistical challenge rather than a fatal impediment.

The first idea for a venue was a steamer, chartered and then sailed out from Melbourne into safe waters. *The Ballarat Star* was all over the plan:

A steamer having been chartered for a pleasure trip outside the Heads on Wednesday, it transpired that the object of the charterers was to bring off a prize fight between Hicken and Foley, (but) the authorities have managed to interpose ... and ... as a clearance could not be obtained, the steamer remained at the Sandridge Railway Pier ... The place selected is understood to be either King's Island, or another in the Straits, and the time early-to-morrow morning ...

The *Newcastle Morning Herald* seemed to know even more, and seemed also to be less approving:

It is understood that the Aldinga steamer goes either to King's Island or

Flinders Island, and the party expect to get back early on Friday

All the pugilist magsmen, scoundrels, and roughs of the country were on the wharf, with a fair sprinkling of respectable sporting men. Many of the crowd of magsmen bore very long faces, because they were unable to procure tickets to go with the party, and others because they had no money to bet on the fight.

It wasn't so much that the fight boat idea didn't get off the ground, more that it never left the wharf. The camps looked for other ways of escaping the court's jurisdiction and Echuca on the Murray, with New South Wales just across the border, held up its un-gloved hand.

The boxers, their trainers and hangers-on, assorted 'sportsmen' and general riffraff boarded, left the wharf and headed to Spencer Street Station, where about 700 of them crushed onto a train for Echuca.

All went well until Kyneton was reached. Hicken, in one compartment, was closely attended by his friends, and Foley and his adherents had another, compartment ...

At Kyneton the already bulging train took on an extra load of ballast – bookmakers who'd fielded at the town's races the previous day.

... they were on the platform in full force; but the ubiquitous [Police Sergeant] O'Meara was there taking stock, and it soon became evident that he intended to make one of the party. As he got into the train the hopes of the fight being brought to a successful issue became much slighter.

On arrival at the Echuca station, however, a considerable crowd was found, and amongst them a number of Melbourne roughs had assembled. Foley ... [and] ... his supporters, at once proceeded to Spearing's Palace Motel, which they made their head quarters. Hicken and his friends betook themselves to Giles' Echuca Hotel.

The New South Wales police were waiting across the newly liberated bridge with fresh warrants to arrest any principals who engaged in any prize fight and with the camps remaining in their respective digs, '(m)essengers ran at short intervals between the head quarters, and several councils of war were held.'

Echuca was abuzz! There's always been an allure of the shifty, an appeal of the larrikin and Echuca was, for now, the epicentre of the nod and the wink. 'The members of the sporting party are at present strolling about the town, or forming centres of little crowds of curious idlers.'

On the night of 19 March a large group headed upriver shadowed by the New South Wales police on the northern bank. Hicken and his backers had left the Echuca Hotel, and Foley's had also decamped but they'd melted into the darkness and weren't amongst those heading east.

Many persons were sent up the river under the belief that it was to take place near the junction of the Goulburn with the Murray and it is understood that the New South Wales police were got off in that direction on a false scent.

The fighters however, with backers, selected followers and bookies headed west and grouped ten miles down on the southern side of the river.

About one hundred persons assembled at 4 a.m. on the Victorian side, and they were taken over in leaky home made boats, 2/6d per head being demanded for ferrying them across.

Amongst the mob was the ever-vigilant Officer O'Meara who'd been joined by local cop, Sergeant Hayes. By twelve minutes to 7 am a flat site had been cleared, a ring fashioned, and the preliminaries done.

... the men stripped, and it was, at once seen that they were both in splendid condition, Foley is the heavier and more athletic looking man, and if the common belief that hair on the limbs and body indicates strength was true, he must be a very strong man.

Before the commencement bell had sounded, one of the crowd stood up.

Senior Constable O'Meara having satisfied himself sufficiently, called on all to desist, and warned them that they were about to engage in an unlawful act. The seconds, however, replied coolly that they were outside of Victoria, that he had no authority, and defied him to interfere with them. Of course it was no use for O'Meara to proceed further, and from this out he was a passive spectator of what occurred.

And what occurred wasn't pretty! The first round lasted for twenty-two minutes and, after sixteen rounds lasting almost an hour and a half, and with Hicken's 'eyes … closed up, his lips blistered and swelled, and his nose knocked out of all shape', the Victorian's corners threw in the sponge.

Larry Foley returned to Echuca with the title 'Champion of Australia'. He also returned with bundles of loot.

The stake itself was for £1000, £500 a-side. But both the men and their backers invested additional money, and this was but a secondary consideration, as the bets had totalled a considerable amount over that sum.

He'd been the underdog against the older and more experienced Hicken, but Larry Foley had backed himself for a fortune, a pile of cash that would see him buy his own pub, the White Horse in George Street in Sydney.

News of the savage bout, the out-manoeuvring of the police, and the money that'd changed hands made newspapers all around the country and the world.

A newspaper across the ditch concentrated not so much on the fight but on Larry Foley's fabulous winnings and its alleged headline has become a timeless catchphrase for which we can thank this town and its punting pub founder, Henry Hopwood. Next time you use it or indeed just feel it, think of Echuca and another debt we have to a publican. The headline simply read: 'Happy as Larry!'

Which brings me to Ned Kelly. There's a persuasive myth that Ned Kelly and at least one of his gang, Joe Byrne, attended the Foley–Hickey fight. It's been propagated and mindlessly repeated by writers who fashion themselves as 'historians' and 'sport historians' and 'boxing historians'.

Ian Jones, in his 'authoritative' *Ned Kelly (a Short Life)* claims, 'The tradition of Ned and Joe's (sic) presence is highly credible …see J. Alex Allan, *Men and Manners in Australia* … 1945 p 145. Allan was a keen student of Australian boxing and no admirer of the Kellys, but recorded the story.'

Well, er, no, not exactly. Allan simply, without explanation or quoting any contemporary sources repeated that, 'Among the ringside spectators (at the fight) *were said to have been* the bushrangers Ned Kelly and Joe Byrne.' (Emphasis added) This phrasing stands in stark contrast to many other assertions in the book that carry no such equivocations.

Jem Mace, Foley's backer, was anything but a shrinking violet and he sure didn't mind dropping names. In his memoirs, his notes and his autobiography, Mace includes mentions of meetings with the famous from the Marquis of Queensberry to Wyatt Earp.

After the Foley–Hicken fight Mace and Foley embarked on tours of country towns, fighting exhibition matches and talking of their lives. Unlike the illegal title bout, these shows were advertised well in advance. In *Fifty Years a Fighter* Mace indeed mentions meeting Ned Kelly:

We were showing 'for one night only' at a little bush town [and] had just concluded our last performance when a horseman cantered up – a big black-bearded chap – followed by three others, all armed to the teeth. I noticed an uneasy movement amongst the crowd … I stepped forward and civilly asked him his business. 'We want to see your show,' he replied …

Mace explains they've finished but the bloke on the horse explains they've ridden forty miles to see the show and eventually agrees to pay for his own encore.

We set to, and gave our regular show … and when it was all over the big-bearded man came and thanked me and shook hands with me. 'You're a celebrity Mr Mace … we ought to be each of us proud to have met the other.'

The four rode off and Mace asked, 'Who is he?'

'"Ned Kelly", answered one in the crowd in a half-whisper, fearfully.'

No mention of ever seeing him again. No mention of having seen him before. Certainly no mention of Kelly and any of his mates either, just Joe Byrne or all of 'em at the fight.

Jeremy Pooleman, Mace's great-great grandson inherited his ancestor's notes. These too carry a story of a meeting at a tent exhibition between Mace and Ned Kelly. Again it was at a pre-publicised event and, though it varies greatly in detail from Mace's autobiography, it doesn't involve stretching credibility that the continent's most wanted man just happened to be in the area of a fight the location and timing of which had not been publicised and not even finalised until just four hours prior to it coming off.

It's a fun story, a bit like Jack Riley back at Corryong being the model for the Man from Snowy River, but it's fiction.

CHAPTER 27 – TORRUMBARRY

DOES 'WEIR' COME FROM 'WEIRD'?

Fourteen kilometres west of Echuca I swing right onto Point Road and ride north to where the river does a wide sweep 180-degree turn from south-east to north-west. The banks at this narrow stretch aren't steep enough to stop access to the water.

It was here at Dead Horse Bend that the fighters and punters, the urgers and the smart money, paid their 2/6– fees and crossed the river for the Foley–Hicken fight. No monument marks the spot of this escapade and on the other bank, there's no sign of the history of the place.

Quarter of an hour later and I'm passing the Torrumbarry Hotel, a low-slung bunker of a pub on my right, but I keep going for another 5 kilometres or so and then follow the signs right to the Torrumbarry Weir.

I'm expecting a quiet 7 kilometres of sealed back road to the river but when I turn north just on 4 pm, I face an oncoming regular pulse of utes and 4WDs heading the other way, more than a few not too happy to share the narrow tar strip.

The original weir and lock here were built in 1924 and its associated gravity feed irrigation system, replacing the expensive pumps, was a cornerstone in establishing the Murray Goulburn Valley as Victoria's food bowl.

The structure did pretty nicely until 1992 when the walls began to leak and a replacement was finished in 1996. So the first stab lasted sixty-eight years, the more recent effort's last barely twenty. A 'major refurbishment' to the lock began in November 2017.

An October 2017 press release from the professionals at the Murray Darling Basin Authority included this gem: 'Executive Director, Andrew Reynolds said the closure of Lock 26 would only affect the lock operation and river traffic. "It is expected that the lock closure will cause minimal disruption to river traffic," Mr Reynolds said.'

So, er, the lock was going to be completely closed to all traffic but that traffic would only suffer 'minimal disruption'. About as clear as the riverbed after a swarm of carp have come through.

Andrew Reynolds from the MDBA promised that the work'd be finished and the 'minimal disruption' caused by a total closing of the lock to river traffic would be done by April 2018. Needless to say that didn't happen. Five months later in September 2018 our Andy was in celebration mood announcing the lock was reopening after the conclusion of the works (that'd taken twice the time he promised). 'It's been a great effort to get the lock back up and running so close to the winter deadline.'

So a year later when I front up, I'm kinda excited to see the lock and the weir in full-on operation mode, maybe even get some shots of a houseboat or paddle steamer going through the lock.

When I park Super Ten there's only one other vehicle, a whizz-bang camper with a pair of inquisitive Germans onboard in the car park, and the entire riverside is behind cyclone fencing and 'Construction Zone' signs.

See, sometimes it's worth waiting for a job to be done right, sometimes the inconvenience and aggravation is worth it, worth the wait for the job to be done right. With the MDBA in charge this was never going to be one of those times. In February 2019, just five months after the galah, sorry, gala reopening the lock was locked again. This time with no sunshine delivery date.

There's no-one else around so the three of us head through an open gate and onto an open grassed area about 50 metres from the weir that gives an unobstructed view of the river, the weir and the Lock 26. The only sounds are the waters churning over the weir gates and the birds roosting in the afternoon glow. Then all hell breaks loose!

'Get outta there! You've gotta get outta there!' A bloke in MDBA fluoros comes charging at the three of us from a cottage on the other side of the grass.

'This is a construction zone. You're in danger! You have to get out!'

'Mate, all the constructors have knocked off, and if this is a danger zone shouldn't you be wearing a hard hat?'

We're in open parkland with only old trees overhead and the nearest piece of construction machinery more that 100 metres away.

'Get out! Get out! Read the signs! You have to get out!'

I look at the Germans, the Germans look at me. We all laugh and shrug and retreat to the car park, grateful that his hero has risked his life to avert a possible catastrophe.

I'm now almost halfway down the Murray. At pretty much every stop the conversation's turned to water, its mismanagement, its theft and its misuse and every time the MDBA has come up. I've not yet heard a compliment about 'em.

I turn the bike back and head to the highway, then backtrack 5 kilometres and park up right adjacent to a sign proclaiming the space reserved and warning that others 'will be crushed'. Sounds threatening but at least it's not a construction zone!

There's just one other vehicle out front, a silver ute, driverless but with the engine running and the front windows open. There's a mutt inside looking like it'd much prefer to be out.

Inside behind the bar, Wayne's wondering what I'd like and the dog's owner's thinking he'll have another. When I suggest he bring his dog in Wayne interjects that dogs aren't allowed inside, 'only guide dogs and horses'.

It's too late for the dog owner to pretend he's blind, so he and I just exchange 'What the?' looks.

Gunbower, just up the road has been holding its race meeting annually since 1881 and now it's fixed for October each year. Last year, or it may've been the year before, or even before that, Wayne's not sure, the pub sponsored one of the races and a horse from Echuca took it out.

The connections had a few celebratories at the course and on the way back (with their sober designated driver) decided it'd be the gracious thing to drop in and thank the sponsor.

'I was just here behind the bar on my own this Saturday afternoon when the doors opened and these guys are standing there and there's a bloody horse sticking its head through the opening. They asked if there was any sign saying horses were barred and I told them there wasn't so they just brought the thing into the bar. Big chestnut. Real well behaved for a thoroughbred. Went over real big. No-one rode it and it didn't have a drink but, yeah, was memorable.'

Wayne's not able to confirm whether it was the last gelding to chest the bar, or if he is, he's not about to share that with a blow-in like me.

Torrumbarry township started in the early 1870s and in April 1874 a post office was created in Tolhurst's store. The *Riverine Herald* mentioned, 'the Torrumbarry Hotel' the next year and it wasn't until 1880 that George Tolhurst was able to announce the opening of his 'Post Office Hotel'.

In 1939 there was a 'back to Echuca' festival back upriver and the local paper called for recollections of the area from old-timers. One who responded was George Tolhurst's son, whose memory seemed to be pretty good in places:

> *I arrived in Echuca in 1873. My father ... selected land at Torrumbarry ... (and) opened a store ... and before long the post office was established there ... I think there were about 60 hotels in Echuca at the time. A few years later my father obtained a victualler's licence and started the Post Office Hotel at Torrumbarry. There were then five hotels within five miles for some years. They gradually closed excepting the Post Office Hotel, which still exists.*

The Torrumbarry Hotel actually outlasted the post office pub. The structure stood for years after the business had closed down. Eventually the shell, just south of the present pub near where the servo now is, was pulled down. One of the blokes who helped reduce it to rubble is the bloke who's now pulling me a beer.

Wayne was born in Torrumbarry, just how long ago he'll leave me to guess but he took over the pub in 2012. It's ticking over okay but like pretty much every pub in the bush it's for sale, both the lease and the freehold, and he's not too sure what he'll do when he offloads it.

The Torrumbarry's a single bar hotel, with barrels and tables and high stools. The pock-marked ceiling is covered in graffiti and a few notes, including a few lobsters all stuck with drawing pins. It's a thin haul right now but the ceiling is brimmed with the scars of previous donations. Each Good Friday the money's all taken down and donated to the Royal Children's in Melbourne. It's never less than a couple of grand.

It's what I call a 'raw' pub – a place where you're considered well-dressed if your thongs match; and sleeves, well sleeves are something that only really old blokes and visiting dignitaries (and racehorse owners no doubt) might wear.

There're five screens around the walls but they're all mute, only turned on when someone asks and, as it suddenly gets busy with half a dozen blow-ins rocking up, no-one's even slightly interested in them.

As Wayne is showing me an old sepia photo off the wall of a flock of 65,000 sheep on a station which the drought has now seen completely destocked, a bloke in a black wife basher singlet, who obviously eats way more regularly than he bothers to shave, and who's just come in with this mate whom we'll just know as Bintang Man, looks at the image and dryly observes, 'Lotta cutlets there.'

You know that moment when you realise that the session's about to go downhill on skates? This was that time that afternoon.

These two are up on one of their regular fishing jaunts from Melbourne, sleeping in their caravan and livin' their dream. They don't give a bugger about the eternal closure of the lock up the road – they fish just upstream from it – but they do have a laugh about it's never ending status: 'The drought'll break before the lock's fixed.'

I don't know how, but somehow the talk gets onto tattoos, specifically the one on Bintang Man's left shoulder.

'We were on the way to the Bathurst car races and it was the day before the Grand Final. We were playing the Swans and we hadn't won the flag since nineteen-bloody-fifty-four. So I made a bet with my missus, well not so much a bet as a promise. If we got up I'd get the mascot tattooed on my arm.'

The Western Bulldogs beat Sydney by 22 points and ten days later when Bintang got home from his Mount Panorama picnic, he headed to the tattoo shop.

'They sit you in the chair and say it's not going to hurt and that's a bloody lie but once they've started and you find out it's bullshit, it's too late, you're committed.'

The whole job took five hours. 'He did the outline of the bulldog first and once I saw that take shape I figured the pain was worth it. We kept having a break then going for another hour and then he coloured in the dog and finally did the writing. Took almost five hours all up but now it's a work of art.'

With his gold chains and matching earring he pauses for effect and smiles, 'And so am I.'

Disbelief, derision and laughter spread through the bar like herpes in a high school.

Bintang Man looks at his mate. 'At least it's better than that rubbish you've got!'

Black Singo's got this skanky mark on his arm that looks like a bad attempt at doing a cane toad dressed up as Ned Kelly. That he's done himself. I stand by for a tale of woe!

'Well my wife said she was going to get her ears pierced and I told her that if god had meant you to have holes in your ears, he would've put them there. And besides it's bloody painful but if she wanted to do that for me, I'd get a tattoo for her.

'So she did, and when she came back I'd had a bit to drink so anyway I went down to this tattoo parlour and said I want a tattoo and the bloke there said what sort of tattoo do you want and I said I don't give a rat's toss, I just need a tattoo. So he said just go through this book and find one you like and can I get you a drink and I said fine and so he went down the road to the bottle shop and brought back some beers.

'So I picked out a tattoo and it hurt like hell and I wanted it in yellow but the next day there was no colour in it so I went back to the bloke and he said, ah yeah, if you have too much alcohol in your blood the colour won't stick. I'll do it again for you. I told him no effing way and so I've got a great body with a rubbish tatt and he's got a decent tatt on a rubbish body.'

These two decide my next book will be hugely enhanced with a centrefold and I tell 'em that could work. 'Of us!'

I'm now a bit more dubious so they line up in what could well be described as a 'spooning formation', concerned that I'm shooting them from their best angle. I tell 'em their best angle's probably from out front of the pub as they drive away to the river, which they reckon is harsh.

Now I never thought I'd say this about a Harley rider, but a bit after the sound of a bike pulling up outside cuts out, in strides a bloke in faded fluoros with the sleeves buttoned down against the sun. He looks more like Ned Kelly than the skanky tattoo and he wonders, with a smirk and a glint, who owns the blue bit of crap that's parked in the Harley Only Zone

Bintang chimes in with his agreement that my bike's rubbish. 'Doesn't even have a stubby holder!'

Colin has a vineyard a bit up the road and the Harley's his pub ride. He has no idea who put up the parking sign but it ain't serious, and from below a fading photo of maybe a dozen bikes out front of the pub, he laughs that any bike out front is a welcome sight.

He has 15 acres under vine, specialising in shiraz, which is available across the bar here, but not by the glass. The local jury tell me it's a bloody good drop but again the talk soon turns to water.

Colin uses drip irrigation from Netafim in Israel, the market leader in targeted water-efficient delivery, but despite his water management with the absolute minimum wasted through evaporation or dispersion, he's worried about his future access to his allocation. I tell him about my MDBA adventures up at the weir and he just shakes his head in total belief.

Apparently it's getting to that time in the afternoon when fish jump onto bogan hooks so people start to make a move. I tell Colin I'll clear his space and Wayne promises to call me next time there's a horse in the bar.

They ask where I'm headed and I pull out an old newspaper clipping. It's dated September 1880 and it's top half is the first advertisement for Tolhurst's just opened Post Office Hotel, the one Wayne helped demolish. Below it is another pub advert. This promises 'Good Stabling ... and every accommodation for the travelling public.' It's for Tracey's Hotel and Store at Gunbower, of equine fame, just ten minutes up the road. I tell 'em all that I'm on a mission to drink at every place listed in this 1880 newspaper, in order, but Bintang Man reckons he finds that a bit hard to believe.

His mate nails it: 'It's probably a lie but it's the most believable lie that's been told in this place all afternoon!'

No comeback to that, so I hit the ignition and turn Super Ten around. Time again to head west into the sunset.

CHAPTER 28 – GUNBOWER

NICKNAMES, ALIASES, A KILLER DOG AND SHANKS PONY

As folks in big cities will know, a lot of the quality of a time at a pub depends on the personality of the door bitch. Doesn't much matter whether they're 120 kilos of scowling tattooed male menace or a slim female with a smile and personality, their style of guarding the entrance, demanding identification, and permitting entry can shape all that comes after.

A quick, 15-kilometre north-west squirt involving just one slight bend on the Murray Valley Highway and I'm slowing for Gunbower. Hanging by chains from the town sign is a well-constructed protest board. At the top it reads: 'No Water No Food No Farmers No Future' and someone's added a scrawled 'no fish'. Along the bottom is a plea: 'Vote for a politician that cares'.

No town, no community, no part of this country is spared from the issues of water, its mismanagement and its theft. Like so many nights already down here, I know that this stay's going to involve talk of water, talk of rotten administration and talk of inept government in far-off cities.

Then, under an increasingly cloudy sky which has robbed the afternoon of any semblance of heat, I park out front and walk to the other corner of the pub to replicate an old shot I have of this place.

Not yet time for the after-work crowd to be here, the car park's empty and as I head over to the front door I come face to face with, yep, the door bitch.

Meet Max, just under fifty (in human years), head security at the Gunbower Family Hotel. A golden retriever who's obviously an expert in character profiling, Max judges me with one eye and moves nothing from

his warm bed on the front step, totally confident in the knowledge that he's going to get a pat and a rub and a gentle scratch on his ears.

Just what the dwarf statue of a smirking, closed-eyed Italianate waiter standing to the left of the doors is doing there is anyone's guess but he adds a bit of quirk.

One gentle canine eye follows me as I push inside where I become the first customer of the afternoon, which is fine because it gives me time to scout around and to have an immediate yarn with Richard 'Call me, "Bones"' McGillivray, the owner.

See, everyone, no exceptions, (well except maybe Max), everyone here has a nickname. On the bar wall is the Punters Club Board, which is looking damn healthy with $6780 in the kick. There're twenty-two members of the club including Bones. Amongst the others there's Flippa and Goa, Talk a Lot (who's rated a 'Legend') and Ace. There's Billo and Slave (rated as 'New Legend'), Papoose and Break Even. And there's Tank, and Moon, Ron Jeremy (don't ask) and there's Frog (who's rated in the 'Elite' class).

I very soon realise that while Golden Max at the front door might be more laid-back than an Egyptian mummy, the real bite in this place comes from the boss, and if I was permitted just one adjective to describe him after two minutes of chat, it'd have to be 'passionate'. He's passionate about the pub and what a pub should be:

'I went to Birdsville, I'd never been there before. Terrible. Been completely bastardised. No natural characters left. Pubs are about folklore and their histories and the characters you have in the place. It's about a home for the locals and a respite for travellers. If people think they can put

150

some Crocodile Dundee type horns on the wall and a collection of hats and some bras on the ceiling and think they have a country pub they can fuck off!'

And he's passionate about the way big companies are screwing over the bush:

'I was in this marquee at the races one day and the boss of Fosters was there and I said you're lucky I'm not the boss of the AHA because I'd bar you and your kegs from every pub in Australia ... you are treating me and bush publicans like me like we're heathens. You've forgotten where you all came from and where your businesses came from. I told him that you people and your squeezing of country pubs is part of the ruination of the bush. He just said get out of the marquee!'

He's got a bit of prepping to do. There's a group of fifty coming in tonight wanting finger food and another group of ten wanting dinner and possibly some others and since he's the cook he's gotta get the makings ready. He makes sure I'm right for a drink and then leaves me to scout around the place.

The walls and various shelves are covered with pub and personal memorabilia, photos and trophies. It all has the feel of some bloke's man-shed and includes a framed set of what's effectively the family tree of the pub.

In April 1907 version one of the Gunbower Hotel burnt to the ground. The Melbourne *Argus* covered it:

> At Gunbower early this morning the hotel, store and shops of Mr. Matthew Treacy were completely destroyed by fire ... The flames ... spread with much rapidity owing to the strong wind [and] the occupants of the hotel adjoining had barely time to escape with a few articles of clothing. The row of buildings was completely destroyed, together with the stock of both store and hotel, and the contents of the post office and the Co-operative Butter Factory's office which were also located in the building.

It was rebuilt the following year and lasted until 1940 when the current Art Deco joint went up.

A bloke comes up, introduces himself and says I need to talk with him. He's wearing a blue crew-neck jumper with the kind of shoulder patch that shooters fancy and apparently he's the only local famous enough to have his portrait included on the mural on the side of the pub.

The painting covers the entire eastern side of the building – just maybe the best external pub mural on the river – and it features a cormorant and a seagull against a backdrop of water and river gums. I photographed it when I arrived and don't remember it featuring any bloke's mug. So I give him my 'Don't bullshit me' face and he invites me to step outside. Not like that! In a nice way!

I grab the camera and follow him out past Max, still on his mat, and around the corner where the bloke asks if I've checked out the Punters' Club board, which I tell him I have.

'Well I'm "Frog",' he croaks, 'and this is me!' He points to the amphibian on the bottom left of the painting. I tell him he looks like an afterthought but he claims he asked artist Jimmy Dvate when he was doing it if he'd include his namesake and it was in the design all along.

Back inside Kenny tells me he's been checking out the bike. He's got Ag bikes and he's just back to riding after a stint off 'em.

In 2018 he was out in a paddock, checking on a neighbour's cattle:

'I was concentrating on checking the cows and wasn't paying attention and I rode between these two posts. I didn't see the single top wire that was still there. The bike had no screen or anything of course and the wire was just that bit higher than the bars on the bike. So it hit me first in the chest and I had deep bruising all along my body but then the speed of the bike dragged the wire up to my throat and it was the weakest link so that's what got cut and pulled me off the motorbike and cut my throat'.

He shows me the ear-to-ear scar.

Kenny, of course, isn't Kenny. He's really Richard. Since the necking he's been known partly as Kenny. The second part is Knievel.

'I woke up laying on my back, my bike was on the ground about 30 metres away there was blood all over my T-shirt and it was flowing very fast and I knew I was bleeding from somewhere. So I took the T-shirt off and tied it around my neck like a tourniquet and went over to the bike but I couldn't get it to start.'

He knew he had to keep his heart rate down so calmly he walked into town 'slowly and almost very casually', concentrating on staying calm. His wife raced him to hospital but they immediately understood his injuries were too serious and he was transferred to Bendigo.

'They told me that I was half a millimetre from severing the artery which would've killed me on the spot in the paddock, so I was lucky. They did some plastic surgery on me and they took some tissues from the neck

and they glued it onto the artery to strengthen it up and now it seems to be all good. And a nurse at Bendigo told me that they get about a dozen cases each year almost the same, farmers riding through fences when they're paying attention to their cattle or something else and forgetting the wires are there. Usually they're their own fences that they've forgotten they'd put up.'

So did it teach him to give the bikes away?

'No, but it sure taught me to keep just one eye on the cattle and the other on the fences!'

The bar fills up and the noise level goes off the scale as the big groups rock up and families and singles front for a drink and for dinner. We're not far enough in the bush yet for the evening meal to be 'tea'. All seem to know each other and enquire earnestly about their health and their families.

Bones disappears to the kitchen where he's the head chef, dishing up what 'pub food' should be: in place of a list of deep-fried stuff that's arrived pre-cut and pre-battered, the menu tonight features slow-cooked pork belly, double-roasted duck, a range of 'McGillivray's Aged Steaks', Thai curry, arrancini, and penne with chorizo.

Bones taught himself to cook and if my perfect rib eye which I order in the middle of the mayhem but which arrives in ten minutes is any measure, he's both master teacher and gifted student. And that's probably because, like pretty much all of what this bloke does, it's not a job, it's a passion.

Later he explains:

'In the morning one of the first things I do is cut all the steaks for the night. I'll cut them all and then stack them in sequential order, then I place it on a tray. If I know that Colin's coming in for dinner and I'm pretty sure he'll be having the rib eye I'll keep the cut that he likes because Colin's a customer and his preferences are important to me. And I know that Colin's not going to order his meal because he anticipates being hungry in an hour. He orders food because he's hungry now! So he has to have his meal in twenty minutes or else he's already not going to like it. And I always get people's names so when we bring it to the table we can say, here you are Brian, enjoy.'

Eventually people wander away and as the noise winds down, Max turns up for a pat and a scratch. Meals done, Bones reappears, comes to the civilised side of the bar and Suzie gets him a staffie.

Next morning, as agreed we meet in the bar for a brew before we jump in Bones's battered beast for a tour of his cattle property down the road toward Kow Swamp. He's running Black Angus and speckled park cattle, and we're joined by Marcus who's about to keep an eye on them while Bones and Suzie take a few days break.

We spend an hour taking 600 kilogram hay bales out to the various fields. The cattle all know Bones but they're wary of a stranger with a camera. And then we head over to Gunbower Island where the old abattoir still stands but closed due to issues of offal removal. Its closure is a setback to plans to raise cattle across the road, slaughter them just across at the island, sell them through the town's butcher and serve them at the pub. With the place closed the footprint is far larger but it's the best the boss can do.

Then it's back to town and the last steps on the tour. As we cross the street to check out Richard's cousin's butcher shop, a white ute cruises up and Bones explodes, 'It's the fucking militia!'

Last night Bones'd reckoned it was a pity Brownie wasn't in – I would've liked Brownie; and the bloke driving the ute is the legend himself.

I'm keen to talk Gunbower militia but Bones tells Brownie what we've been up to and Brownie first wants to talk water. Water's more serious than crime.

He's got dairy cows a bit up the road, had the place for thirteen years but right now, for the first time, he's got no milk.

'First time since we've had the place we've had to dry out all the cows. Like the sign at the end of town says, no water, no food, no farmers.

'We got done over eleven years ago when the Victorian government unbundled the water from the land. We were given iron-clad assurances that we would not lose our sales water. My father has a copy of a letter from Thwaites saying absolutely that no more than 20 per cent of the sales water would be going to the environment and that we would always have access to the 80 per cent. Well that was a lie. Simple.

'We're all operating on one third of what we used to. We used to get an allocation plus 200 per cent that was called sales water. On one occasion in '67 this was knocked back to 100 per cent and then in the millennium drought it was cut for the first time. We haven't received sales water since except once when we got 5 per cent.

'We've been kneecapped. If the fuckers had told us we'd not get sales water any more we could've made plans and arrangements, changed our methods and practices, but they lied to us and told us we'd get this water and then just took it away.'

(Thwaites was John Thwaites, deputy premier and Minister for Environment, Water and for Victorian Communities. He was a keen skier and was investigated over allegations that he and his family had been given free accommodation, lift passes, food and drink at ski resorts over a period of five years without declaring it. The family stayed at government-owned apartments at the invitation of the management boards, which Thwaites had appointed.)

Brownie isn't on his Pat in being outraged at the handling of the water issue. Every person in this town, every person who lives along this river is dependent on its health either directly or at short arms' reach. And pretty much everyone's angry.

It's not a political issue, it's a survival issue. The disdain for all political parties and government instrumentalities, this outrage over riparian rorting, bureaucratic hopelessness, greed motivated by self and vested interests is deep and wide. And it's anything but new.

Way back in 1885 the *Bendigo Advertiser* reported a meeting at the Wee Wee Rup Hotel at Gunbower. A large meeting of ratepayers passed motion after motion expressing outrage and dissatisfaction at the state of water regulation. One resolution read:

That we, the ratepayers here assembled in public meeting, protest against the proposed [water rates as being] wholly extortionate, as we have hitherto received not the slightest benefit by any expenditure the Swan Hill Water Trust has gone to.

Another noted that:

We were included in the trust area without our consent and against our wishes, and we have no confidence whatever in the trust.

And another pushed that the locals would be fair if the government did its bit, begging:

(t)hat, while we again most respectfully and emphatically protest against the Swan Hill Waterworks Trust receiving any fresh loan, or other moneys, to spend on our behalf, we wish to place on record our willingness to be fairly rated, on the Government providing a constant supply of water for irrigation purposes, and to this end we earnestly request the Government

to take immediate steps to keep the Gunbower filled from the River Murray at times when the natural overflow does not operate.

We move onto other stuff and I ask Brownie about the fabled Gunbower Militia. His boiling eases to a simmer and he chuckles. He reckons it's been mentioned in State Parliament but I can't find it anywhere in Hansard. Sure sounds like if it hasn't been, then maybe it should.

'Vigilante mob' isn't a term Brownie's all that comfortable with. He prefers something more like 'neighbourhood watch on steroids', but whatever you call it, it's about the community looking after itself, about keeping the residents and their stuff safe and it's about guarding the natural resources of Gunbower.

He's had a bit of a sleepless night.

'I got a call from a mate who said there was a mob from out of town fishing up at the weir. He described 'em to me and I knew they'd be keeping anything they hooked. Fair dinkum, some of these bastards are like cormorants, they'll fucking eat anything. So I dropped fifty on them and headed up there but they'd gone. See, what they do is get there at dusk and fish all night, take anything they can no matter how small or how prohibited and then scarper before morning and get away with it.'

He's going to head back up tonight and then next week on the same night to try to get some rego numbers.

'We've gotta look after the river because it's our bloody life-blood!'

I ask him about militia membership and he full-on laughs.

'Aaah we're always looking for recruits. Let's say we're a bit under platoon strength but want to get to battalion strength! We're looking for 800 men. We don't need infantry or horses but if any of 'em still have their grandfather's 303s lying around, that'd be helpful'

They have more success in the town itself and Bones is a fully active member.

'We've got a lot of problems with theft out here, stealing fuel, drilling holes into the tractors to get through the baffles to get at the fuel, mostly theft but a bit of vandalism too.

'If I see a strange car I chase 'em now, get their number plates, drop fifty on 'em and then I follow 'em. I'll go and sit off behind the car with my lights on him and when he moves, I move and keep my lights on him and he'll get on his phone and ring his mate and then he has to pick him up and then I chase 'em out of town. Chased one car back to Torrumbarry one night. Got this old girl up to 180. Mate said to me, you'll get yourself shot, but I don't care, we don't want them here and we've gotta do that, we've gotta do that as a community, the cops are too busy doing the rest of their jobs.'

I flash back to Frog last night and wonder about that shooters' jumper he was wearing.

There's still a single officer cop shop in Gunbower. It's been there since the 19th century and it's hit the news itself a few times. The weirdest story was in 1885 when, er, well I'm gonna leave it to the Melbourne *Argus* to tell you:

An extraordinary charge has been laid by two bird catchers, named James Smith and John Sheppard, against Mounted constable Shanks, who is in charge of the Gunbower police station ... Smith and Sheppard state that on Thursday afternoon Shanks passed their camp, being engaged, they believed, in serving jury summonses. At about 7 in the evening he again visited their camp, and asked them to go to an hotel at Gunbower, about a mile away, and have a game of cards, but they both declined. Shanks then left. At about 1 o'clock on Friday morning one of the men was awoken by hearing some-one striking matches outside the tent in which they were sleeping. He awoke his companion with the exclamation, 'The tent's on fire.' Both rushed outside, and saw a man running away. Smith told Sheppard to put out the flames, and followed the fugitive, Sheppard afterwards joining in the pursuit. The fugitive ran into a ploughed paddock, and Smith picked up a clod and threw it at him. The man turned round, drew a revolver, and exclaimed, 'Stand where you are.' Smith and Sheppard then gave up the chase, went into Gunbower, and visited the police station, which they found, they allege, unattended, with the doors open, and the papers in disorder. The men then went to ... a magistrate, and stated that they recognised the man who ran from their tent as the same who had accosted them in the evening ... Today Detective sergeant Charles proceeded under instructions to Gunbower to make a thorough investigation into the matter. Shanks is a young constable, and has only been at Gunbower a few months.

Hmm! For a start, let's just take from this story the fact that the mounted constable, i.e. a copper on a horse, has the surname of Shanks, and that raises major issues: was his horse called Shanks's pony? If, when he was in the saddle he was on Shanks's pony, was he also, like everyone else in the country, on Shanks's pony when he was walking and not on Shanks's pony?

Call my editor if you have a solution!

Anyway, Brownie pulls out and as we head over to the butcher shop I ask Bones what 'dropping fifty' means. He looks at me like I've asked, 'What's a sheep?'

'Mate, that's when you call the cops or the fisheries. In the old days you'd have to use the public phone and it'd cost you fifty cents which you'd slide into the slot at the top of the machine so making a call is dropping fifty. Geez there's some gaps in your education eh?'

On the wall of the pub last night, I'd taken a shot of a stained old poster for the pub surrounded by adverts for local businesses. It was undated but John Reid, a bloke who should know, later tells me it's from the very early '50s, soon after the pub was built. The Gunbower Hotel, it advised, served breakfast from 8 to 8.45, lunch for an hour from 12.30 and dinner, including high tea on Sundays, from 6 to 7. 'Punctuality for meals will be appreciated by Management and staff', reads a footnote.

Forming the left border under the heading, 'Pleased to MEET you, MEAT to please you!' is a sub-header advising that 'the Choice Meat you eat in this Hotel is supplied by D. C. McGillivray'.

DC was the grandfather of Bones and today, beside the front door of this meat house is the current emblem of the shop. Under a portrait of a Hereford is what bikers call a 'kicker' and in smaller letters above the 'QUALITY BUTCHERS' is the name of the current custodians, 'G & G McGillivray'. So it's been in the same family for well over half a century.

Richard, who's known as 'Bones' or 'The Professor' but never as Richard introduces me to his cousin whose name's Robert, but who's known as Tom and never called Robert. I'm beginning to wonder if these are nicknames or aliases. Tom and Bones are cousins – their dads are brothers and DC was their dads' dad.

On the wall of the butcher's is a gallery of laminated photos and old newspaper clippings. Bones, who's really Richard, tells Robert who's really Tom that he's just after some bacon for our breakfasts and then we check out the decorations. There's a couple of shots that these two especially want me to check out. Both of 'em are butchers and both of 'em could move. The first one's their grandfather and the other's a bloke who adopted the town and their common bond isn't just the town of Gunbower, it's also the Stawell Gift professional foot race.

In the late forties and fifties David Crump (DC) McGillivray made his money running the pub. Before that he made his money by just running. Family lore is that at the Stawell Easter Carnival of 1929 he ran slowly in the heats, only just qualifying for the final of both the mile and the half mile. He then backed himself big time with the bookies.

His prize money of 65 sovereigns was dwarfed by his sting in the gambling ring and when he got back to Gunbower, after diverting to Bendigo where he again took out their mile and half mile races, he had enough to buy the family farm, which formed the base of the property that Bones now runs. This bloke was something special.

McGillivray was considered by some of the oldest and best critics on the ground as one of the finest mile and half-mile runners in recent years ... During the past twelve months he has developed into one of the finest distance runners in the Commonwealth. He did the hitherto unaccomplished feat of winning the half mile and mile at Stawell and following it up two days later at the Bendigo carnival. He shows the determination in his running and great judgement in tackling the leaders over the final lap.

From behind the counter Tom recites the achievements of his grandfather as Bones points me to the relevant clippings tracing DC's progression from runner to cattleman to butcher and publican. I'm in a local museum that serves meat on the side.

You'd reckon, wouldn't you, that when D. C. McGillivray opened his shop in a village the size of Gunbower, he would've been the only butcher in town who'd won the Stawell Gift? Well, no!

Bones points out another laminated double spread from the *Herald Sun* of 2005. The headline reads: 'Barney's sprint from Gallipoli to Stawell'. It's a two-page story about Archibald Cashmore who won Stawell nine years before McGillivray. And this being Gunbower, of course his name wasn't Barney, it was Archibald.

Anyway, the *Herald Sun*'s story details the unique feat of Cashmore in winning the Egyptian Expeditionary Force 100 yards championships during WWI after being evacuated from Gallipoli with septicaemia from a gunshot wound to the hand. After winning the race in the Egyptian sands, Cahsmore caught typhus and his parents were telegraphed to expect the worst, but he recovered and returned to the family home near Baccus Marsh. Nine months later he won the Gift and the 75 yards sprint on the same day. His prize money was £114 but he too took much more than that from stinging the bookies at Stawell. He was no doubt proud of his running but even happier with his punting.

His father had gone broke on a government 'closer settlement' block so Barney helped him sell up and they moved. In the mid '20s Barney arrived at Gunbower. A lack of any apprenticeship or other qualifications didn't much trouble him and he opened his butcher shop across from where the current one stands.

Then his bloke who'd fought at Gallipoli, been shot, run and won at Stawell and who didn't mind a beer, turned up the 'real Aussie' dial even further. In the back of the butchers he and his wife, Fanny, who of course never used that, preferring, 'Fatho', opened the town's SP bookie's shop.

They ran it for over twenty years before D. C. McGillivrays became the only joint in town.

Tom's chosen and rolled out bacon so Bones and I head back to the hotel where he rustles up breakfast as I pack the bike. Farmer Bones has been up and working for almost five hours and is about to start his day as a publican.

'These mornings are for the soul – out in the paddocks with the cattle who never complain, never demand and then catching up with the locals on the street, this is my oxygen. It's my therapy!'

Suzie's taken Max for a slow walk so I take my leave from this story-filled town and from this passionate publican and continue west thinking that it's pubs like this, people like this that so enrich this life of mine and all who share time with them.

CHAPTER 29 – BARHAM

DON'T TAKE YOUR GUNS TO TOWN, SON

In 1896 there had to've been at least two pubs in Barham. The Barham Progress Association held its meetings at the Federal Hotel run by a bloke named Dunne. But a wry, dry report of workers cashing their thirty-day pay slips mentions that, 'Their monthly pay took place at Naughton's Hotel, Barham township last week.'

And they didn't stray far to spend it:

After getting hold of the cash the boys speedily forgot all the good resolutions they started with, their promises to remit regularly to their hard up wives and families ... One or two exceptions there were who found relief for their pent-up feelings in a burst of religious mania, but the great majority found a more congenial safety valve in a prodigious spree. They held a lively time for the greater part of two days, but the first day completely satisfied mine host, Mr E. Naughton.

The only way he could get rid of 'em was roll the last remaining keg out onto Murray Street and lock the doors. That keg didn't last long and, 'After the beer was demolished they repaired to Dunne's Federal Hotel and polished off five cases of whisky and a few gallons of beer — all there was.'

Sometime between 1897 and the turn of the century, the Federal Hotel closed and in 1898 Naughton sold the only pub in town, the Barham Hotel, to Martin Donovan, who seemingly didn't take well to two things.

One of them was drunks. Years later when he was offloading the pub, the local rag lamented his leaving and noted that 'it is not too much to say

that if all the publicans were like Martin Donovan, there would be very few arrests for drunkenness.'

The other thing that Martin Donovan didn't much care for was competition. For almost seven years he enjoyed his monopoly in Barham but then in 1905, Sydney Norwood, the licensee of the White Lion Hotel over in Deniliquin, applied for a license for a second pub in town.

Donovan, of course fought the idea:

Martin Donovan said he was the licensee of the Barham Hotel. He had been the licensee for six years and nine months. During that time he never refused accommodation to anybody. Since the opening of the bridge in October his business had decreased. ... He knew that his accommodation business had decreased by half, scarcely two persons staying on an average nightly since Christmas ... two hotels ... would mean ruination to both.

The Barham Hotel had been near the punt but much further from the new bridge and Norwood considered his proposed location for the new hotel a positive. He was sufficiently savvy to understand the importance of 'location, location, location':

Sydney Herbert Norwood, licensee of the White Lion Hotel, Deniliquin, stated ... [that a] new bridge had been opened over the Murray river lately. It was in front of the land on which he proposed to erect premises ... He had made inquiries and formed an opinion that an extra hotel at Barham would be a convenience to the general public.

Despite objections from the police who just may've been in Donovan's pocket:

The bench, after retiring to consider their decision, announced that the application would be granted. The records showed that the present hotel was well conducted, and no complaints were made against the licensee, but it was considered by the court that the travelling public would be better served with two hotels.

Martin Donovan's worst fears had been realised and he faced certain 'ruination'.

Tenders were called for a 'Brick Hotel at Barham' for H. S. Norwood Esq.', but then nothing happened. No plans were submitted and no building was commenced. Maybe this'd been a bluff ploy. Maybe the Deniliquin raider was hoping to intimidate Donovan into selling out cheap. If so it didn't work. The Barham Hotel had fought hard and won, and for the next four years continued to enjoy its position in the town. Donovan and the pub were at the centre of much of the town's activities. They sponsored (and catered at) the major sporting days – athletics and football – and they were the meeting place for all local associations. Things were humming!

Then, in February 1909, the piper at the Licensing Court suddenly was reprising an old refrain. Another application was before the bench from another Deniliquin publican for a licence for a second hotel in Barham and the news wasn't good for Martin Donovan:

The local licensing bench, after two days' consideration, decided this morning to grant a petition in favor of licensing a second hotel at Barham, in view of the increased population and the growing importance of the town.

Maybe this time the town would get a second drinking hole. The site at the corner of Murray and Thule streets had remained untouched since 1905 but it was still earmarked for the new hostelry. It wasn't until the end of the next year that final plans were submitted to council and on Monday 21 November 1910, the *Riverine Herald* announced a curiously related local development: 'Barham was much astonished on Monday night when the news flew round that Martin Donovan and the Barham hotel were to shortly part company.'

Donovan, who'd lost his long battle to keep his monopoly on the New South Wales side of the river, had found someone from away with more optimism than understanding, plus a wallet containing £6000, and had decamped to higher financial ground before the tide of competition rose too high.

Just two days later the *Herald* gave confirmation of the reasons for Donovan quitting:

New Hotel, Barham —

As first laid out, this would have spoilt the bridge approach and the fence would have slightly encroached on the road at one end but as the result of interviews with the proprietor and architect it was agreed to put the building 14 feet back from both frontages. It will also be advisable to put the fence of the bridge approach back in line with the south side of Murray-street.

And a fortnight later they reassured the Barhamites that this time it was fair dinkum:

Operations at the new hotel at Barham have now been resumed. The bricklayers and laborers commenced work on Tuesday last, and the foreman of works, is making arrangements to push the building on without further delay.

Problem was, they still didn't have a licence, but the building went on. The following October, the ever-reliable *Riverine Herald* gave a good insight:

A roundabout method was adopted to overcome difficulties put in the way of obtaining a license by the licensing authorities, but the end sought justified the means, and it speaks well for the business acumen of those responsible for it that they succeeded in gaining their object.

Some time ago the Sandhurst hotel at North Deniliquin was sold, and it soon became known that the buyers – a Bendigo firm of brewers – proposed to close the premises and get the license transferred to Barham. An architect was commissioned, to draw up plans and specifications for the new hotel, a contract was let to Messrs. W. W. Moore and Sons, and in due course the building has been completed ...

[then] ... an application was made to the Licensing Bench on Thursday by John Moloney, to transfer the license of the Sandhurst Hotel at North Deniliquin to Barham.

Deniliquin would now have to struggle with just eighteen instead of nineteen hotels while Barham's number just doubled.

Meanwhile, down the street the Barham Hotel wasn't marking time. In March 1911 tenders were called for building additions to the pub. The battle was on.

The new pub, the Royal, must've hit the ground running. In January 1912 the Farmers' and Settlers' Association moved that its monthly meetings, held for years at the Barham Hotel, would now alternate between there and the Royal.

It didn't take long for the Royal Hotel to hit the national headlines. In July 1912, barely six months after opening, the pub had its first in-house killing:

A dramatic and sensational encounter between Constable Lacey and a man named John Patrick Casey, at Barham on Wednesday, resulted in Casey being shot dead. The latter had interfered while Lacey was arresting a man named John Kelly, assaulting the constable and threatening to 'do for him.' Lacey followed Casey into the Royal Hotel, and the latter rushed at the constable with a jug in one hand and a knife in the other.

I'm not sure if that's two deadly weapons or just one, but anyway, the report went on:

The constable told Casey to stand back or he would fire, and fired a shot into the wall to frighten him. This infuriated Casey, and he threw the jug at the constable, but missed. He was rushing at the latter with the knife when Lacey fired two shots in quick succession. Both took effect, one in the right shoulder and the other in the left, and Casey died within twenty minutes.

The two pubs sparred for the next ten years or so, keeping the peace during the First World War, staying pretty much out of the limelight, but then in 1923 an application for the transfer of the licence of the Barham Hotel returned the place to the spotlight of notoriety.

Florence Gent was the applicant for the receipt of the licence transfer but was refused because she was:

a married woman living apart from her husband, but who had not obtained a judicial separation or obtained a divorce or obtained a protection order under the deserted wives and children's act.

Now Flo was a woman of resolve. Getting a divorce was expensive, a judicial separation could be messy, and a protection order would involve time and effort in a world she didn't know. So that left ... ah, let's think of the options.

Let's just say that when she re-applied for the licence, Florence Gent:

stated she was a widow lately residing at Birchip, in the State of Victoria, where she was licensee of the Commercial hotel for seven or nine months ... [and she] ... had two daughters aged 15 and 13, respectively, and the elder was now of great assistance.

Just how Florence became so fortuitously widowed, is not on the record. Some people, I guess, are just lucky! But how could a court, any court, refuse the request of a hard-working suddenly single mother of two young daughters just trying to make a quid?

Florence took over the Barham Hotel in 1929 and if her £10 fine and conviction soon after for 'suffering offensive water to run to the street' was not much more than a trivial annoyance to her, the next year must surely have been memorable!

In October James Anlezark, who'd been a licensee of the Barham Hotel showed he conducted a pub better than he conducted electricity when he was struck by lightning and died.

But lightning-strike killing was pretty mundane compared to events outside the pub early the following year. The irrigated farms along both sides of the river attracted migrant workers, especially those from south and western Europe prepared to do the hard, hot, dirty work that young Anglo-Celts thought themselves above.

The young thugs amongst the Britishers and their native-born descendants didn't take too kindly to the migrants on their patch. If the reffos had work they were resented for taking jobs from 'Australians'. If they didn't have work, they were despised for bludging off 'Australians'. Hmmmmmm!

Alleged Member of "Slattery Gang" Shot in Barham Street

SPANIARD WEEPS WHEN FREED

(FROM "TRUTH'S" DENILIQUIN REPRESENTATIVE.)

"*OH, I am a gay caballero,*
  "*And an expert at shooting the dago. . . ."*
SO sang William Patrick Smith and a companion as they strolled
  through the night on the peaceful banks of the Murray.
"*OH, I am a gay caballero . . ."*
THEY passed Alfonso Munoz and another man, and they sang
  on—
". . . *Expert at shooting the dago.*"
A LITTLE later William Smith died with a bullet tearing his
  vitals, amid a rout of scurrying men in a street in Barham.
AND Alfonso Munoz stood his trial on a charge of murder.

VIVID tales were told in court,
  tales of peaceable foreigners
harassed by violent gangsters.
Munoz sat all day with bowed
head, and when the jury at length

The leading mob of street thugs in Barham in the 1930s was the Slattery gang and one evening a group of 'em came across a pair of Spanish farm workers on the banks of the Murray where the wharf now is. One of the Spaniards was named Alfonso Munoz. There'd already been ugliness and intimidation by the gang toward the workers, including a confrontation in the town's cafe the previous Saturday between Munoz and a Slattery thug named William Smith. As the groups passed, the gang headed for the Barham Hotel and the Spaniards on the way back to their camp, a couple of the gang members, including Smith burst into song:

> Oh I am a gay caballero,
> And expert in shooting the dago

Munoz hurried back to his accommodation at the tomato farm, picked up a small handgun he'd brought with him when he left Spain sixteen years previously and turned back for Barham.

The gang was hanging out on the corner of Murray and Noorong streets, in front of the Barham Hotel, hassling guests and other visitors. According to later testimony of one of the gang at the subsequent trial they were:

> in front of Gent's Hotel, we were listening to the election results [it was Election day] at about 10.30 p.m. ... Munoz came up and asked me to step aside, and I did so. Munoz then fired point blank at Smith, who fell to the gutter. Men scattered in every direction, most of them running into the hall of the hotel.

Heroes! Nothing like sticking up for you dying comrade!

The town's doctor was alerted:

> Dr. Hay, of Barham ... told how he was called to the scene of the shooting, and found Smith in the gutter before Gent's Hotel, in a desperate condition. An operation was performed in the hospital immediately but Smith died shortly after.

Munoz went home, changed into nice clothes and handed himself in to the police. He was charged with murder and remanded in custody.

The Sydney *Truth* newspaper, the standout muck-raking scandal rag of its time, went big on the trial. Its coverage, credited to its 'Deniliquin Correspondent' – really? Deniliquin had enough murders, adultery, fixed races and crooked politicians to justify a correspondent? – was totally in line with its editorial policy of always erring on the side of sensational.

Its triple-barrelled headline began screaming: 'Dramatic Story of Street Shooting told in Court'. Added the mandatory scandal in caps: 'SANG ABOUT "DAGOES" AND DIED'. Then backgrounded a bit: 'Alleged Member of "Slattery Gang" Shot in Barham Street'. But then not even a bloody spoiler alert and they gave away the ending again in caps: 'SPANIARD WEEPS WHEN FREED'.

The trial was in front of a single Supreme Court judge (maybe they couldn't find the makings for a jury of twelve honest men in Deniliquin) and he took no time in acquitting the shooter, although he resisted what must've been a temptation to rule costs against Slattery's mates. And, no, it's not recorded whether Munoz got back his pistol and the four unused bullets.

But a quick note on Florence Gent who was minding the bar when the gun went off. Quite apart from her wonderful skill of becoming a widow when it suited her licence application for the Barham Hotel, she seems to've been the most promiscuous publican you're ever going to find.

Not that sort of promiscuous! This was a woman who loved pubs but who, well, who seemed to lack some sort of long-term commitment!

She had the Barham Hotel for less than a year from late 1923. Then she was the boss of the Commercial over at Birchip as we've said, for 'seven or nine months' from March 1925 before retaking the Barham's licence in November that year. She stuck that out for a while – must've loved the town, or maybe she was just paying off a debt to a local in connection with the convenient death of her husband.

Then in March 1933 she became host of the Clifton Hill pub. She didn't stick with that long because by February 1936 she'd rid herself of this place, taken over the Farmers' Arms at Yarrawonga and moved on from that one as well. Two short months later she took over the licence for the Earl of Lincoln Hotel in Richmond, Melbourne, kept it eight months and then offloaded the place.

In June 1937 she was granted a licence for the Club Hotel in Albury and on 20 August that year had plans approved for extensions. Three days later she sold the licence to a bloke from Holbrook and picked up the papers for the Corio Hotel at Geelong. In June 1939 she applied to transfer that place to someone else.

That, folks, is a person with consummate skills at buy-fix-sell-at-profit and move on, or it's someone with a very short concentration span. I'd ask her husband to clarify her talents but I understand he's not around.

Despite their rivalries and mornings spent washing blood off the walls and outside footpaths, the two pubs of Barham have historically got along just fine.

In 1927 an application was made for a third pub in the town. Wasn't going to happen! Not on Flo's watch! Florence Gent called in the heavy artillery – the bosses from the pub's owners, Carleton & United Brewery were enlisted.

Flo didn't seem to have friends, only allies. The next one signed on for the battle was a bloke who'd never been in Florence's hotel, but had campaigned outside it. R. J. Atkins Esq. was the town's chief wowser and head of the Barham branch of the New South Wales Prohibition Alliance. It didn't much matter that his reasons for not wanting a third pub in Barham were so different to Mrs Gent's only that, for now, in this, he was on her side.

And of course the owner of the Royal Hotel, Mrs Mahony and her licensee, were part of the publican's platoon. In the end, Florence Gent did what she did best: made the problem disappear, and almost a century later, the town still embraces just a brace of pubs.

And, reckons Arnie who's worked off and on, part time and full time at the Royal since 'sometime in the eighties', and who's just pulled a cold one for me, the two pubs still work in pretty much harmony, providing their different takes on the tastes and needs of the town, never white-anting the other, just getting along three blocks apart on the main drag.

He's survived, he reckons probably a dozen publicans and licensees, some good, like Alan and Julie who run the place now, and some not so. 'And it's funny how the ordinary ones seem to follow the good ones. Hard to get two really good bosses in a row,' as he loads the glass washer and moves on to probably the best he ever worked under.

'A good publican is a person who relates to their customers, and Len who ran the place with his wife, Sandra, around 2002–03, he used to tell the drinkers here, "This isn't my pub, it's your pub, you're the people who make up what this pub is like, not me, you make the atmosphere and if you want something and it's in the realms of possibility I'll get it done."'

Len and Sandra owned a pub over in Wang and they'd started this Buffalo Brewery in the pub. They started winning awards and then they took over the Royal here at Barham.

'Len was a bloody good publican and a champion brewer and when he took over here he said, "You won't see any changes", but one day he said, "You know what I might start up a brewery again", and his wife was deadset against it. He wanted something to draw people to the town, not just to the pub, and it'd worked for him over at Wang.'

I'm guessing Len had no idea that he wasn't the first brewer to own the pub, that the original owners of the place, almost a hundred years before him, were also into hops and yeast up to their elbows.

'So anyway he told his wife, "Nooooo I'll be okay". And he went out and got the gear and it was big time, vats and all out the back of the pub here. He'd started out making ginger beer, and one day we sat around the bar and we all thought, what are we going to call it, and there was four of us and we kicked around a lot of names and we each ended up with a favourite but no-one liked the other blokes'. So we came up with 'Codswallop' after the fish in the river and we made up flyers that we sent all over the place even up to Queensland. And we got up the artwork of the old cod that used to have a pair of horns that could break through the reeds and through nets, massive things, and it was just amazing how many people would come in here from the city and be amazed by the stories about these old fish that are so bloody hard to catch because they can bite through any line or net. Had to harpoon them.'

I chuck in my two bob's worth. 'Sound more dangerous than drop-bears.'

Arnie doesn't miss a beat. 'Mate that's for sure. They're the reason there's no bunyips around here. The horned cod would wait for them at waterholes and swallow the buggers whole.' (I'd mention the bit about their horns being poison spikes like a platypus's but I don't want to add to any alarm.)

But then around 2006 Len and Sandra sold the pub and took up dairying. For the new owners, brewing was too hard, the rewards too small and the benefit to the town not of such concern.

'It was going like you wouldn't believe.'

Like I wouldn't believe? Really?

This bloke's just told me about horned cod that eat bunyips whole and he's saying I wouldn't believe that freshly brewed beer and alcoholic ginger beer might've been selling like, well like good freshly brewed beer in a bar full of thirsty holidaying fishermen. Anyway ...

'We had hotels in the big cities wanting to buy truckloads of the stuff but that wasn't the idea of it. The idea was to get people to come to Barham for it and we had it on tap here – a whole set of taps at the end of the bar with the beer and the ginger beer – as well as bottles. We still get people coming in here asking for it. But the new owners just shut it all down. Sold off the equipment, or they might've just given it away. And that was the end of Codswallop.'

Then Arnie reminds me, 'See, I told you about how hard it is to get two good publicans in a row!'

Julie the boss, well half boss, has clocked on and wants to know if I want another and I want to know what the three little dunnies are doing on the shelf behind the bar.

There's Boxhead's Outhouse, Arnie's Long Drop and Julie's Powder Room. Stuck to their shelf is a sign that mentions the Koondrook Tennis and Swimming Clubs.

'The people from over there came to us and asked for help with some funds. They maintain the park and the recreation areas and especially in the winter when there's no tourists, the money gets tight so we run raffles every Sunday. Winner gets to pick which dunny they want open and they have either a mystery prize, a dinner voucher or cash which jackpots fifty bucks each week.'

The pub sends about $400 a month across the river and that's enough to cover all utilities plus some change. The river here's more like a stream running through the middle of a single town. Julie, 'he's not my partner he's my business partner' Alan, and all the staff live on the south side and so have had the pleasure of crossing the bridge works every work day for the last nine years.

I head out to get some external shots, hoping to get an angle showing the pub and the bridge where the renovations have outlasted four publicans. A table of five blokes threatens extreme violence if I don't take their photo. I can't be certain none of them is carrying a one-hundred-year-old pistol and four rounds of ammo they've found lying around so I take a couple of frames.

Then Arnie lifts a lid on the footpath and tells me he'll follow me down the old steps, 'be very careful the last one's missing' to the cellar.

I don't know how original this dungeon is but I'm guessing very close. The keg slide is a pair of double river hardwood rails, each driven into the mudbrick walls with a pair of bolts. The stairs in the runway between the rails have just been hacked and kicked into the stone. How many thousand kegs have been rolled down this slipway? How many glasses been filled and emptied? How many stories told, arguments had, fights started?

Old disused cellars, more than other parts of pubs, maybe because their entrances are so seldom opened, seem to retain their ghosts and their stories, hold them tighter, tantalising the intruder with secrets that you know are so close but which will never be revealed. Oh for friends who can keep secrets like an old pub cellar.

Back in the bar, Joey, who's got a touch of the Glenn McGraths about him, is working and I take his suggestion of a hot stone steak and chips, oh and another beer.

Joey shares his working time between the pub and the sawmill across the river that I really should check out 'If you have time in the morning'. I tell him he's one of the few sawmillers I've met with ten full fingers and he shows me his flattened one that was crushed under a roller maybe twenty years back but which stayed complete. 'But you're right. There's a few blokes over there with less than ten nails that ever need clipping.'

The steak's spot on and I take the finished plate and my empty glass back to the bar – that'll do me for the night – and head to the gents'. And I don't mean Florence's! Anyway when I get back there's a fresh beer waiting for me.

'Joey, whatcha done? I didn't ask for another beer did I, mate?'

'Yeah you did. You left your glass standing on the bar and that means you want another one.'

'I was just being tidy. I left my plate there too but you didn't give me another steak!'

Joey chucks me one of those, you're an idiot looks and explains the local beer glass on bar etiquette.

'Around here if you put your empty glass on the bar that means every time you want another one. If you don't want a refill you havta lay it down on the bar. And if you want a fight, just put it on the bar upside down.'

Nods and yep-murmurs all round.

'Unless you're a woman.'

Go on.

'If a woman upturns her glass on the bar it means she wants to take you with her when she leaves. And she wants that to be soon.' Pause. 'You don't see that all that much.'

More nods and yep-murmurs.

I drain it and lay it down, 'Getting the hang eh?' And head outside and down the street.

No gang of thugs, no justifiably irate fruit pickers on the street. And no stray keg being rolled along. The Barham Hotel, lit by the orange and blue street lights radiates solid respectability as I get some shots of where the murder must've gone down. Out here there is no legacy of Alfonso Munoz and his killing of a local.

Half a dozen men are in the front bar. Each looks sideways at the visitor as I invade their space. Not a single one has a neck that can swivel and acknowledge a new face.

A wooden door, still with 'Ladies Lounge' in gold print leads past the back bar to a lobby where redgum stairs lead to the accommodation. At the top, on the sideboard, there's a laminated A4 sheet welcoming guests who've negotiated the stone-cold reception, paid their board, unloaded their bike or car and hauled their stuff up these steps so they can drop it in their room before returning for an end-of-day cleanser or two.

It requests that 'guests' (read 'out-of-towners') like me park across the road so 'patrons' (read 'locals') don't have so far to walk. Now that's a long time to hold a grudge against foreigners!

Tonight there'll be no relaxing back into the succour of any spree, prodigious or otherwise. I head back up to the Royal's drive through for a bottle of vino (they have no Spanish) which I take back to sample on the superb old balcony of the Barham Hotel, across from one of the best old Bills troughs you're going to see, as the rain begins to fall and the broken blinds flap in the wind.

And I raise my glass to the fortunate timing of Flo's widowhood and I toast the wisdom of a judge who exonerated a bloke who'd shot a coward right below the rickety table that's right now a haven for my feet.

MAAAAATE, I'M STUFFED!

It means two things when a publican like Julie at the Royal 'Bridge' at Barham 'highly recommends' a nearby hotel: firstly they're generous of spirit and secondly their neighbour's definitely worth a visit.

So after a sloth morning then a brew and pastry at the Riverside Cafe, where Fiona who was working in the pub last night is again hard at it, I flick Super Ten over the bridge, keep left at every junction and soon I'm passing an exquisite old timber hall and pulling up beside a restored old railway station complete with carriage in the siding waiting for a locomotive that's never going to come.

The pub – maybe 100 metres down on the other side of the imaginatively named Main Street (probably decided by a committee after a process of community consultation and several long meetings) – isn't showing any signs of life just yet.

In late 1878 to appease the thirsts and needs of members of the growing army of red gum timber-cutters setting up operations along the river west from Gunbower, the Shire of Swan Hill proclaimed new Licensing Districts including the township of Koondrook.

Less than eighteen months later John Singleton – no, not *that* John Singleton, an earlier version – advertised that he'd opened his Royal Hotel boasting 'first class hotel (with) every accommodation for fishing and shooting parties' at Koondrook in 1880.

The hotel was, subsequent advertisements proclaimed, near the town's new wharf and while 'family parties (would) find all the comforts of home ... gentlemen desirous of sport (would) find plenty of amusement with their gun and line without much trouble.'

I think that translates roughly as 'don't matter if you look in the air, the water or on the ground, there's lots of stuff to kill around the place'.

And there must've been a decent bit of 'without much trouble' killing going on. Two years after Singo had opened the pub, a bloke named Wilson was advertising that he was based at the Koondrook Hotel and was a cash purchaser of 'hides and skins'.

From the start in the 1880s business here throbbed to the beat of axes and hummed to the low squeak of long saws felling trees and the staccato ejaculations of rifles and shotties felling wildlife. If you weren't human, it wasn't important if you breathed or photosynthesised, Koondrook wasn't a place to be making long range plans.

In 1888 tenders were called for the building of brick extensions to the Royal and by 1891 the town even had its own brewery to keep the pubs well stocked. A punt across to Barham had been built in 1884 and a decent old trade corridor had been established. To link up with the trade route to the markets of Melbourne in 1889 a private consortium funded the building of a private tramway to meet up with the government railway head at Kerang and it's here that I've pulled up to have a kick around and wait until opening time. The private tramway down to Kerang worked just fine for over sixty years but it was taken over the by the government in 1952 and folded before the end of the next decade. Nationalisation can be like that.

Just east of where I am, the Gunbower Creek, another anabranch of the Murray which broke from the main channel way back upriver above the Torrumbarry Weir, rejoins the main flow of the river.

Just downstream from this confluence are the Arbuthnot Sawmills that Joey told me last night in the pub at Barham that I should check out. Ron the manager's got time to show me around so he fluoros me up and we head over to the mills that were started in 1889 or 1890 by Alexander Arbuthnot, who had the street to the mill named in his honour, and twenty-seven descendants of whom are still shareholders of the business.

At one end, massive redgum logs, each one tagged with a Forestry Department selection number are piled for cutting either into standard planks or custom lengths for feature work. At the other there're twin towers of sawdust and chips. In the midst of it all Joey's flat out at his day job doing the initial slices on the red trunks of wood so dense it won't float on water. By the time I've stopped annoying Ron and checked out the stunningly designed pontoon a car's pulled up at the pub so I wander down.

It's a classic low-slung single-storey job with corrugated iron roof and a verandah giving shelter along its entire length. But up on the facade, right on the corner, there's a grandiose representation of the Royal coat of arms of the United Kingdom. In flyspeck Koondrook.

On the left a lion's wearing a crown and on the right a horse is pretending to be a unicorn. They're both pawing a central globe which is surrounded by the standard notched garter with the French inscription: *Honi soit qui mal y pense* which roughly translates as 'May he be shamed who thinks evil'. At the bottom there's the Latin *Dieu et mon droit*, motto of the Monarch of the UK (apart from Scotland who excused themselves from this craziness, because when your national animal is a unicorn, you don't need more stupid) and it means, 'God and my right'.

Some Royal hotels, it seems, take their royalty more seriously than others!

To amplify the incongruity of the display, the coat of arms is flanked by the established name of the pub, 'Mates' (to the left) and 'Royal Hotel' to the right. 'Mate' and 'Your Highness' sharing a wall. Damn sure they've never shared a spoken vocative sentence!

But if unicorns and Latin and mates on the outside wall of a pub beside the Murray seem as inappropriate as a dash of milk in a schooner, I pretty soon realise that it's time to seriously dial up the weird filter.

Turns out I was wrong about the new car signalling the arrival of the boss – Slippery's been inside, he reckons, for hours – I should've just knocked on the window like the locals who need a drink after legal opening at ten but before official start at eleven, do.

It's hard to have a beer at a pub along the river without coming face to face with a massive cod staring straight at you, mouth agape, seemingly in disbelief it fell for the old worm on the hook trick. Sometimes it'll be behind the bar, sometimes over your head when you settle at a table by the wall, the date of the catch and the weight and the name of lucky bugger who held on and landed the thing all listed in plaques of varying sophistication. Some pubs also have snakes or spiders in bottles – I've even seen a scorpion or two and of course the croc skins and long horns once you move north. Some places have just the one, others maybe up to a dozen, but there's no pub that comes closer to being a shrine of taxidermy than the Koondrook pub.

'This,' says Slippery Shane, 'is Hamish,' pointing to a massive caribou stag whose snout oversees the entrance to the bar. 'He's the father of the collection, the first one we, well the first one my wife, picked up.'

I nod but Hamish doesn't nod back. Aloof and off the hoof!

But if I want to know his full story and about the other foxes and raccoons and deer and stags and things I'll have to ask Suzy and she'll be here in a bit. So instead, I tackle Slippery about the Mates bit – isn't it a bit jingoistic and heavy hammer to give it a moniker like that?

I'm off the mark for the second time this morning – it's not that sort of mate! It's not exactly clear when, but sometime after 1918 (probably in 1920 when it was advertised for sale) the Mates family first took over the running of the Koondrook Royal. In 1922 Lila Vickers Mates transferred her licence to Roy Albert Mates who kept the place for three years before offloading it. Meanwhile Lila Mates had taken over the Cherry Hill Hotel in Richmond, Melbourne.

It was during this period that the place became known as 'Mates Hotel'. Somehow Roy Mates took the place back over but in 1939 transferred it again, this time to a bloke named 'Donaldson' who then transferred it in 1942 to Kathleen Monica Mates 'of Koondrook, married woman'.

The Mates kept the pub longer this time. In 1951 a syndicate headed by 'R. Mates, Royal Hotel Koondrook' and called, 'I don't want it' won £290 in the lottery. The previous year this same R. Mates and his wife announced the engagement of their daughter Patricia June to Russell, the youngest son of Mr and Mrs A. T. Robinson. Following their marriage, the newlyweds took over the pub and it was from them that Suzie, who's just swept in, and her ex-husband bought the place in the early 1990s.

The car that I thought signalled opening time belongs to Colin who, in his standard blue singlet has assumed his standard morning position on the burl at the end of the bar. He used to come here as a kid fishing with his dad and his uncles and when he got to retiring, there was only one place to shift to, so around 2007 he made the move to the river.

He's at 'his' seat at the end of the room where the redgum bar is extended out by a stunning polished burl slab. 'No girl on the burl is the rule here,' and he goes through who'll be in each of the other stalls as the day ticks through, and Suzie backs him up.

'The local legend is that ladies who sit at the burl will quickly become pregnant, so this is strictly the men's end.'

'Like a woman putting an upside-down glass on the bar?' I ask but it's not quite that drastic, dramatic or immediate.

When Suzie's marriage passed its best-before date, she and her ex leased out the pub and she met Slippery down south and they went into dairying. Then in 2012 he reckoned he was done facing udders at 5 am and figured running a pub couldn't be any harder.

'Since then,' he chips in from the side, 'I've had an average of one day off each year.'

And when I ask, 'So who's more stuffed – you or Hamish?' I get the eye roll, wry smile and would I like another drink? I succumb to Suzie's insistence that a coffee'll do me wonders and steel me for the trip through the game lodge.

Colin's seen it all before and Slippery's got work to do so we head off through the passageway where eight beasts, among them a moose, an elk, a deer and a caribou stand sentry from on high.

'This,' explains Suzie, 'is known as the "hall of death"', and then it's into the dining room where again the tables are stunning polished redgum burl and walls are filled with old images of the area topped off with more.

Beside the door is an old walking stick that was rescued from the rubbish when they first moved in.

'I just love taxidermy. I find them and buy them. Some are at auctions, word of mouth, and then I went to the hunting and fishing expo and this bloke had a couple for sale and he put me in contact with other collectors and people who have surplus to their needs and I chase them all over. The ones on the back wall come from Ballarat.'

Any taxidermy work is done by a bloke over in Mansfield. His place, my hostess swears, is in Deadhorse Lane. (I'm not funny enough to make this stuff up!)

There're nineteen pieces at the moment and all have names, usually the name of the person who sells them to her – names like Nick and Eric and of course Hamish.

'And there's still lots of room between them to squeeze in at least that number again – they're herd animals so they're used to living close.'

But there'll be no zebras and no kangaroos, that'd be a bit too close to home.

I tell Suzie that it's, er, interesting and maybe not my cup of tea. 'No,' she shoots back, 'yours is the coffee.'

Back in the bar Colin's about to shoot off but makes a point of saying he's been promised not to become an addition when he shuffles off his coil. I ponder this and realise I've never been in a pub with the ashes of old patrons in urns on the bar and for a moment am tempted to suggest it to Suzie. But then I opt out. She might take me seriously.

The quirk factor can be seriously under-appreciated. When it's done well, it makes for an unforgettable hotel. Just having a pub known as 'Mates' would make the Koondrook Royal special enough, but to have an extensive bizarre collection of stuffed animals creating an atmosphere so foreign, so distant to its physical location, makes this place one of the most memorable on the river.

Is there another place like it? Stuffed if I know!

CHAPTER 31 – COMMERCIAL HOTEL, LAKE BOGA

THE WRITING'S ON THE WALL

In June 1942, just four months after the Japanese bombed Darwin, the RAAF established a flying boat repair depot on the southern shore of Lake Boga. The lake was large enough to allow the Catalina flying boats to land and take off and the 6-acre site was also considered beyond the reach of Japanese bombers.

A bit to the south-east of the base, known as 1FBRD, and across the main drag to Kerang, was the town of Lake Boga, where the mechanics, engineers and pilots gave good business to the Commercial Hotel.

The pub wasn't one of the really old hotels along the river. When the flying boats started arriving, the pub still wasn't old enough to drink. The Commercial Hotel, Lake Boga Pty Ltd company, with a launch issue of 20,000 shares at £1 each had only been created in 1928.

In 1936 the company sold the hotel to Jack Ryan who kept it for about eight years and welcomed the influx of flyers. But he soon sold the freehold to a bloke named Modge Roberts. Now Modge had two daughters, Hilda and Madeline. He liked the town, liked the people, and liked the pub and as he was getting on, he wanted the pub to stay in the family. So he gave each of his daughters a six-months go at running the place. Hilda did better so she took over the hotel.

I know this stuff because Tony's fronted while I'm having a cool one at the bar after a scorcher day on the bike. He looks pretty stonkered himself and drains a longneck like he's earned it. Which he has.

Tony runs BT Performance over in Swan Hill. It's an automotive and marine engineering joint, and has evolved a specialist stream of rebuilding Ford GT's, many from barn finds, but they do other stuff like old Monaros, and right now he's stripped down a Holden Premier of its 186 and replaced it with a 350 Chev, or something like that. He reels off the numbers of engines, of blocks, of donks, details the specs of inter-coolers and afterburners,

hits me with stuff about overhead cams and turbochargers and I just nod. I think I fool him that I understand.

This is a bloke who probably lost some skin in the delivery room when he was born and whose covering's had at least half a dozen scabs, scars, cuts, bruises and lesions somewhere on it every single day since. Today he's got recent bleeds on a couple of knuckles, both forearms and there's a bit off the back of his neck.

He speaks engines better than I speak English. He asks for another, slides a hand that's never going to be free from grease residue through his full silver mop, and continues explaining the family tree of the place.

'Hilda – hey there's a portrait of her out the back that you should see – had a childhood sweetheart in Melbourne, Frank Smith. They got married and then Frank went off to war. He was sent to Bougainville in the Solomons but was on the far side of the island when the Japanese invaded. He caught malaria and wasn't too well but Frank managed to leave the island in a small boat with seven others. Ironically, he was picked up by a black cat, a Catalina – the same sort of plane that was getting fixed back here – off the coast of New Guinea and eventually came back here. He and Hilda had two sons, Michael and Geoff.'

Tony slows. Inhales. The eyes that were focused on me turn upward and he sucks his teeth.

'He had a lot of issues after the war and just before Mike, his son, got married to Jeanette, Frank took his own life. Out in the stables at the back of the pub.'

The afternoon sun streams through the front windows of the pub. Groups of after-workers come in and take their pews, some at the bar, some at the barrel tables. Phones ring and laughs resonate. A small brown-and-white dog, breed indeterminate, sidles up and sits under Tony's stool.

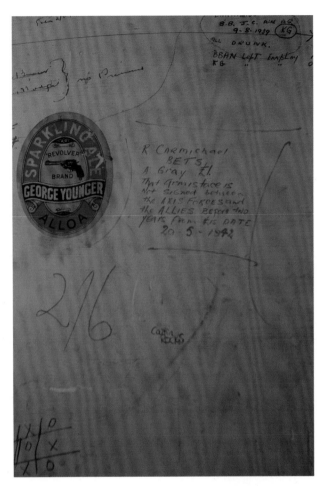

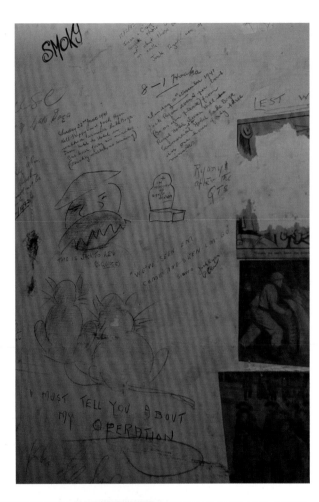

He's glad of the distraction. 'This is Bella. Pub dog and chief rodent inspector.'

Bella's not too sure of me.

Tony goes on:

'So Hilda kept the pub after Frank died but then in '95 or maybe '96 she was playing golf one day and had a massive heart attack. They got her to the hospital and she seemed to be sort of okay. But that night she had another one and that killed her.

'Older son, Michael, with his wife Jeannette, took over the pub, while raising two girls, Megan and Nikki. But Michael had a bad motorcycle accident and lost a leg. It affected him badly and sadly ...'

That same pause. That same look away. Silently, to myself, I say, 'Oh shit'.

'Sadly, like his dad, he took his own life.'

Jeannette, his widow, wanted out of the pub – too many memories and ghosts – so daughter Megan became the fourth generation of the family to own it when she and her partner bought the freehold in about 2003. They put in managers and licensees but when the last bloke, a licensee, did a runner one Sunday night they decided to take on the running themselves. Megan's partner's the bloke who's been telling me all this – Tony.

'On the Monday the liquidators locked the place up but we broke in, changed all the locks and told them we'd taken it back.'

Possession's nine-tenths and they retained the pub.

'The place was an absolute shambles so we advertised to all the locals for fifteen bucks an hour to help us clean and everyone, and I mean everyone, came and chipped in and we were open on the Thursday. That clean-up did wonders for making people around here feel that they had a stake in the pub.'

The new chef needs a word with the boss about the new menu she's designing – a bit of advice about ingredients and local tastes. Tony listens to the issues, smiles and tells her that she was hired for her skills and experience – he trusts her judgement and to, 'back yourself and I'll back you'. Reassured and confident, she heads back to the kitchen where she'll be cooking dinner tonight for people who'll be eating in Hilda's Bistro or in the Catalina Lounge at the side of the pub.

He looks down at Bella on the floor between his feet. 'If I don't have her on a leash, why would I have my staff on leashes?' And would I like to see a portrait of Hilda?

The bar set-up's obviously changed over the years and we head down past the bar, Tony retrieves a key from its resting place and opens a door into what was once, he thinks, the after-hours bar, where residents and overnight guests would have their night caps.

The promised portrait of the woman who took over this place in the early days of WWII, who began a dynasty of publicans, now three generations strong, well there're two of 'em in the room. But they're not in frames and behind dusty glass. They're graffitied straight onto the walls. The main portrait of Hilda Smith is of a long-necked, hair-up woman wearing earrings and pince-nez and announcing the dreaded, 'time gentlemen please'.

In the second the same woman, this time with specs, is depicted across from the caricature of an almost cat-in-the-hat bloke, fag in mouth who's asking, 'Ar yer there, Jack'. Hilda's word balloon reads, 'Come on Carr-ee, Squizz is going crook'. The bloke in the hat seems to be 'Squizz' and he must've been a value-adding part of the town.

Now, if those were the only drawings here, this'd be special, but there's way more and what's here transcends the merely 'special'. Seems that from the early days of Lake Boga's Commercial Hotel it was accepted common practice to use the walls as the medium to record public wishes, private commitments, notable local achievements and to stick newspaper clippings and old beer labels.

Sunday 22nd June 1941.

Kell Guppy and Jack Ryan
Walked around Lake Boga
From Hotel to Hotel in
One hour forty six minutes.
(Quickly walked, no swimming)

Some of the notices are light-hearted and yet, in retrospect, extremely poignant:

BARMANS PICNIC
B.B. J.C. A.N, A.G.
9-8-1939
ALL DRUNK

Just twenty-one days later, Hitler invaded Poland, Britain and France declared war on Germany and the world would change forever. Locals like B.B, J.C, A.N. and A.G. wouldn't be having carefree staffie binges again for a long time.

Amongst the locals to sign up was 'Squizzy'. High up on the wall an inscription reads:

WISHING LES (BETTER KNOWN AS SQUIZZY)
A SPEEDY AND SAFE RETURN
FROM ALL AT THE COMMERCIAL

Below is a signature of sorts:

VX 41191
L.C. Taylor
21/14 Field Regiment

I later ring the Victorian RSL where Fred the librarian immediately checks. The VX Number belongs to Arthur Dudley Earnest Mckenzie, born in Bristol, England. What his connection is with the town or the pub, is shrouded.

The walls reflect the understandable preoccupation of the pub's patrons with the war and their wishes for it to end:

W.H. Bets R that
America will not declare
War three months from
11-3-41 4 Bob

In red, 'R' has added, 'Lost'.
Another:

R. Carmichael
BETS
A Gray £1.
That Armistace is
Not signed between
the AXIS FORCES and

the ALLIES BEFORE two
years from this DATE
20.5.42

W. H. and R. R. Carmichael and A. Gray may've cared about the timing of America's entry into the war and when the horror would all be over. But not all those mentioned had such concerns. Les 'Squizzy' Taylor, didn't have the wished for 'speedy and safe return'. Between his likeness and that of Hilda a different pen has written:

'Squizzy' Departed this life
26-6-40

These walls and their messages, safeguarded behind a locked door are a window into the minds of drinkers over seventy years ago. Tony's not sure what he's going to do with them, just that they have to be well looked after.

I'm not staying in any of the pub's ten rooms tonight. I'd been welcomed to the town by an almost blindingly coruscating lake and then, suddenly, the waterside camping ground was to my right. Empty. There was only one place I was going to be sleeping. I'd swung Super Ten into the driveway and up to reception. Of course I could go right back up to the far end. Of course the tent'd be fine to set up and leave – but they'd keep an eye on it anyway. And no problem at all about turning off the sprinklers in that part of the grounds. So my digs were all done before I'd headed over to the pub, but cooking wasn't on my menu.

'Have the steak sandwich.'

I do as told. It has to be in the top ten, probably top five best steak sangers I've ever had.

'Alice does them. Her speciality, been doing them here for years and people come over from Swan Hill just to have them. Lot of people have nothing else, just one of Alice's sangers and a beer or two.' That, I'm certain is not a Murray myth.

Alice, like all the staff, is twenty-something, no itinerant, not a backpacker, and that's policy. Tony and Megan employ locals, and as far as possible, senior locals with other jobs.

'People who know what a day's work is. People who're connected to the town. People who I can trust to be left on their own and who have initiative and know how to use it. There's a place for training staff but there's also a place for being away and knowing the place'll be running smooth.'

When the war finally finished in September 1945, with Frank home from Bougainville and his malaria under control, with Squizzy Taylor buried in a far-off field, with R. Carmichael a quid richer and with R 4 Bob poorer, 1FBRD down from the pub was full of broken flying boats – Catalinas, Mariners and Kingfishers – and nothing much to do with them.

So the ADF stripped them of any worthwhile instruments and engines and put the carcasses up for sale. Most were bought for scrap but most were not immediately totally disassembled. So how do you chop a flying boat? Vertical or horizontal? Do you fillet it like mum's scone or do you cut it like a pizza? Turns out that it's both, either or neither.

Advertisements began appearing in the press headlined: 'THE IDEAL HOME ON LAND AND WATER'. With just the wings and tail off and internally gutted, the fuselages were easily converted to houseboats.

With the top half cut away along the entire length they were put to industrial use. A lucrative trade in river gums was expanding along the river and the long hulls, strong, lightweight and waterproof were ideal for shipping Murray gum logs out of the flooded forests. So the tops were cut from the fuselages and sometimes an engine and tiller attached but many were also used as simple barges, pushed and pulled by other tugs.

And then some inventive genius, no-one's sure who was the first, realised that chopping a Mariner vertically could turn it into a, yes, caravan, or as they were known, Marivan.

The highest profile dealer in the scrap planes was a bloke named C. Charlton who enthused that the boat hulls 'give you a mobile home of five rooms for £100.'

And the dealer's address? 'Commercial Hotel, Lake Boga'.

I take my last beer around to the Catalina Lounge and mull through the history of this place and its interwoven connections with the flying boats. I thank Alice for the sanger and head over to thank Tony for his hospitality and for caring for the wall documents. I tell him he looks like he could do with a good night's sleep and he concedes running two businesses doesn't leave much time for that. He's had a few approaches to take over the pub but he and Megan have never felt 100 per cent about the folks showing interest. But it'd be bloody good to pass the place into good hands.

Outside, the sliver of a fingernail moon is the highlight of a clear sky. Beside my tent I thank the Squizzy Taylors with their bravery, the Frank Smiths with their horrific demons, the Catalina pilots with their courage and all the others whose efforts made this life of mine, of ours, possible.

A couple of months later I rock up again on a warm weekday arvo and a pair of new faces shine from behind the bar.

Daphne and Honey came up from their homes in Whittlesea with their families for a holiday in 2015 and fell in love with the lake just as I did. They all returned each year and in 2018 Daphne bought a place beside the water and one long afternoon during their 2019 sojourn and over a few drinks these two started playing the 'wouldn't it be great to run the pub here' game.

They ran it by Tony who was receptive and the fantasy became a plan. In December 2019 Honey quit her personal carer job and Daphne (who'd managed a pub for thirteen years a while back) got out of disability support and the plan became a reality.

Now they have a long-term lease with the option to buy the freehold, plans to supercharge the food service, reinvigorate the entertainment, and magnify the links with the community and service to the holiday-makers who make the pilgrimage each year.

'We're really honoured that Tony and Megan trusted us with this place. We know the special traditions of the pub and won't be changing them,' says Honey, 'but we also know which bits we can tweak and turn this into something even more special.'

And, once Daphne's kept us waiting for ten minutes as she sorts her hair and I get them organised for a photo, Honey laughs, 'We're just a couple of old moles who're having a go!'

CHAPTER 32 – FEDERAL HOTEL, MURRAY DOWNS

WHAT'S 308 YARDS BETWEEN FRIENDS?

'**I**t was a bookie who really got Gary back on his feet.'

'Pidge' leans across the high table in the middle of the betting area of the Federal Hotel at Murray Downs, over the bridge from Swan Hill, looks at me but nods at his mate perched on his stool at the end of the table where all the odds screens and race monitors can be surveyed without bending his neck.

It's Saturday afternoon, there's a new mob of hayburners bursting out of the starting gates on the monitors every coupla minutes so Gary ('make sure you only put one 'r' in that') is hard at work.

With Johnno over his shoulder he's checking the form for the next, working out which nag might break his run of picking three straight seconds after backing them straight out. He hears Pidge's comment and smiles as I wonder just how does a bookie get a punter like Gary 'back on his feet'. I figure he must've picked a few more winners back then than he is today.

I've joined Pidge and Gary and Johnno and Greg, who's Gary's boss of sorts, at the gambling end of 'the Fed' because in an historical landscape where, pre-TAB, pretty much every pub in Australia had an SP bookie in the corner of the bar and a couple of cockatoos outside, the connection of this pub with sly gambling is unique.

The scale and longevity of illegal betting and gaming at the Federal Hotel and the resilience and ingenuity of the operators were so great that it brought about changes in the law not just of this country, but of the entire British Empire!

When our old mate Major Thomas Mitchell came through this place in 1836, the first white man to do so, he wrote in this journal that the stretch of the Murray which was to become the site of Swan Hill and Murray Downs was, 'a sort of Paradise … certain to become, at no distant date, of vast importance to a new people.'

Two years later the overlander Joseph Hawdon, on a trip from Seymour to Adelaide stopped here and wrote that, 'it is the first situation worthy of a grazier's notice that I have seen since leaving the depot at the Goulburn [River].'

So, let's just accept this is a pretty place, eh.

Within twelve months Hawdon's nephew, John Hawdon, had taken up a squatting lease along 18 miles of the Murray's northern frontage and extending for 150,000 acres. He named the spread, 'Murray Downs'.

By 1847 Murray Downs was in the hands of the Jamieson brothers, Hugh and Bushby, and it was the vines they planted in the homestead's garden that helped convince the Chaffey brothers some forty years later to embark on the creation of their schemes at Renmark and Mildura.

In 1862 the station was taken over by the Officer brothers and one of them, Suetonius, settled there, marrying in 1866 and, because a bloke with a name like that can pretty much do what he wants, then set up an 80-acre ostrich farm on the property.

Two years after Victoria passed *The Chaffey Brothers Irrigation Works Act, 1887*, Walter Smith erected, and obtained a licence for, his Federal Hotel on the northern bank of the Murray across from Swan Hill and on the edge of the Murray Downs Station.

A trip to the larger neighbouring town involved a voyage on the aging (born 1840s) punt but years of campaigning bore fruit when the bridge, reliable and free of tolls, was opened in December 1896. The Hon. J. W. Taverner cut the ribbon and the parliamentary party, following a riverside picnic, then spurned the half-dozen pubs on the Victorian side and returned to the Federal Hotel. They must've been doing something right on the north bank!

The new bridge opened up a whole new pool of customers for the pub – customers who'd not had to shell out a fee for crossing the punt. And for a certain type of entrepreneur, the crossing also represented a new business opportunity that could be exploited through the pub's special geographical location.

The cops later summed up the special attractions of the place when they opposed the renewal of Donald Urquhart's licence of the Fed in 1911:

> ... the crowd leave Swan Hill and cross the bridge to this hotel, so that the Swan Hill police (can) not touch them ... The nearest police station in New South Wales was about 50 miles distant. It (is) therefore a difficult hotel to manage also for the police to supervise.

One bloke's problem is another bloke's opportunity. While the police were working out how to overcome their business problem, the entrepreneurs had been busy carrying on theirs. Their business was based on the neat circularity that the money the Swan Hill crowd had saved by not spending it on the punt, could be put to better use: punting.

In 1904 Mary Frame, who'd inherited the licence when her husband carked it the previous year, was the first publican to be busted for the new income stream. In court she 'pleaded guilty to five informations of gaming, and selling at prohibited hours. She was fined in the aggregate £15, with £1 4s 2d. costs.'

The place was getting a local reputation for gambling and for after-hours trading, with police just a rock throw away across the river but powerless to break up the partying.

And then in December 1917 the *Swan Hill Guardian and Lake Boga Advocate*, reported a raid on the pub:

> At a quarter past ten on Saturday night Senior-constable M'Callum and Constables Kenneally and Walker made a raid on the Federal Hotel, *and took the names of 23 persons for being on licensed premises during prohibited hours. The cases will probably be heard at Balranald.*

But this raid was special – it involved three police who were from Victoria and the pub was in New South Wales.

The paper's report continued, interestingly but without explanation, that the hotel was 'situated within 500 yards of the common boundary of the State of Victoria and the State of New South Wales, such States being adjoining British possessions.'

The police forces had had enough of their borderline officers being hamstrung by the river. They'd had it up to here with their brethren like O'Meara and Hayes who'd been intimidated and dismissed by the crowd at the Foley–Hicken fight back at Moama in 1878, being ridiculed and laughed at while what they saw as crime was being carried out with impunity under their noses. They put up with it for years, for decades, but the goings on at the Federal Hotel at Murray Downs were the final straws.

The Fugitive Offenders Act of 1881 was beefed up in 1915. Section 20 read:

> Where two British possessions adjoin, a person accused of an offence committed on or within the distance of five hundred yards from the common boundary of such possessions may be apprehended, tried, and punished in either of such possessions.

The Federal Hotel was 308 yards from the Victorian bank of the Murray and Victoria and New South Wales were both 'British possessions'. Finally the Swan Hill cops had been dealt the hand they wanted.

In its coverage of the subsequent trial the same local paper listed the convictions and those who'd had the charges withdrawn before noting, 'As far as we know, this is the first occasion on which a raid has been made by Victorian police on a New South Wales licensed house.'

The Federal Hotel in flyspeck Murray Downs, was nationally famous.

The effect on the pub's extracurricular activities and its after-hours service were more 7 ounce than schooner.

In 1924 the *Riverina Recorder* reported the conviction of George McCallum for being at the pub on a Sunday The single paragraph story was wedged between one reporting the case of a G. E. Fitzgerald, charged with driving a motor car at a speed dangerous to the public in Balranald, and who begged leniency because he'd 'only received his license the day before' (some things never change!), and the case of George Baldwin charged with 'failing to give notice of travelling sheep'. (And some things do!)

The Federal Hotel bubbled along, serving when you wanted if they could get away with it, and promoting traditional Aussie sports, and occasionally they had surprise company.

September 1932:

A successful raid on a two-up school was made by the police on the main stock route from Balranald to Swan Hill, beyond the Federal Hotel, Murray Downs. Four policemen, two from Moulamein, and two from Swan Hill, surrounded the 'school,' which scattered in all directions. Some attempted, to cross the Murray, but found it too strong to negotiate, and 20 names of offenders were taken, who will appear before the Moulamein Police Court later on.

This was a minor setback, a cost of business, and the game went on and the Federal Hotel, with the special assistance of one man, was to see its fame and notoriety launched fully onto the national stage.

That man's name was Dennis Hayes – same surname as O'Meara's offy at the Hicken–Foley fight.

On 28 July 1933:

Thirty-four charges against six defendants were listed for hearing at the Moulamein Police Court on Thursday, 20th July, before the P.M. Mr. G. J. Johnstone. Owing to lack of time the cases against two defendants only were dealt with, and the remaining cases were adjourned until the next sittings of the court. The prosecutions were the outcome of a raid made by the Victorian police on men who were allegedly engaged in street betting at the Federal Hotel, Murray Downs (N.S.W.).

The punters had done more homework than the constabulary. The Victorian police certainly now had powers north of the Murray, however, 'The men were tried at Swan Hill, but the charges were dismissed on the ground that arrest, trial and conviction should take place in the one State.'

The police weren't chucking in the towel quite that easily:

The cases were subsequently taken up by the New South Wales police. Ambrose McConnell, who pleaded guilty to three charges relating to

March 4th, 11th and 25th, was fined £20 on each charge; in default 121 days' hard labour. James Hayes pleaded not guilty to four similar charges. The P.M. convicted defendant and fined him £40, with £22 18s costs; in default 128 days' hard labour.

Charges against the other four, including James Hayes's brother and our hero Dennis, were adjourned until the next sitting in September and all pleaded guilty. Their solicitor, Mr Rowan, sought leniency and understanding. His argument was interesting:

Mr. Rowan said all the defendants who were pleading guilty realised the position in which they were placed and were sorry for what they had done. He pleaded that the offence was not as serious as it might appear. The men did not bet in the town or where there were a lot of people. They went into the bush across the river into New South Wales and only those who wished to bet went there. There was no great moral wrong in having a bet — he liked a bet himself — and did not care who knew it. It was not so much an offence against society as against the law.

Plod (in the shape of Inspector Bourke) was having none of it, testifying that he:

… would be amiss in his duty if he did not stress the seriousness of the cases of street betting with which the defendants had been charged. [Dennis] Hayes was the principal in the case about which evidence had already been taken … These men went across the border and carried on betting with impunity. They flaunted the law and defied the police. Hayes in the witness box previously said in answer to a question 'Oh! The police! We don't take any notice of them.'

Dennis Hayes was in Inspector Bourke's sights and he didn't miss. The Magistrate found him guilty on all five counts, twenty quid a time plus court costs and witness expenses. In default, ninety-eight days of hard. Hayes and the rest argued for time to pay. They didn't have that sort of money and they needed to earn it. Time was granted.

So how's a bloke like Dennis Hayes going to earn a quid? Yep! Two months later Hayes and Inspector Bourke ran into each other again:

180

A successful raid on a two-up school was made by the police on the main stock route from Balranald to Swan Hill, beyond the Federal Hotel, Murray Downs. Four policemen, two from Moulamein, and two from Swan Hill, surrounded the "school," which scattered in all directions. Some attempted to cross the Murray, but found it too strong to negotiate, and 20 names of offenders were taken, who will appear before the Moulamein Police Court later on.

Dennis Hayes, a resident of Swan Hill pleaded guilty [in Balranald Court] to a charge of street betting on the Balranald-Swan Hill road on the N.S.W. side of the river … In opening the case Inspector Bourke said that at a spot opposite Swan Hill, known as Murray Downs, a constable attached to the Victorian police force made bets with the defendant on the roadway in front of the Federal Hotel. 'A large number of men congregate there' said the Inspector, and the defendant acts as a bookmaker. Complaints have been numerous and steps were taken by the police to suppress it. The offence has been committed openly and in defiance of the police …

But it would seem that Inspector Bourke was the one who was ignorant of local customs and was disrespecting local customs:

Mr. Davies, for the defendant, said 'his client had not openly flaunted the authorities as had been stated by the police. Murray Downs, where the betting was said to have taken place had been the meeting place of a large number of men for a long time for the purpose of making a bet. They had enjoyed the privilege and the immunity of police interference.

Dennis Hayes, though had, 'realised the error of his ways and had definitely given up betting on the New South Wales side of the river and there will not be any repetition of the offence in the future.'

Hayes was again found guilty and despite his heart-rending expressions of remorse, this time was hit with a twenty-five quid fine plus costs. Then his day got worse.

'Perjury Charge' screamed the page 1 headline in the *Rivernia Recorder:*

Dennis Hayes Committed for Trial

At the Balranald Police Court … Dennis Hayes and his brother, James Keyes Hayes was charged with swearing false evidence at a hearing of street betting cases heard in the Moulamein Court in July last year.

George Elder Puddicombe, the licensee of the Federal Hotel, testified that he'd run the hotel for fourteen years and knew both defendants. Betting was conducted in front of the hotel but never in it or on its verandah.

Betting had been going on for about two years and a crowd gathered there

for that purpose on Saturdays mostly, and Wednesdays. The attendance would be 30–50 – there would be more on big race days.

Dennis Hayes was committed to stand trial in Deniliquin the following March 20th with bail fixed at a paltry £20. Ten days before he was due to front the ever reliable *Riverina Recorder* carried news which wouldn't have cheered Inspector Bourke:

Alleged Perjury Charge

The Attorney General has declined to prosecute in the case of alleged perjury charge against Dennis Hayes of Swan Hill. Hayes was committed for trial at the last sittings of the Balranald Court to stand his trial at Deniliquin General Sessions on the 20th March. The charge arose out of evidence given in the Moulamein Court in connection with certain street betting charges and it was alleged that Hayes then made a false statement in sworn evidence.

Inspector Bourke moved on, times changed and Dennis Hayes and his mates mended their ways and adhered to the straight and narrow. Yeah, right!

In June 1937 it was the usual suspects doing the usual things in the usual places:

Street Betting

Further proceedings by the Police against Dennis Hayes, James Keyes Hayes, and Thomas Griffiths Bradbury, were mentioned and Mr. McHugh for each defendant asked for an adjournment for one month. The charges are for street betting arising out of a raid which occurred last February at Murray Downs. Mr. McHugh on behalf of the defendants, gave an undertaking that they would not bet illegally during the period of the adjournment. The application was granted.

All three were busted and then a year later the fun opposite the Federal Hotel was raided. Sixty men were arrested, about half pleaded guilty at court the following Monday and were each fined about £2 plus costs. Two of the principals of a two-up game were sent to jail for a month each and Dennis Hayes was remanded on bail.

The following week:

... as the sequel to a gaming raid carried out by Inspector Kemp and district police at Murray Downs (New South Wales) ... Hayes appeared before Mr. A. B. Collins, P.M., in Deniliquin Police Court on the charge (of using a place for the purpose of betting.) He was convicted and fined £65 with £7/15/0 costs in default 146 days' imprisonment.

The stakes were rising and an appeal was immediately lodged with the court and the hearing came around in August 1938. The new sheriff, Inspector Kemp testified that:

... he was on a piece of land opposite the Federal Hotel, Murray Downs, where he saw Hayes standing by a table at a tree calling out the names of horses racing that day at Moonee Valley. He saw men go up and, make bets with Hayes and when the wireless announced that Veiled Prophet won defendant said he would pay on that horse, and did pay money to several men ... The paddock was part of Murray Downs Station, with no other houses, apart from the hotel, nearby ... Between 200 and 300 people were there on a well-worn patch the area of the court-room. He saw only one bookmaker, but there were also two-up, crown and anchor, and 'tote' games in operation.

Mr Hayes had expanded. This was no street betting, it was now a fully-fledged casino in a paddock! The problem for the prosecution was that this paddock across the road from the Federal Hotel, didn't confirm with any definition of 'place' that was included in the legislation.

Without requiring Hayes to respond to the police testimony, the magistrate addressed the court:

I am bound by the remarks of learned Chief Justice in the case of Prior v. Sherwood (3 Commonwealth Law Reports, p. 1051), viz.: 'It follows that the place used if it is not a house, office or room must be some specific area of land which is in the actual occupation of the defendant or some person by whose permission he makes use of it.

The space in the paddock across from the pub wasn't sufficiently specific and so:

... it does appear to me ... following I hope properly the words of the learned Chief Justice, and also of my dear old friend. Sir Edmund Barton, that this is a case where the appeal should be upheld and the conviction quashed.

Dennis Hayes was in the clear and the Federal Hotel was known coast to coast.

Whilst Johnno and Pidge and Gary have been trying to pick their winners, Greg, a strong, solid, squat bloke has been telling stories of the old weekend schedule of 'the Fed'.

'This place used to be a real bloodhouse pub and to try to keep a lid on it, the owners stuck a full regulation boxing ring out where the beer garden is now. Once a month there'd be pickup bouts between locals or locals and visitors, and you'd back yourself with the other camp and win enough to get you through the weekend.'

He's not sure of the legality of it all and eventually it faded but the Saturday night music gigs endured longer. Greg lost three siblings in short and tragic succession and recognises now that he had anger and hostility issues.

'It got to the stage that I'd be in a blue most weeks with someone who looked at me the wrong way, or brushed me as they went past. If it was on Saturday night fair dinkum the band would have a break while I had a fight and once it was over, they'd just start playing again.'

This bloke looks more like a body double for one of the Beach Boys than a block living all his life a long way from the coast. He's shorter than I am but damn, I'd want him in my corner if things turned pear-shaped and he reckons he won a lot more than he lost, both in the ring and in front of the music.

He got his act together, went mining in Kalgoorlie where, down to a work ethic instilled by his father, his love of physical labour and the piece-rates that were being paid, he became the highest earning miner in the goldfields for three years straight.

He returned to Swan Hill, settled down 'a bit' and set up a concreting business which now employs, among others, Gary, and he reckons he's finally lined up all his ducks. He leaves the Saturday arvo gambling to the others, just enjoying 'the beer and the bullshit'.

Pidge and Gary meanwhile, have been in this part of the river all their lives and for as long as Pidge can remember, they've been betting on the horses. Dennis Hayes was long gone by the time he placed his first schoolboy bet at the old car – he thinks it was a Humber – parked across the road from the pub in the shade of tree that was cut down when the track was widened. The bloke inside with the pencil and the ledger book was Donny Kelly, and no-one knocked on the car window more than Gary.

He reckons his system now is to follow trainers rather than horses and when a horse from one of his target stables gets up in the last stride in the sixth at Somewhere and pays $14 he's in a mood for another Great Northern and a chat.

So I buy a round from Daisey – one of those top barkeeps who only need to know for whom I'm ordering and she heads to the taps and the fridge and then points which schooner and which bottle belong to whom – while Gary reaps his winnings from the gambling terminal attendant.

'We never had a TV when I was a young kid and so I used to go across the street to my Gran's who used to watch the trots on her tiny black-and-white set with the rabbit ear antennae. She loved a bet and that's how I got interested. Back then I stayed over at Swan Hill and bet with an SP in the bar of the White Swan where Target is now.'

The bookie was Norm Poole and Gary reckons he laid his first bet in the front bar of the White Swan just under fifty years ago when he was about fifteen. Pretty soon he switched drinking holes to 'the Fed' and started betting with Donny Kelly in his car across the road.

'Donny Kelly used to work every Saturday and most Wednesdays and of course on big meetings like the Melbourne Cup, and Friday was always settling day back over at the White Swan, when your winnings would be in an envelope with your name on, or more likely when you'd hand over your debts to Donny … and he never smiled. He had this sort of upside-down mouth with the ends turned down and he always looked miserable. But one time after I'd started phoning my bets in, I was having a serious session with a mate over at the White Swan, and ringing through new bets every couple of minutes. We even extended it into betting on Perth races. Anyway the next Friday it's settling day at the White Swan and Donny sees me and he lets go of a little smile, first time I've ever seen him smile and the last time too. And he hands me my envelope out of the back of his hand – you know, just a little slip pass – and it's about an inch thick. I'm thinking, shit, I've really backed a few here.

'So I open it and there's two foolscap pages of bets, one bet to a line, that's how many bets I'd had – two complete lined pages full of horses' names and my wagers. And folded in there's about 12 dollars of cash as well. Lot of hard work for a few pennies! But at least I made Donny smile!'

When Gary knew he wasn't going to be able to get to the car on a Saturday, he'd ring his bets through during the week – a system that worked well. But then one time Kelly didn't pick up his phone. Gary kept ringing – he had a sure thing running in Sydney. Each time the phone rang out until on the second day of ringing a different voice answered with the news that Don Kelly was seriously ill and wouldn't be working that coming weekend. And wouldn't be settling at the Swan on Friday.

Two weeks later Donny Kelly, Swan Hill's last great SP bookie was dead. And Gary had a dilemma.

'I owed him $340 and I'm a bloke who always pays his debts.'

But Don Kelly had no family, no wife and no kids. Gary didn't want unpaid owings on his conscience so he came up with an honourable solution.

'They had the funeral at the church over at Swan Hill, and there was a decent roll-up and it was an open-casket thing and everyone filed past before they sat down in the pews.'

As he neared the open casket, Gary reached into his pocket.

'I had this cheque for the 340 bucks so I just slipped it into the coffin. It's been years now but strangely enough it hasn't been cashed.'

Gary grins and as the rest of the table explodes, he takes a swig and gets down to the business of picking his certainty for the next at Somewhere Else.

I get around to telling him that it's a bit cynical paying a dead bookie by cheque, especially since Pidge reckons it was Kelly who got him back on his feet. The rest of the table goes quiet. This punting demon needs a swig before revealing this story.

'Yeah, Pidge is right. I used to have this car that I loved and drove it all over the place. Then I had a bad trot and owed Donny more than the price of my wheels so I had to sell it to pay him out. Then I had to walk everywhere. So yeah, he put me back on my feet alright!'

It ain't going to get better than that. I buy a round and start to pack up. These blokes are going nowhere. Still two races in Sydney and three in Adelaide. Perth will be starting soon and then there's Hong Kong.

I say my goodbyes and Gary looks up from the form guide.

'You coming back again some time?'

'Yeah,' I tell him, 'you can bet on it.'

CHAPTER 33 – SWAN HILL TO THE EDWARD

VIA NOT THAT SPEEWAH, THE NYAH BRIDGE AND TOOLEYBUC

About twenty minutes out of Swan Hill I almost miss the sharp right onto Speewa Punt Road (wouldn't have mattered, there's another turn a bit farther on) and then it's just 5 kilometres to only the second interstate punt on the Murray. The punt's on the other bank and I wave to the bloke in high viz not to come over to collect me. Just wait until someone else turns up, because there's something we have to get straight before we cross the river.

Listen up: Speewa ain't Speewah! It's a pity and I wish it was, but it isn't. For a start, Speewa, where I'm sat watching the river, actually exists. The other place doesn't. Unless it does. Or did. And if it did, there's one bloke I'd especially want to have a beer with (if I was strong enough to hold the massive tumblers they must surely have served it in).

The incredible exploits, the legends, the tales and the yarns of Crooked Mick of the Speewah put the myths like that of Jack Riley's connection to the Man from Snowy River and Ned Kelly's attendance at the Foley–Hicken Fight at Echuca firmly in the shade.

In 1937 in the *Shoalhaven News* a writer with a fake name lifted the lid on the true story of how Crooked Mick got his name:

He was called Crooked Mick, not because he was an unfair dealer— for a squarer shooter never lived— but because it was he who, with his team of bullocks on his way to 'The Speewah' had made the big bend in the Darling River by pulling it crooked. It happened this way: Mick was crossing the river when it was low, with his team of 100 bullocks. A man with Crooked Mick's reputation scorned to drive a team of less than one hundred. When they got to the middle of the stream they became bogged,

and before they could get out, a fresh team was seen coming down about half a mile away. Mick and his off-sider, not daring to look be hind, flogged their team ahead: It was slow going, and they wondered why they were making so little progress. When they landed on the further side they found they had pulled a big bend in the river. Whenever Mick told the story, he always added, 'We pulled her crooked right enough.' And so he was known as Crooked Mick.

I first met the legend when researching the life of Julian Stuart, a true leader and giant figure of the Great Shearers' strike of 1891. Stuart, who was chairman of the shearers' camp at Clermont, was arrested for conspiracy and shipped by train for a trial at Townsville and was then jailed on Australia's Alcatraz – St Helena Island in Moreton Bay.

Julian Stuart wrote on serious labour issues and Indigenous rights, but the folklore of this country also intrigued him.

In a column in the Queensland *Worker* in 1926, Stuart detailed the 'mighty deeds of a mythical personage':

I first heard of him on the Barcoo in 1889 ... [and one night] ... when 'Dusty Bob' got the flute I sat up in my bunk and listened, for I knew him to be the most fluent liar that ever crossed the Darling.

His anecdotes about 'Crooked' Mick' began and ended nowhere, and made C.M. appear a superman—with feet so big that he had to go outside to turn round. It took a large-sized bullock's hide to make him a pair of moccasins.

He was a heavy smoker. It took one 'loppy' (rouseabout) all the time cutting tobacco and filling his pipe.

He worked at such a clip that his shears ran hot, and sometimes he had half-a-dozen pairs in the water pot to cool.

He had his fads, and would not shear in sheds that faced north. When at his top it took three pressers to handle the wool from his blades, and they had to work overtime to keep the bins clear. He ate two sheep each meal—that is, if they were small merinos—but only one and a half when the ration sheep were Leicester crossbred wethers ...

Between sheds he did fencing. When cutting brigalow posts he used an axe in each hand to save time, and when digging postholes a crowbar in one hand and a shovel in the other.

Once, when taming a Dawson River brumby (which had killed or crippled every man who ever tackled him) he nearly died of starvation.

The outlaw had kept on bucking continuously, and on the third day the rider yelled for food.

His mates cooked a lot of preserved potatoes, which they threw at him when they could get near enough. He caught some open-mouthed, but a good deal of the food was wasted, as the horse bucked sideways and in circles.

Lumps of the spuds lodged in Mick's beard, which reached to his waist, and on his moustache, which was so long that he used to tie it at the back of his head.

In a 1951 article Alan Marshall shared more tales of Mick:

Once, the boss, annoyed because of Crooked Mick's rough handling of some wethers, strode up to him on the board and barked, 'You're fired.'

Crooked Mick was shearing flat out at the time. He was going so fast that he shore 15 sheep before he could straighten up and hang his shears on the hook.

But old Mick didn't just have empathy with the sheep, he almost became one:

HIS later days were saddened by a serious accident. He was washing sheep when he slipped and fell into a tank of boiling water.

Big Bill, who was standing beside him, whipped him out, tore off his clothes, then seized two wethers and cut their throats.

He ripped the hides off the wethers, and wrapped them, flesh side in, round Crooked Mick's body and legs.

When they got him to a doctor three weeks later, the doctor took one look at him and said, 'Boys, you've made a wonderful job on him. It would take a major operation to remove these skins. They're grafted to him.'

So the doctor left them attached to his legs and 'they took Crooked Mick back to the Speewah and shore him every year after that. He made 22 pounds of wool.'

But it wasn't just Crooked Mick who was larger than life, the entire Speewah was, well *almost* biblically beyond belief. In 1953 the *Newcastle Morning Herald and Miners' Advocate*, a journal which only ever reported the facts, revealed that:

The Speewah was cursed with every plague.

Rabbits were there in millions.

They were so thick you had to pull them out of the burrows to get the ferrets in, and trappers had to brush them aside to set their traps.

On some of the paddocks they had to drive them out to get room to put the sheep in.

Galahs, too, were bad.

When the big drought broke the Speewah remained dry as a bone, though the rain fell in tor-rents above it.

The first clap of thunder had scared the galahs into flight, and they were so thickly packed as they winged over the station that not a drop of rain reached the ground ...

Hundreds of men worked on the Speewah.

In fact, there were so many that they had to mix the mustard with a long-handle shovel, and the cook and his assistant had to row out in a boat to sugar the tea.

When shearing was on the boss had to ride up and down the board on a motor-bike.

But, ah, that Speewah isn't this Speewa, and the punt's left the northern bank for a car that's just pulled up beside me, so I join in behind, hoping the ferryman's name is 'Mick'.

It isn't.

Plagues Become Folklore

The Speewah was cursed with every plague.

Rabbits were there in millions. They were so thick you had to pull them out of the burrows to get the ferrets in, and trappers had to brush them aside to set their traps . . . Galahs, too, were bad. When the Big Drought broke, the Speewah remained dry as a bone, although the rain fell in torrents. The first clap of thunder had scared the galahs into flight and they were so thickly packed as they winged over the station that not a drop reached the ground.

A flock of them, swooping under Crooked Mick's hut to avoid a hawk, lifted it off the ground with the wind of their wings and carried it 30 miles. Mick finished his breakfast while going through a belt of cloud at 20,000 feet, the gal-ahs still pounding along just beneath him . . .

A tall yarn? It is one of several bushmen's stories which Alan Marshall, in "Australia Writes," says make American folk tales look like sissies.

"Australia Writes," publish-ed to-day, is an Australian an-thology edited by T. Inglis Moore for the Canberra Fel-lowship of Australian Writ-ers.

WITHIN the limits of the 300-odd pages allotted to him Mr. Moore has suc-ceeded in giving a good cross-section coverage of Australian literature history, way of life, idiom and outlook. He has also preserved a good balance between veteran and fledgling

● Somewhere over the range, Australian folk tradition says, there grow bigger cattle, wilder horses, greener grass — and there good bushmen go when they die.

LIFE'S TOUGH AT SPEEWAH

DON'T talk to me about Pecos Bill and Colorado Jack and that giant of the lumber camps who picked his teeth with the trunk of a tree.

The heroes of American folk tales are sissies compared to the men of Australia's mythical station, the Speewah.

Why, Crooked Mick of the Speewah, a man who would sooner have a fight than a feed, used Ayer's Rock to stone the crows and he was no giant by the Speewah standards.

No, give me the Austra-lian folk heroes every time.

Tales of them have been told from Cape York to the Orkeys, from Brisbane to Broome Where teamsters met or drovers gathered, tales of the Speewah were handed on and men, push-Speewah, and it still appears on the map as such, thus giving rise to some argument as to whether it was not the original Speewah from which all outlandish places and events took their origin."

Whatever its origin, it is pos-sible, from the stories told about it, to get a picture of the mythi-cal station and of some of the men who ran it.

The hundreds of stories told about the Speewah are fairly con-sistent when it comes to giving an idea of its size, and though many men feature in the tales, one or two crop up regularly, giving the impression that they

CROOKED MICK FROM THE SPEEWAH

MIGHTY DEEDS OF A MYTHICAL PERSONAGE

Tom Mann, in his memoirs, men-tions that when in Queensland about 20 years ago, he was told of a shearer who had shorn 340 in a day. He ad-mits a doubt about it, and his in-credulity is justifiable, for neither then nor since has Jacky Howe's tally of 321 been beaten. Probably the figures quoted belonged to Crooked Mick, a mythical personage, whose mighty deeds have been recounted in sheds, mostly for the benefit of new chums.

Andrew's been driving this punt since 2001, working a roster of four days on and two days off, combining with two other drivers. He's risen to supervisor level and it was he who trained Amanda, who took me across the Wymah punt way back upriver at Granya.

Standard hours are around 6 am to 9 pm Sunday to Friday and until midnight on Saturday, 'but if the bridges in Swan Hill and Nyah are closed, we have this thing going twenty-four hours Probably happened three of four times since I've been here.'

The Murray here's never been so low that the ferry's stopped running but every so often the operators are forced to stop the craft short of the landing and lower the flaps to connect with the concrete approaches, creating a bridge over the river mud. And he's seen high water reaching up above the concrete so that the vehicles load straight on from the bitumen. All that's manageable, but when the winds blow strong against the current, things get more interesting.

'I've seen one-and-a-half-metre waves rolling up the river and that can seriously scare the bejeesus outa ya,' he says with a laid-back grin as we chat while waiting for business.

He usually doesn't work alone. Leah his English sheepdog and Wally who's got a bit of blue in him, have their perches in the boathouse, Leah on the bench and Wally under the desk.

He shows me a copy of the local rag who've just done a story on the punt.

And he's not too impressed.

'I told 'em that we carry eighty to a hundred cars a day so they've written that we travel 180 kilometres a day. The river's about a hundred metres wide here so that would make 18,000 crossings a day. Impressive eh?'

When I was parking Super Ten on the New South Wales bank I'd seen Andrew's house ('it comes with the job') and noticed his green Kawasaki bike which he rides whenever. Andrew pulls up the calculator on his tablet.

'That works out a bit under 1300 crossings an hour for a fourteen hours day – twenty-one a minute! Mate, if there was a freakin' bridge here, I'd be hard pressed doing that on the green monster! You'd think the journo would've done the maths eh?'

I tell him a feat like that would probably've even been a stretch for Crooked Mick. We both laugh, the dogs bark, and the alarm warning of a vehicle on the far bank begins to wail. Time for him to get his feet off the desk and for me to get moving.

Handshake, dog pats and I'm walking up the slope as Andrew secures the gates and heads over to the south bank. Just twenty more crossings in the next sixty seconds and he'll be on schedule. The blokes at Speewah would be impressed.

I head north of Speewa Ferry Road and then west on Speewa Road and then pull aside before the Armco side barriers at the approach to the Nyah Bridge.

In 1914 the locals began campaigning for a bridge here:

At a meeting held at the Poon Boon homestead ... it was unanimously decided to petition the New South Wales Government, asking that a bridge be constructed over the Murray River at Nyah.

Just over 1000 days later, the people got a, er, punt. By the time it finally started its interstate shunting it was way too little, far too late. Oh, and it wasn't all that buoyant! Soon the push was back on for a bridge.

In 1926:

an indignation meeting was held at Nyah ... to protest against the inefficient punt service ... [it] had been sunk on several occasions ... and caused great inconvenience ... [there is] a pressing need of the erection of an inter-state bridge to meet the progressive demands of the closely settled area.

The governments remained ever responsive and proactive and they swung into action. It took just eight years for the governments to announce that they'd agreed to the project and that work would be commenced, 'in the near future'.

Work began in 1938 and finished as war raged in Europe in 1941. In opening it, J. A. Lawson MLA noted it had been:

[p]lanned in peaceful ... happy days (and) has reached its completion under the shadow of war, and the stress of adversity, but it will remain like the hearts of the people, strong and true to give service long after the war is over and victory won.

As I walk down on the downstream side of the approach road to the stately well-kept lift-span bridge, the clapping rotors of a small, elegant pocket twin-side paddle-steamer cuts through the quiet as it U-turns and then noses into the bank maybe 100 metres upstream from the bridge.

A man, obviously the only person on board, secures his boat to a tree with a rope and heads to the bridge with a measuring tape in his hand. He hangs over and extends the tape to the bottom of the span, takes the reading and then extends it to the river's surface.

'Making sure I can get her under safely,' he volunteers and then adds, 'God there's plenty of room,' before returning to his stupidly cute boat.

A few minutes later the immaculate *Billy T*, Aussie flag limp on its stern is chuffing under the bridge. Later I look at my photograph and realise that apart from a pair of gas bottles at the side and some solar panels discreetly on the roof, this image could've been taken at any time in the last three-quarters of a century.

I watch *Billy T* disappear around a left bend in the river and realise it's time for a brew myself! It's not a total fire ban so I fire up the Trangia and fill the coffee plunger beside the silent river. Not a water bird in sight.

And then it's a quick trip west to rejoin the Murray Valley Highway and in 16 kilometres I'm hanging a right and then another quick right into the park beside the Tooleybuc Bridge.

I've a bundle of good memories of the Tooleybuc pub, but for now it's changed. I climb through the bush to get a shot similar to my oldest image of the pub, get some other drone photos of the bridge and check out the old punt master's cottage and then climb back on Super Ten.

Half an hour later I'm being forced into the dirt shoulder by a speeding B-double on the side road into Chislett Farms and the confluence where the Edward rejoins the Murray River. A bloke at Chislett Farms helps me find the track in and when I arrive a fella from the Victorian Rivers people is hauling out his dinghy after a day of surveying the river.

The river gums all wear markings – like the ankles of people who've been in the sun for too long wearing socks – showing the level of the last great flood, and today the waters of the two rivers are a similar shade. I look at the tip of land between the two rivers and wonder again just why this is not an island.

Then it's time to retrace. With the sun on my back, it's down the MVH to Nyah, across the bridge – this time with no cute boat adding value – then cutting through Tullakool to the home of the great ute muster.

CHAPTER 34 – DENILIQUIN

THE BUNCHA, THE GODFATHER AND THE EFFECTS OF BAD BRANDY

Deniliquin, top town on the Edward River, owes its existence to two things: very ordinary hotel service and the free-range activities of a scarcely scrupled Godfather figure who rode roughshod over anyone and anything that got in his way to business success, social influence and control of every level of the town.

In the early 1840s Benjamin Boyd established a run on the northern side of the Edward near one of the most easily crossed sections of this anabranch of the Murray. He named his run 'Denilikoon' after the leader the local Aboriginal tribe. Slowly it developed, but the crucial first step in the place's development toward being a settlement was the 1847 opening of the Wanderers Inn, named after Boyd's personal yacht and run by one of Boyd's lieutenants, Anthony Faulkner.

Faulkner didn't figure paying the licence fee for this outpost pub, beside the northern approach to the river crossing, was totally necessary and lost the place when two other Boyd employees, Bloxham and Daniels, took it over.

The Wanderers Inn slowly expanded and became the hub of the tiny township as it grew north of the river. It was the only place where meetings could be held, business conducted and the Bench of magistrates began holding hearings in the main bar. Made it easy to sit in judgement of others and then do the disrobed bench-to-bar-to-bed trip in a matter of staggered paces.

In 1854 the New South Wales Government Gazette of 31 March gave notice that:

NOTICE is hereby given, that a General Meeting of Justices of Petty Sessions acting in and for the Police District of Deniliquin, will be holden at McKenzie's, Wanderers Inn, at Deniliquin, on Tuesday, the eighteenth day of April, 1854, at the hour of noon, for the special purpose of taking into consideration such applications for Licenses as may be lodged with the undersigned.

Meanwhile on the south side of the Edward, a young bloke named John Taylor was having a real go. He started out as one of several shepherds working for a squatter and when one of his workmates left, Taylor offered to take over the second flock as well, but on double pay and double rations. When a second shepherd also quit, Taylor again stuck his hand up and again demanded the full entitlement. So now he was getting triple money, which he could save, and triple rations, which he couldn't eat. So he stored the surplus flour.

When drought hit after a couple of years in early 1850–51 Taylor sold the flour back to his boss for 300 quid, around ten times what he'd paid for it. That was serious money. With the £300 Taylor bought a couple of blocks of land on the south side of the river and when he saw how well the local Highlander Inn was doing, built up his abode with its ceilings not much higher than 2 metres from the floor, and obtained a licence for it in 1855.

John Taylor knew how to grease the right wheels of society, knew that employment meant power and pretty soon, with the cash flow from the pub, had opened a sawmill, some brick kilns, a blacksmith's and both butcher and baker shops.

His business ethics and practices are well illustrated by Bushby in his history of Deniliquin, when discussing just a fragment of his empire:

> Taylor was operating in opposition to an established blacksmith, Simpson ... who naturally resented the intrusion into yet another field.
>
> Simpson's price for shoeing was £1 per head but Taylor undercut him and the price gradually dropped to 2s per head, with the latter throwing in a glass of grog. Both men displayed signs showing their progressive new prices but these were being torn down ... Simpson ... advertised a reward of £25 for information leading to the identity of the culprit. Taylor called on Simpson admitting his guilt and claimed the reward.

The reward wasn't paid but, 'Taylor gained a great deal of amusement at his opposition's discomfiture.'

Back over at the Wanderers Inn, business was humming, and it must've been a nice little earner to have magistrates with their social elan staying at the pub and holding their hearings in the bar. But with a beast like John Taylor roaming the paddocks, it was too good to last. As a subsequent writer for the *Sydney Mail* recalled:

> The magistrates ... met on the north side in the Wanderers Inn ... there was then no court-house and there was scarcely a lock-up. Their worships, after dispensing justice one morning at the hotel ... took offence at the inferior brandy ... and the want of courtesy of the then landlady, so in a fit of high dudgeon the magistrates, without a moment's hesitation, appointed an hotel on the south side, at which they would henceforth hold their courts, so from that day the north township was doomed to be a village.

And that, is how rudeness and bad booze killed a town! That simple act is why the main guts of Deniliquin is still on the southern side of the Edward River. Well, probably with a little help.

The beaks didn't opt for the long-established Highlander Inn – no, they decided to bunk up at John Taylor's.

> An 1856 column in the *Sydney Morning Herald* on proceedings at the Deniliquin Petty Sessions noted that: *The Bench held its sitting at the Royal Hotel, South Deniliquin, where, for the present until the projected Court House is built the meetings of the magistrates will in future be held.*

> The Post Office has also been removed to this house.

The locally published *Pastoral Times* was no friend of Taylor and published, probably with tongue firmly in cheek, a 'Directory of Government House'. It ran:

> PUBLIC OFFICES – ROYAL HOTEL
>
> POST OFFICE – First window on right of hall between Parlour and Coffee room.
>
> TELEGRAPHIC OFFICE – third door on right down the yard past bar and Dining Room.
>
> POLICE SUPERINTENDENT'S OFFICE: First floor, turn right twice, No 1 on left at bottom of passage.
>
> POLICE BARRACKS – Ground floor, down the yard between kitchen and the stables.
>
> POLICE COURT – Between the bank and the lock-up, Taylors Hall.

John Taylor was in court almost weekly, as a plaintiff, as a witness and usually as the defendant. When facing a charge he would stand before magistrates who were staying free of any cost at this hotel, listen to evidence from police who were stationed on his property and call witnesses who were, in the main, his employees.

But Taylor craved not just influence, he ached for social acceptance. And he was canny enough to know he needed a rock solid spiritually pure facade to mask his business dealings. So he branched out on an evangelical and philanthropic quest to build, and therefore be identified with, the town's churches and social bastions.

In 1859 the *Wagga Wagga Express* reported that:

> Deniliquin for the last three days has been honoured by a visit of his honor the Chief Justice of Victoria, Sir William Stawell, and has been the guest of our worthy P.M., J. Kelly. Esq. During his stay here, he visited our different new buildings, the Church of England, the Catholic Chapel, Court-house,

Masonic Hall, which [are all] being rapidly built (by Mr. John Taylor of the Royal Hotel).

So the ducks were lined up for the Godfather of Deniliquin (note the initials). When you have a magistrate in your house, you have him in your pocket, and along with the police barracks paying you below-market rent you pretty much have an open licence to run as you wish. (The police hierarchy in Melbourne decided it judicious to remove the barracks from the Royal Hotel so Taylor responded by simply making the owner of their new home an offer they couldn't refuse and took it over.)

When John Kelly, the 'worthy' Police Magistrate who'd escorted the Chief Justice around the town, was dismissed for misappropriation of funds, the local paper reflected that any hope of a new dawn had been dashed:

A new magistrate, James Giles, was appointed. And when he arrived there was a backlog of cases against John Taylor: illegally crossing cattle over the Edward, for assault, for refusal to pay wages in money. The first case was dismissed and the others failed through Taylor's non-appearance. Thus the old order remained unchanged.

In 1864 William Gannon selected 295 acres under the Robertson Land Act on the north side of the river and spent the first year improving the property and erecting a cottage facing the road with the aim of opening an inn on the site.

By now Taylor had bought the Wanderers Inn and didn't want any competition so Taylor set Gannon up on a charge of selling liquor without a licence. The case was heard by James Giles PM, who at the time was living rent-free at Taylor's Royal Hotel. Giles decided the offence – which involved a stooge buying liquor and returning the bottle to local cop Senior Sergeant Devonald who happened to be accompanied by John Taylor – was proved.

Three weeks later Gannon applied for a licence. PM Giles claimed the supporting testimonial signed by fifty residents was a fake and the application was rejected on the grounds that Gannon had been convicted of selling grog without a licence. Gannon cut his losses and sold his farm and cottage. The cottage was converted to an inn and a licence was obtained for it in the name of the Carriers' Arms. The buyer was John Taylor.

Later that year Taylor heard that an outsider named Proctor had plans to open an inn further up the road so he grabbed one of his tenant cops and went for a ride. With Constable Scott hiding outside the shanty, Taylor went in, bought four glasses of gin, and whistled for the cavalry. Proctor was fined £30 and jailed for thirty days. With such a conviction there was zero chance of him ever getting a licence.

Then in 1867 Taylor and another bloke were charged with conspiring to drug a man named Whalon and extract from him a cheque for £70. As Bushby notes:

Taylor ... challenged so many jurors that men had to be called from the body of the court. Most of these were Taylor's employees – the jury returned a verdict of Not Guilty.

John Taylor, Godfather of Deniliquin, had free rein. But he overextended, made a few very wrong enemies and in 1870 the banks began circling. He was forced out of his jewel, the Royal Hotel.

(T)he contents of the Royal were offered at an immense furniture sale at the Highlander Inn in March 1870 ... the mortgagees, the Melbourne Trust and Agency Co bought the Royal Hotel for £3,900.

Taylor and an acquaintance were sued for conspiracy to defraud Taylor's creditors, and '(t)hey were convicted by the jury on what appeared clear evidence, and a sentence of two years' imprisonment, with hard labour, in Darlinghurst gaol was the denouement.'

And as Bushby almost wistfully records:

When Taylor crashed, the town crashed with him ... the mayor at the time went down with Taylor, having backed him on a 'note' when Taylor bought the Exchange Hotel. Giles, the Police Magistrate, was also in on the deal – he held the mortgage at 17½ per cent. The Pastoral Times *made the comment that 'Giles, P.M.' should be the name above the door [of the hotel].*

In April 1870 PM Giles sued the *Pastoral Times* for libel. A stream of witnesses testified:

... that Mr Giles was living on John Taylor without paying him anything for his board and lodging, I had no other particular reasons that I know of. I have heard it generally asserted through out the district that gentlemen avoided the hotel in consequence.

And:

It has been generally reported in the district that Mr Giles had been under obligations to John Taylor for accommodation received at his hotel.

And:

John Taylor was before the court two or three times a month, and always got off – there was always a loop hole for him to escape, or ... he received a very light sentence.

With Jones the publisher pleading 'truth and public benefit' and with Giles not having the jury sway enjoyed by his mate Taylor, the action failed.

John Taylor, Godfather of Deniliquin was out of business. The *Pastoral Times* ran an editorial:

Deniliquin ought to be one of the most flourishing of our country towns, but for monopoly, bribery and corruption. We defy any person to show that Deniliquin has a rival in the colonies.

The hangover of the original bad brandy served at the Wanderers Inn, beside the road leading to the northern approach to the river crossing, is clear to every traveller: the town followed the self-important magistrates across the river and stayed there.

The enduring legacy of the altruistic side of John Taylor, the original Godfather of the town, can be seen in the two churches and the Masonic Hall that he funded and had built. Any inheritance the place may retain of his business dealings, of his 'monopoly, bribery and corruption' is not the province of this yarn.

In October 1876 the local bench of magistrates met in Deniliquin and granted a licence to Henry Willmoor for a pub close to the northern bank of the Edward River at Denilquin. And as I sweep south toward the Deniliquin bridge, this same pub, officially known as the Edward River Hotel, is on my left. And inside the Godfather lives on. Well, sorta.

Behind the bar there's a stylised image of Marlon Brando as Vito Corleone in Francis Ford Coppola's timeless trilogy and a chalk scoreboard for the 'Godfather Challenge'. So what's that all about?

Chris, who's obviously got a poor mirror and an even more ordinary hairdresser, is behind the bar and in the shadow of Coppola's Don. With his partner, Taron, he took over the Buncha in 2016. It's their first pub and, with their four kids, they're settling in just fine.

He grew up in Hobart and, 'When I was eighteen there was a pizzeria and it was called the Godfather Pizzeria. And it was tiny and they did it all from scratch and they had this dinner-plate sized hamburger that they used to serve. It was a monster and what we used to do was on Friday nights we'd order one and take it home and eat half and then leave the other half and then go out. Then when we got home if we were in a state to eat it, we'd finish it off, otherwise we'd have it for breakfast.'

Chris thought it'd be an idea to have a food challenge at his new hotel.

'I didn't want to make it unfinishable, I wanted to make it a bit better presented than the one we used to get. It took us twelve different tries to get the nine-inch bun just right and then we just filled the baby up.'

Equalling about five standard with-the-lot burgers, and with sides of chips and onion rings, the burger is the challenge. It has to be eaten by one person with no limits on time or the amount of water or soft drink taken to wash it down. Get through it and not be in a food coma, you only pay ten bucks and your next two drinks are on the house.

Down it all fast enough to break into the top three, and you'll pay nothing, but be paid $50 instead. To do that, as it stands, you'll need to be licking the plate within half an hour of starting.

I cut mine into quarters – finished the first, plus a handful of chips and rings in just on four minutes. Was on championship pace! The second quarter took me almost ten minutes and I. WAS. BEATEN. The thing is a monster and I was no match.

I asked about the reigning champ:

'Matt was a local boy and that was his first attempt and he was doing the right thing and supporting his wife who went on a lettuce diet and she wanted him to join her on it for the week for some moral support. So he did and it got to Friday and they'd eaten nothing but lettuce and so Matt's wife said thank you so much, you can have a cheat night. So Matt knew about the Godfather here and he got on the phone and ordered one for seven o'clock and he turned up with a bit of a following and he walked in and it was ready and he cut it in half and didn't stop eating. Was extraordinary. His mates carried him out!'

Matt's time is almost two full minutes clear of the nearest challenger and then Chris wants to tell me about the tenth placed athlete, listed as (Korean Guy).

'He was amazing. Was a real slim guy and he just went for it and I wasn't watching all the time and when he got through it I checked his bag and under the table and in the bathroom to see if he'd stashed some of it somewhere but nah, he'd eaten it all. Best pound for pound performer so far by a mile.'

If you're tempted to face up to the Godfather of burgers, ring ahead as they take an hour to 'assemble'. And bring a friend to help you once you've surrendered to the bun!

Chris knows the story of this place, is keen to show me the old photos on the wall and explain how the renovations and extensions were added and the outside grounds subdivided. And he knows the story behind the most mythical episode in this pub's history and how, after 100 years of being The Edward River, it became known to one and all simply as 'The Buncha'.

'What I was told by Alan Christian who had it from '81 to '83 was it happened about ten years before he took it over and the town drunk used to drink here and he would turn up, get drunk, play up, get kicked out. Happened every day. Every day the same thing.

'This one time he came in and pulled a bar runner when a bloke down the bar was about to grab his drink and the drink fell over and so he got kicked out and as he was walking out he grabbed a big burning log out of the fire and threw it onto the bar and turned around on his way out and said, "You mob are nothing but a buncha". So that caused a bit of commotion and they cleaned it all up and no-one saw him for a couple of years, they think he went to another town maybe. Anyway in those days they had about maybe forty or fifty regular drinkers all day every day and a couple of years later someone saw him outside walking past the pub and they were wondering if he was going to come in for a drink. So he suddenly swung around and came down and opened the front door and shouted, "You mob are still nothing but a buncha ..." closed the door and walked off.

'Everyone in the bar had a great old laugh and a lot of them went home and told their families and then their friends and the story got passed down and so the place just became known as "The Buncha".'

'The Buncha' isn't the only valuable contribution the Deniliquin drinking set has made to the Australian vernacular. In August 1856 the *Sydney Morning Herald* ran the first report I've come across about hooning on the streets. Its story about two drunks on a single horse introduced a wonderful new word:

Two lushingtons were charged with being drunk and with furiously riding through the township of South Deniliquin. They were both riding on one horse, and the Court fined 'the man in the saddle' 40s., and his mate 20s., or 43 hours' imprisonment. The fines were paid.

Ah, 'lushingtons' – Deniliquin we are in your debt!

Anyway, it was lucky that the Buncha even existed. In the great floods of 1917 and of 1956, the water flowed through the bar. Chris reckons:

'The place was sandbagged at the doors but they opened the windows to let the water in or the windows would've broken under the force of the water. The bar was all under water and the publican was in here with a half full keg that was floating and an old pluto portable beer tap having a beer ... just kept serving and a couple of regulars were in here soaking it all up.

The pub survived the swirling waters but then just four years later it faced a very different threat, this time from the Licenses Reduction Board. The inspector advised the court that:

the hotel contained 12 bedrooms, four of which were used by the family. There were three parlors, a dining-room, billiard room (un-used), kitchen, a 12-stall stable, and six loose boxes ... [and that it was] ... clean and fairly well furnished, but in his opinion it was not required for the convenience of the travelling public. [It was] principally used by working men. The licensees of the Royal and Tattersall's hotels did not provide accommodation for the second-class population.

In reply, Mrs Donovan, who obviously knew her business and was aware of the priority courts put on accommodation over liquor sales testified:

... she was the licensee of the Edward River hotel since the death of her husband In March of this year. She had a lease of the premises until 6th August, 1924. She had five permanent boarders, and had accommodation

for 18 or 19. The premises were always full at week-ends. She received more from boarders and lodgers than she did from the bar.

Her arguments were persuasive and the pub survived, while five others in the town, the Royal Mail, Victoria, Union Club, Oddfellows and the Carriers' Rest (quite possibly the old pub kidnapped by Taylor) were ordered shut down.

The 'second-class population' still had a place to go in Deni and one winter evening fours years later in July 1925 members of this outcast group assembled at the Edward River Hotel:

NEW A.L.P. BRANCH

At a meeting of the electors of Deniliquin, held on July 18 at Donovan's Edward River Hotel, it was unanimously decided to form a branch of the A.L.P. Mr. Arthur Sullivan was appointed President and Mr. John Donovan Secretary. As this part of the Riverina is practically unorganised, much good is expected to be done by the new branch.

Another four years cemented the relationship of the pub's patrons and publicans with the 'second-class':

At a meeting of the Deniliquin branch of the A.L.P., on Friday evening, Mr J. Donovan, of The Edward River Hotel was chosen as the Deniliquin nominee for the pre-selection ballot to determine which shall be the selected Labor candidate for the Murray seat at the next election.

The wheel had turned. Once again a publican was seeking political influence, only this time he was going through the front door.

Chris reckons there's not a lot of politics spoken in the pub. He's not sure if it's because people are too busy trying to eat things bigger than their heads or if they're watching out for madmen chucking burning logs onto the bar. But he is sure that the brandy and all the drinks he serves, and the service he and his staff provide is right up there with the best. And thinking back to the magistrates who decamped from the Wanderers he smiles and says, 'But this time you can be the judge.'

CHAPTER 35 – PRETTY PINE

HOW TREES GROW AND HANGING (OUT) FOR A BEER

The first time I came to Pretty Pine was back in 2010 and I had trees on my mind. Specifically gum trees and how they grow. I'd known since high school science they grow one way, basically from the top. In fact I was certain of it, but then, on the way down from Lockhart I'd dropped into a famous old property researching a passion of mine, the great shearers' strikes of the 1880s.

The boss wasn't home but he'd left his fourteen-year-old son to look after me and show me around the old shearing shed and wool scour pond. This was the spot where, in 1888, the Riot Act was read for the first time in New South Wales when the station was owned by the anti-unionist, William Halliday, the Chris Corrigan of his time.

Then the fella asked if I'd like to see the shear tree. 'The what?'

He took me across from the shed and over to a massive old gum, I'm guessing it was a spotted gum.

'When the boss refused to employ unionists in the strike and they started arresting the shearers, one of them turned around and wrapped his shears around the tree and said, "well I won't be needing these".' He pointed up the trunk about 5 metres, 'And now they're risen right up there and are inside the tree mostly.'

I peered up and there, about 30 centimetres apart, standing out like nipples, were the very tips of a pair of old shears. Obviously they'd been wrapped around the stripling tree which, over the 130 years since, has enveloped the clippers and no doubt broken their back in a way that Halliday had broken the spirit of their owners.

Fascinating, but no. He was too nice a kid to argue with, so I took my photos and thanked him for his time and headed into Deni with trees in my head. See, I'd been taught way back in school that a distinguishing feature between shrubs and grasses is that shrubs (and trees) grow from the top while grasses grow from the bottom. That's why bamboo is a grass.

And yet here was this earnest young fella telling me that these shears had ascended the tree as it grew, rising maybe 3 metres or a bit more in the century plus since they were placed around its narrow limbs. I could get my head around them being broken as the trunk gained girth, but back then the tree to be that slim to have the shears wrapped around it, wouldn't have, couldn't have been that tall.

And besides, the trunk blazings of the explorers have never risen since they were cut into the bark. The scars of Indigenous canoe and waddy trees remain at the height they were originally cut. It had to be wrong.

I filed it under 'things to be investigated further' as I headed to the historical museum to meet a bloke who'd promised to help me researching some other stuff.

Bill Muleham was a giant of Deniliquin. A gently spoken, erudite, immensely knowledgeable man, as generous with his time as he was masterful in his understanding of the events and forces of the past. Unfortunately, Bill has passed away and the town and the region are much the poorer.

That day Bill went through the old copies of the *Pastoral Times* that he had filed and well-guarded in his offices, and filled in all the blanks I had on many issues. Then at the end, he asked me where I was headed and when I told him it was Pretty Pine, he urged me to, 'have a look at the old shear tree out there'.

I'd not mentioned my morning to Bill so I feigned ignorance of such things.

'In 1914 when one of the young shearers from out there was off to join the army, his mates had a picnic for him on the side of the road to Pretty Pine. At the end of it he turned and cut his shears into the side of a young gum tree saying, 'I'll leave 'em here till I get back.' He never returned.

Bill gave me detailed instructions on finding the tree but then warned, 'As the tree's grown they've gone up with it, so you'll have to look up about six yards or so.'

Now Bill was a bloke I was comfortable being sceptical with so I told him about my morning, about a tree he'd not previously been aware of, and I told him about bamboo, grass and stationary blaze marks.

But Bill was adamant. The *Pastoral Times* had a reporter at the shindig, and there was a piece in the paper about it. If the soldier had stood on his horse or if he'd thrown them high up into the tree, the reporter would've written that as part of the story. No, they were inserted at chest level and have gone up the tree as it's got bigger.

We both had other commitments so Bill couldn't find the clipping. I headed north from Deni, followed Bill's directions, and right where he told me, pulled up the bike and looked at the gums. Bill's shear tree was the first one I inspected. It was different to the morning's – one blade was fully visible whilst the other fully embedded, this time, I guessed in some sort of ironbark. Strangely, disconcertingly, the shears were at a very similar height to the first nipple pair. Something's going on.

Since then I've found other shear trees, along the rivers and in the dry outback and I've heard a dozen explanations. Not a single one of them is totally satisfactory. Not one of them explains each detail and leaves no contradiction. For me shear trees remain an enigma of the bush, part of the rich mysteries of the unknown.

In the afternoon light in October, the pub at Pretty Pine looks misnamed – Gorgeous Jacaranda Hotel would be hugely more apposite. Just to the right of the main entrance a beautiful specimen is peacocking its purple display against the lowering sun.

In the car park, beside the Cobb Highway a pair of John Deere headers, their trays tucked in behind, is parked together with the wide-load warning ute. Inside three blokes are chatting to Denise – joint boss of the place with her partner, Twang – who's behind the bar. They still have to get the combines another 40 kilometres over to Conargo before dark and then they'll be heading back in the ute, hopefully in time for tea. They're from Rowena and they're another face of the drought that's ripping into the country:

'We've all got our own farms carrying wheat, chickpeas and barley but we haven't sown at home for two years. We've come down to try to find some work down here to pay some of the bills. Had a little bit over at Warracknabeal near Horsham but then there was a late frost and that put us out of business and then we did some for a bloke over at Carrathool. He's actually from Narrabri and we knew him from there and he gave us a few days' work. The same bloke has some land over at Conargo so we're walking the headers over to there. We started out at Warracknabeal and doing 30 kilometres an hour it's a pretty decent trip.'

Yep. Decent. Three decent blokes forced to leave their families and their properties to go searching for work where the grass is just that bit greener. Denise is almost aghast that they'd think they might miss out on some chaff.

'Whenever you get back, I'll make you dinner. Don't rush, you'll get a feed!' Relieved, they smile and head out for the last stretch to the town where, just weeks after the breweries cut off credit a few years back, the pub burnt down.

Denise reassuringly sees them out as you would guests from your home then hurries back to make sure there's a stool at the end of the bar, just around its corner.

'Nipper's just parking.'

Nipper lives across the road on the site of the old school but cardio issues mean he drives over. Later he confesses, 'I could walk back because alcohol thins my blood like aspirin and I'm good for the trip home but it's getting over there when I've not had a drink that's the problem.'

Yep, makes sense.

Anyway, he sits down on his perch and gets his stubby without having to tell Jade, an Irish visitor who's also working tonight, what he wants.

'I only ever have to tell them once, on the first day each of 'em is here,' he explains with the laid-back comfort of a man who's right at home. 'From then on they know that I don't drink anything else.'

Especially not stubbies of VB.

'They're the old-style stubbies with the short neck and I'm used to these new stubbies with the longer necks. So when I have a VB I keep coming up short and missing my mouth. Too messy!'

Jade, whose surname happens to be the same as mine, pulls me a beer from the taps on the back wall and I ask what's in the cookie jar on the high shelf of the back wall.

They're homemade brownies and Canadian Rebecca, the other backpacker currently working here, but who tonight's having a shift off and is on this side of the bar here chimes in, 'The last backpacker working here was also Canadian and she missed her grandmother's brownies so she asked for the recipe and then made up a batch and they were popular so when she left I took over the brownie-making role.'

Nipper's not into the brownies and reckons they can't be too crash hot. I ask him why and again his barristerial logic shines through:

'If they were any good, the jar'd be empty.'

I ask him about 'his' stool and he reckons he's not protective or territorial about it, at least not like some blokes get. 'I remember the Colosseum in Heidelberg in Melbourne when it first opened and a guy walked out and said, "You're in my chair", and I said, "You have to be joking", and all the people in the bar stopped talking and were looking at me, so I moved. That place was a blood house.'

He smiles at the memories. 'But it never got any of my blood!'

Nipper was four years old when he started coming up from Melbourne to Pretty Pine with his dad who was a mad keen fisherman. Each time they'd spend time in the pub but it wasn't until he was sixteen that he had his first drink.

On one of the walls is a laminated list of all the publicans and the first Nipper can remember is Phyllis Lotty who had the pub from 1965–67. She was the woman who served him his first beer and as we go through the list of owners, Nipper has a story about each and can name their partners.

'Most of 'em left because their marriages broke down. There was a lot of jumping over the back fence by neighbours to visit the wife whilst the husband was busy or away in Hay or Denny.'

He laughs, 'Yes, a lot of that went on and every time they'd get caught and suddenly the pub'd be on the market again.'

After he left school, which was some time before the scheduled graduation, Nipper found a job in a paper mill in Melbourne working four days on, four days off, and pretty much each time he'd pack the car and head to Pretty Pine.

'I had no licence and the car had no rego. We'd just lift the rego sticker off the family caravan and stick in on the windscreen and I did that for years, never got caught, never got stopped.'

When he was fifteen he met Jill and fell in love. A year later a mate told him about temporary tattoos and he thought it'd be an idea to get one.

'I was told they'd last three years and then just fade away. Did it myself. Just an ordinary sew-up-your-pants needle and then you wrap cotton around the bottom of it and dip it into a bottle of Indian ink and jab, jab, jab. Hurt more than you realise. A few of us did it and of course they didn't fade, but truly when you're that age, they made you feel ten per cent tougher.'

They got married in a traditional shot-gun wedding at Moonee Ponds one Friday night and on the Saturday he packed the car and had a solo honeymoon at Pretty Pine. The marriage ended on the Monday but the fruit of the union, Nipper's daughter still visits him regularly.

He went to work in a wastepaper place in Melbourne, 'and we used to get piles of brand-new books and magazines that the newsagents hadn't sold and I'd put some aside and bring them up here and leave 'em at the pub for people to read. I used to have a huge collection of *Playboy* and *Penthouse* still in their plastic covers but my second wife – well I call her my but we never got married – anyway she stole them when she left. They'd be worth a million bucks now.'

Nipper, it's clear, hasn't been too lucky in love.

And he may not've been busted for driving without all those times he'd use the caravan's rego to fool the cops, but that's not to say he's managed to avoid the law like he did his last three years of school. For many years he rode motorbikes.

'Once I got pulled up leaving here when I was about nineteen and I was on a Triumph Daytona 500 I think it was and my mate had an Austin 1100. We were all going to the Globe Hotel in Deni so off we go and I'm flat chatting it and then slowing down to get some clear road and then flat chatting it again and one of the exhaust pipes started coming out of the cylinder. Anyway this car came up behind me and looked like they wanted a drag so I flat chatted it and the pipe blew off but I kept in front of the car for fair way until it overtook me. It was a Mini Cooper S and it was the copper from Deni.'

Nipper got pulled over and pleaded his case. The cop was decent and told him he'd bury the bluey for a year or so and if Nipper kept out of mischief for that long, he'd chuck it.

'Eighteen months later I was up here in a car and had a local sheila with

me and this local bloke saw the sheila and came over to the car and asked her what she was doing in a car with a desperate like me. I said who're you calling a desperate and turned out he was a detective at Denny, probably the boyfriend of the girl. Anyway when I got back to Melbourne the next week a letter arrived telling me to front court up at Deni for speeding eighteen months before. So the D's gone back to the station and dug up the ticket and decided to get even with me for having his girl in my car. Cost me seventy bucks and that was a week's pay in those days. Lot of money. The mongrel.'

Irish Jade, like, she reckons, all the travellers who lob at the Pretty Pine hotel, is going to be sad leaving this place when her time's up. When times are quiet in the bar, Denise and Twang ring around for properties that can use a free hand.

Jade's found herself helping at harvests and rousing in the sheds at shearing time. She's even been on the long paddock for a bit, moving cattle.

'I'm going to be getting back to my mates in Melbourne, who've done nothing much but earn money on one side of the bar and spend it on the other, with all these amazing stories about life in the bush. When I get home people won't believe some of the stuff I've been up to and about how good the people all are.'

I tell her and Canadian Rebecca that it's not always been a friendly place for strangers and that a part of me wishes they were French.

The first 'watering hole' on the road north from Deniliquin was at the 'Eight Mile' for which a bloke named Coleman obtained a new licence in 1866. He transferred the freehold three years later to George and Charlotte (sometimes known as 'Grace') Stephenson who changed the name to Carriers' Arms and it became, let's say, not known for being genteel, refined, peaceful or law abiding.

In 1871 George Stephenson and a mate were charged with the murder of a woman guest at the inn and Stephenson, who beat the charge, was stripped of his licence but not of his ownership of the property. In 1873 Robert Holloway, a Cobb & Co driver, took over the lease and renamed the place Hit or Miss. If he'd considered the behaviour of his landlord, he may well've considered calling it the 'Hit the Miss' instead.

In addition to the murder charge of 1871, Stephenson was fined for drunkenness, obscene language and resisting arrest in 1872; rape in 1879; rape again in 1880; obscene language in 1883; furious driving in 1884; and domestic violence against his wife in 1884. This is a bloke who's termed,

'known to police', and I'm not even alleging, this is his full rap sheet.

Later in 1884 the place closed down. Its infamy though lives on.

Meanwhile the location of what's now Pretty Pine was originally known as 'The Junction' for its location where the road north from Deniliquin forks – north for Wanganella and Hay, and west for Moulamein. Later, in 1887, the *Pastoral Times* ran an explanation of the name change:

> *... about 25 years ago a certain well-known judge ... made a habit of stopping the [Cobb & Co] coach at this particular [spot with the] tree when travelling from Deniliquin to Hay ... and would invite other passengers ... to a seat and a picnic under ... 'the pretty pine tree'.*

Gradually the name shifted and when Robert Holloway, who'd run Stephenson's blood house down the road, opened his own inn at the junction in 1875, he named it in honour of the Pretty Pine. From then the name of the place was assured.

Holloway died in 1878 and the Pretty Pine Inn was taken over by his wife, Anastasia, who must've had a thing for Cobb & Co whip men, marrying another coach captain, Matthew Hole, in 1881.

The pub pretty much kept out of the papers and under whatever quiet places and things kept before the radar was invented, for the next twenty-five years or so. There was the odd inquest held there of travellers who'd died, and notices in the papers when licensees changed.

The first time the pub hit the big city papers was in 1882 when Anastasia Hole made 'an imputation of unchastity' against one of her staff and the Sydney papers reported on the resulting slander trial. Damages were claimed for £200 but after the jury found for the servant, she was awarded just £30 and costs, indicating, obviously the judge considered her 15 per cent as pure as she made out.

But then, as the Melbourne *Argus* later reported, in October 1883 a:

> *... hawker, named, 'Mizon' was returning home to Victoria, after a long trip through New South Wales, with his waggon and two horses on the day of the murder he called at the Pretty Pine Hotel, in Company with a teamster, whom he treated and with whom he left ... The hawker shortly afterwards reached Stephenson's shanty, two miles nearer Deniliquin, where he stayed the greater part of the day.*

Not long after the hawker left the Pretty Pine a Frenchman arrived at the pub, 'but being already drunk the landlord refused to supply him. He then walked on to Stephenson's, and was seen staggering along the road in that direction.'

The *Sydney Morning Herald*, in a detailed report, informed its shocked readers that the next day Mizon was found dead:

The body was found yesterday, covered with sheepskins, alongside of a waggon. Indications in the vicinity of the wagon point to the fact that Mizon was sitting in the vehicle when the fatal blow was struck, and that the body was dragged to the opposite side of the waggon from the road, and then covered with sheepskins and bags.

Two local coppers, Sargent Rowe and Constable Burrowes, grabbed an Aboriginal tracker, Mitchell, and headed out to investigate. The police found the body and a 'shingling hammer ... covered with blood, with apparently human hair attached to it. I also found the stick produced about ten yards from the waggon. It has hair on it and a little blood.'

Tracker Mitchell found two sets of footprints – those of a man and of a woman.

An inquest was soon held and:

Mathew Hole, licensee of the Pretty Pine hotel, stated the deceased came to his hotel on Wednesday morning, had two drinks, and went away about 11 o'clock. His horses, with the harness on, came back to the hotel at about 12 o'clock at night. A foreigner was at the hotel for about five minutes in the morning, and left in the direction of Deniliquin.

But the more telling evidence firstly came from George Stephenson, keeper of the Eight Mile blood house who swore:

the deceased was at his house about a mile and a half from Pretty Pine on Wednesday at 2 o'clock. He left between 3 and 4 o'clock. A foreigner was also there at that time. A fight took place between him and the hawker. Witness separated them. The hawker took a shingling hammer from his waggon to protect himself.

And from his wife, Charlotte who claimed that:

The foreigner ... went away but before going he said he would murder the hawker, whom he had known in Victoria, and had it in for him, and would burn witness's place down.

The regional press noted even at this early stage that Stephenson and his wife were 'evidently prevaricating for some unknown reason' and that they 'had told different stories relative to their dealings with the deceased.'

Five days after the body was discovered Joseph Cordini, a French national, was arrested in the Kangaroo Hotel at Mathoura after trying to cash several cheques which'd been traced to the dead hawker. He was remanded to Deniliquin Gaol.

During his four months in prison, Cordini was given no access to an interpreter, no support from the French consul in Sydney and no legal representation for him was appointed.

Cordini went to trial on 17 April 1884. The first major witness for the prosecution was George Stephenson who, under cross-examination, 'admitted that he had been tried for one murder, and also had been suspected by a coroner's jury of murdering his first wife.' (Curiously the instrument of choice in both these murders was a tomahawk.)

The second major prosecution witness was Stephenson's wife, whose testimony to the coroner had, '(been) given in a very unsatisfactory manner, and the fact was severely commented on by the coroner.'

Meanwhile, the one witness who could've thrown shade on these two shadies, tracker Mitchell who'd identified tracks belonging to a male and a female, wasn't called to give evidence and his findings weren't mentioned. The fix was on.

The jury deliberated for just on thirty minutes before returning a 'guilty' verdict. Judge Windeyer in passing sentence said:

Prisoner, it is useless to deny your guilt. It is certain that you committed the crime of which you have been found guilty, and I am glad to find that the jury have found as they have done. Your statements were lies from the beginning, and only children could pay any attention to what you might say.

Mr R. W. Pennefather, the barrister who'd been appointed to defend Cordini but who'd only been granted access to his client the day before the trial was so incensed by the process, by the trial and by decision, that he petitioned the government and the French government representatives in Sydney.

The case was debated in the New South Wales parliament and provoked an inter-colonial slanging match between the newspapers of Victoria (who attacked the decision) and New South Wales (who defended it). It was all as pointless as sowing good seeds on bad soil. Joseph Cordini was hanged in Deniliquin Gaol on Friday, 13 June 1884.

About twenty spectators were present, including the press and medical men. A considerable number of persons collected outside the gaol walls ... The condemned man, with his arms pinioned, left the cell on the stroke of nine, and ascended the platform of the gallows with a firm step, accompanied by the executioner and clergymen ... On the drop being reached, the cap was immediately pulled down over his eyes, but at the request of Father Hanley, was removed, as he thought Cordini might wish to say something. The cap was then taken off, when the condemned man made the following statement:– 'I did not hurt anyone, and I do not know anything about it, and as you can all see, and that is all I know about it.'

The reports even gave the technical details, noting that 'the fall measured between 8 and 9 feet'.

The day after Cordini was judiciously murdered, J. W. H. Wyse, editor of the *Pastoral Times* interviewed 'Nosey Bob' the executioner. (I'm guessing the chat didn't begin with, 'So, how're they hanging?')

He'd inherited his nickname after a horse kicked him in the face while Bob was driving a Hansom cab back in Sydney. He shared insights into his work and stressed the importance of hang time and hand distance. '(Cordini) was allowed 7 feet 6 inches. He was 10 stone ... [and] ... took a deal of stretching ... if I'd given him two more inches his head would have come off.'

The *Pastoral Times* (probably wisely) thought the interview so sensitive that they delayed publication for nine years.

This was the third and last execution at Deni Gaol and in a nice touch each of the three had been given his own bespoke scaffold. Reports failed to mention the type of wood used.

Jade pours us another round for Nipper and me as the blokes from Rowena come through the door, and with the headers safely parked over at Conargo, it's time for a feed and a cold one or several.

Denise grabs their food orders and disappears out the back; when I float the question of how things grow and explain about the shear trees, it's like striking a match in a tinderbox. No two people have the same opinion. I show 'em shots of the Pretty Pine tree just down the road. They've not seen it before but are pretty much agreed that in 1914 it wouldn't have been as tall as where the shears are hanging. But trees don't push up from the bottom so the shears are fakes. Added recently.

I show 'em the shots from the old station. They can't have been late additions. It's agreed the tree would need a century to envelop them as it has. But again they're sceptical of their height from the ground and the tree being that tall in the 1880s.

As we're all laughing about the conflicting theories and I'm telling them it's somehow fitting to be having this discussion in a place called Pretty Pine that actually features a pretty jacaranda, Denise fronts with feeds for the header fellas.

'We've actually got a little pine tree out the front that hardly grows in any direction because our goat keeps escaping from out the back and eats the thing.'

'You've got a pet goat?'

'Yeah, we've got a billy,' the boss explains and then sums up the glorious craziness of this place where trees grow backwards, a massive island just down the road isn't considered an island and where innocent people are hanged on the word of criminal publicans: 'His name's "Horse".'

CHAPTER 36 – THROUGH MOULAMEIN

ALONG THE EDWARD

About 9 kilometres west of Pretty Pine I bend left onto the Old Morago Road to again check out the old shear tree in different light. Its secrets and mystery remain mute so a right onto Eastmans and it's not long before I've rejoined Pretty Pine Road.

Soon on the left is the sign for Barratta Woolshed and then for the homestead. This extraordinary station property, started by the Gwynne Brothers in the 1840s was the venue for one of the great literary soirees in our history. It's where three true Australian writing icons: Frank Clune (our first great travel writer and author of such titles as *Try Anything Once, Rolling Down the Lachlan, Roaming Round the Darling* and *Try Nothing Twice*), Miles Franklin (*My Brilliant Career*) and Patrick John Hartigan (John O'Brien) who wrote *Around the Boree Log,* once met by happenstance. Today both the still-working woolshed and the homestead – a series of buildings built around a central lawn – are beautifully maintained but hell it'd great to have them host visitors and some sort of annual literary event.

Half an hour later I'm at Moulamein with its fabulous old wharf again giving sad hints to the heights to which the river once regularly rose.

In 1855 Scottish immigrant Lachlan McBean bought Woorooma which I'd passed ten minutes east of the town for £12,000 '… all the money in gold which he took over from Adelaide to Melbourne personally, most of it in a leather belt which he wore, this being done to save the exchange.'

He did quite nicely thanks and scored himself a knighthood. When he died in 1894, in addition to landholdings in four states, he owned both the pubs then in town – the Royal and the Moulamein Hotel.

One niece, Mary Ann, was given the first pub and another niece, Isabella, inherited the other. The Royal was in prime position, across the road from the wharf where I park Super Ten. Isabella must've known her business because forty years later, when the pub was completely rebuilt, reports still listed her as the owner.

But its days of glory are gone – shuttered and bolted and seemingly deserted, a flaking painted sign, fading under each morning sun, the scant reminder of its existence.

Diagonally across, Tattersalls is struggling along. When I first lobbed back, probably around 2010, the guts of the place, its bar and its back rooms were stunning – well-maintained and well-staffed. Old images including the classic 'Bogged' by the 'Pommy Jackaroo', Reginald William Sharpless, including an accompanying framed explanation of its photographer and how he came to take this iconic image at Willandra Creek in 1925, crowded the walls.

The last time I rocked up an itinerant from Europe was basking in the afternoon sun, doing her nails, and would I mind waiting for the lacquer to dry? The patterned glass windows, chipped and holed back then, are still needing fixing and many of the images, including the Sharpless explanation, have vanished.

After checking out the old courthouse I head over the river and yes, the 'big tree' is big. Then west on the Balranald Road, the Edward kissing the road a dozen or so times and countless tantalising tracks leading off into the bush where cognoscenti no doubt gather for good times out.

And then around a right sweeper the Kyalite Pub – get that right, it's not the Kyalite Hotel – emerges on my right.

CAMELS, DIVORCES AND MORE SHOOTINGS

Three months after I finally got around to interviewing Ken, co-owner of this pub with his partner Victorine, after being here maybe half a dozen times, I dropped in again.

It was around noon on a scorcher. A bloke I didn't recognise was at the bar. Turned out he was Vic's brother. Three weeks after I'd last been here, and just two days before the thirty-year anniversary of the couple owning the pub, Ken stood up, cried out in pain and fell. The ambos came fast but couldn't save him.

I went out the back where Vic was packing and cleaning. She'd found a buyer, a caring good couple from Balranald who were taking over the place. She was glad to know it'd be in good hands. Apparently they even like Victorians.

I tell her how sorry I am and she looks at me. 'I had to sell it. I just couldn't bear to stay here with the memories.'

Vale, Ken. Your special character will be missed.

One of Australia's first high-profile divorces was very messy. It involved the usual allegations of mental cruelty but, sensationally, it also centred on charges by one party of several instances of inappropriate behaviour by the other with a camel. In fact, more than one camel. And the first alleged occurrence of this shameful behaviour with said camels was at the river at Wakool, across the road from where the Kyalite Pub now stands.

The 1860 dissolution of the Burke–Landells relationship transfixed and scandalised the entire country.

In 1858 George Landells was in the business of exporting horses from Melbourne to India and was looking for cargo to fill his ship's holds on the return journey. He heard the colony's government was considering a camel-breeding program and Landells wrote to the powers suggesting they commission him to import some from the subcontinent. They took up his offer and when Landells's ship returned from Karachi, thirty-two camels were glad to be back on firm ground.

Meanwhile, the Royal Society of Victoria had been having trouble raising funds for the expedition of Burke and Wills but by the time the camels arrived, the delayed departure was imminent. The breeding program of Ferdinand at the Botanical and Zoological Gardens was put on hold and Burke was permitted to take his pick of the humpbacks.

Burke proved not to be greedy, only taking twenty-six of the thirty-two. The Royal Society decided the camels needed expert care and appointed Landells to the expedition on higher pay than the leader. Probably a wrong move. These two had just met and apparently things went fine until Burke tried to load the camels to a degree that mahout Landells objected, and as the group headed north after leaving Melbourne on 20 August 1860, the relationship between Burke and Landells went south.

Long story short, Landells stuck it out for a bit under four months and the group was near Menindee where he penned his resignation:

Upon mature consideration, I have arrived at the conclusion that my only course under recent and present circumstances is to tender the resignation of the appointment I now hold under you as second of the expedition under your orders.

I beg, therefore, to adopt that course upon the understanding that sufficient time be allowed me to permit my reaching Melbourne, the spot from whence I commenced my present duties (say a fortnight) as I shall have to travel slowly until I reach Swan Hill where I hope to find the mail coach. I hope you will not deem me too exacting in requesting a certificate that I have performed my duties well up to this date.
    G Landells

A month later George faced an extraordinary meeting of the Exploration Committee and sheeted it all back to the camels and to Wakool.

... permit me to refer again to the chief point of my complaint – viz., [Burke's] constant interference with me in the management and movements of the camels: even Wills was allowed to interfere. And here I feel I cannot do better than quote instances in point from my journal:-
    While crossing the Wakool Punt, Wills's interference with my arrangements in disembarking the camels caused an accident to one of them, and nearly led to its total loss.

Maybe Burke and Wills should've left the crossing of the camels to the expert and taken themselves up the cliff for a drink. Four years earlier John Talbett had advised all and sundry that he'd opened a 'first-rate Punt on the Wakool River' and that he was one of the fabled 'Pub 'n' Punters', also being the owner the adjacent Wakool Inn.

If they'd delegated and had a cold ale, things might've turned out differently. And by 'differently' I mean better.

Anyway, they all moved unharmoniously north, leaving John (sometimes referred to as 'Henry') Talbett (sometimes called 'Talbot' or 'Talbott') to run his pub beside the Wakool, variously named the Edward and the Kyalite River.

The year after the desperates and their dromedaries had crossed his path, Talbott's own path was crossed by the court at Balranald where he was censured 'for misconducting his house, and warned that his license would not be again renewed unless the police reported a considerable improvement in his establishment.'

Talbott took it on board and didn't get the cops offside. Good move, because nine months later, in January 1862, the Wakool Inn and the Balranald police were in contact again.

On Thursday night, the 9th instant, Henry Talbott's Wakool Inn, situated on the Wakool River, in the police district of Balranald, was 'stuck-up' by two armed men, who, after a severe struggle, in which the barman received two shots – one in the hand, the other in the shoulder succeeded in robbing the house of considerable property. The Balranald police, on receipt of the news, at once started in pursuit and on Saturday captured the two men on the Poon run, who answered to the descriptions they had received of the offenders. Some of the stolen property was found on them. One man has been identified as the man whose shot took effect in the barman's hand.

Unlike back at Pretty Pine where Cordini (variously called 'Cordene' or 'Gordon' or 'Gordini') was stitched up for a killing he had no part in by the actual murderers, abetted by a judge who took the path of least resistance and was happy with wasting the life of a foreigner, this time the right person had been fingered and justice was brutally swift.

In April:

Benjamin Allerton was indicted for assaulting, in company with some other person unknown, David Elliott and Henry Talbot, near Balranald, putting them in bodily fear and robbing them. It appeared that Talbot kept the Wakool inn, and Elliott was in his employ. Allerton and another man came there, and, after having supper, produced pistols, and 'stuck up' and robbed both Talbot and Elliott. The latter, in making an attempt to wrest the pistol from the prisoner's hand, was shot in the hand and back.

The verdict was 'guilty'. The sentence was 'death'.

In May:

ON Monday the last dread penalty of the law was carried into effect on ... Benjamin Allerton, convicted of shooting at and wounding David Elliott, at the Wakool Inn, in the Deniliquin district ... The requisite preparations being completed, the bolt was withdrawn, and [Allerton] passed from this world. [He] struggled violently for about twenty seconds, and when taken down was found to have died from strangulation.

That's probably enough information from the scaffold but when I mention it to Blinky at the bar of the Kyalite Pub he tells me the place's maintained the relationship with the police up in Balranald. He promises to tell me a story about a shooting down here later but meantime:

'In the old days here the publican, when there was a big night planned, like an all-nighter, would ring up the cops up at Balranald and tell them there was big trouble brewing up at the Homebush pub (about 30 kilometres north of Bal). So they'd all head up there and the party would rage all night.'

Problem was that the host up at the Homebush twigged and started returning the compliment and the police would begin turning up at Kyalite, and they weren't often happy.

'So they agreed on a ceasefire and everyone, specially the coppers, was happy.'

Blinky fell out of the back of a ute on his eighteenth birthday, puncturing his left eye on a piece of wire.

'I broke every bone in my head and spent the next six weeks in hospital. The only thing that saved me was that I was so drunk and relaxed when I hit the ground, and for the first ten days I was in total darkness and wasn't allowed to move. They got some photos of me so they could recreate my face and they did a pretty good job. They did their best but couldn't save my eye and the doctor told me that two eyes are a luxury, one is a necessity and to look after what I had.'

As soon as he was sort of fixed, he headed back to shearing and just a couple of days later someone in the shed dropped the nickname on him and he's been 'Blinky' ever since. I'd let you know what he was called before that but he's not keen on revealing what his mum and dad saddled him with over fifty years ago.

He shore for twenty years or so, only using a brace for the last four and then gave it away around the turn of the century.

He's down here on a night off from droving – 500 head from Penarie (home of the Homebush Hotel) to Swan Hill. He's on his own with just five dogs to help and he's taking it slow:

'... doing 3 kilometres a day with a special slow progress permit. The cattle are so placid that the cars have to beep them to get out of the way. There's almost zero pick on the roadside but we're lucky to be there. I'm the last drover on any TSR at the moment. Every other one has been closed because there's just no feed.'

Travelling stock routes have watering and yards every 20–30 kilometres but these are too far apart for slow progress herds, and besides, almost none have any water. So Blinky's forced to fill a water tank each morning at the river and then eke it out to his cattle through each day. Not much Banjo Paterson romance in droving in this drought.

Once he gets the cattle home, he's planning on picking up the shears again, out in the bush with his mates, 'just blowing it off, working as hard as you can in the real world with real people ... making new friends and catching up with old ones.'

And he wants to see just how much he's got left in him. Two hundred and forty-nine was his best one day and he's done eighty-five in a run. He's been around too.

'I've shore in three states,' he brags. 'Drunk, sober and indifferent, I'm probably at my best when I'm indifferent. I shore my first two hundred on Remembrance Day 1991. It was my first season after coming up from being a rousie,' another shed job that he'd taught himself and loved.

He could toss a fleece onto the table backwards, picking it up cross-armed and tossing it over his head.

I tell him about a young woman in a shed in Wilmington South Australia who could throw a fleece and make it look like a flying lamb. Blinky wants to see a photo of that and when I find it, he says, 'I take my hat off to that. Truly a great effort.'

While we've been jawing, a group of five blokes has arrived, got some coolant and some change for the pool table. They don't seem to be Lindrumesque. A ball flies off the table and bounces on the wooden bar floor.

Blinky turns and calls to them, 'Dollar in the Legacy jar!'

They want to know what he's talking about and Blinky explains the house rules: 'Hit a ball off the table and it's a dollar fine in the Legacy jar on the bar there.'

One of them, who's wearing an unimpressive T-shirt, impressive watch, wedding ring on his right hand and a hat the brim of which he later reveals he likes to use as a beer coaster (yep, the one who I wrongly think looks the least non-sensible of the quintet), comes over, pulls a fiver and folds it into the container. 'That'll save us coming back every coupla minutes, eh?

Then Blinky has a lightbulb moment. 'Talking of hats, you've gotta see mine. Be back in ten minutes.' So I head over to the pool table.

These five fishing mates can't agree on which footy team to follow (though they do agree it's not Collingwood), don't much like each other's politics, drink different beers and each prefer different bait when they're

on the river and seem to have a consensus on just one thing. They love each other's company and they treasure their times together. They seem like any mob of mates who're away in the bush without much of a care and having a well-earned when they are. They've been coming here for years but the last couple have been a bit different.

One of 'em's a cop, not from Balranald but from down on the Murray. For years he's worked on the domestic abuse unit and it's taken it's toll.

'I now go to the shops and I see an old man with a young child and I don't see a loving granddad and his grandson, I see a paedophile and a victim, and I have to shift the filter. It stays with you. It's stuff you can't turn off at night, or when you clock off. You suspect people who have no cause to be suspected. You think bad stuff about people who are only doing good, and going home to my kids at night after a day dealing with this stuff is real difficult.'

So his mates stay close and each year kidnap him out here for a week of good times, bad pool, cold beer and no night sweats.

One of those mates has travelled a different life path:

'I did some time at one stage and when I was going for parole they were asking me about my family support when I got out and I told them the truth, my oldest brother's a copper and my sister's a copper too so that should stand me in good stead. And the parole officer said, "So what happened to you?" and I told him, "I decided to help 'em out and keep 'em both in a job."'

In the middle of the laughter, Blinky fronts with a couple of Akubras. One's his seventeen-year-old Rough Ride working hat and the other's a Snowy River model he wears on formal occasions. Like tonight.

Blinky points at the stains on the barely held together working model with an air vent in the top of the crown.

'You make sure you tell people those marks are my sweat. Those stains ain't painted on,' and I tell him consider it done but what happened to his story about a shooting?

Blinky points to a tattoo on his right shoulder. It's a line drawing of Ned Kelly with a pistol in his right hand and under the grip of the gun, the only filled in section of this work of art, there's an indent into his burnt skin.

'That's a bullet hole,' he mentions nonchalantly. 'I got the tatt done a few years back to hide that bullet hole. Was tired of everyone asking me about it.'

'Well I have to ask you too.'

'I was asleep in bed and my missus at the time was on the drink and shot me. Woke me up pretty quick. Was lucky she hit me, if it'd missed me it would've hit me son.'

I tell him about Benjamin Allerton who shot the barman here. Blinky just laughs and drains his glass again.

We've been served all night by Dylan, a young bloke from Tooleybuc who's been filling in for owners Ken and Vic, but when I surface the next morning the pub's being guarded by a black Labrador and a bearded bloke is hooning around on yet another John Deere ride-on mower. He's pretty busy but he'll just take the load of rubbish down the back and join me inside.

I soon learn: that the dog's name is 'Get out of here you bastard', usually shortened to Cassie; that it's not a croc skin on the wall, it's a Wakool goanna; that the punt gun on the wall is real; that the place's official name is the Kyalite Pub because it's not a hotel, hotels are things in England which rent out rooms with beds; that the cellar door might be strangely in the middle of the back bar's floor but that's because the pub expanded around it; that amongst the first things they did when they bought the place thirty years ago was stop the bikers doing burnouts in the bar; that living here all that time doesn't make you a local but it helps locals know your name; and that visitors from New South Wales are the best because, 'When Victorians leave home for a holiday up here they take one pair of undies and one ten dollar note and when they get home they haven't changed either.'

I head down to the old punt landing. There's not a camel in sight. But across the river a victim of the last floods of the Edwards/Wakool lies smashed against the gums at the line of the highest water and causes me to smile.

One hundred and sixty years after Landells fought with Burke over what he took to be damaging treatment of his camels, at this same spot there's something that was originally intimately connected with those ships of the desert – ironically and incongruously it's a broken caravan.

CHAPTER 38 – THE MURRUMBIDGEE CONFLUENCE

THE RIVER GAINS STRENGTH

Just on 40 kilometres after weaving through Tooleybuc and then onto the MVH, I take a right onto the River Track and I'm into the reserve. Four kilometres of twisting two-wheel track through river forest and the river rejoins me on the right and then, across the flow the mighty Murrumbidgee is emptying its grey-green waters into the brown Murray.

Not a person in sight. I've passed no other vehicles or campers or hikers.

I put Super Ten to rest slap opposite the inflow of the Bidgee, the only major river in this country that was permitted to retain its Indigenous name – the only one that's not been burdened by the moniker of some governor, explorer or far-off monarch. It's supposed to mean 'big water' in the tongue of the Wiradjuri and for sure its written history is punctuated by floods, including the disaster of 1852 when almost ninety people died at Gundagai (and many more were saved by two Indigenous blokes named Yarri and Jacky).

But here, today, where the Bidgee finally ends its beautifully symmetrical struggle of 1500 twisting kilometres involving a descent of right on 1500 metres, it's a lazy purgative push of clay filled water. I take a seat in the dust.

Somewhere, a long time ago, I remember reading that some expert had calculated that by the time a person's reached less than my age now, each breath they take – and not necessarily a super inhale, just a normal breath – well each inhale contains at least one molecule of air that has been in that person's lungs at least once previously. I was much younger then but

I recall thinking not how did he work that out, but *why*. And sitting here just maybe ten metres downstream from the junction where these two rivers join forces, I'm convinced he was wrong.

The air's too pristine, too fresh, too new to've ever been used before by anyone let alone me. The odours of the bush – the timeless scent of the gums overhead, the eternal whiff from the water's edge of mud newly exposed and the acridity of something that's died a distance off to my left – they're all there but it seems that I'm the first person who's ever sucked them in.

Far off, across the Murray the mandatory dog is yelping. The corellas are fighting over the best branches for the night and a pelican patrols the confluence.

I wait for that magic hiatus when the cooling evening pushes the flies under their leaves but the mosquito squadrons haven't yet left their hangers. And then in that brief break, it's safe to chuck up the tent and get it zipped bereft of insects.

Light up the Trangia and put on a brew. Somewhere back down the highway a bit, maybe 15 kilometres or so, the Murray River off to my right and unseen, had reached the halfway point on its 2508 kilometre journey from source to sea.

I set up my cameras for some night shots and smile. It's all downhill from here.

MT DISPERSION
NAMED BY
MAJOR MITCHELL
ON MAY 26TH 1836.
AFTER AN ENCOUNTER WITH
ABORIGINIES AT THIS SPOT

CHAPTER 39 – MOUNT DISPERSION

HIDDEN HISTORY

Just on 2.5 kilometres west from Euston on the Sturt Highway there's a nondescript turn to the south. There's no standard white writing on green national-standard direction sign of what this rural road might lead to. And there's no white on brown tourist route sign indicating anything of interest along this track.

Just an anonymous road leading off to who cares where. Well, I do.

Fourteen kilometres and the sealed section gives way to corrugated hard packed dirt which lasts for a further ten and then the road rises around the edge of a small hill and on the left is the reason I've taken this route.

In May 1836 Major Thomas Mitchell, leading his third expedition, was camped near this spot. He had been trailed for days by a large number of the owners of the land and their noises and gatherings over the previous days since the party left what is now Euston, spooked him.

Mitchell later wrote to Governor Bourke:

… on the morning of 27 May they were following us closely along the river with tumultuous shouting, and our own safety and further progress evidently depended on our attacking them forthwith. But it was difficult to come at such enemies hovering in our rear with lynx-eyed vigilance of savages. I succeeded however … Attacked simultaneously by both parties the whole betook themselves to the river, my men pursuing them and shooting as many as they could. Numbers were shot swimming across the Murray, and some even after they had reached the opposite shore as they descended the bank.

The massacre prompted a Legislative Council enquiry that December at which Mitchell and some of his party defended their actions.

The event has raised debate and discussion ever since. Academics and historians who are professionally bound to cite their sources and evidence have often been in conflict with popular writers who have no burden of peer review and no obligation to substantiate their claims. (Very much like the rubbish written by journalists posing as historians back at Echuca and the myth of Ned Kelly at the Foley–Hicken fight.)

One brilliant rebuttal of a simplistic popularist was written by John Read of the Major Mitchell Commemorative Project:

he uses two pages of selective information, clever use of words, innuendo, subjectivity and contrived journalism, to make Mitchell out to be untrustworthy, brutal and complicit in the rape, murder and the massacre of inoffensive aborigines. As a Journalist, [he] does not [have to] disclose his sources … [and] his views are not supported by thorough historical research.

Whatever the causes and the catalysts, irrespective of how terrible was the body count, what's certain is that a mass killing occurred here and it included the shooting of Indigenous owners who were in retreat – many swimming and running and others already across the river. This cairn memorial beside the road should be publicised and signposted. The lack of recognition, the lack of facilitation for visitors and travellers to visit this site isn't just lazy, it's disrespectful.

Major Mitchell named this place Mount Dispersion and as I kick around this cairn, erected some 2 kilometres from the actual killing site by the Mildura Historical Society in 1963, the flies and insects have all gone silent.

CHAPTER 40 – GOL GOL

A MEMORIAL TO BRAINS AND STUPIDITY

Very shortly after what became known as the Liverpool Riot of 1916 in which soldiers stationed at Casula refused to comply with orders for extra duties, marched on nearby Liverpool, ransacked the hotels and then commandeered a train and drove it to Central Station where one was shot dead by armed military police, the New South Wales government succumbed to wowser pressure and introduced six o'clock closing of all hotels 'as a war measure'. The other states apart from Western Australia and Queensland soon followed.

The War to End All Wars (which didn't) came and went and then the Second World War decimated a generation of the world's youth. Those who returned from these fights for freedom, like those who'd never left, were confronted with laws which continued to forbid the serving of alcohol in pubs in anything resembling a civilised manner.

In 1947 New South Wales held a referendum on the issue but it returned the status quo. Many publicans campaigned against longer hours because they knew they'd make little more than they did in the 'one frantic hour' of near bestial imbibing. But four years later the government appointed Justice R. V. Maxwell to lead a Royal Commission into licensing laws and liquor trading.

It took him three years, but eventually Maxwell was scathing of the effects of early closing. To quote Diane Kirkby's analysis of Maxwell's findings:

Maxwell ... described drinking conditions in the metropolitan area as 'deplorable' and early closing ... as an encouragement to the practice of sly grog and after-hours trading at black-market rates. Reform of the licensing laws seemed imperative as the solution to a state of affairs that had another judge reportedly saying 'the breweries were a law unto themselves' and 'NSW publicans were arrogant, rapacious and contemptuous of their customers.'

The New South Wales government figured it was time for another poll and passions ran high. Six days before the plebiscite, the Sydney *Sun Herald* ran an editorial that started out recognising the incongruity of part of it:

NEXT Saturday electors will decide whether liquor bars are to close, as now, at 6 p.m. or remain open until 10. On polling day, the hotels will be shut.

Could there be a more ironic commentary on drinking habits in N.S.W. than the fact that, in theory at least, the people cannot be trusted not to abuse the consumption of alcoholic liquor while they register their decision on trading hours?

And ended with a very clear statement of position: 'Six p.m. closing has failed to provide rational drinking conditions. It is time to give 10 p.m. a trial.'

Two days before voting day the *Sydney Morning Herald* also weighed in:

The only sensible approach to the question of later closing is that it is the necessary first move — but only the first move — which has to be made if drinking conditions are to be brought into line with civilised practice ... Six o'clock closing has had a fair trial, and it has failed. Its failure is demonstrated not only, or even most significantly, in the '6 o'clock swill' of which so much is heard, but also in the circumstance that it has enabled hotel-owning interests to 'get by' with the minimum of facilities ... Late closing is not a bold new experiment; it is standard practice in most civilised countries, and it has proved its value in creating communities which regard liquor as a social adjunct, not – as too often here – as an end in itself. The crux of the matter is surely contained in Mr. Justice Maxwell's warning that 'there are evils associated with 6 o'clock closing which ought not to be tolerated in a civilised community.'

The vote was so close that initial reports had the status quo being retained and it took a week to announce the decision that the ten o'clockers had just scraped home. South of the Murray, meanwhile the government trod water.

The Melbourne *Argus* took aim:

MR. CAIN, Premier, obviously believes that it is not necessary to take a referendum in Victoria on hotel closing hours.

And how right he is.

Every Victorian could, tell him, without benefit of a costly poll, that the State's liquor laws are just a practical joke on a modern community.

Why they have been continued in their present lumbering, ugly, out-of-date pattern is something that no-thinking citizen can understand.

New South Wales's laws were ejected by the bouncer of public opinion early in 1955; Victoria waited more than another decade. It was bad news for Victorian drinkers but especially good news for a band of enterprising business folks north of the river.

And it's down to one of them that soon after riding across the top of the Trentham Cliffs, I pull Super Ten to the left, down the side of the Gol Gol Hotel and into the car park beside the new kids' adventure playground. Then it's around the low wall with its nameplate wall proclaiming this the 1877 Lounge Bar & Dining and onto the rear deck, reserve a table with my helmet, head in and grab a chardy at the bar, too dedicated to gambling for my liking, and nod to the old sepia photo mural of some cool dudes on their old bikes. Back to my table in the sunshine, because there's only

one place to have a cold refresher at this place – just the one place where you can have a suitably reverential drink and maybe a meal from their top-notch kitchen.

Way down the bottom of the well-kept wide lawn, maybe 80 –100 metres away and through the trees, the Murray flows by – importantly, from the left to the right, reminding me I'm in New South Wales.

I raise my glass to a smart publican and a dumb government. Without them both, this magnificent behind the pub, where kids play, pick-up games of cricket and footy are played, weddings celebrated and memories made wouldn't be here.

Two weeks after the New South Wales vote, with the narrow decision still bubbling, and with Victoria still in love with the six o'clock swill, this magnificent beer garden, or at least a precursor to it, made a mention in the Melbourne *Herald* under the heading, 'GOL GOL IS GETTING READY'.

New South Wales hotels on the Murray River are planning for heavy trade from nearby Victorian towns when the ten o clock closing operates. The tiny hotel at Gol Gol, five miles from Mildura, will have its bar extended to provide for the expected demand from Mildura people. Mr H. Wilkinson, proprietor of the Gol Gol Hotel, said today that he would establish a beer garden if the trade from Victoria was as good as he expected.

This pub had a good track record in profiting from the stupidity of the legislators. When the Chaffey Brothers brought quasi-prohibition to Mildura, Gol Gol was the closest township outside the proscribed area.

In 1898 an ex-resident of Mildura wrote to his local paper in response to an earlier editorial:

strictly speaking, Mildura has never had Prohibition. The settlers there were always able to get whatever liquors they fancied from ... Gol Gol, on the New South Wales side of the river, [where] there was from the first a public-house, where every Mildura resident could get whatever they wanted; that they did want it often, and in large quantities, is shown by the fact that the licensee of the Gol Gol Hotel (a little roadside house that, before the advent of the Chaffey Bros., could count his clients on his fingers) retired at the end of four years with, a competence!

And half a century later they obviously still wanted it, wanted it often and in large quantities. Today the beer garden that H. Wilkinson, publican, established back then in response to Victoria's recalcitrance to ditch its repressive drinking laws is a testament to a smart operator and a memorial to the fall of wowserism.

And it's a great place to take a break before the traveller dives into the territory deeply scarred by a pair of Canadian wowsers who might've known irrigation but didn't know people. Or their thirsts!

THE
Gol Gol Hotel
N.S.W.
(Within half-an-hour from Mildura),

Has been leased for a lengthy term by Geo. H. PAYNE, who contemplates making extensive alterations and improvements, which, when completed, will afford first-class accommodation for travellers and visitors.

Travellers on the Victorian side of the river can put up their horses at Brighton's stables, opposite the Hotel, and can cross by the Ferry there, thereby saving punt fees.

Arrangements are being made to convey Mildura visitors from the Punt to the Hotel.

ALES, WINES AND SPIRITS,
Of the Best Brands only,
KEPT IN STOCK.

Geo. H. PAYNE.

GOL GOL IS GETTING READY

MILDURA, Today
New South Wales hotels on the Murray River are planning for heavy trade from nearby Victorian towns when the 10 o'clock closing operates.

The tiny hotel at Gol Gol five miles from Mildura will have its bar extended to provide for the expected demand from Mildura people.

Mr H Wilkinson, proprietor of the Gol Gol Hotel said today that he would establish a beer

THE LONG ESCAPE FROM TEMPERANCE

In 1885, after a drought had parched Australia for the previous eight years, Alfred Deakin, who was later to be the country's second prime minister (and its fifth and its seventh!) visited the irrigation projects of California. He met the Caffey brothers, George and William, and early the following year, George Chaffey arrived in Melbourne.

George visited the Murray Valley and returned to Melbourne, where Alfred Deakin assured him that the Victorian government would make a quarter of a million acres of crown land available to him and very favourable rates. Chaffey cabled his brother and told him to sell everything in California and head down under to what must surely be a liquid goldmine. In October, the Chaffey bothers signed a deal with the government for the land, undertaking to spend £300,000 on improvements over the next twenty years, but giving them enormous rights over things from land sales to water distribution and social engineering.

It was to be the first real instance of Australians selling the farm. The government passed the *Waterworks Construction Encouragement Act 1886* and Deakin introduced a bill in November to validate the agreement, but the waters didn't run smooth.

Parliament wasn't too impressed by the sweetheart deal with the 'cute Yankee land-grabbers' and the matter was put out to tender. No tenders were received. Not a single one.

So in 1887 the Chaffeys (having meanwhile done a similar deal with the Downer government in South Australia for another 250,000 acres in Renmark), signed the forms with the colony of Victoria and Mildura was theirs.

The brothers firmly believed that crops, might be better off irrigated, but workers were more likely to flourish when parched like a dryland backblock.

Part of the deal was that the settlement would be without pubs and the availability of liquor and alcohol would be as limited as possible.

In July 1890 the Victorian Parliament passed 'An Act to consolidate the Laws relating to the Licensing of Public Houses and the Sale of Fermented and Spirituous Liquors'. Section 176 read:

... an irrigation colony is about to be formed in [Mildura]....and it is desired that the sale of liquor in such colony should be placed under special restriction ... [and] ... no license authorising the sale of liquor in [that] part of Victoria ... shall be granted other than a grocer's license a colonial wine license a brewer's license or a spirit merchant's license ... and no license at all ... shall be granted ... except with the consent of the Governor in Council.

And so began the legacy of the Chaffey brothers along the Murray ...

The problem was that the gentry felt they should be entitled to imbibe after a day of supervising their workers and so a loophole was inserted. The restrictions of the 1890 Act did not apply to 'any person occupying premises bona fide as a club which the Licensing Court ... has certified to be a club within the provisions of this Act ...'

And it defined a 'club' as 'any body association ... of not less than 50 persons united for the purpose of providing accommodation or and conferring privileges and advantages upon the members thereof ...' And so the clubs of Mildura were born.

The Settlers' Club opened in 1893 and was the hangout of more successful small landowners and other town professionals.

Back in July 1888 W. B. Chaffey, who'd been so instrumental in restricting the flow of alcohol in the settlement, had assembled a bunch of notable and well-bred businessmen to found the Mildura Coffee Palace Coy with himself (of course) as chairman. The £10,000 seed capital was quickly subscribed and in September tenders were called for the 'erection of a Coffee Palace at Mildura.' The plans included a billiard room, dining room, offices, smoking room, kitchen, storeroom, servants' quarters on the ground floor and large underground cellars. Upstairs there were twenty-one bedrooms. Two months after opening the place was already needing extensions.

The Mildura Club, aimed from the very start at satiating the civilised tastes and thirsts of what passed for the Mildura aristocracy, was created in 1894 and took over the premises of the Coffee Palace. It stayed ensconced there until 1901 when it removed to the basement of the Cultivator Building before having its own premises built in 1920. (Just ninety-six years later in 2016 the Mildura Club took the extraordinary step of allowing women to become members!)

The Working Man's Club was established down the road from the Settlers' Club and in 1895 George Leonard applied for and was granted certification that the Mildura Working Man's Club, formed the previous year, was bona fide within the definition as stipulated in the Act of 1890. It's still going strong.

In the 1970s it claimed to have the longest bar in Australia but in 1995, in a clear reflection of how the place balanced its love of avarice and the respect for unique history, the bar was demolished to make way for more poker machines.

With the Mildura Club having moved out in 1901, the Coffee Palace began slowly campaigning for a more lenient liquor permit. In November 1906 a Dr Robertson of the Victorian Health Department rocked up on an official visit of inspection. If his early comments rocked the wowsers' boat:

Mildura is peculiar in that it possesses no hotels ... [and it] is a hot, dry, and dusty place, and in warm weather one naturally develops a thirst ... [and] the visitor is practically forced to avail himself of the ... clubs ... No

provision is made ... for the refreshment of the woman visitor, who must content herself with water not above suspicion or warm sodawater ...

His conclusion: 'From a visitor's point of view a well-conducted hotel, under municipal control would be infinitely preferable to a coffee palace, plus clubs.'

Hit them like a multi-wave tsunami. A sample letter to the editor:

For cool cheek the [report] would be hard to beat ... Where he got his notion that the Murray water is 'suspicious' and 'of poor quality' we know not ... [and the issue is] not likely to be helped very materially by the suggestion that women visitors should be assured some alcoholic refreshment ...

The first nail in their coffin of righteous outrage was hammered in just a fortnight later when the Licensing Court decided by a majority of the Bench to grant a colonial wine licence to the Mildura Coffee Palace. Civilisation was about to crumble. The local council had been blindsided:

At a special meeting of the Mildura Shire Council to-day, held to consider the granting of a colonial wine license by the licensing bench at Birchip, it was decided to take no further action. It is reported that steps will be taken privately to test the legality of the bench's decision.

It took almost a decade for sisters, Mrs Annie Yule and Miss May Williams, who'd run the place since 1904, to get a full licence. Young men who'd spent weeks, months, trapped in frozen trenches in the battlefields of Europe dreaming of getting home to a warm welcome and a cold beer were rejoining their communities and they weren't about to settle for a wowser's lecture and a lukewarm cordial.

In 1919 the evolution from Temperance Hotel to Coffee Palace to Mildura Club to Grand Hotel Mildura was complete. By now the place had 120 rooms and occupied an entire city block.

Advertisements began to appear in the press for the supply of poultry and ducks, for other supplies such as firewood and in August the secretary of Mildura Grand Hotel Ltd sought the services of a qualified manager, promising a 'first class salary will be given to a thoroughly competent man.'

Women were welcome in the Ladies Lounge, and as lower employees behind the bar and no doubt cleaning the bedrooms and insanitary amenities, but they had to know their place wasn't in management, not in this pub and not in this town.

Mildura was still a man's domain but it'd finally shaken off the temperance shackles and its pub opened for business late that year.

And doesn't seem too much has changed. The Grand Hotel now occupies an entire block, dominating the river end of town. The only real bar, apart from the modern, unconnected Brewery, is a betting venue, and on this Saturday afternoon it's overflowing – truly out of the door – with a gang of uncomfortably past middle-aged blokes in loud shirts shouting at screens and each other. Not a woman in sight.

Back in the late '70s I was in Mildura with a good mate, Geoff. He didn't like tomatoes but we both loved burgers – this was way before ordering one without pickles and could I have the pattie just lightly done please is enough to cause a meltdown of a nice young person in a freshly ironed uniform. Nah, this was back when there was one type of lettuce, not a single person had wondered if coriander is the same as cilantro, when those brown furry testicle-sized things were Chinese gooseberries, chicken was a treat kept for Sundays, food allergies were almost unheard of and hamburgers were only ever beef and always came 'with the lot' unless you wished otherwise. And told the fella in the T-shirt early.

So I asked for a burger with extra beetroot and Geoff asked for a burger without tomatoes. The fella looked back at my mate and in one of the most stunningly unforgettable statements of logic I've ever come across uttered, 'Mate, we're out of tomatoes, do you want it without something else?'

With the pub so unappetising and on a pilgrimage for a burger I head up the road to the Langtree Cafe with its first-floor deck overlooking Langtree Avenue. Yes they do have hamburgers and yes they do come with beetroot and yes, we'll make sure it has extra tomato.

The burger doesn't block out the horizon like the Godfather at Deni, but it's damn fine. And the tomatoes? Geoff doesn't know what he's missing! And the local wine that washes it down? Well all I can say is the modern equivalents of those irritating irrigators – the Chaffeys – they don't know either.

Aborigines of Australia.

Domestic occupations in summer season
on the Lower Murray River.

CHAPTER 42 – MERBEIN

MARNGROOK ON THE MURRAY

'**I** reckon I know just where that is,' is the instant reaction when I show Toney a copy of an old etching while we're sitting in the bar, the only bar of what's left of the Merbein Hotel.

Toney's just been elected for his seventh term as President of the Merbein Magpies Aussie Rules (and Netball) club, founded in 1910 and so older than the pub itself. He's been off the booze for years, 'except for weddings and premiership wins' so as Mick – resplendent in checked shirt, buttoned cuffs, traditional barman's waistcoat and Lord Kitchener moustache – gets him a Coke and pulls me a beer, Toney tells of the history of the club and the full-on job of being president of a bush footy club. How he used to go fishing on the bank of the river maybe five times a week but now's lucky to make it once. How being a father to some players, a brother to others, an accountant to always several, a marriage counsellor to too many and an ear and shoulder to pretty much all of them at some time has filled in every spare moment away from his paving business.

But he's not complaining – it's a job his father had for a long time and as we talk messages and calls come in from players needing a chat about things but none seems urgent so he'll call them all back.

He keeps looking at the old etching as he talks and his certainty that it's a place near where he likes to drop a line firms.

'I'll take you down there.' But then a call that has to be answered comes in so he ducks outside to sort it.

The bar's a classic Art Deco curved counter with a tiled front. Mick explains how it used to be a complete island bar before the wall was changed and one end was trashed.

On the inside rim of the bar, there's a lower counter which is Mick's favourite perch to lay back on as he tells his story and listens to those of others. He's been in pubs for just short of fifty of his sixty-six years and

that's more than half the lifetime of the Merbein Hotel, whose creation was marred by allegations of vested interests and tall poppy cutting in the early 1920s.

When Mick started all the town's grapes went to the dried fruit industry, a labour-intensive operation and the workers weren't backpackers working in the bush to extend their visas.

'Back then if you were on the dole in Melbourne and you were considered fit enough you had to get on the free train from Melbourne to here and you had to go grape picking or you'd lose your dole. Lose your benefits ... When the trains would arrive and all the pickers would get off and official types would herd them into groups for each blocky and then onto old buses to take them to the vineyard. Once they were clear, there'd be a couple of dozen would get back on. They were the real bad characters. See the Ds were always keeping an eye on them and they'd weed out for the crims in the days after they arrived and they'd round them up and keep them together for shipping back to Melbourne so it wasn't our problem any more.

'There were pickers' huts out on all the blocks with beds and kitchens and showers and they'd all work for piece rates, get paid on Saturdays and then come into town. Was nothing back then to go through 12 to 140 eighteens every week. Tops was 167.'

Toney's sorted the problem for the player on the phone so we gather up the gear and head out in his ute for the site of the etching, but first he wants to show me the new footy oval and the juniors' oval behind. They play in the Sunraysia League against the likes of Mildura and Robinvale and most of the Mapgie players, especially those who've left school now live in one of those places but consider Merbein home and so play for the place they grew up.

This is as grassroots as it gets: Toney's committee do the catering at the ten to fifteen annual meetings at the local speedway and do a similar number of functions to raise the roughly hundred grand that's needed for costs and players' wages. No wonder he doesn't fit so much fishing in.

We cut down to the Merbein Common on the edge of the Murray, past the old racetrack that closed long ago and was taken over as a training facility by a trotting trainer until he was 'charged with engaging in conduct that corrupted a betting outcome, engaging in conduct that would corrupt a betting outcome and facilitating conduct that corrupted a betting outcome.' Like that bloke's career the track has now gone to dust.

We talk about the dozen or so Merbein football players who've gone on to senior AFL ranks, but the town has links to one famous player who took his first kick at an oval-shaped ball, and played his first ever 'rules' game at Merbein West Primary but whose family shifted before he was old enough to play for the club. This kid had only ever played soccer before arriving at the town in 1986 but had to switch to 'rules' as it was the only winter sport. He went on to win two AFL premierships, two Brownlow Medals (including one playing for the losing side) and was selected four times as an All-Australian. He went on to be a role model and a respected leader and representative of his people, and of all Australians, and in 2014 he was selected as Australian of the Year.

That kid was Adam Goodes. But it's not because of his connection with the town that I'd been keen to catch up with a person connected with Aussie Rules whilst at the pub at Merbein. It's because of the original of the old etching which I'd shown Toney back in the pub and which we're now tracking in his ute.

The year after Goodes won his second Brownlow Medal, researchers in Mildura were backgrounding for an upcoming exhibition on the work of German-born explorer Johann Wilhelm Theodor Ludwig von Blandowski, known as William Blandowski, who led an expedition to the Murray–Darling confluence in 1857.

Blandowski's expedition left Melbourne in December 1856 and spent eight months camped beside the Murray 'close to the current town of Merbein – probably on what is now the Merbein Common'. Blandowski was a member of the Victorian Philosophical Institute and spent the time documenting in words and sketches the flora, the fauna and the activities of the traditional owners, the Nyeri Nyeri (or Yerre Yerre) people.

While Johannn Wilhelm Theodor might've got along great with the Indigenous people, he seemed to lack the interpersonal skills and social sensitivity to get along with his colleagues, but it was enough to make him the sort of bloke I find interesting.

He named newly discovered items after fellow members of the Philosophical Institute which I would've taken as an honour but there was offence taken by the egghead after whom he named one fish which he described as, 'Slimy, slippery fish. Lives in the mud. Is of a violent bluish colour on the belly. The whole upper surface is of a dirty olivish-green colour, with numerous irregular dark patches.'

And another got peeved when his namesake was labelled, 'A fish easily recognised by its low forehead, big belly and sharp spine'.

(Blando was treated more kindly. He's commemorated in a genus of marine fish (*Blandowskius*), and of the decent-looking Murray River perches (*Blandowskiella*).)

Blandowski's artistic skills weren't much better than his diplomacy and his sketches were sent to others to enhance and improve. James Redaway created several but the bulk were returned to Germany where Gustav Mützel produced *Australien in 142 Photographischen Abbildungen*. It was this collection that the research committee unearthed in 2007 and in which the etching Toney's holding is contained. The print features a foreground of Aboriginals seated around three separate fires, some cooking some painting and in the background an important depiction of three tall men fishing with a long net.

But in the mid-ground six youths, in two teams of three, are playing a game. One of them is kicking an object with his left foot toward the other group. It's believed this is the earliest image of the game of marngrook, described in 1858 by William Thomas, assistant protector of Aborigines as:

> *a favourite game with boys and men ... the ball is kicked into the air not along the ground, there is a general scramble at the ball, the tall black fellows stand the best chance. When caught it is again kicked up in the air with great force and ascends as straight up and as high as when thrown by the hand.*

We skirt the edge of the Murray on our right, past numerous beautiful free camping spots until Toney pulls up and we get out. In front of us a small riverlet crosses our path. When the river is higher it leads to a billabong and on the far side is a rising bank similar to that in the etching.

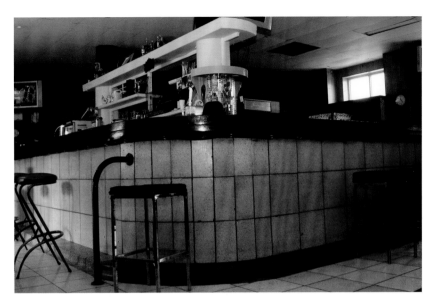

'Soon as I saw that photo, I thought of this place. It's for sure not the river and it makes sense that it'd be here because this is the only billabong and so the blokes in the background would've just spread their net from one side of the other, walked up the water and then circled the fish inside. It's still better to fish in a billabong than in the river when the water's up.'

His eyes and face ping-pong from the etching to the landscape and back again. And again. He's convinced this is where Blandowski stood over 160 years previously.

Toney's proud that there's more Indigenous players in the Merbein Magpies than any other club in the comp and he'll be keeping the print to show them when pre-season training starts.

The connection between Marngrook and Aussie Rules is disputed and controversial. The story of Tom Wills, the professional cricketer who helped frame the first rules of a game to keep cricketers fit over the Melbourne winters is for another time. Enough to say here that he co-wrote the first set of rules for the game in 1859, two years after Blandowski's spectatorship of the Merbein marngrook football game.

His entire extended family and some other settlers (nineteen in all) were killed in the Minerva Hills outside Springsure in Queensland in the biggest massacre of whites by blacks in Australian history, but he returned to Melbourne and managed the first Indigenous cricket team. It's established that he had good and regular relations with the Mukjarrawait people in Geelong, where he'd grown up, but he made no recorded mention of playing any game with a possum-skin 'ball'.

Greg de Moore, who wrote the definitive biography of Tom Wills, claimed shortly after the discovery of the Blandowski etching:

it's the first image of any kind of football that's been discovered in Australia. It pre-dates the first European images of any kind of football, by almost ten years in Australia. Whether or not there is a link between the two games in some way for me is immaterial because it really highlights that games such as Marn Grook, which is one of the names for Aboriginal football, were played by Aborigines and should be celebrated in their own right.

And so it should. As should Merbein on the Murray, poor cousin of Mildura but the home to the earliest known image of a truly Australian game and the place where one of the greatest Indigenous players to ever pull on a boot, kicked his first oval football.

Back at the pub, Mick's still lounging on the bar and wants me to take a squiz at the enormous cellar with its rare powered beer ramp, 'just be careful of the feral cat that's sometimes down there'.

Toney's never been into the cave so he comes down and checks out where in its heyday, long gone, this place went through twenty kegs a day. Now it'd do that in a good month.

Back on top he finishes his Coke and gets ready to head. He folds the old print into his pocket.

'I've fished that spot for years, mate – even know the giant goanna that lives up in the tree there that scares the hell out of you if you leave a caught fish laying around for too long – but I'll never look at it the same again.'

IN REMEMBRANCE OF
THE RUFUS RIVER
MASSACRE
ON 27TH AUGUST 1841
AND THE 2 TRIBES
BARKINDJI/MARUARA
WHO OCCUPIED THE
LAKE VICTORIA AREA

THIS STONE UNVEILED BY
REPRESENTATIVES OF THE
BARKINDJI/MARUARA COMMUNITIES
ON THE 26TH OCTOBER 2002

CHAPTER 43 – RUFUS RIVER

SOBERING

I head west from Merbein, then north to the river. Cross it at the Abbotsford Bridge, then on through Wentworth where Mick back at Merbein told me all the pubs have secret tunnels to the old Customs House. But the place is strongly on the Darling River and so'll have to wait for the next book! Instead, I head down to the confluence of the two rivers. Pelicans eye me suspiciously under a bushfire-bronzed sky and the waters of these two mighty rivers are mirrors to the heavens.

Two kilometres north of Wentworth I turn left off the Silver City Highway and immediately I'm in the glorious empty harshness of this country's timeless heart. Ten minutes later I pull Super Ten up in the middle of the thin sealed strip which is Renmark Road, turn off the engine and take off the helmet. It's hot and, with even the flies seeking respite, I'm immersed in immense silence.

I try again to imagine the white explorers trudging this land without pity, forging on in the hearth of the day with the sun at its highest, clad in unsuitable clothes and leading struggling horses forever needing water and always in want of food. Sobering country this.

Just on 32 kilometres of bitumen later I bend left onto Rufus Road, where the bitumen stops and then a comfortable journey of similar distance of placid gravel and I'm swinging over Frenchmans Creek and very soon my destination is on the right.

The Murray River is now the source, the font of immeasurable joy to countless people, but its white discovery, exploration and development sure wasn't easy or straightforward and it certainly wasn't without tragedy. What came to be known as the Rufus River Massacre was one of the great tragedies of white encroachment into this Indigenous land and I pull Super Ten up beside the massacre memorial on the banks of what we know as Lake Victoria.

The Rufus River hardly warrants the moniker. It's a maybe 5-kilometre thin waterway flowing from Lake Victoria to the Murray, entering the just downstream from Lock 7, and in most years it's not much more than a line of waterholes which afforded the early overlanders easy passage.

As they journeyed west or east through this area with their flocks of easily speared sheep and cattle, confrontations grew and a cycle of violence and retribution began to turn. In October 1839 a party was attacked near Morgan and the overseer killed. In retaliation at least eleven Indigenous locals were murdered with a South Australian investigation failing to find and charge the perpetrators.

The next month on the Darling another overlanding group was attacked and sheep killed. Again in retribution their camp was ambushed and Aboriginals killed and injured.

In 1841 a confrontation on the Rufus River resulted in at least eight black deaths and in June that year Charles Langhorne's group lost four members and killed five. Two months later, again on the Rufus River, William Robinson's party killed fifteen Aboriginals after claiming to have been attacked. The next day a force led by Matthew Moorhouse, the Protector of Aborigines, headed to the area from Adelaide. They caught the Indigenous warriors, their women and children in a classic pincer trap. At least forty were killed in what is now known as the Rufus River Massacre.

A subsequent governmental 'Inquiry into the Circumstances attending the death of a number of Natives on the Murray', chaired by Charles Sturt, feigned indignation and exonerated the perpetrators.

A couple of snippets from the proceedings:

Mr E. Stephens: 'It appears ... Mr Moorhouse, that no hostile proceedings or act of aggression on the part of the blacks had taken place before the order to fire upon the blacks was given by Mr Shaw?'

Mr Moorhouse: *'No'*

...

Mr Stephen: *'You did not think the loss of life was in any degree wanton, or that any man fired unnecessarily'?*

Mr Moorhouse: *'Certainly not.'*

'Then they only fired on the armed men, and when they were in the order of battle?'

'Yes.'

...

Mr Stephen: *'As Protector of Aborigines, you consider that what was done was not only decidedly necessary, but merciful? '*

Moorhouse: *'It was decidedly merciful, as far as I could judge.'*

...

Mr Eyre: *'Do you consider them a brave people?'*

Moorhouse: *'I do not.'*

...

Mr Eyre: *'Do you think the natives meditated redress for the aggressions of former parties ...?'*

Moorhouse: *'I believe they have been aggrieved; but I think they were merely looking for plunder, and not in pursuit of revenge.*

So, the 'Protector of Aborigines' nicely managed to confess that the first shots came from his side; lie that only armed men were shot despite the evidence of dead women and children; claim that killing people is an act of mercy; deride the courage of the warriors; and dismiss any notion that past injustices against these traditional owners may've been part of the motivation for the attacks while the recent history had shown that revenge was the prime motivation for similar attacks by whites on blacks.

Without so much as an adjournment to consider the evidence, the Board of Enquiry then moved:

> *That the Bench of Magistrates, after a full and careful examination of all the evidence brought before them relating to the late affray on the Rufus between the Europeans and Blacks, are unanimously of opinion (so far as they have had an opportunity of forming one) that the conduct of Mr Moorhouse and his party was justifiable, and indeed unavoidable in their circumstances; and that much praise is due to him and them for the great forbearance evinced by the force when placed under circumstances of the most trying nature.*

And yet Charles Sturt, the first white man to lead a party through this area and the Chairman of this Inquiry must've known this was fanciful.

Cumpston, in his *Charles Sturt – His Life and Journeys of Exploration* writes of Sturt's progression through these parts:

> *On 24th January they passed without trouble the Cadell Rocks below Wentworth. On 26th they passed the outlet stream connecting Lake Victoria with the Murray, and Sturt named it the Rufus River, after Macleay's red head ... From the Rufus River to the Merbein rocks they had no trouble, although they still saw natives: in the rapids round the Merbein rocks the natives actually helped them with the boat – one of them being the same 'remarkable man' who had intervened on the critical occasion at the Darling mouth.*

(These would've been the same good people amongst whom Blandowski lived for eight months without trouble and whom he drew fishing and playing marngrook.)

In 1923 the *Murray Pioneer* carried a feature interview written by Walter Ogilvy with John Coombs, 'mail coach driver, stockman and bushman' who'd lived and worked in the area for most of his seventy years. It includes a long segment on the 'Rufus Massacre'.

'I was only a lad', said Mr. Coombs, 'when the massacre of the blacks took place. It happened this way. A party of drovers under a man called Robertson or Robinson were overlanding cattle, and on arrival at the Rufus they were informed that the natives were going to spear some of the beasts. The drovers took up a position, and John McKinley sent post haste to Murrundi below Blanchetown for troopers from the barracks there. On the patrol's arrival McKinley escorted them round to the Rufus and placed the troopers in such a position that they and the drovers' party caught natives between two fires. There was no get away for them. Hemmed in by the drovers on one side and the police on the other, and also subjected to cross fire, the boys were shot down like dogs. Caught in a death trap men, women and children perished.

'I had a boy on Moorna station with me called Monkey and it was from him I obtained the story. Frightened by the sound of firing, Monkey at first could not understand what was going on. Presently his father and mother

and other relatives fell, shot dead. All his family except Monkey were killed. Terrified, he leapt into the Rufus amongst the dead and dying people.'

Jack Coombs says that Monkey always maintained that practically all the natives present were wiped out … The Rufus Creek affair, says Coombs, was murder. As a youth he spent many years amongst the boys, and only once was he set upon, and this was by a native at Salt Creek who, when refused more liquor, rushed at him and attempted to strangle him.

John Coombs was less than 'only a lad when the massacre of the blacks took place'. He wasn't born until eleven years after it happened but the rest of his story aligns with other contemporary and independent accounts.

The banks of Lake Victoria, with the education centre about the massacre and also the WWII plane buried below its waters with all hands, is a solemn place. Today it's quiet and I can raise no-one to help me immerse into its story.

I make a brew and take in the history and progress that I hope we've made. I pick some pebbles from the tread in Super Ten's tyres and then climb back on, glad to've come to this, this special place.

"I had a boy on Moorna station with me called Monkey and it was from him I obtained the story. Frightened by the sound of firing, Monkey at first could not understand what was going on. Presently his father and mother and other relatives fell, shot dead. All his family except Monkey were killed. Terrified, he leapt into the Rufus amongst the dead and dying people."

Jack Coombs says that Monkey always maintained that practically all the natives present were wiped out.

Continuing his narrative, Mr. Coombs said that at this time already most of the country had been taken from the blacks, and many tribes did not quite know where they were going to live. They had not, however, commenced to die off. Many of the families were growing concerned and trust in the white man was undermined.

The Rufus Creek affair, says Coombs, was murder. As a youth he spent many years amongst the boys, and only once was he set upon, and this was by a native at Salt Creek who, when refused more liquor, rushed at him and attempted to strangle him.

CHAPTER 44 – RENMARK

INTRODUCING MEGGS'S 'FIRST LAW OF FRUIT PICKIN' BEER DRINKIN' SYNCHRONICITY'

'**W**hen you get to the pub, if there's a black three-wheeled scooter parked under the window, left of the entrance, I'll be inside.'

'And', I ask, 'how do I find you?'

'Got a beard and I'll be wearing me hat and a fluoro top,' Peter adds. That, I'm figuring isn't narrowing the field down too much, but then he adds, 'Oh, and I've only got one leg.'

It's not much after 10.30 when I pull up at the Tourist Info Office beside the river and across from the wondrous Art Deco beauty which is the Renmark Hotel. This is probably the most stately pub on the entire river. It presides rather than simply stands on the western side of Murray Sreet, facing the morning and the river. The pub has a grandeur that befits its story and its unique position in the history of hotels not just in South Australia, not just on the river, but in the entire country.

Its opening on Monday,8 March 1897 was the result of a long, bitter, decisive but not divisive campaign. If the few puritan and vested-interest opponents who'd argued that this would signal the collapse of river civilisation as they knew it had been hoping the first day would be an exhibition of their most dire predictions of wholesale drunkenness, they were to be disappointed:

The Renmark Hotel was opened at noon on Monday last ... Owing to the number of roughs about who are employed grape picking, it was expected that there would be some rodyism. Although there was plenty of noise however, there was no disturbance that would have called for the interference of the police, if it had been available. Considering that Trooper Teate was away, and the character of the strangers in town, the Committee are to be congratulated that they got over the opening without trouble and damage.

Few pubs in the history of Australia ever had a conception, gestation and birth as difficult, tortured and fraught as did the Renmark community hotel. It grew from a seed planted by the editor of the local newspaper, the *Renmark Pioneer*, was irrigated by leading citizens of the town and was finally harvested by a joyous, celebratory and thankful community.

In June 1895 the *Renmark Pioneer* carried a small, cryptic paragraph regarding a raid by the town's policeman: 'Constable Teate made a raid on a sly-grogery in the settlement and confiscated a quantity of the invigorating beverage for the use of the state.'

Whether the report intended a suggestion as to what purposes the seized hooch was put, or in whose hands and stomachs it would end, we can't be certain but a fortnight later James Ashwell, the editor of the *Pioneer*, fired his first salvo in the battle to have a licensed hotel in Renmark.

The settlement of Renmark was created in 1887 and by agreement with the Canadian Chaffey Brothers, was a 'dry' though not prohibition township. Workers and settlers flooded to the Riverland and, without any legal means of slaking their after-work thirsts, Renmark soon became one of the great sly-grog capitals of the country.

James Ashwell's nascent campaign for a licensed hotel was aimed firmly at the twin targets: the need for a legitimate supply of liquor (together with accommodation, meals and stabling) and the need to eliminate the sly groggers.

His editorial of 15 June 1895 was headed: 'A HOTEL WANTED' and began: 'no other town or settlement in the colony of even half the size of Renmark exists which cannot boast one or more hotels where spirituous liquors may be legitimately retailed.' It continued:

> There is no reason why residents of Renmark should be deprived of privileges enjoyed by other communities of smaller population. It was all very well for the promoters of the settlement to start it on temperance principles, but now a large number of settlers have taken up their permanent residences here there is no reason why the opening of a licensed house should be prevented.

The puritan wowsers wasted little time in hitting back. Tellingly not including his title of 'Reverend' in his sign-off, W. Corly Butler preached that:

> it is not less prohibition but more prohibition that we want. Let us petition, not for abrogation, but for the extension of the law, so that it shall be unlawful for any person within our boundary to make, to hold, or to sell alcoholic liquor, in any quantity without proper authorization ... the introduction of a public house, its agents and agencies, a(re) infinitely more dangerous to the well-being and happiness of a community, than the explosion of many barrels of gun powder ...

No less than three times in his subsequent rebuttal did Ashwell pointedly refer to this writer as 'Reverend'. The battle had started.

(Meanwhile, later that year God rewarded W. Corly Butler for his stalwart stand. In November the Adelaide *Advertiser* reported: 'While bathing in the river on Tuesday evening the Rev. W. Corly Butler thoughtlessly put his arm through a clump of roots by the Waterside, and was immediately bitten in the right forearm by a tiger snake. Mr Butler injected ammonia into the arm, and was seemingly well enough to preside at the meeting of the literary society that evening. He also preached on Wednesday evening, and apparently was suffering from nothing worse than numbness of the bitten limb, but this morning the bite is affecting him considerably, and he is now very ill.' Yep, he works in mysterious ways indeed!)

Slowly the fight for a licensed house in Renmark was refined into a campaign for a community-owned hotel along what became known as the 'Gothenburg System'. The hotel would be controlled by a committee of five local residents and run by an appointed manager. Mrs Jane Meissner had been running her accommodation hotel on the corner of Para and 15th streets for 'about eight years' and she became the linchpin first nominee for licensee.

Finally in February 1897 all the legislative ducks had lined up and the *Pioneer* trumpeted that on 25 February 'Mrs. Meissner will start for Clare, to be present at the meeting of the Licns Bench, by next Thursday's steamer.'

Back in Renmark, the committee, of which James Ashwell was a member, was assuming the success of the application.

> The Renmark Hotel Committee has been busy this week making all arrangements for the opening of the hotel. Two long meetings were held at which nearly every possible contingency was considered and provided for. The beer, wine and spirits, were ordered by Tuesday's mail, to be forwarded on receipt of a wire saying licence was granted.

On the morning of Wednesday 3 March Jane Meissner telegraphed the *Renmark Pioneer*:

> Mr. W. Culross today presented the petition and applied to the Licensing Bench for a publicans' licence at Renmark, and after consideration, his worship, Mr. Johnston, S.M. Chairman of the Bench, intimated that the Branch had decided to grant the licence in respect of the existing premises, subject to Section 47, of the Licensed Victuallers Further Amendment. Act, 1896. It was pointed out to the Bench that it was intended to improve the premises in accordance with the plans as filed. The application was fully explained by the counsel for the Committee. Owing to its novelty the application created considerable interest.

Renmark had a hotel!

The committee moved quickly. 'On Wednesday afternoon a telegram was dispatched confirming each order, and the first instalment of the stock should arrive by the *Ruby* tomorrow morning.'

But the opening of the new hotel would have to be put on ice for just a little longer. 'As Mrs. Meissner will not return till Monday by the *Pearl*, it was decided that the hotel be not opened till noon on that day … The temporary bar, with two beer engines will also be fixed up by then.'

When she returned to the settlement and stepped off the paddle-steamer, she was feted like a heroine and as I head into the bar, Jane Meissner's name tops the list of the wooden honour board in the lobby listing every manager of the 'Renmark Community Hotel'.

The one-legged, fluoro-wearing, scooter-driving bloke I'm looking for is also connected to that honour board. Known to everyone, including occasionally the police, simply as 'Meggs', he just happens to be Jane Meissner's great-grandson, the son of Jane's daughter's daughter.

When Raymond 'Meggs' Johnson had his first beer in this pub back around 1964 when he was 'fifteen or sixteen' it didn't go unnoticed by local Detective Sargent Max James who booted him out with a warning. But then the copper had second thoughts.

'I had this mop of flaming red hair – that's how I got my name – and fair dinkum, I stood out like dogs' even when I wasn't doing anything wrong, which wasn't often. And old Max decided that it was safer for all concerned if I was in the pub where he knew where to find me than out somewhere else getting into trouble, so he told me he'd be sweet if I behaved myself.'

And in the more than half a century since, Ray's pretty much kept on track, never being barred and only once or twice getting kicked out. He tells of the most recent:

'Out here if the staff think you've had enough they'll give you a pint of water and won't serve you any more grog until you've finished off the water. Well one day I came in here and someone had told the barmaid, Sarah here, to give me a glass of water and insist I drink it. Well I was totally sober, hadn't had a beer all day so I just blew up! Sarah was brilliant and wouldn't budge and in the end the manager told me to leave!'

'Yep,' adds Sarah from across the bar, 'that was a memorable.'

So now, pretty much each and every day, Meggs is at his regular perch at the bar here, and since 2006 when a mate suggested he get off the full-strength West End, he's been on the light beer, always in schooners – straight glass, no handle!

'See, it stands to reason – most bar staff are right-handed and I'm right-handed so when they pour a handle they then hand it to you with their right hand and then the handle's on the wrong bloody side! I've got better things to do than rotate my beer every time I get new one so to save the aggro I only drink out of straight glasses.'

His glass size has also changed. 'Everyone used to drive ponies, seven-ounce beers so they'd still be cold when you got to the bottom but when they installed air-con in the bar, that didn't matter so much so we all switched over to schooners – better value!

And then he introduces me to 'Meggs's Law of Fruit Pickin' Beer Drinkin' Synchronicity'.

'When I first started drinking, a schooner cost 16 cents and fruit pickers were paid a dollar an hour. So for every hour you worked you could have six beers. Today a schooner is four bucks and the pickers get $25 dollars an hour. They can still buy six beers for every hour they work. Over the years, that's never been changed. Pickers have always been paid six beers an hour!'

Digesting that demands a beer chaser. As we're waiting to catch Sarah's eye, Meggs expounds on bar etiquette:

'It's how some of these blokes pay that is just completely disrespectful. They'll stand around while the beer's being poured and only when it's in front of 'em they'll dig into their pocket and then lay a mitt full of change on the bar and just look at the girl and expect her to count it out for them. Then all the extra goes back into the same pocket and next time they'll do it all again. Takes three times as long to get served and meanwhile I'm down the end of the bar with my money ready and my throat dry!'

I ask him about his transport, complete with Harley Davidson emblem out the front. It's a Gopher, designed by a bloke in the Riverland, and I tell him about Rex Beaver and his ride-on mower back at Jingellic. He laughs at the thought of Rex cutting the verge grass on the way to and from the pub but reckons his electric mobility scooter is a better deal.

'See, a ride-on mower is classified as "plant" and has to be registered and you can get breathalysed when you're driving it but with the Gopher, I'm legally the same as a pedestrian. If I have a session and head home on it, I can be charged with something like drunk and disorderly if my ginger genes come out but I can't be hit with DUI.'

I share a story about the ex-publican at Willawarrin in New South Wales who'd lost his licence and then copped a heavy fine for carrying a slab home on the back of his mower, so that part of the story at least is true, but Meggs swears so the Gopher immunity!

He shows me a folded, tattered sheet of paper, a print-out of a section of the South Australian road rules that seems to prove his case. 'I carry it with me because I had a couple of run-ins with the local cops, mainly new ones when they first arrive in town, and a friend of mine who actually works at the police station looked up the rules and made me a photocopy.'

The Renmark Hotel is still governed by a committee of five and is still community owned. Members don't have to be local residents but they all receive discounts, special deals and 'even Christmas cards'.

But for Ray the structure is problematic:

'The trouble with community ownership is that some people from the community think that they're entitled to more than people who don't own a part of it. They want some sort of secret extras, just a bit more than someone else and a lot of 'em don't understand the charter of the place. And they say it didn't make a profit but that's not what the place is all about. And if the board is doing its job they it should be breaking even and not paying any tax on profits.'

When I ask if he gets anything special because of his bloodlines, he slaps his leg and laughs, 'Ninety-nine percent of people have no idea that I'm connected to Jane Meissner – it's not something I talk much about.'

I have to head; first there's the museum upstairs that I'm keen to check out and then there's another bloke I need to see in the town but my offer to buy a parting drink is refused.

'I never shout, and never get shouted,' he explains. 'I've seen too many group shouts end in tears – always someone who arrives late and leaves early, getting a few and then pissing off before their round.'

I have a ceremonial schooner of water and leave a schooner's worth of money on the bar, telling Sarah that if Meggs changes his mind, to take it out of my change, if not, consider it a tip.

Upstairs, the museum is another Art Deco beauty, the walls filled with framed old photos, a biography of the pub, and several glorious large display cabinets are chock with crockery, cutlery, more photos, menus, cards and books. It's obviously done with love and commitment and a sense of custody and connection.

I'm in a pub that owes if not its very existence, then certainly its creation and establishment, to the editor of the local paper so I figure it'd be interesting to catch up with the Paul Mitchell, the current editor. It's one of the two weekly deadline days and Paul can't get to the pub so I head up to his offices.

Other than changing its name from *Renmark Pioneer* to the current *Murray Pioneer*, the paper's been published continuously since the heady days of the campaign for the pub and is now in the hands of the fifth generation of the same family.

We get onto the changing face of Renmark and the Riverland – how, back in the days when the agitation was on for the hotel that the locals were vocal, with a healthy disdain for the ruling classes, and how the IWW even initiated strikes amongst the settlers.

But now, in a curious boomerang to the culture of the great shearers' strikes of 1891 and '94 where the shearers were disenfranchised because they were not permanent residents in the towns where they shore and fought for better conditions, nowadays, the advent of the 457 visa and the backpacker economy has also seen most local workers having no rights on polling day. The character of the median local voter, and hence politics, has moved to the right.

Paul reckons he tries for balance and a reflection of this community and, with its footprint stretching throughout the Riverland and down through the Mallee to places like Pinnaroo, and taking no syndicated copy, the focus is fully on local issues.

Renmark has the highest methamphetamine usage rate in South Australia and yet there is no permanently manned police station in the town, the nearest one being down at Berri. The legacy of Constable Teate and Detective Max James has faded and died. This issue of policing plus the management of the Murray-Darling Basin are the two major issues right now.

I ask him about the paper's relationship with the hotel and he thinks for a bit:

We've both been around since the start of the town, like two foundations. We're a bit older and had a role in their creation and we're privately owned and the pub's community owned but I hope that people see us both as serving the community in different ways.

I thank him for his time. He has pages to check and outside the shadows are getting longer. I head back to the river to soak in the dusk. A squadron of pelicans carves across the sky and the scooter's gone from out front of the pub.

MEISSNER'S HOTEL

Corner, Para & 15th. Streets,
RENMARK.

Offers the best and most comfortable Accommodation for

Visitors & Tourists.

Patrons will find every
COMFORT   &   CONVENIENCE
looked for in a first-class

hostelry.

Mrs. MEISSNER
Proprietress.

The Pioneer.

SATURDAY, NOVEMBER 2, 1895.

SLY-GROG
v.
LICENSED
HOUSES.

Cannot some action be taken with a view to the establishment of a licensed house in Renmark? The sly-grog shops seem to do a thriving business, and it is extremely difficult for the local police to take adequate measures for its suppression. If a legitimate trade could be carried on the shanties would have to close. They would get no support and the

PASTS WITH NO PRESENT

Direct routes are for surface skimmers who're in a rush and that sure ain't me, so rather than head west on the Sturt out of Renmark, I retrace it east with the morning sun right in my face for the first bit and then just on 13 kilometres to a right at the sign pointing to Loxton, another 17 kilometres to a similar one and five minutes later I'm at the Lyrup ferry.

Off to my left's the largest mob of pelicans I've yet seen – patrolling the flow in their elastic pairs. The punt's on the other side, empty, but I signal not to come across for me – this scene needs soaking up. So I get out the cameras and try to do the scene justice and then a couple of cars are needing to be brought over to my side so the pelican that's in front of the punt condescends to get out of the way and the humans start to move.

Then it's back up to the Sturt and then just 5 kilometres into Berri with its singular hotel.

Berri acquired its first legal drinking hole in 1913 when William Henry Wade successfully transferred his licence to the town from his pub to the west near Saddleworth. (He was no relation to L. A. B. Wade who'd been appointed Commissioner for Water Conservation at Leeton just six months earlier.)

William Henry was a forerunner of the opportunistic solely profit-driven exploiters who, eighty years later when Juan Antonio announced the awarding of the 2000 Olympics to 'Seed den nee' formed vulture mobs who travelled rural New South Wales buying up pubs and their pokies, removing the machines, transferring the licences and closing the hotels. He moved to the new township of Berri in 1909 and worked on irrigation for the Chaffey brothers in both Renmark and Mildura. He was smart enough to realise his hometown needed a hotel and the easiest way was to import one from outside the area.

In 1911 Wade took over the dud lease of the Royal Oak – a fine looking old building in the dying settlement of Tothill's Creek – from the long term but retiring Ted Knowling, a locally beloved identity who'd had it for over twenty years. Wade obviously had no plans to support that township for the long-term.

The Adelaide *Register*: 'the purchaser of the (hotel) business almost immediately applied for, and eventually obtained, the transfer, of the licence to the irrigation settlement of Berri.'

At the hearing William Wade 'stated he was a justice of the peace (and) gave evidence in support of the application. He had been conducting the Tothill Creek house at a loss.'

Well of course it was running at a loss! That's why you bought it!

Anyway, testimony from the residents of Tothill Creek that the hotel was required in their township was rejected on a technicality and after a short deliberation 'the chairman announced that the application would be granted.'

Billy was in business! He didn't so much hit the ground running once he'd opened his pub at Berri, it was more a case of just, well, hitting the ground:

CREATING A DISTURBANCE

Raymond Scott, a labourer, at Berri, was charged on the information of Mr. W. H. Wade, proprietor of the Riverside Hotel, Berri, with creating a disturbance on his premises at about 1 o'clock on October 9.

William Henry Wade ... deposed that defendant was lying in the bar. Witness requested him to get up and a room would be found for him. Stooping he put his arms round Scott, who assaulted him ...

The accused in defence stated that he was sitting in the bar of the hotel when Mr. Wade tried to get him out. He resisted and would not go. Wade called for assistance, and an all round struggle then took place. He was only trying to defend himself. The flannel shirt was torn off his back.

Wade had purchased most of the ground on which Berri township came to stand from its first white owner, William Marshall, but before long returned it to the government in exchange for 50 acres of vine country on the edge of town.

Meanwhile, his pub rode a roller-coaster and 1920 was a tumultuous year beginning with its licence renewal hearing:

The application was opposed ... Constable Jones stated that ... 'for the last 12 months it had been a common occurrence almost any day to see five or six men lying drunk about the hotel premises and in the sheds and on the lawns ... Had every "drunk" been arrested there would have had to be 50 cells provided to accommodate them' ... On one occasion witness counted 18 drunken men coming out of the hotel, and five of these had to be assisted out. These were placed in motor cars, of which there were three usually standing at the door, and they made their living by conveying drunken men from Berri to the camp at Lone Gum.

The board of management convinced the court that they'd get their house in order and managed to hang onto the licence. But just three months later 600 men from the irrigation works went on strike for higher wages and for better meals and sanitation in their camps.

Publican H. G. ('Bert') Rodgers had been profiled in the local paper when he took over a short time before the men went. The article noted that, 'a few years ago, Mr. Rodgers was at Port Pirie and at that town he was prominently connected with labour matters, being at one time president of the Trades and Labour Council, and chairman of the labour party.'

The law wasn't about to take any chances on where this unionist's loyalties lay:

... the police served Mr. H. G. Rodgers, the licensee of the Riverside Hotel, with a notice to close his premises. The order read as follows:—

'I, Matthew Guy, a justice or the peace, being of opinion that a tumult is expected to take place at Berri as a result of a strike among the workers, hereby direct under section 151 of the Licensing Act of 1917,

one H. G. Rodgers, a person holding a publican's license for the premises known as the Riverside Hotel, Berri, to close his licensed house until further advised to open the said premises.'

Rodgers took it in his stride, improved and regularly expanded the pub and completely changed its face. In 1927, a 'Special Representative of the Adelaide *Register*' scored a junket to the river and was well impressed:

Splendid accommodation for the travelling public is provided at Berri by the Riverside Hotel, situated, as its name implies, along the bank of the Murray ... (T)he proprietor, Mr. H. G. Rodgers has ... completely carried out his objective to make the Riverside hostelry one that is famed throughout the State for comfort, courtesy and good management. He has much to be proud of in the beautiful gardens and lawns available for the comfort of tourists and others. Within the hotel the note of refinement and comfort is apparent also. It is artistically furnished throughout, and is, moreover, scrupulously clean, a virtue much appreciated by travellers.

In seventeen years of slog, Bert Rodgers had dragged the pub back from the threat of loss of its licence to being 'famed throughout the State' for its amenity and professional running.

When the lease was put out for tender in 1934, his efforts were rewarded by the management board with his tender being rejected and the business being handed over to a Mrs M. M. Leahy. Ah loyalty!

But just back up the river the community hotel model of the Renmark Hotel was proving successful and popular so the board got to work on their new licensee. First they tried to buy the freehold from under her but they failed, so they began negotiations. But they lacked the numbers to carry their resolutions, so they adjourned a special meeting for a fortnight, signed up a tribe of sycophants and then made Mrs Leahy an offer she couldn't refuse.

And since 26 June 1937 Berri's had its own community hotel – a pub with a fascinating back story full of colourful characters, shady deals, questionable motives, rough-house tactics and no doubt some altruism and hard yakka.

I pull up the bike on the river side of the road out front of the pub and beside River Jacks Cafe, one of my real favourite caffeine 'n' scrumptious must-goes along the river. Each time I rock up here, I arrive with high expectations and not once have I been disappointed. Double shot, homemade quiche and a dive-bombing seagull done and I head across the road.

There's maybe ten people in the back bar, and about the same number of blaring racing screens and the barman tells me the bistro up the front is the only place if I want a quiet drink.

So I head up there and it's empty, order a South Australian pony of light from the young gentleman who's not interested in having two words let alone a conversation with me. He can't tell me about the history of the place, knows nothing about the management structure of this community hotel and 'sorry, mate, can't help ya' with any details about when the last extensions were added.

I sit down in this room with all the personality, appeal and character of a melted vanilla ice cream, and realise I could be anywhere. Pick any leagues club in New South Wales, any rissole in any state and I could be there. Nothing here connects with anything other than the present. It's safe and it's antiseptic, as colourful as those cubes that lie in the bottom of urinals. And no more appealing.

I head back for a second sobering drink and the barman meets me at the taps.

'Same again please, mate.'

'What is it you're drinking?'

Since I ordered my first, not a single other person's entered the room.

'On second thoughts, don't worry.'

A wander around behind the quite gorgeous Art Deco accommodation reception desk reveals a wall of old images of the pub but the receptionist can't tell me anything about them or when a board member might be able to have a chat about the place.

I was booked in here for the night. As I head back from the photos in the hallway, I cancel. There has to be a better place down river.

At the cafe my seagull mate is attacking the chips on a young kid's plate. I gear up and swing Super Ten along the river then right and a quick elbow left and I head to Loxton. (When I get home I write to the pub with some of my thoughts about the disconnectedness and impersonality of the whole place. The reply comes back without a name, signed off anonymously in unsurpassed impersonality simply as 'The Berri Hotel'.)

In December 1907 the Rose Family of Oakbank submitted plans to the Licensing Court for the first licensed house in the new town of Loxton. A year later, citing difficulties created by the place's isolation and difficulties in sourcing materials and tradies, they begged for an extension to their contracted launch date.

The family, which had incorporated a management company, finished the construction in November 1908 and immediately advertised for tenders for a five-year lease on the pub. The lease was taken up and as the town expanded, the pub put on extra rooms and an extra bar, eventually even an extra storey. Business chugged along with a succession of licensees working for the out-of-town owners.

In May 1922 the first threat to its monopoly surfaced when Morris Coffey, secretary of the Loxton Residential Club, applied for a club licence for premises that the club proposed to erect. The Licensing Inspector objected and:

> *Although the objection was made by Inspector Davey, the real objectors were the Loxton Hotel Company, who had spent many thousands of pounds in the erection of a large and up-to-date hotel.*

The challenge was beaten off but the locals were getting restless and agitated for a second pub. In April 1930 a local option poll had resulted in 59 votes for a reduction (from 1!), 107 votes for retaining the status quo and a whopping 482 in favour of a second hotel.

By law this cleared the way for a second licence for Loxton and the campaign cranked up, beginning with a community meeting in the Loxton Institute in July 1930 where the feeling was divided on the need for another pub for the population of 3500 but 'unanimous that if there is to be another hotel it should be run on community lines'.

One local, obviously having studied the progress, development and success of the Renmark community hotel and with his finger firmly on Loxton's pulse hadn't waited for red-tape formalities of community consultations and deep-into-the-night discussions. As soon as the poll result was announced Hurtle Horan (now that, folks is one hell of a name!) put down his drink, headed to his solicitor's and lodged an application for the town's second licence. The *Murray Pioneer* and *Australian River Record* covered the agitation exhaustively:

MR. H. L. HORAN said he had taken his cue from the result of the local option poll. The people by that poll had practically demanded another licence in the town. The result of the poll gave the Licensing Court the power to grant two more licences. Barmera got in first and secured a licence. That left one licence which could be granted.

Hurtle by name, hurtle by nature. By the time of the meeting, he'd already gone straight to the top.

Horan [advised the meeting that he] had spoken to [Mr Hill, the South Australian Premier] over the phone [and the Premier had said] ... he would assist in securing a licence for Loxton. Mr. A. G. Cameron, M.P., who was present with them that night, had also given an assurance that he would do all in his power to get another licence.

Old Hurtle then showed the lessons he'd learnt from Jane Meissner up at Renmark:

[Councillor] Scott-Todd had entered into negotiations with the [Mr Horan]. These had resulted in Mr. Horan offering to hand over the licence, if granted, to a committee, providing that body would reimburse him to the extent of £19/8/, which was the cost of the drawing of plans for the new hotel, and advertising and legal expenses (applause) ... The plans of the proposed new hotel, said Mr. Horan, were good ones, and the building would cost about £19,000. It would not disgrace 'the town. (Applause)

One councillor played stick in the mud:

Cr. Petch said he held that if two licences were held in Loxton one would die a natural death, or would be bought out by the other, or the standard of the two houses would come down.

Eventually this meeting and the subsequent council meeting bought it. All fell in behind Hurtle Horan's application before the Murray Bridge Licensing Court. Ah, and that's when it all went pear-shaped.

On Wednesday 20 August 1930, 'Hurtle Lawrence Horan (represented by Basil Harlord) applied for a publican's and billiards license for a new hotel in Loxton to be called the Producers' Club Hotel.'

Several opponents to the application were heard and countered but then counsel for one of them broke the script and sought confirmation from Horan about a detail of his recent past.

'Yes,' he confirmed, 'until four days ago' he'd been a bookie.

This scandalous revelation caused an immediate adjournment and on resumption Basil Harlord: 'said that in view of the evidence learned in cross-examination he had conferred with his other witnesses, including A. G. Cameron, M.P. They desired to dissociate themselves from the present applicant and application.'

Gambling? Drinking? Together? How shameless!

The Bench had no option: 'The magistrate said that the application would be dismissed (partly) on the ground that the ... applicant was not a fit and proper person to be granted a licence.'

Hurtle Horan never got to build his pub. No-one else did either but seven years later, in January 1937 Loxton finally had its much-cherished community hotel and Councillor Petch, who'd warned of a war if two licences were granted, was pretty much vindicated:

a committee of Mildura citizens bought the lease of the Loxton Hotel, Loxton (S.A.), and converted it into a community institution. An option of purchase has been obtained. All profits will be devoted to local welfare. This is the second Murray River town to adopt the community hotel idea. The first was Renmark.

The committee created a management vehicle, the Loxton Club Hotel Ltd, and a dozen years later, with everyone involved squeaky clean and free of gamblers or bookmakers, the deal was complete.

'Loxton Club Hotel Ltd. has purchased the local hotel from the proprietors, J. A. and A. G. Johnston, of Oakbank, for £32,000.'

From the car park in the middle of East Terrace, the Loxton pub's a damn fine-looking building. Double storied brick with balcony running along most of its frontage, the balustrades tastefully done and well maintained.

In past the large montage celebrating its centenary in 2008, past a photo every rider would love of a motorcycle group of three rigs and five single riders when ATGATT (an acronym well-known to motorcycle riders and standing for, 'All The Gear All The Time') was still way in the future, past the frosted glass door panel etched with '1908' and into the ... no, this can't be right, into a formula soulless bistro.

I U-turn and find the bar at the side. Six odds screens and three action screens, no-one behind the bar and just the one bloke down in the front row seat watching his 'investment' treat him poorly.

In a pub that was denied a licence because the publican-elect was a bookmaker. There can be no more blatant denial of one's roots.

I head back into the sunshine.

NON-PUBS OF DIFFERENT TYPES

The road downstream from Loxton bends north with the Murray close by to my right, and then suddenly on my left a bit over 25 kilometres into the ride, a little back from the current road, a glorious ruin surveys the scene. Stately, gorgeous and evocative, it demands attention like a stunning older woman at a cocktail party.

It appears to've once fronted the edge of the road north and at its southern end there's a pair of metal posts, maybe 3 metres high with wooden cross beam at the top – obviously once the supports for a sign facing the traffic from the nearside of the road. Not something you usually find on a residence.

Inside there's a massive old wood-fired stove in one room and magnificent old fireplaces in pretty much every other room and behind the failing render the old stone mud construction is revealed, together with the split log roofing under the corrugated iron roofs.

Out the back is an incredible cellar with original hessian ceilings above beams of local trees and some newer reinforcements of corrugated iron. Behind the front building are the remains of a large yard or building, possibly stables.

My later searches for any mention of a pub at Moorook prove fruitless. A clipping from 1919 complains that 'at Moorook … there (is) no accommodation at all for the travelling public. So this must've been a residence, possibly of noted early settler, Mr. H. Drogemuller, but whatever, like the woman at the cocktail party, the secrets here are part of the allure!

I again head north, then after ten kilometres a right onto the Sturt Highway. The river's still just to my right as I cross the wide bridge, then it's a right into Cobdogla, down past school and back to the river.

The first time I ever came here the day was a stinker – well into the 40s. I was riding my beloved red Ducati and wearing a shell armour suit over a merino long-sleeved T. In the biking communities there's endless discussion about the best methods of keeping cool on such days and one method I, well I guess I invented was put to use that day.

So I pulled up at the Bruno Bay boat ramp, shed my boots and socks and just waded into the water. The armour shell floats, as do my armoured riding pants, so I just floated there in the glorious cool of the river. Could've dozed off!

Completely refreshed and re-energised, socks and boots back on and start riding. The merino layer holds water better than cotton and certainly better than any poly fabric and it takes a bit over an hour to fully evaporated on a scorcher at 100 kilometres per hour. During that hour I'm well within cool and it's then I begin looking for another bit of easy access to the river (or someone in a town watering their lawn!).

Normally this would've been a short, simple chapter on the ride from Loxton and the backtrack to Bamera and points beyond. But tonight I'm stopping here, not at the impersonal Cobdogla Club with its pokies and betting screens and no-one who can tell me much about the town, but down beside the river under a clear star-filled sky.

See, 'Cobby' is a place of great stories and history. This town was the confluence of the great counter-influences of the history of pubs in this part of the river. It was the focus where the various interests, vested and free, faced up and fought their battles for the souls and what they considered, without much consultation, the wellbeing, of the population. This tiny place is the epicentre of myths, legends, history and battles between the forces of religion and those of free will. To go past it without comment would be to ignore the core issues in the history of this area.

I cut Super Ten's engine at the entrance to the designated camping areas along the riverside.

William Napper is a bloke we'll meet formally in the next chapter when we get to Lake Bonney but he arrived in South Australia in the 1840s and with his wife headed out to the river. In 1929 the *Murray Pioneer* interviewed two of his daughters, then living in Renmark. They detailed, amongst many other things that Napper's first wife, 'after some 18 years hard pioneering work on the river, died at Cobdogla in 1869, and her humble headstone may yet be seen just off the main road which leads between Cobdogla and the Kingston punt.' And they continued that, 'she was a woman who ranked high in the esteem of all who knew her. She was a true pioneer in every sense of the word.'

The cairn beside me, on the riverside of this track that was once the main road, is this 'humble headstone' of William Napper's first wife. Some rodent has removed the plaque from its front. Even in its anonymity, poignancy survives.

The township's named after the original white station in the area and the Napper sisters went on to share one of their beliefs about the origin of the name:

> *One day the 'Scrubber,' 'Fisherman Jimmy', and others came up to the hotel leading a very old black who was quite blind. The young fellows all wanted to go hunting and asked father to take care of the old black for the day. Father told the old fellow, who had white hair, to sit down in the sun. He fed him, and the black dozed most of the day. At night the hunters returned, and as they walked past the hotel one behind the other, a voice called, 'Cobdogla', 'Cobdogla'. The old black got up and joined his tribe.'*

So, er, just a couple of questions: firstly, what were you girls doing up so late? And secondly, 'the hotel' was beside a lake and was ten kilometres from here so why was did this place beside the river and more than a short horse-ride distant get anointed with the name? Sorry but that fails the pub test and I ain't even at the pub!

Another version is:

> *that when the station was being fenced, a group of blacks came down the river, which was in flood, with fish and wild fowl in abundance, and to illustrate the good living, exclaimed repeatedly to the white men, 'Copdogla', meaning 'land of plenty'. The whites, according to the story, painted or chalked the name on the back of their cart, and it was soon transferred to the designation of the station, the 'p' being perverted to 'b'.*

However it got its name, it's a bloody nice change from the endless string of places named after governors, parliamentarians, explorers and surveyors. And it's designed to be said out loud!

Around the time William Napper arrived in South Australia, copper was discovered over in Burra, 170 kilometres to the west in South Australia. Miners from Cornwall flocked to the town, dug caves in the soft clay of the riverbanks, and so spent most of their existence underground. When floods and disease drove them out of their troglodyte existences, they were moved to the nearby government township of Redruth, whose major claim to fame was that state's first prison outside the capital.

The copper didn't last and the mine was closed in 1877. Burra and especially Redruth dwindled, hardly surviving.

Forty years later in August 1919, Redruth's Courthouse Hotel was doing it very tough in a near ghost town and its publican, the more than adequately named, John Alexander Wolseley Robertson applied to the East Midland Licensing Court for permission to remove his publican's and billiards licences to the new settlement of Cobdogla where prospects looked more rosy (or should that be rosé!).

These were boom times for the new irrigation areas. World War I had finally and mercifully ended the previous November and returning soldiers – boys who'd become men, all of whom had lost mates, often brothers,

in the battle, were central to the government's post-war plans, especially along our greatest river.

Sam McIntosh, South Australia's Director of Irrigation, saw an unlimited grape-fuelled future for an industry powered by returning soldiers, claiming it realistic to expect between 10,000 to 20,000 people to populate Cobdogla making it 'a second Los Angeles'. (Reality check: current population is south of 300.)

The Diggers, finally out of uniform and thankfully out of harm's way flocked to the river, all prepared to exchange a hard day's yakka for fair wages and decent conditions, and to serve the country in peace as they'd done in war.

Hotels had to provide four things: the first was accommodation and as down at Moorook, there was no accommodation at Cobdogla (or at Kingston). The nearest hotels were back at Berri or 40 kilometres downstream at Wailkerie. Even the Director of Irrigation had argued in court that 'more accommodation was urgently needed at Cobdogla'. Commercial traveller Robert Fox brought laughter from the Bench when, in answer to magistrates' question of how he had found Cobdogla with regard to accommodation, he replied, 'There is nothing to find.'

The second requirement was stabling and the site on which J. A. W. Robertson proposed to build had ample room for horse stalls out the back. The third criterion was meals, which Robertson had served throughout his time at Redruth so that wasn't an issue. And finally was a need to provide refreshment. Robbo was sure happy to tap the kegs and uncork the bottles as often as needed and the soldiers wished that was much sooner rather than later.

Importantly, unlike many applications for new licences or transferals, there wasn't a single petition or testimonial, not even a solitary lone voice from a single local opposing Robertson's plan to create an establishment that would satisfy an agreed and established need.

Seems a no-brainer doesn't it? Yeah, nah!

Robertson's first problem was that the map of local option electorates had been redrawn two years earlier and Redruth and Cobdogla were no longer in the same control areas. There was no provision in the Act for the removal of a licence from one to another, only the movement of licences within the same area. Basically not much more than a thin strand of red tape that the Licensing Court could easily overcome.

But then, enter the wowsers. Five months before Robertson's first hearing at the Midland Licensing Court, the Methodists had held their state conference in Adelaide. Amongst the pious, yet business-minded clergy who decided that things were so dire in Burra that it would be expedient to sell the remaining land that the church owned in Redruth were the Reverend John Pearce, secretary of Methodist Home Missions, and Reverend George Shaw, ex-president of the Methodist Conference.

When the application for the licence was being heard, these two just happened to be in Renmark, on a church-appointed expedition 'enquiring into the conditions of soldiers' settlement in that district.'

The fact that Renmark was a different 'district' to Cobdogla didn't stop these two from chucking in their two bob's worth. They sent a telegram off to the Honourable J. G. Bice, Chief Secretary of South Australia, 'Protesting strongly ... in the interests of the soldiers employed at the construction camps ... against the granting of a licence at Cobdogla.'

Adelaide's more liberal *Daily Herald* felt obliged to comment on the perceived 'interests of (these) soldiers':

> We are quite sure that, had not the necessity for an hotel at Cobdogla been so obvious and urgent, and had not the residents there been strongly in favour of the granting of the application, opposition would have been catered. As there was no opposition before the Court, it is reasonable to assume 'that no one in the immediate neighbourhood was opposed to' the granting of the application.

The irony and hypocrisy didn't escape them either and the paper posed a couple of questions for the chief secretary:

> Is it not a fact that the Government (of which he is a member) recognising the importance of the wine and brandy industries to this State has advanced thousands of pounds for the erection of brandy distilleries on the banks of the Murray: And is it not also a fact that the same Government is making a special provision in the agreements with returned soldier blockers that portion of their lands must be planted with brandy grapes?

And it then went on to observe, 'If such is the case, then according to the Minister it is wrong to sell in an irrigated area the principal product of that area, which is absurd.'

As judgement day neared, the Methodists kept up the pressure. Their

Synod of the Middle District met in Gawler and agreed that:

Owing to spirituous liquor materially affecting work in the irrigation construction camps, along the upper Murray, thus hindering repatriation, the Government was asked to do all in their power to prevent the prospective settler waiting longer for his land and paying more for it, owing to this obstruction. The Synod was under the strong conviction that the granting or the transfer of the hotel licence from Redruth to Cobdogla would be disastrous to the work of repatriation in the latter district and to the general welfare of the settlement. Belief in the need for the prohibition of the liquor traffic was affirmed.

Faced with this zealotry, the court's eventual refusal of the application in a majority 2–1 decision, with the chairman dissenting, was not much more than a moot charade. In response to the two alien reverends' pre-hearing telegram, Bice had informed them that, 'the issue of a license was one within the jurisdiction of the Licensing Court, and in which the Government could not interfere,' but assured them that they should lose no sleep nor waste any prayers. The wowser-controlled powers-that-be would do their bidding, Thy Will be Done!

... the policy of the Government [is] against the erection of licensed premises in irrigation settlements, and in the event of the application in question being granted, a Bill [will] be immediately introduced into Parliament dealing with the matter.

Later that year, despite the plans of John Robertson to personally survive and supply a wanted service being scuttled, the government moved to alter its Licensing Act of 1917, section 119 (1) of which began:

No licence shall be granted in respect of any previously unlicensed premises situated in that portion of the said State which is comprised and described in 'The Chaffey Brothers Irrigation Works Act, 1887,' and in the schedule thereto ...

Those 250,000-acre defined areas did not extend to Cobdogla and the government was taking no chances.

A letter to the Adelaide *Register* from 'Commonsense' put it all pretty nicely: 'For pretty cool wowserism give me the Bill before Parliament to stop hotel licenses for irrigation areas. Has some one put a pair of dark glasses on the Premier?'

Eventually in 1932 Act 2083 was passed. Its preamble read, 'An Act to enact that section 119 of the Licensing Act, 1917, shall apply in relation to licences granted in respect of premises within the Cobdogla Irrigation Area ...'

And so the deed was done and Cobdogla was officially out of danger. No threat of a privately owned, publican-operated place with personality ever existing in this town baby!

Cobdogla's story is similar to many towns along this part of the river where the government believed that young men were capable of making a decision to risk their lives for their country and were equipped to commit to shedding sweat toiling to improve it. But when it came to deciding how to spend their leisure time, when their shoulders were briefly off the wheel, the prohibitionist Protestants knew best.

So tonight I won't be in some small pub with a connected, involved, caring publican on one side of the bar and long-term locals sharing stories on the other. No, I'll be down beside the wonderful river under a blanket of stars, with the regular slaps of fish jumping, no doubt the mandatory far-off dog barking and the endless calls of a storm bird across the river.

FAITH JUST AIN'T ENOUGH

Trucks haul past all night on the highway to the north and I change camera batteries three times during the gorgeous night. Pelicans glide past as the low sun hits the far bank in the morning and I pack it all up and head out. The place I'm headed is just 10 kilometres away so plenty of time for the scenic route, and I head east to Bamera then cut down to the water and follow Lake Bonney anticlockwise on Queen Elizabeth Drive until I'm at the north-west corner of the lake.

High on the hill to my right is a modern homestead but to my left, probably ten metres above the level of the lake, and maybe 100 metres from its edge today, is the place I'm seeking. It's never good to see a pub in ruins, but sometimes it's beyond good to see the ruins of a pub. This is one of those times.

A quick detour: in 1920 King George V, who'd during the war changed his family name from Saxe-Coburg-Gotha to the current 'Windsor' to hide his connections to the enemy 'Hun', dispatched his son Edward, Prince of Wales to the antipodes to instil some post-war cheer amongst the colonies.

This is the bloke who became King Edward VIII. He'd had measles in his childhood and this created er, a fair degree of erectile dysfunction once he hit and passed puberty. He countered his problem by having relationships only with married women whom he believed were more sexually experienced and therefore more likely to be able to arouse him. He ended up with Wallis Simpson, a manipulative American, and ended up abdicating and living pretty much in exile.

Anyway, he came out to Australia in 1920 on a goodwill visit and was invited up to a property north of Coonamble in central New South Wales. Between the town and the property was the Tyrone Hotel and on his way up the Prince dropped in. About a dozen locals were inside. He'd been

schooled on what it takes to be instantly popular in an Australian pub and he announced that he'd like to shout the bar.

Instantly he became the 'Digger Prince'. He then headed up for some days of shooting native animals and when word got out he was headed back south, just short of fifty people were stretching the walls of the old pub. Again he obliged and bought drinks all round. 'Not a Wowser' shouted the Mudgee paper.

Now this is, as far as I can work out, unique in the history of pubs in this country; the only time a monarch or future monarch even rocked up to a bush pub like this, let alone put bank notes and coins featuring his old man's head on the bar and cleared everyone's slate.

Sounds like a place worth keeping eh? Well less than a decade later the Tyrone Hotel sold its last drinks and the licence was transferred over to Armatree. Something I can understand – the reality of business and changing populations. Armatree was a new railhead with silos for the wheat crops.

But, and here's what I just can't get my head around, in 1934 the papers carried reports that the pub was being totally demolished. This unique landmark was razed to the ground, not because the bricks and other materials were needed elsewhere. Just, it seems, because!

Ashley, who's doing such a brilliant job at the Armatree Hotel nowadays, got me the number of a bloke he thought might have some details about the Tyrone Hotel and so I rang Adam Macrae who confirmed he did and told me where and when to meet up with him.

Adam's one of the most vocal and knowledgeable leaders of the fight to guard the purity of the Artesian Basin and other underground aquifers. He is at the forefront of the Lock the Gate Alliance against CSG and the forced routing of gas pipelines through farmers' properties. In the hour trip in his ute it becomes very obvious this bloke knows the land, knows its history, understands what's under it, is across the Indigenous connection to land and he knows exactly where the old Tyrone Hotel once stood.

When we get to the site there's nothing much apart from rubble, some evidence of foundations, some beautiful old drink bottles and a single rock bearing a plaque. It was placed there by Adam's father maybe forty years ago and it reads:

The site of the
Tyrone Hotel
About 1895 to 30.5.1928

This erudite, loquacious bloke is speechless – as I am – at the demolition of this place. The destruction and the mindset behind it is incomprehensible, the loss immense. And so when I see ruins of the Lake Bonney Hotel on the south-eastern corner of the intersection of Morgan Road and Queen Elizabeth, my spirit rises.

In 1855 William Napper and his wife, Anne, arrived in Adelaide after a six-month cruise from England. On the trip William got matey with a bloke named William Parnell. They were both timber-cutters and general labourers and pretty soon after landing in Adelaide they all struck out east for the river country.

They lobbed at Cobdogla near where I spent last night and began working as timber-cutters, hewing sleepers for the new railways from the river red gums along the Murray banks.

According to an interview with two of William Napper's daughters published in 1929:

... every week or so the hardy overland drovers came down the Murray (and across the north shore of Lake Bonney) with large mobs of cattle and horses. Later droves of sheep from the Darling station made use of this stock route.

... Parnell realised that the camping ground of these drovers would make a good site for an hotel. He spoke to Napper about it, made a trip to Adelaide, and soon came back with permission to build, and open a house accommodation. Rough plans were made and then the two friends commenced building.

... The hotel consisted of 11 rooms, and ... in its hey day was one of the

important centres between Sydney and Adelaide ... The bar was a fairly large one always neatly kept and well stocked. There were three rows of bottles at the back of the bar together with storage room for beer.

In June 1862 The Bench of Magistrates approved the transfer for the licence of the Lake Bonney Hotel from William Parnell to his mate, William Napper. The place has been known as 'Napper's' ever since.

I reckon William Napper must've already been working at the place before he took over. Either that or he got into the saddle smooth and fast. Because just six months later the Adelaide *Observer* was lauding his track record of hospitality in a report on the Lake Bonney races:

The day was unfortunately extremely hot; but nevertheless the races went off with great eclat. We were agreeably surprised as to the number of fair equestriennes who were present on the course ...

The day's amusements were wound up by a substantial dinner at the Lake Bonney Hotel, which was served up in Host Napper's usually correct style. This was followed by a ball, which was attended by a large number of ladies, who with their partners, in spite of the heat, kept up dancing with indomitable spirit until the small hour of the morning warned them of the necessity of taking their departure.

The dancing was in the 'eating room' which could hold about a dozen for meals, a lot more for dancing and 'comfortable beds were provided' in all accommodation rooms but one. In the tradition which we first came across way back up at Tintaldra, Napper's had their version of a 'dead house' and though it had more than just straw on the floor, it still wasn't fully salubrious.

The interview with the daughters noted, '(I)n the 'rowdy' room, where stockmen and others who had kicked over the traces a bit were locked up by the management until they were sober, only bullock hide beds were used.'

William Napper's first wife, Anne died in 1869. The anonymous, vandalised cairn which I photographed last night just up from my camp beside the river, is her modest headstone.

Napper and his new wife, Eliza set about maximising the potential of their pub and got to work on the entertainment and the grub. The daughters again:

This man [Johnson] had been knocking about the river for some time when one day someone asked him if he could play the piano. He answered yes, and walking into the dance room at a race ball played all night for the tireless people who 'would not go home till morning.' But Johnson soon showed that he could do more than play a piano and taking over the kitchen at Lake Bonney fed visitors as they had never been fed before on the Murray.

But nothing stays the same. On the back of western expansion of settlement from Sydney and north from Adelaide, stock routes changed and the one across the north of Lake Bonney and past Napper's became less used. The pub at Overland Corner was now on the major trade route and got all the business and began race meetings on the alluvial flats between it and the river.

In late 1876 William Napper faced the reality of his hopes dying and closed his pub. It stood empty for five years while he, dreamer but realist, took over the licence of his competitor at Overland Corner. His wife died the following year aged just thirty-eight and it seems that Napper must've lost the enthusiasm required to be hospitable, especially in another's pub. Without notifying the owners, he sublet to a bloke named James Spedding. The landlords took him to court in 1881 claiming that he'd allowed the pub to 'fall into disrepair, and … a dilapidated and ruinous condition.'

Napper lost the case, was turfed out of the pub and, now without income, was forced to pay costs.

He returned to his old hotel at Lake Bonney and, though without a licence, opened an B&B accommodation-only operation and experimented with irrigation and with various fruit trees.

In 1892 a South Australian parliamentary delegation visited the area. Adelaide's *Express and Telegraph* reported their time at Lake Bonney:

The Speaker and the Commissioner of Crown Lands met an old acquaintance in Mr. Napper … During the hour that a stop was made [his] garden was thoroughly inspected and it indeed presented a marked contrast to the surrounding country. Around the house were a number of almond trees, which were planted seven years ago and had not been irrigated. They have grown remarkably well, and at present have a heavy crop. Orange trees … also showed a fine growth … The vines … have done exceedingly well, and last year a fair amount of fruit was obtained from them. Apricots, plums, mulberries, apples, peaches, figs … are thriving admirably … Vegetables, including cabbages, lettuces, onions, and thousand-headed kale, have all been grown successfully, while lucern seems to thrive amazingly.

William Napper, visionary pioneering publican, passed away in either May 1907 aged eight-one if you believe the plaque at the ruins, or a year later but year younger if you trust the contemporary *Renmark Pioneer* which noted his death in June 1908:

A very old riverside identity passed away on Tuesday in the person of Mr William Napper, who died at his residence on Lake Bonney. Mr Napper, who was eighty years, of age, had lived on the Lake for the last half century, keeping the Lake Bonney hotel until it was closed some 20 years ago. He has left a family of two sons and three daughters, none of whom are married.

I'm going with the paper if for no other reason than an article in the same rag three weeks later which noted that, 'Old Mr. Napper … has just crossed over the River at the ripe old age of four score years.' Nicely put!

I'd spoken with the sister of the family who live in the homestead that'd been on my right as I pulled up here. She gave me permissions and instructions on what I was seeking.

So I head a little further north on the Morgan Road and then pull the bike to the side. Off in the middle of a sloping field, green with the sprouting of recently planted crops, possibly 100 or so metres from the road, is a small post and rail enclosure. Two bollards at the northern end have fallen while the two others remain upright. There is no sign, no plaque, no tribute – no indication whatsoever that within this two-metre-square enclosure lie the remains of William Napper, his second wife, Eliza, and those of an infant daughter.

I try to get a shot of the plot with the old pub in the background but the hill's rise prevents it. I walk back to the bike convinced that while the maintained ruins are a valuable testimony to this man's work, surely he and his pioneering wife deserve even a roadside plaque to recognise their final resting places.

But even in the absence of such a memorial, a visit to the ruins of Napper's hotel is as rewarding as any sojourn at any still operating pub along this amazing river.

CHAPTER 48 – OVERLAND CORNER

THE RIVER, AND THE PUBS, TURN THE CORNER

Less than ten minutes of sweet riding, from leaving Napper's ruins, I'm leaning left off the Goyder Highway into Old Coach Road and then pulling up out front of what's known as the Overland Corner Hotel.

It's been a year or so since I was last here but Phil recognises me, heads inside for my drink (and one for himself) and I plonk down on one of the tables not already hosting any of the mob of bikers who're in for a couple of days.

Phil, a Kiwi, and his Netherlands-born wife Renske took over this place in 2012 after coming to this part of the world as a community engagement officer and viticulturist. He first worked in pubs around the age of fourteen cleaning flagons (ah … remember them!) but this is the first one he's had skin in.

And he's very quick to point out that this place is not really a pub at all. 'It's a tourism destination historic site with a liquor licence' and it just might be the only place in the country that's still bound by the six o'clock closing laws.

Renske now does the cooking because, 'we used to get in good chefs but the bigger pubs around the place who could give them more hours kept stealing them from us.'

Phil's got himself a sauv blanc from the range of local wines and as we ease them down we get onto the wonderful and strange history of Overland Corner.

In 1859 John Chambers was given permission to erect and occupy an accommodation house here. Four years before, 'Owing to trouble with the natives and cattle duffers, the authorities in 1855 decided to open a

police station [at Overland Corner],' and in supporting the application the constabulary described the establishment of a hotel next door to their station as 'beneficial'. Just maybe they were talking about their own morale.

It was built in eight months from ancient local limestone by the Brand brothers. Fifty years later Harry Brand would proudly reminisce that, '(t)he present hotel at Overland Corner was built by myself and my brother in '58. We cut and sawed all the stone used in its construction and I think it has stood the test of time fairly well.'

In March 1860 William Brand's application for a publican's licence was successful and the Overland Corner Hotel was up and running. Soon, along with Napper's back at Lake Bonney and Von Rieben's downstream a bit at North West Bend, it became a landmark outpost for drovers, bullockies, intrepid settlers and, some would argue the odd bushranger.

William was the first publican on sufferance. He and his brothers had followed the gold rush to Avoca in Victoria and youngest brother George had struck it best, finding a 52-oz nugget. It was George who most wanted to run the pub but he was still a bit under eighteen years old and so had to wait nearly three years for the licence to be transferred to him.

In 1937 Lucy Maymon Hines wrote of the early days out here and detailed an adventure not long after the pub'd opened by von Rieben's son.

Driving … the sheep to Overland Corner Hotel, they were rounded up, and Mr. von Rieben, hungry and exhausted, sought food and shelter for the night. The hotel was full of linesmen, laying the telegraph line from

The Brand Brothers

James, William, Henry and George

William, Henry and George built the Overland Corner Hotel in 1859 for John Chambers. The Brand Brothers emigrated from Graves-end in Kent, England in 1851.

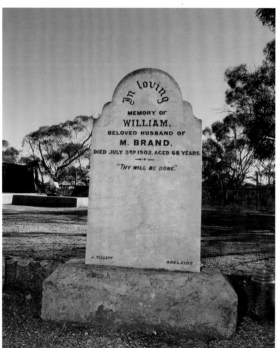

In loving
MEMORY OF
WILLIAM,
BELOVED HUSBAND OF
M. BRAND,
DIED JULY 3RD 1902, AGED 68 YEARS.
"THY WILL BE DONE."

J. TILLETT   ADELAIDE

Wentworth to Adelaide – so drunk and noisy that the noise scared the
sheep. They began to break away, and Mr von Rieben and the drovers had
to sleep near them all night to keep them quiet. They had no blankets, as
the horses were too poor to carry anything but bare necessities, and were
frozen with the cold.

With the sound cranking up from the bikers' amps, I figure it might be wise to rattle my own dags, head down to the river and stake out my claim for the night. I ease through the riders' campsite, giving a few nods to wearers in the usual seemingly mandatory black vests with patches, and out across the alluvial fan flat to the riverside.

There's no room accommodation at the Overland Corner, but the camping down by the side of the Murray is simply superb and the sky is cloudless as I unload the tent, set up the Trangia camp stove, blow up my mattress and do the rest of a solivagant's chores just two metres from the water.

I make a brew as a lone pelican patrols the mirror surface of the river and corellas squawk and squabble in the trees. I'm almost out of earshot of the music, and the unique peace that comes from solitude by water flows over me. And yet, when you're aware of the story of a place, when the legends and the ghosts are nearby, you are never within it alone.

The site is devoid of litter, no detritus or jetsam, and it's safe to leave my home open and unguarded near the scene of one of the more memorable thefts in the river's history. In 1925 the *Murray Pioneer* ran the recollections of Alf Thompson 'an abstemious man himself, [who] probably knows as much about [the] early sly grog days as anyone.' Alf recalled:

During one low river period 50 barrels of beer were ordered with other
liquor to come up by the S.S. Federal. The steamer stuck at the sand bar
near Overland Corner. The liquor was landed on the river bank, and the
hotel authorities were not informed of the occurrence until some days later.
When teams arrived at the Corner to lift the grog they found 25 barrels
empty, and half the spirits had walked. There was only a lonely postal
official living at the Corner then, and on examination he was found quite
sober.

So I head back up to the pub. In 1864, due to the 'indefatigable exertions of the Messrs. Brand' the first of what became a regular annual race meeting was held on this alluvial fan which extends to the river's edge, but today

there's no trace left of the hayburners. Which is a pity! It would still make an amazing country/picnic racetrack.

I blow the froth off an OCG and go through a bit of the history of the pub with my host – how the pub changed hands a few times, survived the police station closing in 1894, but then how 'Bunyip' Palmer pulled the last beers three years later and then pulled up stumps for good.

Later Phil tells me his theory about why the 'Bunyip' let the licence lapse. Since its opening in 1860 the pub's mainstay was the bullockies (or as Phil calls them, 'bullockers') taking fleeces and limestone to Adelaide and bringing station supplies back north. These teams consisted of the bullocky and his offsider, who was generally eight to twelve years old.

'Once the kids got older than that their feet could reach the stirrups so they became riders and, since there was more money in droving, they gave the bullocks away.'

But in 1863 the South Australian government passed, 'An Act to consolidate and amend the Laws for regulating the retail of' Liquor, and for preserving good order in Licensed Public Houses.'

Section 56 read:

Every person licensed to deal in wines or spirits under this Act, who shall
knowingly supply any sort of distilled liquor to any boy or girl under the
age of twelve years to be drunk upon the premises, shall be liable to a
penalty of not less than Twenty Shillings nor more than Five Pounds.

Yep, no longer could eight, nine, ten or even eleven-year-olds throw back a porter or three between sucking on their cheap 'backie rollies' after a hard day of swearing at snorting bullocks! For the child labourers it was a swift switch from depraved to deprived.

The hotel was blindsided! In one stroke this pub, boxed flank to flank with the police station, lost close to half its clientele! And that, reckons Phil, was the major reason why Bunyip Palmer called 'last drinks' at the sadly childless pub for the last time in 1897 and headed for greener, much greener, pastures upriver.

I reckon he may be at the edge of the truth – that there may've been a stronger catalyst. The unconscionable decision to ban sub-teens from drinking may've certainly contributed to the demise of the Overland Corner pub but mopping up the slops of this deeply fermented tale of ale I reckon there may've been other factors.

In an article in the *Murray Pioneer* an old local by the name of Thompson recalled 'Bunyip' as a 'mysterious individual [who] claimed to have the skin of a bunyip in his possession' and who was busted in his room opposite to where the hotel now stands: 'Th(e) sly grogger … was caught and fined half a hundred. He paid the fine into court, and it was whispered that he could have found £500 cash if necessary, so lucrative was his business.'

Two days after Christmas in December 1893 the South Australian *Register* newspaper ran a page 5 article headed 'SLY GROG-SELLING AT RENMARK' which reported three cases being brought against Mr Palmer, 'who pleaded guilty and was fined £50.' Two others were fined lesser amounts, no doubt reflecting Bunyip's dominance of the trade. The report finished with the resigned observation that, '(a) licensed hotel cannot be started here, owing to the settlement being instated on the basis that no licenses be granted.' (Of course, we've been through that a couple of chapters ago!)

This was a year before the cops pulled out of Overland Corner and relocated to Renmark for the explicit purpose of fighting the sly-grog trade. Once they'd gone there was little stopping Palmer serving the young bullocky offsiders and anyone else who wanted a drop. But the chances are that the Overland Corner Hotel was, by that stage not much more than part of the supply chain for his far more lucrative business upriver. More than likely by 1897 he'd sorted out another system of obtaining his hooch and the pub was surplus to requirements, so he just walked away from it.

What a shame! Doesn't he sound like a publican who'd fill an arvo with some yarns?

Anyway in around 1905 an ex-coach driver, John McCormac and his new wife Emily, took out a lease for the old pub building, trying to run it as an 'eating house'. They must've made a decent fist of it. In 1906 a traveling Reverend wrote:

about 6 p.m. [we reached] … What was one time the Overland Corner Hotel, now a mail change eating house [where] we managed to get rid of some of the dirt which had adhered to our bodies, and sat down to a good meal.

But the Licensing Bench, believing it was better to have a permanently closed historic building than to have a young couple doing their best and serving the needs of travellers, refused to give them a licence – and with no cop shop next door, there was no benefit to the police in supporting the application. The Gospel of Overland Corner according to the good reverend concluded with the lamentation, 'the place is shorn of its former glory.'

While we've been talking we've moved outside to a spare table where Phil can watch the bar and we can enjoy the evening as the air begins to cool.

Overland Corner remained 'shorn' and unwelcoming until the old hotel building was purchased by the National Trust in 1985 and, despite the absence of a local police station, was re-granted its licence that same year.

Phil shares a story about the tiny graveyard up the hill where the Brands are buried and I make a note to get up there in the morning. And while we're on bodies, he shares a divine story:

'Maybe five or six years ago this bloke came by and he was well dressed in RMs , he was tall with an Akubra hat, moleskins – the whole country bit. And his little tiny wife came up to me and she asked me if I believed in water divining and I said yes, that I used to work with guys who could divine pipes in the ground and we used to divine wells and she said, well my husband has done that for sixty-odd years in Victoria but he also he can find bodies in the ground, human bones and stuff.

'And I said I'll take you up to the old cemetery up the hill. He had wires and he walked around and pointed out well-worn wires too, and he went to the back of the cemetery and said this is where a lot of young born babies are buried and he marked out twenty sites There must've been a lot of deaths in childbirth and young kids getting sick back then. It's upsetting how many tiny short graves there are when you drive around the country.'

In the nearest cemetery to the pub, just a bit further along the Coach Road, there's the grave of young Walter Brand who died at the age of just four in 1880 so there's no doubting the ravages of infant mortality but, unfortunately, even overcoming my scepticism of divining, there may be another more sinister explanation.

In 1919 the *Murray Pioneer* and *Australian River Record* ran a piece entitled 'The Early History of the Cobdogla District' by their 'Morgan Correspondent'. In talking about the 1860s he revealingly writes:

In these days hundreds of blacks resided in and near Overland Corner where now they are rarely seen. On the hill near the site of the present boarding-house, is an old burial ground where about 150 blacks were interred.

The 'boarding house' was of course, the old pub.

In 1928 the same newspaper interviewed Harry Brand, son of William and Martha and the captain of the S.S. *Industry*. He was a man of stories and he too had some possibly relevant to our body diviner. He told of a deadly fight between a couple of shearers over at Markaranka downstream from Waikerie, and how the body of the dead shearer was buried near the woolshed. But then his interviewer wrote:

> *the captain [said] ... there had been several very suspicious deaths along the river at various times. Pressed for details of these, Captain Brand said he did not care to discuss them but mentioned that most of those who had died or disappeared were women.*

So there's no doubting the hills around here are hiding a lot of bones, secreting many tragedies, outrages and scandals. The mystery is just whose bones they are. Probably a combination of all three.

Our chat's regularly interrupted as Phil flits into the bar to serve drinks or bring out ordered meals that Renske's cooked up. Things become quieter as the bikers gravitate back to their camp and their music ramps up. They base near the pub so they can use the toilets which are open all night and when they leave the rubbish bins'll be packed with rum and whisky bottles they've brought in with them rather than buy here. Phil's resigned to the exploiters and the rule-benders and is happy the riders will all have bar drinks and most'll have tea.

'And they won't knock off the dunny paper. Being with a group that'd be like stealing from your mates and that sort of theft is dominated by the grey nomads who travel on their own'.

Phil tells of the time Renske heard a strange whirring sound coming from a cubicle in the Ladies and peaked over the top from the adjoining seat.

'There was a woman inside with a small battery-operated drill with an attachment on it to hold a dunny roll and she was unwinding the loo paper onto her drill.' Renske was outraged and waited for the woman to come out but she didn't and, losing patience Renske headed down to their million-dollar Winnebago which was surrounded by other vans.

'She just went to all their camp neighbours and told them to watch out for their stuff because the people in the big van were thieves.' The 'bago pulled out in the middle of the night. And hasn't been back.

With all the new homes up on the overlooking cliff pretty much owned by people 'from away' Phil and Renske depend on travellers to make the place tick over. At the start of 2017 they decided to scrupulously record their work time and their expenses. At the end of December they tallied it all up. Over the year they each averaged a net per hour income of four bucks fifty an hour.

With the meals done for the night Renske has joined us and she adds, 'This year it'll be less, probably around the three-dollar mark.'

A couple of late arrivals rock up, hoping they haven't missed dinner and Renske tells 'em they've just made it, sit yourselves down and relax and when they're ready just let her know.

Half an hour later two riders pull up out front, wondering if they're too late for a feed, and Renske tells 'em they've just made it, sit yourselves down and relax and when they're ready just let her know. It's that kind of place – hospitality's in its DNA. Almost a century ago a bloke who'd carted the mails around here recalled:

> *We were a terribly happy crowd ... At the pubs we all met and drank together; everybody knew one another, and the only crime about would be when horses and cattle disappeared; but that was thought nothing of. At wayside houses one was welcomed.*

The latecomers get fed and watered and the riders drift back to their camp. We kick over the remains of the day and share tales of outrageous behaviour of the various National Trusts around the country. In the distance some crows are bemoaning something and somewhere closer a butcher bird is telling them to get a life.

William Brand who built this place had a wife, Martha. Her oldest sister took her first breaths in November 1836, the first white person born in the colony of South Australia and Martha herself, when interviewed by the local paper in 1926, was the oldest living white person born in South Australia.

She spoke of the desolation and the loneliness of the early days, her peaceful relations with the traditional owners, her disbelief in myths about bushrangers in the area and how she came to love this place. Then she quoted her favourite poem. It ended:

We oft' destroy the present joy
  For future hopes and praise them,
  Whilst flowers as sweet bloom at our feet
  If we would stoop to raise them.

The gums and bottlebrushes are in flower and next morning after breaking camp and loading up Super Ten, I head away from the river, prune some of these native beauties and then it's past the dusty-looking bikers, left at the pub and up to the main road. A right turn and then on my left, back from the tar is the cemetery Phil was talking about.

At one side is an unpretentious plot with three headstones, those of William Brand, his daughter Lucy, and in the middle lies the body of Martha. At her feet is a poignant faded plastic rose. Sweet.

Postscript: When Covid hit and the first lockdown was imposed, Phil wrote to the National Trust of SA seeking rent relief. His request was ignored.

On a monthly tenancy, as things grew increasingly dire, he wrote again seeking a temporary waiver or at a minimum, meaningful relief from the rent. Again he received no acknowledgement, no response. But at some stage his landlord, the National Trust, began clandestine discussions with another entity.

He and Renske were given notice during which they were compelled to paint and remove a number of items including the outdoor furniture. They were kicked out of the pub they'd nurtured and developed for almost nine years three days before Christmas 2020.

'There're eleven long weekends a year and they are what keep the pub afloat,' Phil explains from his new home in the Barossa Valley, where he's doing voluntary work at the local school. 'But public holidays also mean penalty rates so the turnover skyrockets but so do the costs.'

'The nomads who can fill the flats down by the river, well, you'd be lucky if they visit the pub – apart from the toilets – more than once every three days. And the aggregation of farms, and the disappearance of family-run orchards and the move away from sheep has diminished the transient workforce, so there's a much smaller pool to draw from.'

Just as the raising of the age of drinking to twelve back in 1863 dissolved a crucial chunk of this pub's clientele and saw 'Bunyip' move on, outside factors have again put the squeeze on the sustaining juices of this iconic pub and seen the demise of a damn fine publican. The population changes are one thing but it's the bureaucratic impaired vision and lack of empathy that leaves a taste worse than tannin.

CHAPTER 49 – REST AND BE THANKFUL

ODES, SONNETS BUT NO BENDER AT THE BEND

In 1803 Willy Wordsworth, who'd been born thirty-three years before in the evocatively named Cockermouth in Cumbria, England headed up to Scotland for a walk with his sister Dorothy and their friend, another poet, Sam ('the man') Coleridge.

They planned to travel across from Arrochar to Inveraray to the west of Loch Lomond. Coleridge couldn't hack the pace and was an early scratching, probably to get back onto the opium that inspired him to write transcendent verse like *Kubla Khan*, but the other poet, the one who'd written that he'd, 'wandered lonely as a cloud', and his industrious sister soldiered on. (It wasn't a marathon, just a mere twenty-odd miles, the first half of which was uphill.)

When they reached the saddle, Dorothy recorded that they found:

... a seat with the well-known inscription 'Rest and be thankful' ... The seat is placed so as to command a full view of the valley, and the long, long, road, which, with the fact recorded, and the exhortation, makes it an affecting resting-place.

When they returned from the wilds to what passed as civilisation, William Wordsworth wrote the sonnet, 'Rest and Be Thankful':

DOUBLING and doubling with laborious walk,
Who, that has gained at length the wished-for Height,
This brief this simple wayside Call can slight,
And rests not thankful? Whether cheered by talk

With some loved friend, or by the unseen hawk
Whistling to clouds and sky-born streams that shine,
At the sun's outbreak, as with light divine,
Ere they descend to nourish root and stalk
Of valley flowers. Nor, while the limbs repose,
Will we forget that, as the fowl can keep
Absolute stillness, poised aloft in air,
And fishes front, unmoved, the torrent's sweep,—
So may the Soul, through powers that Faith bestows,
Win rest, and ease, and peace, with bliss that Angels share.

Fifteen years later another poet, Johnny Keats, took a break from odeing to everything from Grecian urns to nightingales and hit the same high road without doing too much homework:

We were up at 4 this morning and have walked to breakfast 15 Miles through two tremendous Glens – at the end of the first there is a place called rest and be thankful which we took for an Inn – it was nothing but a stone and so we were cheated into 5 more Miles to Breakfast.

I know his pain. I've felt that pain.

Somewhere else in Scotland around this time it's likely that a wee boy bairn was born to the Mackey family who christened him Joseph. Somehow Joseph found his way to South Australia and thirty-two years after Keats had mistakenly assumed that 'Rest and be Thankful' was the name of an inn in the glens of Scotland, Joseph Mackey successfully applied for a licence to operate a hotel by that same name on a stretch of land known as Harry Weston's Flat at the nor-west bend of the Murray. (Later that same day a German immigrant, Hermann von Rieben, also successfully applied to the same court for a licence for his hotel less than 20 miles down the river and around the mighty bend. And a bloke named William Crabb secured a licence for his place over at Murray Scrub. We'll catch up with them both in a bit.)

In 1939 Lucy Maymon Hynes, a landmark chronicler of the river wrote that:

> The title 'Rest and be Thankful' was an Inspiration. It was a commodious one-storey house built of sunny ochre-colored stone cut from the Murray cliffs; the stones themselves were blocks of dark mystery formed of shells. The old inn still stands sturdy and glowing, and is now the homestead of a sheep station owned by Mr. C. M. McWaters ... 'Rest and be Thankful' was built on Government reserve land on top of Murray cliffs that rise 80 feet from the river bed. The rent of the land was £1 a year.

Joseph only kept the hotel for a couple of years before selling to William Mallyon. The locale shed half its name as a snake discards it skin, and became simply 'Weston's Flat' and the pub, as was the wont of such times, assumed the proprietor's name and became known simply as 'Mallyon's Hotel, Weston's Flat.'

William and his wife Rebecca (Britcher) had three sons and four daughters. One son, also William, became a self-taught architect, designing around a dozen churches including St Peter's Anglican Church just down in Morgan.

For the next thirty years, well after William Mallyon had moved on with his seven kids, all subsequent licensing hearings, through a number of owners and licensees, the hotel was referred to as 'Mallyons'.

I take the punt across the Murray at Waikerie, head north and then turn west on the Goyder and ten minutes later on my left's a sign that announces that I'm at Mallyons on the Murray, Bush Cafe and Historic Site, by appointment only. What a pity they've chosen to memorialise the ego of a publican rather than the inspiration of the founder of the place.

It's a bad time. There's been a tragedy in the family and the harvest is happening so sorry, understandably there can be no guided tour today but please make yourself at home.

Adjacent the road, the western end of the long low-slung old pub glows in the afternoon sun, an old wooden mangle at the edge of the rear verandah. Alone it would be evocative but it's not alone. To its south, down a short path, behind a towering gum and overlooking a 90-degree bend in the river is the stunning homestead. A 360-degree verandah under a newly repaired roof, a tantalising stairway leading down to a cellar (surely not a dungeon) and an atmosphere overflowing with the ghosts of many types.

George Schell was the boss here from 1876 to 1881. In 1928 Lucy Hines wrote a memoir of the pub for the *Murray Pioneer*:

> [During Schell's] ownership the hotel became a great country racing centre. The first meeting was held in 1877, and ... One hundred and fifty people congregated for the races arriving in drays, carts, bullock wagons and horseback from Wentworth, Moorna, Lake Victoria, Lake Bonny, Chowilla, Bookmark (now Calperum), Blanchetown, and other places within a hundred miles radius. Over 40 horses entered the lists, mostly untrained.
>
> Dancing to the music of the accordion, concertina, and violin in the large dining room lasted all day and all night for two days ... [but] the dining room was too small to accommodate the dancers, so dancing was done in relays, those not dancing slept in the three spare rooms or in the sheds. Who minded travelling many weary miles, and days, through sand and scrub, camping out at night, when one could meet old friends and have a glorious time for two whole days?
>
> These great race days made very strenuous work for Mrs. George Schell. She had only one servant, and a small daughter of 12 (now Mrs. John Pendle of Morgan) to do the work. The blacks supplied plenty of ducks, fish and turkeys. All other food came from Morgan by steamer. Butter was in kegs; sheep and bullocks were bought from passing drovers at 6/ for a sheep, £8 for a bullock. All spare meat was salted down. Sixteen loaves of bread a day had to be baked in the camp ovens, coming out the size of a small motor tyre. For light, tins were half filled with sand and then filled up with fat. Sticks covered with soft rag were stuck up in the fat and sand to make wicks.

These lamps were what were known as 'slushies' – an integral part of life in the bush.

Back in 1861 Bill Crick, a real legend of these parts, had advertised that his carriage 'leaves Truro for Harry Weston's Flat every Monday,' but, as the South Australian government poured money into Morgan, just 20 miles downriver, and with its railhead and its gentler banks to the river, Weston's Flat lost its lifeblood. Plus, the land transport routes had changed and the bullockies and drovers no longer thundered into town, thirsty, hungry and in need of bed.

Henry Brand, whose brothers George and William had both tried their hands at running the Overland Corner pub, took over the Rest and be Thankful in 1899 but he ended up being the final publican. In 1906 he surrendered the licence and the magnificent buildings were super-annuated into a stately retirement of a private residence for a succession of fortunate families.

Lucy Hines recorded in 1928 that in 1907 Harry Brand sold the unlicensed property to a Mr. M. Coombs who:

used the house as a private residence and for three or four years bred sheep and cattle. He was followed by Mr. Clarence Mann of Eudunda, and eventually the old landmark became the property of the present owner, Mr. C. M. McWaters.

Like the Irish nominative prefix 'Fitz' and the Hebrew 'ben', the Scottish 'Mc' or 'Mac' designates 'son of' and, for mine, a settler out here with a surname meaning 'son of waters' is a bloke who's found his place. I'm soon to have reason to remember this appropriate appellation, but that's getting ahead of myself.

In 1937 the Adelaide *Chronicle* wrote that the '"Rest and be Thankful" still stands sentinel by the road side as it has done for more than 80 years.'

I now rest on a seat out front of the homestead and watch the Murray far below. I do the sums and realise we can now double the years in that claim. And be doubly thankful.

Later I again call the number and yes, Rita isn't going to be off leading adventure tours in the north for her sister's Iconic Tours so the day I'm passing back through will be fine.

When I knock she's busy making a massive pot of vegetable soup and could I please excuse the blood pressure monitor she's wearing? It'll beep every 30 minutes for her to stay still while it measures her health. She reckons she has 'white coat syndrome' where being at a doctor's stresses her so she's being monitored in real-doctor-free-life and all's looking good.

We sit in her kitchen with Narla – her separation-anxiety-infected pug at her feet and Otto, a hyper border collie making it obvious I should be outside throwing a stick – and talk of the history of the place.

'My mother and father-in-law bought it in 1989 as a hobby place with their boat down the bottom, and the other building, near the road was just a complete ruin with the ceiling hanging down. It had become a shearing shed for a bit and was full of junk.'

The verandahs on what was the pub but now the homestead had been demolished so they set about replacing them, removing the rubble that was filling the enormous cellar, restoring the 22,000-gallon rainwater tank. Then they turned their farm organic and now grow peaches, apricots and hothouse cucumbers.

The entire place – just like it was when the Scotsman built it 160 years ago – is completely off grid. The power comes from two banks of solar panels, the drinking water from clouds and the home and irrigation water from the river down below. The thick old walls make air-conditioning redundant but in winter the wood is chopped for the big old fire.

There's a beep and we stop while the machine takes Rita's BP and then head over to the adjacent shed which was built in 1841 and was a resting place for the overlanders and a changing station for Cobb & Co (and just maybe a discreet sly groggery as well). It was this long open room that Rita and husband Nick converted into Mallyons Cafe.

They ran it for eleven years until, 'our kids were at uni and when they came home on weekends I was always working and I just thought, hey this doesn't suit my priorities of family and work.'

And so now the cafe is open only to groups by appointment and if the grub tastes anything like the aroma from the soup bubbling on the stove back in the house, it'd be a damn fine stop.

When I ask what she most loves about this priceless old pub, Rita smiles and says it can be hard work but she loves it all: 'We don't always rest, but we're always thankful.'

June 1860

THE RIVER HEADS SOUTH THE PUBS HEAD NORTH

The Rest and be Thankful is the last semblance of a hotel before the great nor' west bend where the mighty Murray, after its 2200-kilometre journey west changes direction and heads south for the final 330 kilometre run to its mouth.

The Cadell ferry's on the far bank when I arrive so I switch off Super Ten's engine and watch some pelicans paddling the waters. And then the reason hits me.

For days, almost in despair, I've been wondering why so many pubs, ever since Mildura – that's 250 kilometres of road, more than double that by river – have been uniformly ordinary. But the answer is so bleeding obvious.

Way back in 1895 when James Ashwell, editor of the *Renmark Pioneer* wrote his first editorial under the banner 'A Hotel Wanted', and pushed a system of having the place owned by the community, controlled by a trust, he argued that, '(t)he trust should employ a manager who would have no interest in pushing the sale of drink.'

That same year over in Mildura, the Council President, Edmund Semmens, a god-fearing church-going alcohol-abstainer, introduced a motion:

That in the opinion of this Council it is advisable that a clause be inserted in the Local Government Act relative to the sale of alcoholic liquors in Victoria as follows:– 'The Council of every Municipality shall have full power to acquire and retain the sole retail sale of all wines, spirituous and malt liquors within its boundary and all managers or other persons employed in the sale thereof shall be officers of the Council, and shall not participate in the profits derived from the sale.'

I knew all that. I knew that the crucial element in the proposed system was the distancing of the workers, the management from the profits, from the success of the hotels. And I knew that when I ring ahead to a hotel and ask for the boss and then ask them if it's run by the publican, by a licensee or by a paid manager on behalf of an owner or a company in some distant city, that the amount of skin in the game the face of the place has, the more likely I'll enjoy my stay.

And, sitting back in the red dirt beside the road leading to the Cadell ferry, I have the light-bulb moment. The enduring legacy of the Chaffey Bros, the wowser Canadian visionaries who hated alcohol as much as they loved profits, and who cared about people, just not enough to look after their workers when they went bust, their legacy is a string of drinking holes, owned by communities but bereft of character, atmosphere, staffed by no doubt good people but with no interest whatsoever in whether you come back.

It's the Chaffey legacy that enables the young woman behind the bar in Waikerie to tell me without the slightest irony that if I want to drink my beer in the fresh air, the only place is the smokers' area through that far door.

It's the Chaffey legacy that facilitates being told in Berri that if I'm interested in the history of the place then just look at the photos on the wall but, sorry, there's no-one who's available any time today to talk about the place and they probably wouldn't know anyway.

It's this same legacy that permits being told that if I want a quiet spot for a drink in the Workingman's Club at Mildura, away from the gambling screens and the poker machines, that there wouldn't be a problem if I were to nip into the soulless bistro.

It's a tough gig to be interested in a customer's comfort if you have no interest in their custom.

The ferry's done three returns as I've been sitting and thinking about this but now, with head cleared, I crank up the bike and roll down the asphalt approach then up the silver ramp and soon we're in the middle of the river.

Quarter of an hour later and I'm slowing for the first east-to-west ferry crossing. The Murray's turned its corner and, confident in a mate's advice, I'm pretty certain the next pub'll reveal that the nor' west bend, flanked by the Rest and be Thankful on its up-stream edge and Morgan on its other, signifies not just a change in direction of the waters, but a change in character of its watering holes.

CHAPTER 51 – MORGAN

A FAMILIAR FACE AND ROOTS IN THE RIVER

I rock up to the bar of the Terminus Hotel at Morgan on a mission of my own and with a message from a mate, Tony.

He's a water man – a bloke whose enthusiasm for boats, especially old wooden ones, knows no plimsoll line. A few months earlier he was sailing his new obsession up the Murray with his son, Tim, and as they were mooring at Morgan the young fella stood on something nasty and slashed his foot. Badly.

They wrapped it up (yes, gaffer tape was involved) and headed into the pub, a pub they'd never been to before. They were told the town was medico-deficient on Saturdays – the closest qualified help was back at the Waikerie Base Hospital 40 kilometres away. And getting there?

'Not a problem', said the publican. 'Take my ute. There's no keys, just turn the lock and it'll start. Oh, and the windows don't work, the levers are buggered but it'll get you there. Help yourself, it's out the back'

They got young Tim to the hospital and a few hours later, bandaged and on crutches in the 45°C heat, they slid back into the windowless HZ Holden for the ride back to Morgan and the pub.

'When you get to the Terminus at Morgan,' Tony instructs me, 'just tell Phil who owns the place, "thanks" again for helping out and making us feel special.'

Now, three years before, on a seriously foul night on the southern coast of Victoria, another good publican, this one at the Royal Hotel at Portland where I was kipping, made me feel special too. I'd spent the afternoon watching a pair of tugs struggling against the currents, wind and swell of the Great Southern Ocean to get a massive tanker into the harbour.

Eventually they admitted defeat, turned it around and sent it out to anchor until the storm blew through.

Phil decided it was too foul to even leave my bike out in that rubbish so we parked it in the front bar. Memories of special publicans are the froth on the inside of the glass of my mind.

I head up the street between the only two pubs in town, turn left into the parking area around the back near the motel rooms and then walk back to the main entrance of the Terminus.

I open the door and the bloke behind the bar squints at me for a bit and then: 'What're you doing here?' I tell him I could ask him the same question. The two blokes I've just told you about are the same bloke – the fella who helped me on the south coast and the one who'd helped my mate are the same Phil.

Turns out that about five years ago Phil and his partner decided they'd had enough of Antarctic gales full time and bought themselves a place in milder climes a few kilometres out of town here at Morgan. It was intended to be some sort of holiday slash eventual retirement residence for them both, but then in 2016 they fast-forwarded their plans, cashed in their chips and moved into their place near the Murray. He went to work on the Brenda Park Vineyards just south of town and Phil started using a local bloke, Brian, as the courier to service the needs of the vineyard.

Meanwhile, the fella running the Terminus Hotel in Morgan was hating it. He'd only had it a year. It was his first pub and it wasn't what he'd dreamed of. So six months after Phil'd signed on at the vineyards he put the bloke out of his misery and bought the pub.

I give him the news from Tony and he wonders how Tim patched up. The bar's just one long counter with a short end, sort of like a long, reversed L shape, and I'm at the foot.

Pretty much every stool is taken. Some are having a latish lunch, others just a refresher from the heat outside. There's a pile of tables in the room but clearly this is a joint where a seat at the bar is the go. In the middle, right beside the taps sits an old bloke delicately devouring a fish n chips lunch. In the midst of the raucous repartee, the raised voices and the louder laughs, he has an aura of tranquillity, of grace, and it's obvious he's treated reverentially by the staff and by the locals. Now the bar stools at the Terminus are all the same – standard black round tops, without backs, except the one this old fella's perched on.

When Phil took over the pub he set about employing locals and ramping up the food and the service. And he gave Brian, who'd done good work back at the vineyard, the contract to courier in all his booze from out of town. Now there'd not long been an addition to Brian's household. In 2012 his mother had passed away and the following year his dad, then aged eighty-eight, had sold the family home south of Adelaide and joined him at his place some 13 kilometres out from Morgan.

I ask Phil who's the peaceful looking old bloke on the stool with a back and he reveals that this is Brian's father, Alwyne, known to everyone simply as 'Dad'.

'Dad comes in at the same time every day and if anyone's in his seat around quarter to eleven, they'll be asked to move, either by me or one of the regulars. And yeah, he'd be up for a chat for sure.'

His knife and fork are old school – placed together in the middle of his plate despite one fish fillet and a stack of chips remaining so I understand he's done eating and I cruise around. On the back of his seat's support, in white paint, a firm hand has written, 'MR Brian'.

'My son thought it'd be an idea to bring me into town while he was working because I do like a bit of company. At the start I used to share my time between both pubs but since Phil's taken over here I haven't strayed.'

He wasn't all that much of a 'pub person', 'but when I did have a drop it was West End but once I came here I changed to drinking XXXX. Schooners. Pretty soon Phil decided I needed my own seat with a back so he got me this and put my name on the back. That made me feel very special and this really is my second home now.'

'When,' I ask, 'was the last time you had to tell 'em what you

wanted to drink or eat?'

He smiles his soft smile.

'I ask for my dinner because I don't always have the same thing but the food is good here and the helpings are big so I usually can't finish it. They know I don't like wasting any so they always give me the leftovers in a little box. But the beer? Maybe the first day I came here I asked for a schooner of XXXX but I don't think I've ever had to ask since. They all know what I like.'

And that, in a nutshell is what this publican and his pub are about: making people, friends and strangers, feel special and at home.

But it's not just the pub here that's special, the whole town seems to be. After he knocks off and feels like a beer, Phil heads across the road to the Commercial for a quiet one, and it's just as common for their boss to finish his day with Phil pulling him a glass.

When the South Australian government sent their surveyor out to the area known to the traditional owners as 'Koerabko' (meaning something like, 'meeting of the tribes') in 1878 it was more a political than a social justification. The other colonies already had railheads to the yet to be federated country's greatest river (and at that stage, transport) system – New South Wales at Bourke and Victoria at Echuca – and the convict-free settlement wanted its share of the river trade.

The rail line was already being pushed eastward and the first railway engine, the Pioneer, reached the town that April, a month before the first allotments were sold.

The government surveyor mentioned that a pub of sorts already existed and one of his colleagues was, unknowingly, soon to be accommodated within. In October 1878 an inquest was held at the Terminus to enquire into the drowning death of George Harvey, surveyor, found drowned in the Murray. So it's pretty likely the pub mentioned as pre-existing the survey was the Terminus.

The *Kapunda Herald* of 18 June that same year had carried news that a contract had been let for the building of 'Mr Moyle's new hotel ... [which] is to be completed by Christmas.' Can't have been a government contract – it was up and running well before that and in the first week of November the same paper was reporting that an excursion to celebrate the birthday of the Prince of Wales would be provided 'luncheon' by Mr Moyle, 'in his new hotel at Morgan at moderate charges'.

So both these pubs, the Commercial and the Terminus have stood shoulder to sandstone shoulder, like dizygotic twins at the intersection of what are now Railway Terrace and Eighth Street, high on the bank overlooking the first stretch of the Murray after it ceases its flow west and turns south for the coast.

'We're not opposition like footy teams,' says Phil, 'we're slightly different and we both have the same aim of serving the community and doing our bit to ensure out-of-towners come back by making their visit enjoyable.'

There's only about 500 permanents in the town but summer sees that swell to, 'three or four thousand and then we really do need to two pubs.'

Phil's sorted a lift home for Dad and his half-meal has been doggie-bagged for his tea, so I say, 'Seeya next time,' as he heads out to the waiting car of a local who's said he's going past his door but who's probably making a detour or even a special trip to get the old bloke home.

Back in the bar where the walls are filled with old photos of old carts, men in hats, barges and floods, plus a bit of bourbon paraphernalia, a bloke comes in wanting to bludge a rice cooker for a family do. If it's left to him, he'll burn it he reckons. Not a problem! Phil heads to the kitchen and gets it for him. If you're going to sling your car to a stranger, dealing your rice cooker to a local is a no-brainer.

I'm taken on a tour. Phil's particularly proud of the renos in the restaurant. It's a light-filled airy extension outside the original stonewalls at the side of the front of the pub. The space works brilliantly and food's on for what I call lunch and dinner, but which Alwyne calls dinner and tea, every day, prepared by a new chef and Phil reckons he's a 'corker' (sounds like he should be a sommelier).

The arvo's wearing on and I tell Phil about the other fella I'm trying to track down. He sticks his head out the door, surveys the road. 'He drinks across the road and his ute's not out there but he may've got a lift in.'

I then follow his directions and cross to the Commercial and stick my head in the door. When the barman asks if he can help I tell him I'm looking for a bloke in a terry-towelling hat.

'Ah Juice! He must be running a bit late. When he gets here he'll park across the road there and (pause for effect) you'll know him.'

Back at the Terminus I grab another beer and take it outside in the cooling evening to a kerbside table right at the corner. Two mouthfuls later a ute pulls up, dogs yapping on the back, and Phil yells from inside that this is Juice.

'And it's okay, you can take your drink over there, just bring back the glass!

He's wearing a Penfolds issued hi-vis long-sleeved top over a red and black flanny, and his hat's as faded as his blue eyes. He's not expecting me, wouldn't know me from Adam, so I decide to come out firing.

'Juice?'

'That's me.'

'They told me you always wear a terry-towelling hat and that ai'nt terry-towelling where I come from.'

'Couldn't find the bugger this morning, I'll have to start wearing it to bed.'

I tell him what I'm doing in town and he says he'll just get a beer for himself and Charlie who he's brought with him, say g'day to the folks inside and meet me back outside in ten.

Juice has lived here abouts all his life, had his first beer down at the Mount Mary pub when he was probably fifteen or so but disputes that he's here every day, 'just most of them'.

And the Commercial is 'his' pub. 'Often a mate'll drop me down and my wife who everyone calls the Uber driver comes down and picks me up.'

But tonight his wife's busy, 'painting the door of the shed so I've driven myself down and I want to get home and have tea and watch the cricket on the TV.'

His farm is up the road a bit and its water frontage is all that's getting him through the drought.

'We usually carry about 1500 head of sheep but we're down to a third of that because we don't have any feed. I'm on the water so we have stock and domestic and that's enough to water them but we can't use water to grow feed.'

Juice still has forty head of cattle as well and he's just spent over three grand on ten large bales of hay, but 'you just can't continue doing that'. So to augment the animals' diet he's come up with a solution befitting his nickname.

'We discovered the cattle and the sheep love oranges.' He buys the 'seconds', the bruised or skin-marked fruit from the local processors for 'twenty bucks a ton. They'd usually juice them but these are navels and they go a bit sour when you juice them so I get them. Cattle love them. Sheep too. They just chomp it. They love it. Been a real help to get through. Even when they're juicing them I get the peel and they chomp on that.'

And when he can get them, the peel and the rinds that used to go to compost are his for six bucks a ton.

'And the animals never catch a cold or have runny noses with all that vitamin C!'

To keep himself and his family going, Juice has turned more to his second stream – trucking 'sand and metal and all the stuff the railway used to carry.'

He is convinced the water problems all stem from over allocating up stream ('there's not even enough flow to keep the old box trees going') and believes that Lake Alexandrina was always a freshwater lake, the Goolwa barrages simply stopping all the fresh water from running out.

'Typical,' he thinks, 'of the eastern states to blame us for their problems.'

He can't conceive of living away from the river despite hardly using it for recreation. It's the font of all his work, trucking, farming and, with Charlie, who's a boilermaker by trade, fixing stuff, welding, restoring, maintaining many of the luxurious 'shacks' along the river.

Juice is, unfortunately, nowhere near on his Pat in fighting through the dry times, however they've been caused. What does set him apart and the reason I've hunted him down is the depth of his roots in this part of the country and on this bend in the river.

He is the great-great-grandson of William Brand, the bloke who built the Overland Corner Hotel. His mother, who passed away in 2018 just four days shy of her 100th birthday was a Brand and one of his great uncles who still has the 'Brand' brand lives back upriver on a property at Qualco. 'He's

got a son so the Brand name still has a bit of life in its legs.'

It's family lore that William Brand also built a pub out at Truro as well as Nappers over at Lake Bonney and Juice can't remember not knowing about this link of his to the famous pioneering brothers. Then he hits me with a bit I didn't know. His surname is 'McWaters'.

'My grandparents used to run the Rest and be Thankful ... By that stage it wasn't a pub and was known as Mallyons. My old man, his two brothers and his sister were all born there. And dad, whose name was Murray, kept living there after he got married and stayed until I was born there in '52 and then the family moved to town.'

So he's the grandson of the Clem McWaters, mentioned two chapters back. He remembers the school across the road and a few months back ran into a woman who'd been a schoolmate in the late 1950s.

'She used to live on the south of the river and she'd paddle across the water and then walk up to the store out the front of Mallyons and see my parents and then go over to the school.'

I head into the bar and ask for a round, 'A lite for me and one for Juice and Charlie.' I haven't asked what they're drinking, I have no need to know.

The drinks come back with my change. 'That's Juice's that's the Charlie's and you can work out the other.'

I tell Juice that with his pedigree and his surname I can understand why he feels so connected to the river and he explains it's not the whole river, it's just this part of it, this crucial part where, after dithering west for hundreds of kilometres it finally makes up its mind to head south on its final journey.

The cricket from England's starting soon on the TV and beneath the clear sky the night's turning chill. Juice, an addict of the summer game, who'll watch every ball tonight despite working all day, has to get moving.

In a thick crew jumper and insulating beard, Charlie, who first came to this part of town as a kid on school holidays from Adelaide and who now, apart from working with Juice, does what he 'can to support the pub, especially when the tourists are thin over winter,' will be heading too.

The two dogs on the back of Juice's ute voice their excitement at getting home and as they clear out, I head back for dinner or tea at the Terminus.

Next morning, after a wander around this historic and interesting place, right up with the best towns on the entire river, I enjoy breakfast at the Riverview Cafe next door, watching caravanners in the park across the road preparing food they've bought in big stores in big towns, scrupulously avoiding spending any money in the place they've spent the night.

Phil's up early and says he'll ring ahead for me. Next stop is the vineyard where he first worked when he left the Victoria coast. He's sure I'll love the pub there, and the people who'll show me around.

I crank up Super Ten and for the first time on this journey begin the trip by heading south.

A couple of months after my visit, I get a call from Phil and he doesn't sound good. The previous afternoon Alwyne's carer had helped him shower and he'd gone to his bedroom to dress. It was too quiet. Too much time passed. She pushed the door open. 'Dad' was on his bed motionless. He'd sat down and passed away, as peacefully and as tranquilly as he'd lived.

The town was in shock. I thank him for calling and letting me know. I tell him 'I'm sure you helped make his last few years fuller and happier than they may have been,' and the publican, the person, just says he hopes so, 'because that's why we're here.'

I make myself an excuse to head out to the river bend country. I'm told the funeral in Adelaide was 'huge' with people from down south where he ran his bakery for years, people from Adelaide and half the town of Morgan. Alwyne's chair in the pub seemingly hasn't moved, just been changed a fraction. In the same bold script as the original name, someone's added a poignant 'R.I.P.' in the top left corner.

And on the edge of the bar where he sat from 11 am every day in the real sunset of his life, there's a brass plate which simply reads, 'Alwyne 'Dad' Always Remembered'.

This chapter was originally written very much about Alwyne. It remains as a testament to a wonderful man and to the role a pub can play in enriching lives. In my head I have a message for my mate: don't go feeling special in the treatment you were given in the Terminus at Morgan – everyone who comes by gets the same.

A TRUE SHRINE TO PUB HISTORY

In 1849 Hermann von Rieben, then aged forty, his twenty-four year old wife Louisa, and two kids, joined around 150 politically and socially liberal Germans on the chartered vessel *Princess Louise* at Hamburg for the near twenty-week voyage to Adelaide via Rio.

They joined the Buchsfelde settlement on the Gawler but then in July 1854 headed north west to Scotts Lagoon, just downstream on the Murray from the great nor' west bend, where the river ceases its western journey and heads south for the coast near the new convict-free township of Adelaide.

Their settlement wasn't near much else apart from the permanent water of the Scotts Lagoon, a short anabranch of the Murray, but once they'd set up digs the flow of visitors pretty much matched the waters of the river. Their place was on a trade route from the squatted lands of western New South Wales and Queensland and the markets of Adelaide and the ports of the Murray River.

Entertaining an endless stream of blow-ins and blow-hards might've eased the monotony and loneliness for this German family far from its roots and far from other settlers but hey, enough was enough of the free hospitality!

Hermann realised the place's commercial potential and in December 1854 applied to the court for a licence to operate his home as a public house. For some reason he didn't front the hearing and though there were no objections, magistrates Fisher, Campbell, Stevenson and Hamilton didn't much appreciate the snub and refused to grant a licence.

Three months later Hermann got his act together and had his day in court in Adelaide. On 13 March 1855 the licence was granted and Baron Hermann von Rieben was a publican.

Three years previously the Murrumbidgee had flooded, completely obliterating the township of Gundagai which, despite the advice of the local Aboriginals had been built on the lower flood plains of the river. Killing eighty-nine people, it remains the worst flood disaster in Australian history. Cyclone Tracy in Darwin in 1974 by comparison killed seventy-one. Von Rieben must've known about the annihilation of Gundagai. Before building, he sought advice from the Indigenous owners, who told where the highest flood in their memory had reached and Hermann started work above this height. (Unfortunately in 1870 the Murray flooded the house to within a foot of the ceiling and the family stored all their belongs in the loft, living in tents on the hill for eleven months. When things were needed the two von Rieben sons would row to the house and retrieve stuff from the attic.)

Hermann and his wife were obviously gifted and thoughtful hosts. In 1856, just a year after the pub'd opened, the *South Australian Register* ran a piece headed, 'Notes of a Ten Days' Tour to the Murray and the North'. The intrepid correspondent noted that, 'Von Rieben's Hotel is a point of essential importance to the tourist in this district.' It was, 'the only house between Murpka and the North-West Bend [and] situated in a lonely part of the bush, on the bank of a great lagoon, about five miles on the Moorundee side of the North-West Bend of the river.'

The unnamed writer then went on to assure the readers that this monopoly wasn't being exploited, telling them that any traveller, 'will meet with every accommodation, and every comfort he could expect, and more than he could expect. The hostess is most attentive and obliging, and the charges moderate. We ate well, drank well, and slept well at Von Rieben's, and our horses fared well too.'

It was no accident that von Rieben was providing what his clientele of travellers, explorers, drovers and bullockies all wanted. It seems his son was one of these itinerants. Either that or Hermann himself would hit the road from time to time. See, Hermann and his wife decided to name one of their sons Hermann too and newspaper reports of the time fail to identify which Hermann they were talking about in various stories.

A reminiscence of the 1860s and published in 1929 recalled a Hermann droving a large flock and battling a horde of wild dogs which'd decimated and dispersed the sheep. He rounded up all the survivors and reaching the Overland Corner Hotel:

Mr. von Rieben, hungry and exhausted, sought food and shelter for the night. The hotel was full of linesmen, laying the telegraph line from Wentworth to Adelaide – so drunk and noisy that the noise scared the sheep. They began to break away, and Mr von Rieben and the drovers had to sleep near them all night to keep them quiet. They had no blankets, as the horses were too poor to carry anything but bare necessities, and were frozen with the cold.

Young Hermann would've been around twenty by now, and his father into his fifties so this is very likely the son rather than the clan head. Whoever it was, this sure wasn't the sort of hospitality available back at the Nor' West Bend home!

Anyway, the last annual licence renewal was in March 1879 and just two months later on 24 May the death a week prior was announced of Charles Frederick Willis Ethelbert Hermann von Rieben. No cause of death was given.

It was the second time in two days that Hermann von Rieben's name had been in the news. The previous day the *Kapunda Herald* had carried coverage of scuffle at the hotel:

Assaulting a Bailiff.

We understand the bailiff of the Kapunda Local Court (Mr. Parker) was rather roughly handled at Von Rieben's on Saturday last. (I)t appears that Mr. Parker proceeded to Morgan for the purpose of serving an execution in the suit of O'Neill v. Scanziana. On arriving at the Bend, the bailiff learnt that Scanziana was at Von Rieben's, so he proceeded there where he found his man, who is a hawker well-known in Kapunda and on the River. On Scanziana seeing the bailiff, he attempted to drive off as he then had his van

and horses ready to start. The bailiff, however managed to get a seat on the van and after some angry words, took the reins and stopped the horses.

At this stage, we are informed a resident on the River (whose name we refrain from, mentioning at present) came out of the hotel and so incited Scanziana, that he by the aid of his wooden-leg and his whip, knocked Parker off the van, the resident, before mentioned, assisting in ill-using him. Eventually Parker drew his revolver and threatened to shoot any one that laid a hand on him. This quieted matters and the bailiff got his claim settled and came away ...

The article then ended with a regret, 'The most unfortunate part of the affair was that it took place shortly after the remains of the late Mr. Von Rieben had been committed to the grave, which could not have been many yards from the scene of the row.'

I can't work out who exactly owned what in this story but I'm just going to leave you all with the image of a bailiff armed with a small arm being knocked off a horse-drawn carriage by a bloke armed with a big leg.

Back at the Terminus Hotel in Morgan, when I told him they were my next port o' call he rang ahead to warn them of the threat of my arrival. When I pull off the road and into the dusty car park, two figures are waiting beside a well-used ute.

After a working life that includes being a builder, a farmer and a zookeeper, and twenty years of working for Byrne Wines, Geoff, with his wife Lyn became the general manager of Brenda Park Vineyards in 2014. It's obvious from the get-go that they're in love with this place, with the area, with the vines, with the environment and with the history. They can't wait to get me into the ute and down to the ruins. We pass the old woolshed at the top of the rise, before it a pair of huge old steam engines, and then we're weaving down a grey path between plots of vines.

On the way I get a potted history of the area and of the vineyard. It was set up in the '70s by Penfolds as an irrigation property for premium grapes to augment its Barossa vineyards. Byrne Wines, a fifty-year-old family company bought it from the crowd who purchased it from Penfolds.

There's an obvious common thread through everything Lyn and Geoff tell me. They explain how the old binary business model of a primary industry vineyard and a secondary industry wine-making operation has been supplanted by a single inclusive concept involving the understanding of it all being the one process and wine making beginning in these fields.

Their signature grape here is shiraz, using techniques of vine drying and harvesting each vine in two stages. And they tell of how this vineyard had South Australian water allocation licence number one and stop to show the old overhead irrigation gutters up to which water was pumped before gravity did the rest to take it via channels and levees to the river flats.

And then there's the massive area which is being returned to its native state, the eco lodges up on the ridge, the wonderful old home of Sydney Wilcox who owned the place in 1906 that they're slowly renovating to its original state and then before us are the ruins of Von Rieben's pub. Wilcox called it 'Mulyoulpko' which meant 'home by the water'.

And then the remains of Von Rieben's pub, or probably more correctly the Von Riebens' pub, are before us. Facing the track is the almost complete end wall, reinforced no doubt by the fireplace and chimney. This was obviously the hostelry's main entertaining room and next to it, toward the lagoon which is just visible, is the old cellar, muchly filled with rocks and sand from the surrounding collapsed walls. Then another couple of rooms end at the top of the ridge before it slopes down to the waters and then just dry grey dust and bushes. This is what's left of Von Rieben's Hotel, this 'point of essential importance ... situated in a lonely part of the bush, on the bank of a great lagoon.'

When old roos die their lifeless bodies are picked clean by the opportunistic carnivorous scavengers, the eagles, the crows, the wild dogs and the feral pigs until the dry bones only remain. The sun, with heartless heat then attacks the skeletons and dehydrates them to dust. But when pubs like this die the meat has already gone and the elements begin their destruction from even before the heart has stopped beating. They collapse into themselves, seeming to cringe against the elements until eventually they too merge into the topsoil.

Unless, that is, their spirit is blessed and they are rescued, rescued by people like those of the Byrne Wines company and Geoff and Lyn.

As we walk upstream to a small, high-walled enclosure Geoff gently explains what is really his mission statement.

'This place has been allowed to get run down over the last number of years and we really do feel that we are custodians of it and slowly we are restoring it because it has such a great story, such a history.'

And that includes fighting any more decay of the hotel and establishing some ways of making it more accessible to travellers while safeguarding its wellbeing.

The walled enclosure, built strong and solid to withstand floods even of the ferocity of the 1956 benchmark, is a small burial plot. It contains just two headstones. One reads: SACRED TO THE MEMORY OF Hermann von Rieben ... and of his three children, Rolly ... Amelia ... and Malchin.' The other is of Louisa von Rieben who died four years after her husband in 1883.

An old bunch of plastic flowers lies between the plots. The headstones carry no tribute, no biblical text, no touching words of recognition and no trite verse.

As we walk back to the ute, we all agree that the memorial, the shrine, to these two pioneer publicans, who established an outpost which must've brought comfort, rest and succour to so many, so needy, is not so much their graves but rather the ruin of the pub itself.

CHAPTER 53 – BLANCHETOWN

DEAD PUBLICANS' SOCIETY

I n 1937 the Adelaide *Chronicle* ran a feature on 'Romantic River Hotel', subtitled 'Why Blanchetown "Lay Down and Died"'.

Before the opening of the railway to Morgan, Blanchetown was a very busy and important port. All cargo was carted by bullock team and dray from Freeling, Truro and Angaston to Blanchetown, and then by steamer up the Murray and the Darling. Mr. A. Teesdale built the Government bond stores. Mr. Woolley was Customs officer; Mr. Jackson, postmaster; Corporal Ewens was the mounted policeman; Mr. Rossiter had the Blanchetown Hotel; and Mr. W. N. Potter was shipping agent.

This place was first surveyed by whites in 1855 and declared the Port of Blanche Town the next year. It was, just like Rome, built on seven hills with the post office, the police station and the general store having their own mound but the highest hill was grabbed by the aspiring Mr G. Green, who built his hotel on its crest in 1858, after first having a shot at one further down the slope. The licence was transferred from Heywood's Old Whipstick Inn which was first licensed in 1845 a couple of miles further to the south on his Portee Station. In Blanchetown it was initially named the Heywood Arms but later became the Blanchetown Hotel.

It was well needed. In 1856 a correspondent for the South Australian *Register* filed a series, 'Notes of a Ten Days' Tour to the Murray and the North'. He and his comrades spent a night at Moorundee, about 8 kilometres down river from Blanchetown, and:

We were informed that although there was no 'licensed' at Moorundee, it would not be impossible to obtain a bottle of grog. However, we found it quite impossible, although we both went and sent as for as the Government

Location on the one hand and Green's intended new Blanchetown Hotel on the other. Not a drop was to be had, so when we tired of coffee we regaled ourselves with tea.

(I'm guessing next time he went to a ride-through before heading to the bush.)

By 1858 the pub was well-established and in the hands of Thomas Harvey who kept the place until he passed away, when his widow took it over before passing it to James Rossiter – mentioned by Lucy Maymon Hayes in the opening quote – in 1865.

The pub must've had a strong pull on Mr Rossiter. He had the place from 1865 until 1869. Then he returned in 1872 and kept it for three years. And then in 1886 he regained it, this time from William Crabb, whom we met back up at Weston Flat when he secured a licence for his pub at Murray Scrub the same day Hermann von Rieben got his for Nor' West Bend and James Mackey secured his for his Rest and be Thankful'.

This third and (very) final time James Rossiter ran the Blanchetown Hotel for a longer stint – a bit over fifteen years until 1901.

I'd arrived at Blanchetown before the pub'd opened so I found a convenience store in one of the backstreets and asked directions to the cemetery. She'd never been there; lived in town for ten years and thought if I kept going to the T then a left and a right at the T and then a left … it'd be on my right. So I did. And she was right.

The scene was depressing. These are all old graves; many are unmarked mounds but those with headstones, every single one has been vandalised, smashed.

Some have had the headstones re-assembled on the ground and the one I was seeking was onesuch. Above an inscription which reads, 'But when this corruptible shall have on incorruption, then Death is swallowed up in Victory' is the dedication:

In Memoriam
James Rossiter
Blanchetown
Died December 8th 1899
Aged 80 Years

Beside the shattered headstone is a fragment from the other grave in this plot. It's in loving memory of Susannah, James's beloved wife.

Nearby, also vandalised and laying on the ground is the headstone of William Crabb (died 13 May 1905), the bloke who'd passed the pub to Rossiter in 1886. Then across and up the gentle slope there's another plot, this one fully intact. It's the final resting place of the last of the Brand brothers who built the Overland Corner Hotel, who were involved with the Rest and be Thankful and who were so instrumental in the creation of homes away from homes for travellers in the Bend country.

James Brand drowned falling when trying to board a dinghy for a trip across the river. There was just a single witness and the local paper pointedly found it strange that there was no inquest. The headstone reads, 'Erected by his brothers'.

With the pub still open I ride down to check out Lock 1, the first lock on the Murray River. On the downstream side of the weir, the floating safety barrier is chockers with cormorants. Without the noise and the fighting of corellas and without the menacing attitude of vultures, several hundred cram every available space between the flotation buoys. God help any fish that feels stupidly joyful and in need of a quick breach!

A bloke in blue and orange reflective work top, wraparound sunnies and SA Water peaked cap strolls down from across the road. Darren's the master of Murray River Weir and Lock 1. And he's had a call from a couple of boats coming downstream that're needing to pass through. He keeps the body of the lock at upstream level for reasons to do with minimising corrosion and so with the press of his remote, sensors in the upstream lock gates sense the levels are identical and open to accept the two boats – one a tadpole of a thing, pretty much at capacity with a just couple on board, and the other a full-on private houseboat that could take half the town.

Once they're tethered and their details logged – origin and today's destination – the gates closed behind them, six valves 'the size of a house door' open below the downstream gates and the water within the lock drops (today it's 24 metres) to the downstream level. The gates open, the thumbnail putt-putt leads out, both toot and wave.

'Good people. You can tell when they ring what they're going to be like. Most are real good but the rich kids in daddy's speedboat, who've done nothing to earn their lifestyle, they're the ones who'll be smart-arsed on the phone when they ring and then be off-handed when you're helping them get through.'

Darren smiles, 'There's ways of doing this quickly and there's ways that're not so quick.' We leave it at that.

He splits the job with another bloke, working twelve days on then two days off. He loves the river, has been 'in water' all his working life including the last nine here, but those two days are very strictly 'GOOB' days.

'Eh?'

'Get Out Of Blanchetown.'

He looks at his watch. It's just gone eleven and the pub'll be open so we walk back up to the road, say our goodbyes as he crosses to his cottage right opposite the lock, and I head up the hill to the open pub where Danielle is preparing the place for another day.

She runs the place with her husband Wes whose parents owned it from 2004 to 2010. Wes grew up here – worked in the pub as soon as he was legal and when his parents shed it, they moved to Aldinga where Wes worked nights in the gaming room of the local pub, always vowing that one day he'd be back running the pub of his youth.

In 2016 the pub went on the market and they sniffed the bait. The place was doing it tough and in danger of closing.

'They'd put in a manager but it's too small for that. The town's too small. It needs a hands-on owner and we just didn't want to see it close. For us, especially Wes, it's always been the hub of the community.'

So they did their sums and made an offer. In January 2015, with their two daughters and son, they moved back to Blanchie and on the Australia Day weekend, they took it over, hitting the ground running, 'make that racing'.

And things are turning around. Locals who've told Danielle they'd boycotted the place for years, are now regulars. The shackies from Adelaide are having more meals during their weekly pilgrimages and they're both thinking they've made the right choice.

The entire pub is listed with the National Trust including, she thinks, the old stables (now storerooms) on the northern side. They've converted the oldest section with its locally cut sandstone walls with old wooden beams, into a character-filled dining room where today a busload of seniors from Murray Bridge have booked for a meal.

The old thick walls make for a naturally cool and relaxing pub even at the height of summer, while the exquisite deck out front optimises the hilltop position.

I tell Danielle I completely agree with her belief that pubs like this need a hands-on host but that causes me a problem.

The list on the wall, just like the other records shows that Rossiter ran this historic pub for the last time from 1886 until 1901 when he passed it to Charles Botten (who very quickly had himself in court for opening on Sundays and serving a bottle of alcohol to a girl under the legal age of, wait for it … fifteen).

Court records actually show that Charlie Botten took over the pub from James Rossiter in December 1900 but that still leaves a problem for a place that needs an attentive owner. Rossiter's shattered, vandalised headstone showed me an hour or so ago that he was buried a good twelve months before this. Did he just keep on serving beers from the grave?

The 1937 article in the Adelaide *Chronicle* continued after the quote which opened this yarn:

> *When the railway to Morgan was opened in 1878 Blanchetown practically lay down and died. Life revived there during the building of the first lock in 1914, and now a bitumen road from Truro and across the punt on to Renmark brings motor traffic.*

Just maybe, just somehow, it's fitting that in a town that today is doing just fine, and with a pub that's resurgent, but which was once accused of laying down and dying, the pub should've been run for even just a short time, by a bloke who already had!

CHAPTER 54 – SWAN REACH

ENDURING BEAUTY

The history, the old news clippings of most pubs, is punctuated with scandal of some type – court appearances for after-hours or illegal trading, suspicious fires, or for issues of violence or brawls. But the story of the Swan Reach Hotel is pretty much without such blemishes and in their place is a regular stream of compliments and praise unequalled by any other pub on the river.

1905:

'O, could I flow like thee, and make thy stream
My great example, as it is my theme.
Though deep, yet clear; though gentle, yet not dull;
Strong without rage; without o'erflowing, full.'

These lines of Denham came back to my memory on a recent moonlight night, when I gazed from the hotel verandah at Swan Reach upon the playful rippling waves of the monarch of Australian rivers.

1908:

Of the many new settlements on the River Murray which have in recent years come into existence the township of Swan Reach is one of the most impressive.

1909:

The hotel is in a most picturesque spot, being built on a cliff overlooking a fine reach of the river.

When Paul Hasse bought the 600-acre Swan Reach Station in 1895 and brought his family from the Adelaide Hills to live 'on the despised sand-hills ... there was no means of getting horses and vehicles across the river except by swimming the horses and getting the trap across on a boat.'

Hasse had a personal need and he saw a business opportunity and, 'after a good deal of exertion Mr Hasse secured a punt'. It soon turned out to be a good investment. A later testimonial noted that the punt was, 'one of the best paying concerns of its kind on the river'. To service the needs of travellers using their crossing, the Hasses then opened a small store and in 1897 Paul A. Hasse was granted a storekeeper's colonial wine licence.

Again, this must've gone well because two years later, using the existing licence as leverage the Hasse family beat off a challenger for the settlement's pub:

Emma H. Hasse, Swan Reach Hotel, Swan Reach, River Murray. Mr. T. R. Bright for applicant. There was also an application by Heinrich J. Hennig, for whom Mr. R. Homburg appeared. After hearing the evidence, the Bench considered an hotel was necessary, and they decided in favour of Mrs. Hasse.

The Hasse family was a fully paid-up member of the Pub 'n' Punter' Club.

Paul Hasse and his family must've had severe business nous. After he passed away 1911, his estate was eventually offered for sale. It included 'a seven roomed stone house overlooking the township and the River Murray, [with] a cellar, men's room [and] windmill [all on 5 acres]', another three-bedroomed house on two roods, a section of 261 acres of cleared land, another 78 acres of lucerne land, six subdivided half-acre blocks in the town, four full acre building blocks and nine subdivided blocks totalling over 30 acres.

And that was after the pub and the general store had been sold separately. Nice little earner!

But Paul Hasse hadn't just done well for himself and his family. He'd kept his hotel as the hub of his community and created a legacy of social involvement and proper procedure.

I swing left off Murraylands Road and then a graceful right sweep down to the Swan Hill punt which is mid-stream. Behind it, on the far shore, seemingly aloof, almost stately, the Swan Hill pub commands the cliff face as it looks down over the river.

Then, just as I'd lucked-in with the tiny paddleboat coming under the bridge back at Nyah, maybe 200 metres downstream to my right there's a three-blast horn signal from a big rear-paddler headed my way. Frantic rush to retrieve my cameras from Super-Ten's panniers and the five-deck PS *Murray Princess,* the biggest paddlewheeler to ever sail on the Murray and the largest one south of the equator, glides across my bows as my finger stays on the shutter button.

Once it's well clear Peter, who's been driving this thing for over seventeen years, closes the swing gates and again I'm the only passenger on the trip across. In 1925 the *Murray Pioneer* wrote a brief history of this township:

The Swan Reach crossing place dates back to about 1848, when it is said that a party of stockmen rode out from Adelaide, swam their horses across the river where the present punt now is and rode inland some 30 miles. They are said to have encountered many blacks, who were hunting kangaroos on the plains.

Paul Hasse ended the need for horses and cattle to be swum across the river here in 1895 and although it was a great advance, it didn't always run smoothly.

In 1919 a travel writer recalled, 'the puntman gave us the cheering news that he expected the rope to break at any time,' and in 1927 another scribe reported that 'passing on to Swan Reach wonder ... is aroused at the clumsy bulk of this punt as compared with the more modern one installed at Purnong.'

Captain Peter reckons the craft's regular and routine maintenance are the best on the river and should either of its twin engines cause problems,

getting it out and dropping a new one in can be done in under an hour. He's one of five operators who rotate through a series of twelve-hour shifts to keep the punt going twenty-four hours a day, every day of the year. In his time he's never been forced to use the considerable powers that operators have should trouble arise, and he's not sorry about that.

Peter explains the rules of the river, about the rights of way for punts and power boats and the etiquette of sharing the water. It's a good life though the night shifts, when the operators use a donga across the road from the pub for relaxation as they wait for the next siren to advise of a waiting vehicle, can be a challenge.

Then we're across and I'm heading up the slope of Hasse Hill Road past the cafe and left into the car park of surely the only pub on the river sitting on a road named after its founding publican. (A later search for a street

sign to that effect proves fruitless). The entrance is straight ahead and to my right a series of doors opening into the cliff face. Old stables.

Room sorted it's time for a window table, a cleansing Annie's Lane chardy and some kangaroo fillet, chips and a first visit to the salad bar, as the sun lowers and the colours change and down below me, Peter plies his trade back and forth.

I ponder life's big issues – like why the *Murray Princess* is still called a 'PS' when it hasn't been powered by steam for yonks.

The tide of families having tea recedes and Georgie, who runs the place with partner AJ, sits herself and her glass of red down at my table.

She grew up in Port Augusta.

'I was always a country girl and remember musting our cattle in a little Suzuki but my parents sold the farm in '85 and we moved to the Adelaide Hills and went into cattle on 600 acres there. Dad had an engineering business in Murray Bridge and then Mum and Dad separated and Dad went to Venus Bay near Streaky Bay on the west coast of SA. I got married at twenty-four and he was a hay contractor and I was in childcare and I'd help at night and then we managed a Black Angus property at Keith and I loved that but it didn't work out so I came back to the Adelaide Hills.'

And met Anthony 'AJ' Johnston.

'He'd just come through a broken marriage and had two kids and he'd been in hospitality for years, and we just wanted to do something together for ourselves, so I got into the pub game and he got back into the pub game.'

Their first stint was at Coonalpyn back near Keith. They couldn't get the mix quite right but they kept at it, learned the ropes and in January 2015, they took out a twenty-year lease on this place, determined to establish an equilibrium between the pub, the town, their customers and their own lives.

And a key to that was stepping back from full-time, full-on involvement. Now, each Thursday they hand the reins over to Geoff, and AJ and Georgie head out to buy supplies for the bar and the kitchen. Geoff keeps the place ticking until the Sunday when the bosses return refreshed and invigorated from time spent gardening, touring on their Harley, or just hanging out doing zilch or getting involved with other locals in other pursuits.

'At the end of the day, we're custodians who're looking after this place for the community and you have to feel part of the community and we both really love it here, not just as a business but as part of the social network.' And now, 'When we come to work we're not tired, we're not fed up. We're

recharged and because we're happy to be here our staff are happy to be here and that rubs off on our customers and the more we enjoy it the more they do.'

What I take to be three generations of boys look out from the far end of the balcony and I check a clipping from the Adelaide *Mail* of September 1939:

... and then you come to Swan Reach, one of the exquisite places of the world. The hotel where I lunched is the old Swan Reach station homestead with a story added. It stands on top of a limestone cliff, and is built of limestone cut out of the cliffs. You can see the old gear which was used to lower the wool bales over the cliff into river steamers or barges. It is anchored to red gums, and has become elevated as the trees have grown. The gums hereabouts are glorious, and the river is equally so. What a

place for an idle holiday, with a little boating and fishing, and an eye trimmed for the reception of beauty.

New stuff can be great but at times like this, with a cool breeze blowing and a cooler glass in my hand, the beauty and enduring truth of these eighty-year-old words is a reassuring constant.

Postscript: By early 2020 AJ and Georgie had 'run out of puff'. They'd not been able to find the balance they'd been seeking. There was a life out there calling them. No point living the dreams of others, eh? Quietly and without any angst, the fifteen years remaining on the lease was put on the market in March 2020.

In Feb 2021 a local bloke, John, who owns the town's motor museum put in a serious offer.

AJ: 'It didn't take us long to decide. He promised to keep on all the staff and really look after the place, both of which were very important to us. This is no horror story. We're happy, the town's happy and we know that John'll invest money and heart into the place and do a great job.'

On 3 May they flicked the keys and headed to their home at Woodside, planning to travel the state and the country, confident the Swan Reach pub's future is as bright as the place is beautiful.

CHAPTER 55

WALKER (OR WALKER'S) FLAT

I head south from Swan Reach with the river to the west and, though it's far below the road, the water is regularly visible off to my right. In just under 30 kilometres I'm turning into Angas Valley Road and about 100 metre on, I'm searching for a spot to park Super Ten on the slope down to the river.

I'm at the end of a maybe 4- or even 5-kilometre straight stretch of the river, flowing at me from the north-west. Down below the Walker Flat (not Walker's Flat apparently) punt is chugging across the stream, silhouetted in the afternoon sun.

In 1897 a deputation of residents of this part of the river travelled to Adelaide and waited upon the Commissioner of Crown Lands. Led by the ubiquitous Captain Randall M.P. they drew the commissioner's attention to a promise made five years earlier by government that a punt would be provided at Walker Flat. They pointed out that the government had raised the price of land in the area to pay for the punt, that the local people had been paying the levy ever since and that the government had kept the funds and punted the ratepayers.

They were told that Swan Reach would be getting a punt the following year and that only then would it be the turn of Walker Flat. But, ah, in the meantime, the levy for the non-existent ferry would remain.

From what I can find this punt has broken down, been washed away, been flooded and has sunk more than any other crossing on any river in Australia – facilitated no doubt by its exposed position on this long, straight stretch of water.

In 1919 it was reported to've been 'on the bottom of the river ... for about three weeks'. In 1917 it was almost swept away and out of service for a month. In 1926 it was closed for a week 'owing to the strong wind and the high river'. In 1932 the 'Royal Automobile Association [reported] that the punt ... ceased work. Extensive repairs are to be made and it is expected ... [to] be

out of action for at least five weeks.' And again in 1952 the RAA advised the 'punt will cease to operate at 10 o'clock ... for an indefinite period'.

Today it's all serene, the water rippling under not much more than a zephyr. My travel guide reads:

> A steeply graded track leads down to the Walker's Flat punt. The river is wide at this point and ... the ever courteous and obliging puntman well earns his toll in propelling traffic ... on the large engineless punt.

In the ninety years since that was written, the road's been sealed, the punt's inherited a motor and I get a personal solo voyage across.

It's only then that the grandeur and beauty of the cliffs I've been on top of reveal their splendour in the afternoon golden glow. The water reflects a tapestry of blue from the clear sky and gold from the cliffs, resembling a rich Persian tapestry.

I ring my hotel in Mannum and put back my booking. When I knock on the door of a riverside camp, Warren answers and yes, it's low season and there's no group bookings so sure I can camp slap beside the water in the hope of grabbing some star shots through the night. 'But the conditions aren't going to be quite right for a real cliff glow.'

Warren runs the Ankara Youth Camp just down river from the punt and knows how rare it is for the cliffs to turn to golden fire in the late afternoon sun. Generously he offers me a shot of his and wishes me good luck for the night.

At dusk the wind gets up and it turns out I've not taken into account the motion sensor security lights, which are endlessly set off by the waving branches. There'll be no star shots tonight but still, a night beside the river, across from such cliffs is a rare and treasured pleasure.

CHAPTER 56 – MANNUM

THE FINE DIFFERENCE BETWEEN A BOGAN AND THE BOGAN

On 14 December 1868 Charles Phillips's application to the Adelaide Bench of Magistrates for a liquor licence for a newly built house in Mannum was supported by 'a memorial numerously signed'. Once his counsel had assured the court that the place had windows and partitions in place, the application was granted.

Just two weeks later Phillips advertised that his hotel, The Bogan Hotel, Mannum was 'ready for the reception of FAMILIES and PLEASURE PARTIES' and that those wishing to pursue the 'real Sport (of) Rabbit and Duck Shooting' would be provided with boats and guns. (Ah ... a mob of city blokes who likely couldn't swim, piling into rough boats they'd likely never rowed, armed with strange guns they'd never shot and with bags of free ammo after a session at the Bogan pub. What possibly could go wrong?)

Apparently at first it was just a single-storey thing because in 1870 Adelaide's *Evening Journal,* reporting the floods of the Murray said, '(t)he river is still very high (at Mannum), the water being level with the windows of the Bogan Hotel.'

In fact, I reckon the first iteration of the pub occupied only where the northern half of the present site is and sometime in the first half of the 1870s a new two-storey addition was added at the southern end, in time for the earliest photo of the place which was taken in 1877.

By 1884 the Bogan had been further extended with '(a)n additional storey [being] built on the older portion ... which now corresponds with the new, and a balcony extends along the whole frontage (115 feet).'

Some time around the 1960s the Bogan pub switched to being simply the Mannum Hotel but, hey, I figure once a bogan, always a bogan and when I go through the front door on a cold Thursday arvo, I've switched on my mullet radar and I'm on the prowl for some.

I pull the door back and the signs are promising for a half-decent time. All the noise, and there's a bloody lot of it, is human-made. No race commentaries blaring over the hubbub, no obnoxiously faux-joyful sound of pokies lifting pension cheques. Just voices, shouting, laughter, and from a room with every seat at the L-shaped bar taken plus many of the stools at the wall and the island tables. It's the end of a cold work day. Beanies, fluoros, vests are de rigueur

At a table just back from the bar there's an ample bloke who could be a shaven Santa enjoying some off time. In a ragged long-sleeved top that originally might've been around cream in colour he's one of those guys who you immediately spot as going to be the centre of any circle that he joins. He's obviously the font of the laughter of the others at his table and as I sit a few tables down and suck it all in, a steady stream of people shimmy up, say g'day to him and move on. He's as glad to see them as they are him.

This, it turns out is Peter Raison and this is his pub in every sense.

In 1984 when he was a copper working out of Hindmarsh police station, he came back from his annual leave with his belt two notches longer to accommodate the effects of a seaside fortnight of food 'n' frothies. One of his workmates tapped his guts and asked whether he was smuggling a beachball under his uniform. Instantly he was known as 'Beachball'.

He left the force in 1998 and tried his hand working in a few pubs in South Oz and up at Tenant Creek but then his marriage went south.

In 2003 he met the woman who was to become his second wife and she suggested they head out to Mannum, where one of the pubs was looking for a manager. He got the gig, liked it and after three months approached his bosses and bought the licence from them.

He's been at the Mannum Hotel ever since, opening the doors most mornings and spending a good bit of most days spreading his exuberant brand of hospitality from the punters' side of the bar most days. And he brought the nickname with him.

'Beachball' was very quickly shortened to just 'Beachy', he confides. 'Most people have no idea what my real name is and most of those who know I'm Peter think my surname must be Beach or something like that.'

On the wall behind hangs a caricature portrait painted by a bloke in Ardrossan of this ruddy boniface with his thumb up and wishing the world 'Cheers'. True to his word, it's titled simply, 'Beachy'.

The first few years after they took over things were comfortable, the pub had its clientele and Peter set about entrenching its niche in Mannum's hospitality scene.

'Mannum's really lucky because it's got a club, and a really flash venue hotel across the road (the Pretoria) and it's got us as a real country pub where we get a lot of locals and there's no point in me being anything other than a country pub. I can't beat them at their game because they have a really flash top tourist venue up there but here we are old style country.

'Country people like to come in and have a chat and to have a host they know and to almost feel like they're in the host's home and we get the farmers and the tradies and they're all comfortable coming in after work in their work gear. They don't have to get dressed up, they can come in here and relax and catch up with each other's news and bring their families and relax, nothing pretentious. But it's wonderful for the town that there's such a choice of places to relax.'

Beachy's genuinely happy for the town, its locals and its visitors, that there's such a choice of watering holes and the venues all work in with each other. But it wasn't always quite so chummy.

For fifteen years the Bogan had the town's drinking trade and accommodation business to itself but in 1884 there was an application by a fella named Bothe for a second pub, the Bath Hotel. The Bogan opposed the application but midway through the process the applicant died and his wife withdrew the motion. (That's some serious sway!)

Two years later another application for a pub of the same name was made by a bloke named Gerloff. It was opposed by both the licensing inspector and by the proprietor of the Bogan on the grounds that another pub would be surplus to requirements. The Adelaide papers reported that there were 470 residents in Mannum and over ninety houses, 'eleven of which had been erected during the past year'. The Bogan's owner argued that the pub accommodation was 'quite sufficient to meet all requirements' and the licence was refused. The bench told Mr Gerloff not to bother applying again for at least twelve months.

The Bogan continued to survive floods and droughts and continued to thwart threats to its monopoly, but in 1892 the first local option poll ever taken in South Australia was organised at Mannum and resulted in a majority voting for 'increased pubic house accommodation'.

The push was on but nothing materialised until 1900 when another local option poll was taken as a result of the efforts of a bloke named Sam Hoad. This one couldn't be ignored. One thousand and one people voted in favour of another pub, which only 205 negatived.

In very short order, Hoad, with the Boer War raging in South Africa and the Transvaal's capital Pretoria under siege, opened his Pretoria Hotel in a town with a heavy representation of Germans (who also had an interest in affairs in the Cape). His choice of name is a mystery but this is the 'flash venue hotel' just up and across the road that mine host was talking about.

As we shoot the breeze about the history of the pub and the current challenges there's a continual conga line of arrivals who detour via our table and shake hands with Peter on their way to their perches around the bar.

Di comes over. This lady's prepared to say her husband's somewhere around sixty years of age, but she's more coy about her own. Hubby took off with one of Di's friends and as she cradles her merlot she explains how she was going to divorce him but hell, no, 'I'll leave all the leg work to him and save myself the trouble.'

But it's not her ex that's the big news in Di's life. She just had a pacemaker put in and reckons my and Peter's lives would be enhanced if we saw her scar. Peter thanks her for the offer. But Di, stop it, there's kids around!

He does the 'face of the place' thing very well but Beachy's only the last in a long tradition of hospitable hosts of the Bogan. Way back in 1882 the Adelaide *Advertiser*'s travel writer lobbed into the place after a less than comfortable trip:

about II o'clock the coach drew up at the Bogan Hotel, Mannum, where a
substantial supper soon caused us to view our previous experiences in a less
gloomy light ... The landlord and his wife leave little to be desired in their
relations to their patrons, and not only is the former a keen sportsman,
but he has evidently wide sympathies for all who come up to have a few
days' shooting in the district, and does not spare trouble in assisting them
in their quest.

But it wasn't just the hospitality that even then was impressive. The writer was also won over by the place's thoughtful design which allowed the pretentious snobs like himself to be kept separate from the, er bogans:

The hotel is the only house of its kind in Mannum, and is built in such a
way that the bar customers are at a considerable distance from the portion
devoted to the convenience of visitors – indeed, unless the circumstances
are very exceptional, there is nothing to indicate that the bar has any
connection at all with the more select part of the building.

Thankfully that rubbish has now changed and everyone's in the soup together, and that's the way they like it.

Peter's fully across the old name for the pub and a few folks have tried to convince to revive the original tag but he's not about to be tempted. 'I don't want to run the risk of having people in here who can't tell the difference between The Bogan Hotel and a bogan hotel.' And I'm not about to argue with that!

Darren comes over from behind the bar for a quiet word with the boss. There's a bloke he hasn't seen before, he's over there on his own at that table under the notice board.

'He just ordered a Jameson Whiskey and I gave it to him in a butcher but he then had a shot glass of his own and he re-poured it into that. He might be undercover checking if we're pouring full measures.'

'Not a problem,' says the boss. 'All our stuff's legit so nothing to worry about but keep an eye on him, eh?'

In the sixteen years he's been here, there's only been two fights and they both started at the other end of town and sorta just rolled into the pub. Once here they both were soon quelled by the ex-cop and his staff. They don't use outside security, relying instead on their experience both in and out of the pub game.

'If someone comes in and they've had enough we either drive them home or tell them to leave, depending on their attitude.' And in a continuation of the 'special hospitality' we first met way back upriver at Tintaldra, the pub has its own special version of the 'dead house' or Tocumwal's 'donkey room'.

'Room 3 upstairs is always the last room we rent out to visitors. It's semi-officially known as the pisshead room, where we put the people who've had too much and who we know are just going to sleep it off. It's near the toilets and it works very nicely.'

Yep, this is the kinda thing that defines a country pub.

Peter's gotta use the bathroom and I use the chance to head over and suss out the shot glass fella. He's a deadset character actor out of central casting for people needing a trawler captain or a lighthouse keeper; just swap his red beanie for a sou'-wester and the look's complete.

Strong blue eyes fix on me from under a red beanie, long, greyed hair cascades down the sides of his face and a wild white beard but trimmed moustache balance the bonnet. His red-and-white flannel shirt is backed up by a similar dark blue and green one underneath. A metal cigarette case in his chest pocket screams 'old school' and his hands and fingernails just as loudly shout 'been working'.

It doesn't start well. The butter that's come with his meal is in one of those annoying little foil-topped sachets that he's struggling to open. I offer to do it for him and he snarls that he's sick of people trying to take over his life, his life's been full of controllers and he'll do it his way thanks very much.

The top comes off, the roll gets spread and I learn his name's Chris. He's a qualified mechanic and he's come to town just 'to check out some old engines and generally annoy everybody'.

I tell him we already have something in common because I've come over to annoy him and he smiles and takes a swig. He isn't from the licensing people, he's just a bloke who prefers whiskey to whisky (Jameson when he can get it) but always neat and always in a shot glass. But he won't take it from plastic or from a warm glass so he carries his own and feels at home.

Sweeeet!

Chris isn't too keen to share his age but his stories put him in the tall fifties, most of which, after his birth up at Paringa, have been spent around the Murray downstream from Nor' West Corner. He's been living 'freelance' since his place burnt down a few years back and as he becomes

more comfortable and less suspicious of my intentions we swap stories of the history of the river, of the water and of the pubs.

He has little time for tourists, especially those with money whom he calls the 'effluent travellers' who 'pull up, camp at night and go talk to other tourists about other towns they're not in, and when they get to those towns they speak with other tourists about other towns they're not in. They're never where they are!'

'They're always in a rush to get to the next place so they can then be in a rush to get to the place after that in their bloody Toorak tractors so they can spend time talking to other people who're in a rush to get somewhere else.'

Then he fixes on me, takes a swig of Jammy and says, 'I thought at first you were humbugging me. You know what that means?'

I tell him I'm not sure, so he explains.

'I worked in the Territory for twelve months and the young black fellas up there have this thing they call 'humbugging'. It means when a white fella comes along and pretends to be interested in them and asks what is this, why do you do this that sort of thing, where do you live, how old are you that sort of thing like they care but all they really want is to take a photo. That's called humbugging, simple as that. I thought you were humbugging me.

'But you're not and so, yeah, you can pick up the camera now but do it quick coz my tea's finished and I've got stuff to do.'

I again apologise for offering to open the butter but he shrugs it off with a smile, shakes my hand, asks about the opening time for the Overland Corner pub because he's headed there in a day or two and then he's out the door, drained shot glass in his pocket.

So I've been in this ex-Bogan Hotel a good couple of hours and all I've met is good interesting people, not a bogan in sight and the ranks in the bar are thinning but I'm called over by a couple of blokes at a barrel table who wonder what I'm up to with the camera.

These two are work mates and they reckon I've missed a good photo by a couple of weeks. That's if I would've liked a shot of a classic 'shiner' of one of their eyes. I'll let the big one tell the story.

'There's this bloke in town and we don't really get on and haven't for a few years now and anyway about two years ago I had a swing at him down at the park. We were pissed and it was a total air swing so I missed and the force of my swing knocked me over and he then had two swings at me and both missed and after the second one he fell over and we were just

both on the ground and later all my mates said that was the worst fight they had ever seen. They told me you guys need to get a grip and fight properly.'

(Ah, I'm thinking I may've finally hit bogan jackpot!)

'Anyway, we were at this baby shower or it might've been a christening and it was 3 am and we'd been drinking that blue label Johnnie Walker and I don't usually drink that stuff, but anyway I went outside for some air and this other bloke was there. So I started yelling at him and told him what I thought of him and he said I'm glad you said that because I've been recording you.'

(I'm pretty sure where this is heading.)

'And I said what, you've been recording me? So I looked at him for about ten seconds to give him an idea of what was in store and said, well record this, so I hit him in the guts. A bit of advice: don't go hitting people in the head, it only hurts your hands and doesn't hurt them, but I hit him in the guts and he doubled over and everyone came running and separated us and that was it.'

(Yep, this is the script I was expecting but where does the black eye come into it?)

'But the next morning I woke up with a sore eye and I've got this shiner and it had this indent in it and I thought, he never got a punch in, I just couldn't remember him hitting me. All I could remember was that one punch to the guts and him going down.'

(So, what about the shiner?)

'So a week later at tea I'm sitting with the wife and she confesses that she was so angry with me when we got home that it was her who punched me and gave me the black eye. She punched me with her left fist and the indent mark was her wedding ring.'

Now, that, I hadn't been expecting.

'I'm forty-three and I really should be over clocking guys at baby showers.'

And there, he might just have a point.

'Just a pity you've got a clean shaved head. If you'd had a mullet,' I tell him, 'a story that begins with knocking yourself over with air-swing punches and then finishes with you getting a black eye from your wife would be a contender for bogan brag of the decade.'

And on that note I head upstairs, past room 3 which tonight is vacant, to my digs in room 6.

It's over 150 years since Charles Phillips convinced the Bench of Magistrates to grant him a licence for the first hotel in Mannum – over a century and a half since 'numerous' people signed the memorial in support of his application.

No doubt they all had high hopes for the place, visions and dreams. But it's doubtful that any imagined that for its sesquicentenary it'd be in such good hands and full of such a rainbow of characters, every one of them not wanting to be anywhere else.

CHAPTER 57 – MURRAY BRIDGE

UNPROVEN NEEDS

Back in the 1800s anyone applying for a new publican's licence in any town had to demonstrate a social need there of both the residents and travellers in the district for that licence, no matter whether it was a first for the area, or for an additional house.

In December 1882 Peter Hooper gave notice of depositing plans with the Adelaide Licensing Branch for a new hotel at the town then known as Bridgeport on the Murray River. In the same notice he advised he'd be applying for a publican's licence for this property, to be known as the Bridgeport Hotel in what became known as Murray Bridge.

He first fronted the Licensing Court in March 1883 and his application was heard in conjunction with that of a Mr H. O. Tauber for his Murray Bridge Hotel. They both failed to convince the hearing of sufficient need and were knocked back on the testimony of Inspector Bee who argued that 'the houses were not required'.

Hooper licked his wounds and in December that year he tried again but 'as the application was refused (back in March) … without liberty to apply again, it was not now entertained.'

Not one to give up easily, Peter Hooper began canvassing local power brokers and the press. An editorial conveyed the local outrage at the rejection and argued that the local need was sufficient and would only increase with 'the altered circumstances which the Intercolonial Railway [then under construction] will be sure to bring … Accommodation here at present … is entirely too limited to meet even the requirements of the hour.'

With influential backing, and good legal representation Hooper again applied to operate a hotel in March 1884 and despite the continued opposition of the Inspector on the same old grounds that the 'house was not required', this time his licence was granted.

He lost no time. Two weeks later tenders were called for 'the erection of the BRIDGEPORT HOTEL, MURRAY BRIDGE'. Just eight months later advertisements appeared for tenders to lease the 'just completing' hotel for a term of either seven or fourteen years. In December 1884 Hooper was granted a full licence for the hotel together with a billiard table licence.

On 1 January 1885 James Potter announced that he was operating Peter Hooper's Bridgeport Hotel and offered 'unequalled fishing and shooting'.

Potter's previous position had been at the Riverton Railway Station refreshment rooms. Thirty-six years later those same refreshment rooms were to become infamous as the scene of a different kind of 'unequalled shooting' when Koorman Tomayoff shot and killed Broken Hill labour leader and MP, Percy Brookfield, in this nation's first murder of a sitting member of parliament. The railway line is long gone, replaced by a splendid bicycle path, and the old station is in private hands but the marks of the stray bullets that struck the building and the door frames are still visible)

Back at Murray Bridge, the new hotel was immediately making its presence. In February 1885 The *Mount Barker Courier* waxed lyrical:

> *By far the most conspicuous building at the Murray Bridge is the large hotel which has recently been built there for Messrs. J. & A. Johnston. It stands on an eminence within a few hundred yards from the Bridge and close by the Railway Station, and from the balcony a very excellent view of the surrounding scenery is obtained … As the house occupies the most commanding site in the neighbourhood a wide expanse of country can be seen from every window. The building contains 28 rooms, of which 14 are bedrooms. All the apartments are unusually large, lofty, and well ventilated, and generally the place is fitted up like a first-class city hotel.*

The cost of the house was £3,800, and ... its present landlord is Mr. James Potter [who] has furnished it in a very comfortable and artistic manner.

It's certainly impressive as I cross the Murray Bridge road bridge, which for some strange reason has two flat top sections and a single camel-back span, and then up the imaginatively named Bridge Street.

At least it was. Well at least it was from the outside. It was extended in 1910 and now it sits at the crest of the hill with the almost regal presence of a monarch on a throne. A poly-canvas banner hangs on the side proclaiming, 'Eat Play Drink'. If you're stupid enough to wonder just what 'Play' entails, the word is stylised as a poker machine display with an old-school pokie lever at the side.

Inside the bar is just a depressing long room with screens and the bar has security bars and it's mostly closed out with safety glass. Once again the priorities of the owners to limit interaction between staff and guests is obvious – there's not a single stool at the bar in the entire hotel.

I tell the assistant I've seen the 'Play' sign and is there any, say, backgammon, or cards or chess or draughts. 'We have crayons and paper for the kids.'

And a quiet place for a relaxing drink? 'Maybe around in the bistro,' is the best she can offer. The only other bar is the pokie room where maybe six of the three dozen machines are free for someone to play with them.

I take the bistro option and have a quiet chardy in a cavernous room with the personality of an old-school television test pattern before moving on.

When I return to Murray Bridge some three months later, the pub's been demolished. It's trading out of temporary premises at the back of what was the car park and will continue like that until the hotel's new incarnation is finished. And it's going to take way longer than Peter Hooper took to have the first edition built in 1885.

Down the street and around the corner, the outwardly gorgeous Murray Bridge Hotel on the corner of Fifth and Sixth holds even greater disappointments for any traveller seeking relaxation in a pokie-free, gambling-free, smoke-free, character-filled environment.

We've come a long way since the 1800s: refrigeration is just one advance. But what's the point of cold beer when it comes without a warm welcome? What sort of advancement is constituted by the abolition of the requirement for licence applicants to convince a court of a social need for their services? And if publicans of Murray Bridge with a population of 22,000 and with a mean income 30 per cent less than in Adelaide, had to prove, like Peter Hooper around 140 years ago, that there was a social need for over 150 poker machines, just what would they say?

Thankfully just twenty-five minutes downstream, past the equally dire Swanport Hotel, there's a pub that prefers to focus on the amenity of guests rather than ease for the staff; on personal interaction and chewing the fat rather than having machines lamb down their visitors in windowless rooms with free coffee and an ATM always handy to withdraw more of your hard-earned.

I buy my fill of some of the best handmade chocolates from Cottage Box around on Bridge Street and point Super Ten south.

CHAPTER 58 – TAILEM BEND HOTEL

THE CHALLENGE OF DRINKING YOUR WAGES

The Tailem Bend Hotel has gotta be the closest hotel to a railway station I've come across that isn't called the Railway Hotel. I mean, the station's car park across Railway Terrace is effectively the best option for pub patrons to hitch their steeds, and that's exactly what I do.

Outside the pub there's a single vehicle, a very well-used red ute right at the front door, and when I go in, there's an even more used old hat, on a very used old head, right in front of the taps. Hanging from the bar beside him there's an old walking stick and if you were going to describe this little bloke as wiry, it'd be the barbed variety.

Yellow, tobacco-stained moustache cascades down to grey whiskers drooping a good few inches past his hidden chin. Filthy spectacles span a nose which has been non-professionally rearranged at least once and a folded, furrowed face that looks like an aerial shot of the channel country far to the north when it's not seen rain for years. For a jockey of a bloke his fingers are long but gnarled with arthritis, age and a life of toil.

Born just back up the river at Mannum but with Scottish heritage, this is Jock. He's been drinking at this pub for the best part of thirty years and he reckons he's even done a couple of years behind the bar a while ago. Sometimes drinks at the other place in town but only when he has to. I'm not too sure just what that means because he says he's never been banned. Must be when this place is out of his beer.

Faded checked shirt and lightweight vest, he cuts a figure and he'd stand out in pretty much any bar as a bloke with a story or two. And that's without his hat. A stained, worn, fraying Akubra that's the real icing on this cake. (I'm guessing it's a sand Golden Spur model and I've seen others that've been retired and nailed to pub walls and ceilings that've been in better condition.)

He's had this one for 'ten, maybe twelve years' (hats apparently age in even years.) 'It's the first thing on in the morning and the last thing I take off at night. I'm never without it, inside, outside, everywhere.'

It took him fifteen years to wear out the last one and the remnants are now hanging on the hallway wall at his place about 14 kilometres out of town. He doesn't just keep to the same brand of hat, always an Akubra, he keeps to the one style.

'See when you buy a hat like this it's just a dome and then you can bash them any way you want and this what I've done to mine is called the western bash, and it looks like the roof of this pub eh?

'One day it was pissing down rain and I had to go out and do something, can't remember what it was but I went back in and felt like the job deserved a beer so I went to the fridge and when I bent down to get my stubbie this waterfall poured off my hat onto the floor. Wasn't a problem, needed a bit of a wash anyway!'

Jock doesn't mind a punt on the hayburners and tells of a day a few years back when he got a tip, stuck a hundred each way on the thing and won five-and-a-half grand. Slowly, inexorably, it's all found its way back into the bookies' pockets but it hasn't dampened his enthusiasm for the neddies.

Each year in September he heads up to Mindarie-Halidon for what's known as the 'Melbourne Cup of the Mallee'. Of course he wears his hat. And in the throng he still manages to stand out.

'They all turn up there in their moleskins which they wear once a year, and their RMs which they wear once a year and their bloody Akubras which they wear once a bloody year. It's like seeing a thousand bloody Barnaby Joyces running around in the paddock, not a mud mark or a sweat stain in the bloody place! Would these people actually know what physical work is?'

We decide that they wouldn't and we decide to have another drink. The image of a paddock full of beetroot-faced disgraced politicians cavorting in front of their pregnant office staff and their bastard children needs alcohol to wash it down.

From his bent back, buckled knees and walking stick I guess Jock must've been a shearer at some stage but I'm wrong.

'My dad got this stick when he buggered his back and when he got old he said to me that he can give me lots of stuff but the most useful thing he could give me was his walking stick. And you know what, he told me a lot of stuff but that was the truest thing he ever said.'

Last time his back really started causing problems he had to see the local doctor.

'He took these X-rays and then put them all up on the wall with light shining through and I said I didn't understand them and told him just to tell me how I was in language I could understand. So he asked when I was born and I told him '49 and he said, you're just a worn-out FJ Holden, they were born the same year and not too many of them still have a good chassis.'

Hopefully the doc was more precise with his knowledge of medicine than cars.

'I didn't wanna tell him that the FX came out at the end of '48 and the first FJ wasn't made until '53 but I got the picture. My wheels were pretty much falling off!'

But it wasn't removing wool that took its toll on Jock's body. After getting out of the army in '72 he worked for years at a foundry carrying 150 pounds (almost 70 kilograms) of molten metal in shoulder shanks for eight hours a day.

'There were six men in the team and between us we'd carry 190,000 pounds of metal a day. It was good money back then. In 1974 I was knocking back 340 bucks a week and paying 18 cents a middie. Was the only time in my life I couldn't drink my wages!'

Jock pauses for a sip from a middie that's cost him around twenty times that price and then looks at me over the rims of specs. His eyes fix on mine.

'But that's not to say I didn't give it a shot a couple of times!'

This spot, front and centre, right beside the taps is Jock's perch, but he's not as protective as some of his own seat; if someone else's in it when he fronts he'll make himself comfortable somewhere else and wait till they leave.

'See, it's not my seat. It's the pub's seat. If it was mine, it'd be different,' he explains and then tells of a time in Sydney back in the '70s when a bloke's seat actually was his seat.

'I was in Sydney and I went into a pub and it was pretty empty and there were all these seats and they were like not the same, every seat was different – different colours and different styles and shapes. And so I got a beer and sat down and this bloke came over to me and he was polite and he said excuse me and I said yeah and he said you're in my seat and I looked around and I said, so has it got your name on it?

'He said matter of fact yes, it's on the back, and it was and then I saw all the other seats had names on the back and he said the rule around here is that anyone can sit anywhere but if the owner of the seat comes in they have to move. See, we brought these seats ourselves from home, everyone brought their own seat and put their name on it and that's why they're all different colours and styles.

'So I asked him where I should sit and he was real nice and pointed out this seat and said the bloke who brought that had died a few weeks before so there wasn't much chance of him coming in and telling me to move. So I finished my beer there!'

Jock's uncle was a long-termer at another pub. 'Didn't never have a seat. He never used to sit down but he could do all these duck calls, had a real talent at it and so everyone just called him Ducky and they put a little brass plaque on the bar where he used to stand and it said, Ducky's Place.'

Jock's glass has been empty for maybe twenty seconds when he reflects, 'a man's not a camel', and we get another round. I'll get back to camels in a bit.

Back in March 1902 the annual meeting of the Adelaide Licensing Branch granted the application by George Hoad for the first hotel in the new township of Tailem Bend, ignoring the opposition of the police who'd argued that it was, 'not required for the accommodation of the public'.

Three months later Hoad (often wrongly reported as 'Hood') was granted a billiards licence. Business was on the up and the pub was quickly becoming the centre of its community. In August a 'large gathering took place at the Tailem Bend Hotel ... to form a cricket club' and the publican was elected secretary and treasurer.

Soon the pub was advertising 'SPLENDID ACCOMMODATION ... [and] boats on hand' and two years later Hoad had expanded his business empire advising that 'Hoad's coaches [leave Tailem Bend] on the arrival of train from Adelaide ... every Wednesday.'

Hoad offloaded the pub to S. O'Hara in 1906 and it quickly hot-potatoed through a few hands until in 1909 it was the centre of one of the bigger acts of bastardry you'll come across.

Hugo Miatke, a good god-fearing man from Moorelands, about 12 miles out of town, was giving a fellow parishioner, Johann Paech a lift back after church. According to a previous issue of the local rag, Johann had just 'erected a fine up-to-date residence and shop (which) is rented by Mr. I Pritchard, fruiterer,'

Hugo decided to drop into the hotel to get some brandy for the trip home. He was observant but by no means an abstainer and his fellow worshipper joined him. They both ordered a flask of brandy.

Miatke was entitled to buy the booze because, living over ten miles from the pub he was classified as a traveller, but his mate lived in town and had no such justification. So Hugo Miatke did what it takes a very special breed of self-righteous jerk to do. He reported his mate to the cops who busted Paech for receiving and publican Mitchell for supplying on a Sunday. Truly!

They were hauled into police court where, thank god (and here I'm not referring to Hugo Miatke's version) the bench dismissed the information against Paech and the charge against Mitchell. I'm guessing church services the following Sunday they sat in separate pews!

(Three decades later this sort of rubbish was still going on. Just short of five months before Germany invaded Poland on 1 September 1939 to precipitate World War II, the pub's host was in court successfully fighting his conviction and fine for Sunday trading. The magistrate was urged to find the original offence either unproven or 'trivial'.)

Later in 1909 Mitchell added seven new rooms to the southern side of the hotel, bringing the total to twenty-seven and in April 1910 he sold to B. W. Richards of Wallaroo. Just two weeks after Richards took over the government surveyor arrived in town. He brought with him two truckloads of camels.

The Adelaide *Chronicle* reported on the subsequent circus:

The presence of camels in Tailem Bend caused excitement among the horses in the town. While Mr. L. Soult, jun, was carting machinery his horses took fright and became unmanageable, with the result that a chaffcutter was thrown to the ground.

The local kids were also excited and queued for a turn to sit atop. Publican Richards must've been a man of action. He'd only had the pub a fortnight but the memorable image of kids atop a dromedary outside his hotel is one of the most enduring of all historical images of pubs along the river. And there, right in the centre of the background is the facade of the pub with his name, 'B. W. RICHARDS' dominating.

By the time Richards bunged on the second storey to the pub in 1912 the place was firmly at the centre of town life.

Jock reckons not much has changed. 'This is the place to come to find out what's going on in the town. This is where you come to meet other locals and to have a yack and a punt.'

It's time for both of us to get going so he gets a couple of takeaways and I say my thanks. We head out together and turns out the dusty ute is his and can I hang on just a moment.

Jock's enjoyed the yarn and has something for me. Turns out he likes writing too – poetry mostly, and he's got a few poems printed up that he'd

like me to have. It's a gesture from the heart. He tells me he's been writing poems for years, 'but never had anything published', and I look at him and say, 'Well that's about to change!'

Enjoy a fragment of 'The Platform' by R. J. Muir (Jock):

Hand shakes all round
And board they did
Youths and men
Uniform clad
Some never to be
Seen again
For their souls
To ride
and ask
those
who go home
to tell them
we gave
our today
for their
tomorrow
To ride
The never never train.

SPITFIRES, SMOKE AND THE LOWEST PUNT

I've met a few Jocks on the road and like my new mate at Tailem Bend, they've never failed to be entertaining. But memories of the story of the first Jock I met have been the most resilient.

Sometime in the late 1970s I was in New Zealand, hitchhiking, strangely enough to their Wellington, from Auckland, and a bloke in a rental car stopped for me just south of Hamilton. This was 'Jock' and he was going two hours along my route, to a small place on Lake Taupo.

Jock was a Scot who'd migrated to Melbourne with his parents and who'd never quite lost his Scottish brogue. He was about the age of my father at the time and this day he was nervous and glad for the company.

Just before he'd gone off to war in 1940, Jock had a girlfriend for a few months, a 'Kiwis lass' whom he really cared about and to whom he wrote weekly letters both on the ship to Europe and for the first year or so of action. He heard nothing back. Not a response. No acknowledgement. Not even a 'Dear John'. The war finished, Jock survived, returned to Melbourne, searched without luck for his old flame, became a storeman, got married, had two girls and looked after his parents as they aged.

Meanwhile, his ex-girlfriend and her family had at some stage returned to New Zealand and two years before Jock stopped for me, her mother passed away. The woman began to clean up her mother's things and it was then she came across a bound bundle of unopened letters she'd never seen before. From Jock.

There were also a few letters that she'd written. To Jock.

On the eve of his departure for the war, Jock's girlfriend became pregnant. The family chose to maintain the pregnancy and keep the child.

But the mother had intercepted all of Jock's letters, just as she'd chosen to keep the messages her daughter had given her to take to the post office.

The girlfriend, who'd never married, opened and read each of Jock's letters. She knew she had to track Jock down – how she did it he has no idea just yet – and explain. She wrote and he telephoned her back the day he read her letter. She told him of his – their – son and their grandchildren.

Jock sat his wife down, told her the story and how he was driven to see his son and grandkids. His wife wasn't impressed – she would leave him if he went to NZ and for six months he wrestled with the issue before making his decisions.

When he picked me up Jock was recently single, both his parents had passed away and he no financial ties – no mortgage and nothing to keep him in Australia other than his daughters who understood why he had to see their half-brother, his son.

At around fifty years old, he was on his way to see his childhood sweetheart and was as nervous as a teenager. After two enthralling hours he dropped me off on the south side of Taupo and I wished him happiness and luck.

To this day I wish I'd taken an address or a number to see how it all unfurled and as I head south again to another Wellington, I have no idea that by the end of the day I'm going to be telling that yarn to a bloke with a different but similar story.

There's a choice of two quick squirts south from Tailem Bend to my digs for the night, but to appreciate the grandeur of the Wellington Hotel, it's best to approach it on the punt so I keep the river on my right, take

the fork right on the Princes Highway and then another onto the B45 for Wellington and Stathalbyn. Past a wall of soft toys. How do these start? How do they take hold? One day I'll time it so I pass one as someone adds to the collection of bras or kettles or shoes or whatever! Then a lonesome ruin of what was very likely an old pub now in the red dust field.

The punt's just pulled out from my side so plenty of time to enjoy the scene from beside an old Southern Cross Number 10 that's clanking in the breeze. A couple of blocks to the right of the punt approaches on the opposite bank, the Wellington pub sits aloof on the cliff, strongly redolent of its mate back at Swan Reach, but more low slung and less regal. Whereas the Swannie, had only a mooring and a steep rock face between it and the river, the 'Welly' has a superb grassed frontage and a gentle path leading down to a flat picnic area for the use of pub guests.

At its left shoulder is the pub's accommodation donga block where I'll be tonight and between the pub and the line of vans, cars and a truck loading onto the ferry there's a reserve where the old approaches used to be.

It's a panorama of riparian relaxation that pulls strongly – that deck at the front of the pub, overlooking it all from a higher vantage point and the promise of a glass of chilled Langhorne Creek white has me urging the far-side travellers to get onto the punt, code-named 'Heron' so I can soak it all in.

Wellington's first hotel, the Ferry House Hotel opened in 1845, a year before the Wellington Hotel, but if the Bell brothers, who opened the Welly the following year were second in the race to establish a pub here beside the Murray, they were the first members of another, far more important and financially rewarding river community.

Very soon after opening their hotel, later in 1846, a public notice appeared in the *South Australian Register*:

> *Messrs Bell beg leave to inform the public that their punt at Wellington ...*
> *is now completed, and in full operation; and they undertake to cross drays,*
> *bullocks, horses &x[sic], with all possible dispatch. The accommodation*
> *this offers to the public needs no comment, particularly with those who are*
> *acquainted with the locality.*

The brothers Bell had created the Pub 'n' Punters Club. They were the foundation members. The hand-driven Wellington punt was the first such Murray crossing and its position on the most direct route from Adelaide to Melbourne ensured business was steady. In the face of this competition from a pub and punt package deal, the Ferry House Hotel didn't last a year.

The Bell brothers weren't in this for love and altruism. They made very little effort to maintain either the approaches to the punt or the punt itself. In 1848 the issue of the operation and the charges for crossing became a statewide concern:

> *We are glad to hear that the road at Wellington is nearly completed, and*
> *that the punt is now in operation. The settlers, however, complain of the*
> *still heavy charges levied; 2s 6d, for instance, for a horse; and trust that the*
> *government will reduce, and henceforth regulate, the scale of fees.*

A year later the brothers had offloaded their income stream to the government and the tolls weren't the top concern:

> *The celebrated Government punt at Wellington has been at length, after*
> *much labour and expense, raised from the bottom of the Murray, where it*
> *has lain for the last twelve months. It now requires the services of a man,*
> *employed at 5s. per diem, bailing it out to keep it afloat, but it is shortly to*
> *undergo a thorough repair, and a regular ferrying staff is to be immediately*
> *established at the crossing-place, so that the settlers may shortly look*
> *forward for more facilities of ferrying themselves and their stock than they*
> *were provided with heretofore. The party in charge, however, will require*
> *to pay a little more attention to his duty, and not spend his time in the*
> *customary amusements of fishing for cod, and chasing the wild ducks and*
> *pelicans down, miles away, to the basin of Alexandria, if the convenience*
> *of the public is to be taken into consideration.*

Wellington at this stage straddled the river and once they had their punt floating and notionally serviceable, the focus switched back to the iniquities of the charges on the 'only place in this Province where tolls are levied on passengers, cattle and vehicles'.

In 1857, eighty-six:

> *inhabitants of Wellington, settlers, stockholders, and persons residing in*
> *the South-eastern District of the Province of South Australia petitioned*
> *the government humbly holding that they 'ought to be relieved from this*
> *unequal tax (and praying) that your Honourable House will sanction the*

abolition of the ... tolls and also ... vote a sum sufficient for the maintenance of the said Ferry'.

The strongest agitators were those living in East Wellington who abhorred the extra impost for crossing the river to have a drink and this only increased when sand drifts invaded West Wellington at the end of the 19th century and most of the population was forced to move across the river.

The pub however stood firm. It was only well after the turn of the century that the sands were controlled and the population returned. Slowly East Wellington withered and West Wellington with its pub and courthouse became simply 'Wellington'.

The old windmill grinds on, the ferry arrives, gets me across without sinking or charging any exorbitant rate and I'm soon parking beside my donga digs and heading into the bar.

Danny has just the chardy I'm looking for and I take it out onto the deck that'd been tempting me from across the river. And it's all just as idyllic as I imagined. Below the punt, the lowest one on what could be considered the main river channel, continues to chug its return journeys and I'm soon joined by Phil who's needing a smoke.

Not usually the stick-rubbing of an enjoyable encounter, but he deliberately sits downwind and parks his 'old man's drink' – a butcher of port – on the table as he lights his durrie.

Born in '51, Phil grew up in Stanmore in the inner west of Sydney. His dad spent the war as a Spitfire pilot based in England but flying countless missions over Europe. When he came home in '45, he looked at Sydney traffic and, even after spending years dealing with the possibility of being shot down, decided it was way too dangerous.

'He told us that at least when he was up in the sky he knew exactly what the Germans were trying to do to him, but on the roads you could never be sure what the other idiots behind the wheel had in mind, so he never got a licence and we travelled everywhere by bus and train and trolley bus.'

Phil and his younger brother became fascinated with the machinery of public transport and we yarn about the old Albion double-decker buses with the chrome pole on the rear deck that you could hook onto with bent elbow as it passed at 50 miles per hour and about trolley buses in George Street, Sydney. But then he switches to trains and really lights up.

'I probably should've given these up by now but geez, I started smoking early.'

Sydney's Stanmore is just west of Newtown and beside the main western railway line from Central Station.

'Me and my brother used to go train spotting. It was near the end of the steam trains and the start of the electric ones and the electric trains would pull out of Strathfield (about 10 kilometres west and the last stop for expresses to the city) real fast and the steam engines would take longer to get going but by the time they got near our place, the steam trains would be really travelling and they would've caught up with the electric ones.

'We'd stand on Petersham Bridge and lean over the edge of the railing – there was no safety rail in those days. The steam trains would come fanging down the outside track belching all this smoke and we'd take a deep breath and stick our heads out right above where we knew the smokestack would be and the smoke would just totally rush up and cover us. For a good thirty seconds on a still day you'd be completely inside this smoke cloud.

'No health and safety in those days. We'd go home and Mum would go crazy at how filthy we were. Some days we'd do that with four or five engines. Probably inhaled more smoke on a Saturday arvo on Petersham Bridge than I do in a month of sucking these things.'

A qualified carpenter, Phil and his then-wife came across to Adelaide in the late '90s and he started working for a crowd re-fitting petrol stations and garages, and they both visited, and liked, Wellington. Then the marriage ended, and in 2001 he got himself a 'big caravan' and parked it permanently at the van park across the road to use as his base while he moved around the state fixing up servos. But the company got bought out and he was shoved out so now Danny behind the bar sees a hell of a lot more of his face.

'So no strings now? No family?'

He lights another. It'll do him less harm than a steam engine.

'Got one son who's a farmer in [NSW]. I didn't find out about him until about twenty years after I broke up with this girl. I always wondered why she stayed in contact with my mum but Mum never let on. She was a country girl and she went back to [her home town] and every now and then mum would let slip something; mention her, and I'd wonder why.'

Then his mother passed away, 'and I found a bundle of letters from the girl and I put two and two together. She came from a very strict Catholic family and I wrote her a letter about twenty years ago and it took a while but she got back to me and basically said, "let sleeping dogs lie" and you have to do the honourable thing so I didn't pursue it. So I have a son out there I know nothing about, maybe grandkids by now too.'

His eyes are narrow slits, closed equally from top and bottom. And he hasn't taken them off mine the entire time.

'Then I got married and my wife was German from the Barossa and she couldn't have kids. We were married for about thirty years until we'd had enough of each other.'

And here he is.

As we drain our glasses, I share the story of Jock in New Zealand and Phil looks out into the darkness. Out on the river, the night's closed in, the lights of the punt bounce of the water, the skeetas have arrived and our glasses are empty. Phil's got an early start in the morning and my day's been a long one so neither's after a refill.

Danny gives me my room keys and as I walk out with Phil I ask him if I can write all he's told me. He'd prefer I don't specify the town his son's in but apart from that just asks that I be gentle. This time I fix my eyes on his and throw him an old line: 'That's the least I can do, and I always try to do the least.'

Phil laughs, we shake hands and as he disappears into the night he turns, 'I bet Jock stayed with her for the rest of his life.'

And I call back that I reckon he's right.

CLOSE TO THE BEST, CLOSE TO THE END

In January 1891 Meningie hosted the Lake Albert race meeting and the papers at the time wondered:

what there was in a little country race-meeting to attract people from Adelaide (a hundred miles away) and others from country towns at distances nearly as great,

before answering themselves:

Some of the visitors were no doubt bent on business pure and simple, and others went for pleasure only; but the majority, it may safely be said, combined the two objects and expected to have an enjoyable outing while not neglecting to keep their eyes open to the main chance. Amongst those hailing from the city were several of the most respectable of the 'bookies' and a few well known citizens.

The ferry bringing most of the visitors was late leaving Milang and, 'a promised telegram to [Mr Phillips] the hotel-keeper [at Meningie] had not been sent from Milang, notifying the departure of the steamer.'

When the fifty or so horsey folks arrived wet, late, hungry, unexpected and homeless, 'Mr. Phillips and his staff were equal to the occasion and an excellent supper was laid for the visitors, who were loud in their praise of the manner in which their wants were attended to.'

Two traditions had been set in train: hospitality of the publican, and a connection with racing.

This pub hadn't had an easy birth or adolescence. In 1866 William Hitch's application for a new hotel at Meningie was knocked back on the grounds that the building 'wanted proper accommodation'. Despite Hitch arguing that it'd been improved since the police inspection, the Bench refused, 'considering the house at present unfit for the purposes of an inn.'

I guess William was used to such, er, hitches and he was back in three months re-applying and this time, over the top of more objections from the police, he was granted his licence. After a celebratory photo out front with four cars and over a dozen locals, the Meningie Hotel was up and running, not that it seemed to enliven the town overly.

Three months after it pulled its first beers the Adelaide *Observer*'s 'own (somewhat bored) correspondent' was scratching for copy for his weekly column:

Things in our small township are at present very dull, and I have nothing very stirring to record this week ... [although] there are ... considerable alterations going on at the Meningie Hotel [and] as this township may some day become a resort for tourists a comfortable hotel will be a strong recommendation.

Just opened and already eyeing expansion – Billy Hitch must've been doing some stuff right at this fishing village on the far side from Adelaide on the banks of the estuarine Lake Albert, a place fighting to be a destination in itself but for now fated to be a lonely stop on the coastal route to Australia Felix. A 1932 memoir recalled:

Meningie seemed to be the last outpost of civilization in the sixties and seventies and early-time travellers who braved the experience had plenty to tell of for many years to come, for there were many real dangers to be encountered on the way, [and] the reports of questionable places of accommodation and of characters of evil repute were not altogether groundless. On the outward trip at Meningie one said goodbye to ordinary civilization till Kingston hove in sight.

At the get-go the pub may've been ready, and it sure was rough, but over time it lifted its game. The same memoir of 1932 applauded:

The Meningie Hotel was anything but a high-class hostelry in the [its early years], but today it is so up-to-date an establishment that it caters admirably for travellers and gives them a good deal of the comfort and attention that its namesake in Melbourne, Menzies Hotel, has for half a century been noted for.

In 1885, the hotel was put up for tender and pushed as being 'well known as one of the best businesses in the colony'. Follow the rule of discounting real estate agent's claims as 90 per cent exaggeration and it still must've been in decent shape.

In 1907 the Adelaide *Advertiser* noted that the 'Meningie Hotel has been much enlarged' and seven years later Adelaide's *Saturday Mail*, ran a yarn about two motorcyclists who'd decided to have a bit of a race from the South Australian capital to Melbourne. They made Meningie comfortably the first day and, '(t)he night was spent with that good host, beloved of motorists, at the Meningie Hotel.'

The two traditions were in good hands.

Bike riders will appreciate the next bit of these blokes' journey:

We had been dreaming for weeks past of the speed trials we would run on our own account when we got on the famous racing stretches of the nine-mile beach. Alas! We were doomed to disappointment, for it was raining hard, and the whole beach was under water. Water ran down our necks, into our boots, and into our carburetters [sic], but we battled along, riding in water all the time. Naturally the pipeclay was like greasy glass, and the machines skidded in all directions.

Ah, and they say that a bad day on a bike is better than a good day off it. But back to the pub!

When I ring ahead to reserve a room I get straight through to Ben, a quietly spoken bloke who tells me he runs the place, laughs that yes there's plenty of place to park my bike under cover and would I like him to organise the pub's historian to drop by on the arvo I plan to turn up?

It's been a long ride down the river and this is the first time I've been offered the company of a pub's historian so I say 'yes please', narrow down my arrival time the following day and hang up with optimism.

The ride south on the Princes Highway from Wellington is windblown under a grey sky and the 10 kilometres from Meningie Lake Albert, once a salty estuary, now effectively a freshwater adjunct to the much larger Lake Alexandrina suddenly appears on my right. Then it disappears for a bit before becoming my companion for the last few kilometres into town.

The pub's busy! Buzzing. A bunch of blokes is packing out the gambling end, another group's filling the middle of the bar and at the end there's a throng of the town's socialites quaffing discreet wines and ostentatious water.

A bloke behind the bar in red and black footy jumper is juggling it all with the help of a couple of others. I guess he's Ben and he guesses I'm me, opens a slate, puts my beer on it and tells me to make myself at home. There's a spare barrel table up near the corner door so I take a perch and pretty soon it's 'Are you Colin the writer fellow?'

Way more effervescent than the half glass of beer she's holding onto, Marianne Cunneen's ubiquitous smile seems only ever replaced by a laugh and her eyes reflect a spirit of adventure. She's the town's semi-official historian and chronicler and it's Marianne who in 2017 wrote the sesquicentenary history of the Meningie Hotel.

She was born here and her education started at the local primary school. In later life she moved away to Murray Bridge for a couple of years but couldn't wait to get back. I tell her I can understand that. She has a copy of her pub history book with her and together we go through the story of this pub and how an unusual number of publicans, beginning with William Hitch the first host, had it, left and then came back for seconds.

She explains how John Menzies spent the year of 1923 handmaking cement bricks out the back and then giving them a full year to harden before using them to build the second storey of the pub. She talks about Henry Botten who owned the pub for thirty years from 1893 and who

likely used it as front for bootlegging operations run by his mother.

Now that's the sort of sordid shenanigans that draw me like an S-bend draws a full flush so that night I go searching for stories of Henry Botten's mum. The smoke is quickly found: in the Adelaide *Advertiser* of January 1902 I soon find an extraordinary public notice in which Elizabeth Botten warns that all persons defaming her character or her house will be *prosecuted*.

But why would anyone defame such a woman? The fire is more elusive but there's a juicy hint in a legal case fifteen years earlier when Botten owned a store in the main street of Meningie. She was hauled into court by one Catherine Robb; wife of J. B. Robb of Coorong who deposed:

On Dec 30th went to Botten's store to pay an account I owed defendant. Said to Mrs. Botten you have charged me with receiving goods I never had. She replied, you have only come to bounce me and I will not be bounced at the same time calling me a dirty slut. I said don't call me a dirty slut; you are only a blasted old washerwoman. She then threatened to knock my brains out and threw a two pound weight which struck me on the arm. I ran outside calling murder and police. I had a very bad arm.

Elizabeth of course claimed to be as pure as the driven:

she said you are a b——— old washerwoman and I am a lady. Told her to go out of my house. She would not go, and I put her out. Did not throw any weight at her. Did not say I would knock her brains out. When she was outside I locked the door, and she commenced kicking. She then went on the road and called me a damnable old harlot. She was three-parts drunk.

Ladies, ladies, stop it!!!!

The bench in its wisdom dismissed the case with both parties paying costs.

The post office where I can get a copy of Marianne's book is closed for the afternoon and as I make a note to pick one up in the morning, we're joined by a real nugget of a bloke. Huge hands, big forearms grown from yakka, trimmed moustache beneath a nose that looks like it could've been rearranged on a Saturday arvo in the park, eyes that fix on you, he's wearing a deep blue polo, camo vest and a peaked cap. He's drinking a 7-ounce of what turns out to be port and which he calls his 'boogidee'. This is Derrick, known universally around here simply as 'Uncle D'.

I ask him if he's a local and he points to his hat with 'Raukkan' embroidered on the crown and he tells me he's a Ngarrindjeri man from up the road.

'I was born at the mission at Raukkan and I lived there all my life until I was seventeen. We had a big family – we're the Gorralls and I had five brothers and three sisters and I was the third eldest and I could see my mum and dad struggling to make a living for us. So I decided to leave the mission station to get a job to help them.

'And it hurt me because I'd moved away from my family and my home. But I kept chasing the work and found myself working on the Nullarbor on the east-west railway line. I was lonely. I missed my family. I missed my friends and so I came back home. Back here.

'I moved from Raukkan to Meningie, just around from here. It was a struggle but I was home. And that was the important thing.'

Uncle D started working in shearing sheds but then in 1984 the South Australian government was looking for Indigenous rangers.

'So I did a three-year course and became a ranger. I graduated and I worked for seventeen years as park ranger in Coorong National Park and unfortunately in 2002 I decided to leave because the government was going away from what being a ranger was all about. You know – talking to people, educating them, taking time to tell them all about your home country. So I felt very sad about leaving after all that time. The park users used to love seeing rangers, you know, saying g'day.

'We had a conference in Adelaide and we all went and they told us they were cutting back the interaction with park users and I couldn't see the point. So I quit. I wanted to talk to people and welcome them to country, not go around booking them forty dollars for dropping a piece of paper by mistake.'

Uncle D married a local woman and they had five kids, four girls and a son. 'Unfortunately we lost our son a couple of years back aged thirty-eight. When he left here he met a couple of girls but one year he came home for Christmas with us and he never went back. He had brain cancer. He'd kept it secret but it finished him fast. I remember saying to him ...'

His strong gentle voice trails off and his eyes moisten and he looks away. We both take a sip of our drinks and right then, it's as if there isn't another person in the place. Existence is blocked out by emotion.

We sit as Derrick goes through the memory and I try to fathom his loss. In time, in his own time, he fixes back on me.

'I still haven't got over the loss of him. I'm still blessed with three lovely daughters. They all live in Meningie. One of them started working in the local surgery and she's been there for twenty-odd years and a few months ago the surgery recognised her for all her service and she's the big boss there now.

'I told her I'm very proud of her. Ellie, she's done it all off her own bat. No special treatment because she's an Aboriginal. Just got it all through hard work and being honest.'

As he's proudly talking of his other daughters, local buck Roy decides to crash our party because he's seen me talking with D and thinks there's stuff I need to know about the bloke across the table:

'Uncle D's a man of a lot of knowledge and he taught me a lot of things. Things about being an Aboriginal and about being a man. When I was young I played footy against him and I had to mark him. I was just a skinny kid and I looked at his huge shearin' hands and thought, what have I got myself into? He taught me a lot about football that day! I snuck a couple of goals in but Uncle D still came out on top of me. He was always at the forefront teaching us young fellas about the town and about the Coorong and we're all better for it.'

D does what blokes do when people say good stuff about them: deflects. He asks me if I have a fifty-buck note in my wallet. Yes I do, so I pull it out, hand it to him and he turns it over from Edith Cowan to David Unaipon and he asks if I have any idea what he's doing? I don't have a clue.

For the second time Uncle D points to the name on the front of his hat. And then to the fifty-buck note.

'This bloke David Unaipon was called the Australian Leonardo da Vinci, and he was born in same mission as I was over at Raukkan. And see that church just behind his right shoulder on the note? Well that's the church up there. Still exactly like that.'

It's my shout so I take the fifty and head to the bar, tell Ben that I need one for me, a boogidee for Uncle and one for Rod, oh and I think I'm going to need to extend my room to two nights. Ben smiles. 'Headed to Raukkan in the morning are we?'

It's rare, as rare as it is refreshing, to hear men praise men to their face in front of other men. It's usually only done in eulogies at funerals and at wakes, or at retirement dinners. But once it's known that I'm not simply just yarning with Uncle D, a steady stream of locals drops by our table because it's important for them that I know what an extraordinary person this bloke is.

But eventually D has to get moving (can we catch up again tomorrow?) and I'm beginning to need a feed so when this special person heads out, I make tracks for the dining room which you have to access from the road.

The much-vaunted Coorong mullet ('only have it grilled') is all that it's been cracked up to be. The relative tranquillity of the restaurant relaxes me and after some dessert I'm ready to head back to the bar, which has thinned by maybe 60 per cent while I've been gone.

So much so that Ben has time for a break on the pleasure side of the bar.

When Ben Reusch arrived in Meningie in 2015 on his fourth hotel resuscitation mission the town's pub was on life support.

'This was my biggest challenge. There were pigeons living on the verandah and in some of the upstairs rooms, the bottle shop wasn't working because the roller shutter door was jammed and there were nine full-to-the-brim 30-cubic-metre skip bins out the back, including one with twenty-eight broken televisions.'

He attacked on two levels: upstairs he replaced all the broken windows, turfed out the pigeons and made the eight guest rooms liveable. They're now all air-conditioned, with fully screened windows and the common room has a fridge, microwave, toaster and makings for your morning brew.

Downstairs he fixed the roller door, replaced the beer pipes and the carpet, fixed the plumbing throughout and gave it all a fresh coat of paint. There're now eight beers on tap. The refurbed dining room where I've just been serves dinner every night and lunch Wednesday to Sunday.

'We wanted to get the pub back to being the heart of the town, the hub of the community, for friends to meet and families to enjoy and we've made progress but we're not close to finishing.'

As Ben speaks he's suddenly grabbed in a headlock and kissed on the cheek by a wild-looking hirsute local in bright yellow cap who doesn't give a bugger if he's interrupting coz there's something he has to say.

'What this bloke has done for this town can't be described. He's a magic person who's set the town alight, made the pub a breathing centre for the town,' he gushes about Ben.

Steve 'Sticky' Ayres, whose seventy-eight year old father Ronnie still plays in the pub's darts team, is a fourth generation Meningie native but reckons that's no claim to fame. 'My granddaughter,' he boasts, 'is sixth

generation. Our family's been here almost as long as the pub.'

'I've been drinking here in this pub all my life. I used to come through the bar door and park my 1950 BSA Bantam here in the bar every Christmas but the local copper objected for some reason. Might've been because the bike wasn't registered and I didn't have a licence. Anyway one day I was doing doughnuts and burnouts in the dining room out there and I leant the bike over too much and the pegs ripped all the carpet up. They told me to park outside after that.'

Sounds reasonable. 'And whaddya reckon about the mowers?'

Ben says he was just getting to that.

Once the pub began to hum, Ben looked for magnets to bring more people to the town. He re-purchased a big block of adjoining land out the back, land which had been part of the original lease in 1867, and then Ben, a long-term petrol head shared his dream with some locals.

When they called him crazy, Ben showed them some YouTube videos of what he had planned and this convinced them. In June 2017 the Meningie Hotel hosted its first annual ride-on mower racing championships.

'I wasn't at all sure how it'd all go – whether people would show up or whether it'd be a disaster,' reflects the publican, smiling at the memory.

He needn't have worried. Over 600 people crammed in to watch more than sixty-five mowers race around the track marked out on the new block out the back. The caterers, who'd been more confident than Ben, had still underestimated demand and sold out in ninety minutes.

Hay bales were brought in as safety barriers and at day's end were distributed to the area's farmers. Over $6000 was given to local charities.

'It was just mind blowing. Race day was Sunday of the long weekend. On the Saturday the caravan park had a rock and roll day so people came from all over for the two days and then recovered or headed home on Monday.'

A very serious team of mower racers from Western Australia took out the top prize in the open division where mowers are highly modified with 450cc motorcycle engines and special tyres and have top speeds of around 150 kilometres per hour.

Out in the old stables behind the pub, Ben got working on the next year's mower using a 400cc Yamaha race bike engine. It was one of half a dozen local special builds for the 2019 races, which had won

designation as the SA State Championships.

'The great thing about this is not just the success of the day and the money it brings the town. It's the way organising it and hosting it draws the community together. The people on the committee can't wait to begin next year's planning and the town can't wait to watch it again.'

If I'm interested he'll crank up one of his mowers in the morning and give me an idea. 'Let's do it!'

I head out early next day to face a gale blowing in over the lake and get some shots of the pelicans doing the same, and then back to the pub where Ben and his good mate, who's had a relationship bust up in the Territory and headed back here and now has his motorhome parked out back and who's doing some bar work to pay his rent, are unloading a couple of the racing mowers.

I tell them about Rex Beaver way back at Jingellic. Same river, same outrageous spirit but very different mowing styles! One of the machines coughs into action and Ben dons his helmet and kicks it into gear.

Yep! It moves! Ben churns up the track, rooster tail of dirt exploding out the back as he gets in some lap time. Just what it'd be like with another dozen fighting for the racing line is incomprehensible. I pencil in June long weekend next year.

After the madness, we head up to the local bakery for a brew and pastry and we talk of his hopes, more expectations, that next year's crowd at the Mower Grand Prix will top the 1000.

I show this publican who's turned this pub, and with it this town, around, a 1924 review of the Lake Albert Races. It opens with, 'Each year a loyal band congregates at … Meningie, for the annual race meeting and the enthusiasm is just as intense as though it were a Melbourne Cup fixture.'

He smiles and says he hopes that'll be written about the ride-on races in a year or so.

And then I get this publican who's reinstated the traditions of boundless hospitality and a connection with racing the original clipping from 1891 in which the scribe wondered, 'what there [is] in … [Meningie] to attract people from Adelaide [a hundred miles away] and others from country towns at distances nearly as great.'

Ben's eyes tighten and his lips curl, 'Wonder no more.'

HOSPITALITY, JUST NOT ON YOUR TERMS

I'd tried maybe a couple of dozen times to ring the Coorong pub but never managed to get it to answer but then Ben back at Meningie had a mobile for Roberto the owner, so I'd tried that and eventually got a result.

I'd told the voice my spiel and yes he could be there at that time, or thereabouts, if he wasn't then he'd be on the way and just hang there. The pub probably wouldn't be open but he wouldn't let me down.

I have a few hours so I take the long way down, south through Coonalpyn and on to Tintinara. 'Fifteen hundred kilometres,' I muse, 'from Tintaldra and all that's changed is three letters!' Then it's a half hour blat back to the coast tempered only by the seeming desire of wildlife to be imminent road-kill and I'm turning left on the Princes Highway and then pulling up across from the Coorong Hotel Motel. And yes it's closed and yes it's deserted.

Sorry, but even the beginnings of this place seemed to have their share of shonk. In March 1861 William Allen's application for the Coorong Inn was knocked back but three months later he scraped in on the promise that he'd erect a stable within six weeks.

In March the next year Allen was granted a renewal but then in 1863 he was back before a sceptical Bench fighting for the future his pub. Allen argued that, 'the delay in the improvement of the premises arose from [him] not having yet been put in possession as owner of the land, but that this would shortly be done. The house would afford great accommodation to travellers in the district.' (This is a year after he claimed to be empowered to undertake the erection of a stable.)

The police were dubious, arguing that 'the present premises were very unclean, and that there were but two bedrooms, each of which was about 12 feet by 6 feet, and contained three beds.' No mention was made of the stability or indeed existence of any stables.

Allen must've been convincing enough to get his paperwork and having talked the talk he walked the walk two years later and offloaded the pub to another bloke with delusions of the place's potential.

This seems to've been the heyday of pubs on this rotten stretch of road. Places like the Tam O'Shanter Inn and the Corio Hotel are mentioned as being along the Coorong but by 1869 the Mount Gambier *Border Watch* noted that:

> *The Gazette contains the names of two Hotels for which licenses have been issued in the South-East for the [coming] year ... Meningie Hotel, Meningie and ... Coorong Inn, Woods Wells, Coorong.*

And so it remains – a hotel at Meningie and what's only ever been an inn at Policeman Point or Woods Wells. I use the time to walk down the side of the pub to the Coorong itself, grey and uninviting under a muted dappled sky that's weirdly birdless as it begins to rain.

When I get back there's a red car out front so I head to the door which is just ajar and a voice invites me in, but please close it behind. I don't lock it and before I sit down a woman comes in wanting a toilet. Wanting it pretty bad I'm guessing.

'We're closed.'

'So, no toilets?' in a disbelieving heavy accent which I reckon is South American Spanish.

'No, we've got plenty of toilets but we're closed.'

He gets me to lock the door.

'Some people have no respect for the "Closed" sign.'

This is Raymond, 'I have no idea why Ben thinks I'm Roberto,' and this is his place and it runs to his rules. And what's more he's happy to let you know at the very outset how this system works:

'We open when we want, we close when we want and we only rely on booking out our rooms to make money. I don't actually want people sitting at the bar getting pissed ... I'm not sitting there for three hours with John Smith hearing his effing sorrows which I've already heard a thousand times from other people about him. I'm not into that. I'm not a friggin' psychologist and I don't want to be.'

All said from behind a bar mat bearing the slogan, 'Fresh, approachable and easy to pick up.'

'This is a hotel, it's never been a pub, and I have to be responsible. I don't want people having too much to drink and then getting in their cars and driving off. It's not as though they can walk home from here. Everyone has to drive somewhere unless they're staying with us!'

Think, residential hotel with bar for residents just so long as they understand the drinks go off at 8.00 pm.

Raymond and his brother started thinking they had the right personalities for the hospitality game back in 2014 during one of their annual fishing trips down to 42 Mile Beach, about 30 kilometres south of here, from their place on Hindmarsh Island.

'We ... saw the For Sale sign and rang the agent and made him an offer and he told me to go and get effed, said that's too cheap and I said its only twenty-five K less than you're asking, so he said he wasn't going to insult the owner by taking the offer back to him. So ... another year goes by and we come back for the annual fishing trip to 42 Mile Beach and the sign's still out there, same real estate agent, everything.

'So my brother and I had a chat about it and thought it'd probably be better if we didn't ring him back as he'd probably remember us so we got a professional negotiator to ring him and after a few weeks we ended up getting it much cheaper than our first offer. We got it for land value. No licence. It'd been closed for three years, operating as a spiders' nest, full of vermin, and we weren't allowed to look inside because we were only buying the land and my brother is a builder and he said not to worry, whatever it is, we'll fix it.'

Sounded like a plan!

'Then we bought it and we came inside and we were horrified by how horrible it was – snakes, spiders, cockroaches – and it took me a year to get it into inhabitable state.'

They began welcoming guests (in their own special way) in 2017 and the place now has four rooms all with ensuites, with parking right outside the rooms.

Tonight there's just the single booking and they say they'll be wanting tea. Once they've arrived and are inside, Raymond'll lock the door just in case a passing traveller might want a feed or a drink to break his journey.

I'm not really concerned that there's not draught here, only cans and bottles. Since I'm not booked in, nothing's available and it's time to move on from this, the last pub on my journey.

Some of the bumper stickers I've collected on this journey down the river have been special; carefully worded to catch the character of the pub. It's a pity the Coorong Hotel doesn't have one. If it did, I'm sure it'd say, 'Don't tell us your story, we don't effing care!'

I unlock the door back out to the rain and thank Raymond for dropping by. And without trace of irony, tell this final publican that like so much of this trip, 'It's been memorable!'

This time it's a 50-kilometre direct squirt back north-west along the edge of the Coorong and soon another famous mullet.

A FIFTY-DOLLAR VIEW AND INLAND LIGHTHOUSE

Under pink morning skies I head south from the Meningie bakery and pull up a few doors down from the pub, duck into the post office and pick up a copy of Marianne's 150 history of the hotel. Then back north, left at the pub where Ben's already water-blasting the front smokers' area, and I'm on Narrung Road.

A bit under 10 kilometres along the southern edge of the lake, the road swings north-west for twenty minutes through lush dairy farms, then it's left at the T and suddenly right in front of me is the Fifty Dollar Church.

And it's a pretty honest job, just a tree added in the background on the note, and one of the chimneys deleted. In 1930 the Lower Murray tribes erected a cairn to commemorate the presence here a century before of Old Charlie Sturt, which I find a bit strange. Then a delish milkshake at the tiny local store and I'm heading east for the final punt of the trip.

The Narrung Ferry crosses the narrow Albert Passage, the strait between Lakes Alexandrina and Albert. Back before the geniuses decided to alter nature and turn these tidal estuarine lakes freshwater reservoirs behind the Goolwa Barrage, the tides ripping through these narrows must've been fun for the ferry masters.

To help them navigate across from Milang and down from Wellington, the Port Malcolm Lighthouse, the only inland lighthouse in Australia and which still dominates the scene, was erected in 1878. Its rotating white light guided passenger ferries and goods barges through the pass until declining traffic mandated its closure in 1931. We had visionaries back then so it wasn't pulled down, and whoever lives there now (lucky buggers) sure keep it sparkling.

The clipping I'd shown Ben just before I left of the race meeting in 1924 went on to note that 'Mr Keith Bowman ... brought off three races,' two of which were taken out by the same horse. Keith Bowman was noted as the owner of Poltalloch Station, on the lakeside just five minutes up from the lighthouse.

Poltalloch Station was first settled by Scotsman Neill Malcolm in 1839 but his plan to stock it, sorry, staff it, with Scottish peasants didn't come off. Maybe there was a backlog with 457 visas or maybe all the slave traders were busy in the Americas.

So he turned to beef cattle, oh, and salt. In 1843 a group of bizoids visited the area and reported that 'water of good quality is ... to be got by digging six to eight feet' and that salt 'of superior quality' in incrustations 'about nine inches thick' were being harvested from a lagoon on Poltalloch. Sounds like a place in balance.

I ring the number on the gate and assure the bloke who answers that I've not been on any other farm, have no other agricultural mud on my boots or tyres and he tells me I'm welcome, just stay away from the residences.

Under racing clouds a gale's blowing in from the lake, white horses are whipped up and lash the old jetty, No damned wonder a gent from Argyllshire on Scotland's wild west coast felt at home here, despite missing his peasants (and no doubt his pheasants).

Gorgeous old stone buildings, twin shearing sheds with domed roofs and a stately homestead are set back from the water while closer to the lake there's a solid rectangular building with the marks of sensitive restorative surgery at its corners and around the windows and doors.

It stands beside a smooth walkway, maybe 50 metres long, to a jetty. This used to be a railway where beasts and produce would be rolled to waiting ferries for shipment across the lake and thence to the markets of Adelaide.

As the waves and wind continue their endless task of wearing down the jetty I have visions of the only things that'd get me through a winter here, things that Neill Malcolm and his non-peasant group no doubt leant on: open fires and malt whisky.

Then it's north with the lake to the west, back over the punt at Wellington and, skirting the northern edges of Lake Alexandrina, through open fields and vineyards, a leisurely ride soon has me at the lakeside parking area at Milang.

GOOD PUBLICANS AND SMART PELICANS

A brief of pelicans patrols the choppy waters and a group of maybe a hundred terns rests from a gale on Milang's two jetties.

Inside the double-storeyed pub across the road there's refuge from the winds and soon I'm talking about the place with a (very) regular habitué.

'The quality of the pub depends on the quality of the publican.'

In a blue short-sleeved work shirt, wraparound sunnies atop a head that requires no comb, beard that's longer than his face and drinking a seven of something dark and dangerous, Doc reckons he's lucky, I'm lucky, we're all bloody lucky to be here having a drink because the, 'bloke who had the licence two blokes before this one did his best to kill this pub.'

'You'd be sitting at the bar talking with a mate about something you'd done and he'd just chime in that he'd done the same thing, only bigger and better and funnier and more dangerous.'

It got to the stage where the locals stopped drinking at the bar, taking their drinks and their laughs to the far tables or even outside. Then they just stopped coming.

'He stayed here for five long years, and I boycotted the place for the last four and a half. Starting drinking at the Langhorne Creek but then that was taken over and they decided to glam it all up and turn it into something else so I started drinking at Strathalbyn. I sure wasn't going to come back to this place!'

He wasn't alone. 'One Friday night we counted forty Milang locals in the bar at Strath, that's how dire he was.'

One night the bloke vanished into the darkness. Disappeared. Gone. He'd joined the patchwork legion of ex-hosts of this lakeside hotel – a list of publicans and licensees whom, in many cases because of, and in more than a few instances, despite, the pub has survived.

The place changed hands again in late 2019 and Doc likes their work: 'No-one has done as much to this place – fix it up – than these two. The beer garden out the back is looking the best since I've been here and there's regular live music like the concert out there tonight.'

He takes a swig from his evil looking seven. 'It's not even what they're doing, just the fact that they're making an effort that's bringing the people back here. It's a good pub again.'

We chew over the elements of a good pub and then I ask him about the eating habits of pelicans. The group I'd been watching across the road before I came in would paddle in a tightly huddled formation and then spread out into a flat line which then bent symmetrically at each end to form a circle which tightened until the birds all dived under to grab their feeds.

'Yep, they hunt in groups and they herd the fish into a tight group and then pounce. They're after baby bony bream which are small but in big schools at the moment,' he explains. 'Very smart birds, just don't feed 'em cutlets.'

'Eh?'

'Last week we had some city slickers here who were catching carp and thought they were doing the right thing by cutting them up and feeding them to the pelicans. But if you look at a pelican swallowing a fish, they always do it headfirst so the scales and fins will slide down their throat. But with the carp from the fishermen they were just throwing the bits back and choking on the bones that were catching on their throats.'

OJ's Corner

I tell Doc about Olly my pet olive python that would only eat live finches when it was young. Olly would grab the bird in its jaws, wrap its length around the bird and squeeze it to death, tightening its hold every time the finch would exhale.

'Then it would know to manoeuvre the bird around and start swallowing it headfirst so the feathers would slide in.'

'Exactly the same instinct,' says Doc. 'So I went over and they were real nice, just didn't have a clue about why the pelicans were all coughing with these lumps in their throats.'

Not sure just how many times I'm going to put that bit of knowledge to use but if a pelican ever pesters me for cutlets, I'll be able to explain that my refusal to comply is for its own good. Authoritatively!

The Pier Hotel wasn't Milang's first pub – by the time George Chalklen was first granted a licence for this place in 1867, the Lake Hotel up the road had already been serving local settlers for over ten years and was old enough to've survived its first serious fire.

But publican Chalklen, whose promotions claimed, 'beds and stabling unsurpassed in the colony', seems to've known how to run a pub and it was soon the town's preferred venue for debates for political office, meetings of local interest groups and pop-up workspaces for visiting health professionals and government inspectors.

In 1871 Chalklen sold the pub to George Cozens whose advertisements lyrically boasted the pub had liquids of quality 'undeniable' and 'accommodation unimpeachable'. The pub became the venue for all coronial inquests into local deaths and for major public meetings.

One of the early ones was hosted by the Bremer and Alexandrina District councils to address 'the Barley Question'. Governor Hindmarsh had permitted John Warren to build the colony's first brewery in 1838 as part of the push to have the new settlers shift their drinking habits from harmful spirits to healthy beer.

Seems the plan worked: over thirty breweries were operating in Greater Adelaide by the mid-1860s and the owners set about encouraging the farmers to sow barley. Problem was, they didn't want to pay a fair price for it so they formed a cartel and forced the prices down to below the cost of production.

Ah, there's a lot of enduring traditions in this country but squeezing and screwing farmers has been there from the start.

'Mr. James Rankine said that ... (t)he farmers had been completely sold by the brewers, who had led them to grow barley, on the understanding that they would get a fair price for it ... [but the] ... growers had now become convinced that they could not grow barley except at a loss ...'

The brewers attacked the quality of the local product, arguing their maltsters couldn't work with it, while the meeting no doubt downed pints of local brew made with imported malt without much thought to the irony.

In 1894 the obviously eloquent publican of the Pier wrote to the Adelaide *Advertiser* complaining of a proposal to increase the tax of local brew:

Sir—I have read the remarks of some of the members of the Upper House re the proposed duty on colonial beer. Now I think instead of any farther tax it would be juster if the Government placed a duty on hop beer, sugar beer, cordials, sodawater, lemonade etc, so that teetotallers might have a chance of paying something to revenue, to help to meet the working expenses of the country and for the protection they receive, instead of loafing on the moderate drinker as they do at present.

Beautifully put!

But then in 1907 the pub's boss was in involved in some seriously bad business. An Indigenous fella named Harry Hewitt was bashed to death at a camp where he lived up the road from the town and another resident, Tommy Lawson was charged with his murder while both were drunk.

At the inquest, Lawson swore that:

(h)e went to Mrs. Baxter's Pier Hotel with the flagon produced. He saw Mrs. Baxter at the back door, and she asked him what he wanted. He said he wanted a flagon of wine, and gave her the shilling and the two fish for it, telling her to book the balance. She gave him a flagon full of wine, and he took the wine to Yates' camp, where he saw the deceased and other natives, and they drank the wine.

Selling alcohol to Aboriginals was illegal and Baxter denied the supply:

Violet Baxter, licensee of the Pier Hotel, having been cautioned by the coroner, deposed that she remembered last Wednesday. She was at home. She knew Lawson, but did not know where he lived. She saw him once only, last Wednesday, in the yard of her hotel. She refused to supply him

*with wine, and gave him 6d. and tobacco for fish which he offered her ...
It was not true that she supplied Lawson with wine, as stated by him.
She did not remember supplying him with anything last week.*

Did you ever supply him with, intoxicants? — I refuse to answer.

The coroner returned a verdict that, 'Harry Hewitt met his death through a blow with a blunt instrument, used by Tommy Lawson, whilst fighting at the blacks' camp, Milang, with the deceased.'

That wasn't the end of the story. Baxter, 'licensee of the Pier Hotel, Milang, was charged at the Police Court ... by Detective O'Sullivan, before Messrs. Fischer, Griffin, and Binny, with having on January 23 supplied Tommy Lawson, an aboriginal, with wine. The defendant, who was represented by Mr. Tucker, pleaded not guilty.'

After a short hearing and even briefer retirement, the court announced that it didn't believe a bit of the publican's testimony and found the defendant guilty. For being instrumental in the cause of death of a person, Violet Baxter was fined a wrist slap amount of £5.

The Adelaide *Register* was appalled:

At Milang ... according to the evidence accepted as trustworthy by local justices, a hotel licensee acts the part of a virulent enemy of the good that has been done, [for aboriginals] and for the sake of a few paltry pence provides the aborigines with what has been over and over again demonstrated to be the most self destructive weapon that could be placed In their hands. The public do well to be angry, and to demand that more effective measures shall be taken to prevent a recurrence of the crime against their better nature.

For contributing to a death, Violet Baxter's licence was never held to be in jeopardy but ten years later, a far more serious offence endangered the very existence of the pub. Yep, the front door was left unlocked!

The *Southern Argus* was in full Terror Headline Mode, screaming, 'Pier Hotel, Milang, The Licence in Danger.' Publican Richard Wall was called upon by the Licensing Court to 'show cause why he, being a person holding a license under the Licensing Act, 1908 ... [and having been] convicted two several [sic] times, within a period of two years should not have his license forfeited.'

Selling beer to white locals after closing time was clearly more heinous than being implicated in a black death!

The defendant, sworn, said that in one case in which he was fined the police visited the house at twenty, minutes past six, and found the bar door unlocked, though it was shut. He had been out to the stable, and in shutting its door had dragged off two nails from fingers of his right hand, and when the police came he was upstairs washing the wounds. The bar door was shut but not locked.

The Bench, after consultation, decided that defendant should have another chance, the Chairman noting that he thought, 'there was not one licensee in a hundred who knew how drastic the Act was.'

Seems that for the next century the landlords boned up on the Act and pretty much kept out of trouble. The four months following the licensee's dark of night scarper in 2018 was the first time the pub'd been closed in its history, but the new owners needed that much time to get it right.

When it reopened on 20 August 2018, Doc reckons there wouldn't have been a single Milangite over in Strathalbyn. Their pub was back!

Doc's a local – had his first beer here when he was about sixteen, can remember about half a dozen publicans, only ever been barred by the infamous disappearer, and is glad the place is back on an even keel.

Not that all the old regulars are back. Doc remembers, 'At that table over there, there was a Kraut, a Pom, a Scot, an Irishman, someone from Belgium, an old Italian and they were all telling each other how hopeless they all were, and just having a great time pretty much every afternoon. But one by one they've all fallen off the perch.'

We talk about what makes a pub good and what doesn't and I mention the frustration of being a blow-in and being ignored as the bar staff serve locals who've approached the beer taps well after I've arrived and not getting served until they're all done. This has long been a criterion for me as to whether I stay or move right on.

Doc hits me with a new slant on the etiquette of service order.

'It's not that simple – they shouldn't feel obliged to serve people in order of them chesting the bar. The right way,' – and it's obvious that he's given some thought to this – 'is to first serve the person who's just come in from outside, from working in the heat. See, we all need that first drink but we only want the second one and need beats want every time.'

I feel ashamed, humbled before such wisdom. Over fifty years of drinking and that bit of common sense has never occurred to me.

Just up the bar a pair of blokes are having a laugh and a beer – like they've been doing for, they think, about fifty-six years. Nangkers and Alan have never had a blue, 'except when I jammed his head in a door at Loxton one time ... Oh and he once pushed me out of an almond tree.'

Nangkers reckons he has to be nice to his mate, if for no other reason, there's a long debt: 'This bloke here, he taught me to drink when we were both teenagers back in the '60s. He must've been a good teacher or I must've been a gifted student because ...'

His mate Allan cuts in to finish the sentence that's obviously been told more than once: 'He only needed one lesson!'

Alan is a Dunn – part apparently of a tribe of them in these parts.

OJ chimes in that 'there's so many of them they've renamed the Nine Mile road to Strath the Dunnbarrel Highway.' Everyone, at least all the men in the family are known as 'Dunny' but Alan's 'Dunny One' because 'I've been here the longest, been drinking here since I was sixteen and the legal age was twenty-one.'

But by the time he had his first pot here at the Pier, Dunny One was an experienced drinker.

'We used to take cattle down to the show in Adelaide, sleeping in the back of the cattle trucks, having a great time. When I was twelve my job in the evenings was to be barman for the team and I had to keep their drinks topped up out of long necks that we kept on ice. So I used to leave a bit at the bottom of each bottle and when I went back to get a newie, I'd swig the dregs of the old bottle. We slept in triple bunks and this one morning I woke up feeling very crook in the second bunk up and they'd tied me to the bed. Wasn't punishment, they reckoned it was for my own safety.'

Which gets OJ, looking fairly decent for eighty-three years old, started on his initiation:

First time the old man took me to the pub we were rabbit trapping, that's how we earned a living in those days and I was fourteen and I had a little bit of bum fluff and he said don't shave, I'm going to take you to the pub tonight when we're done.

Used to get two bob for a big one, one and thruppence for a medium one and nine pence for a small one. We used to have a bench in the old shed at the back and we'd skin them and Mum would wash them and Dad and I would look after the skins and hang them in the sunshine to dry them out.

Anyway off we went to work, we used to set 200 traps a night and a trap would go off and you'd run over get the rabbit and reset the trap and bring the dead one back to base. So after about six hours we were done for the night and we got to this pub and we had X amount of money. Me dad noticed this big bowl on the shelf behind the bar with this agitator in it, mixing it sort of thing and Dad said, 'we'll have two of them' but then said to the barman we were out of money. He said to the bloke behind the bar 'Are you interested in rabbits?' And the barman said, 'Yeah, I could use a couple' so Dad said, 'So we'll be right if I bring you in a pair of rabbits?' and the barman said, 'Sure,' so Dad went out and brought in two rabbits.

So I spent my first night on the grog drinking on the rabbits' account. Rabbit economy works just as good as the beer economy!

OJ tries to work out how long he's been coming to this pub and thinks it's gotta be a bit over fifty years. He graduated from rabbiting, moved to live in Port Lincoln and signed on with the railways, pulling up disused lines, and he figures it was in the '60s that the job brought him to Milang.

He and his boss used to drink out the back in a small room known as the Snake Pit, a small alcove with a table and just four chairs, and they'd drink there with a pair of local girls that they got 'tangled up with'.

Back home one time in Port Lincoln OJ's phone rang. His girlfriend was pregnant.

'I came down when she was in hospital having the baby but we weren't allowed inside in those days so I stuck a bunch of flowers on the fence and said they were for her.'

OJ kept in contact with the young woman, meanwhile having two sons with his wife in PL and then in 1988 a letter arrived. 'It was from Jodie, my daughter. Before I could write back the phone rang and it was her. She said she'd like to meet her father so I came over here from Port Lincoln and met them both and then I went back to Port Lincoln and stayed there about ten days and thought about things. Then I told my missus she could have the house and the life, I was moving to Milang. I've been here ever since.'

OJ religiously drinks just three days a week: Sunday, Wednesday and Friday. He says it's not just about him – he also wants to give his wife, whom he calls the War Office, respite from his madness.

Dunny One chimes in: 'My doctor told me to have two days off each week and I told him that when they invent nine-day weeks, I'll stay dry those extra two. I tried OJ's routine for a bit but I kept getting confused so it's just easier to have a drink every afternoon.'

From the end of the bar another old mate chimes in. I tell him that in his flannos, beanie and long beard, he could be a Bhagwan Shri Rajneesh doppelgänger.

'Just don't call me Grizzly Adams,' warns Rob when I tell him of my thoughts. 'A kid called Jethro took my photo and had it published and called me that and I hate it.'

Rob's been living in Milang for twenty-five years – started coming here in his school holidays to visit his grandfather who'd been given a government shack down near the lake as thanks for his service in the war. Took a liking to the place and when he could, moved up.

He has a close connection to the water and saw me photographing the terns down on the jetties before I came into the pub. 'They're the sign that there's bad weather on the way. When the terns visit it's for shelter,' and he warns me to get off the road before the weather sets in.

He reckons he can remember the benchmark flood of 1956 which washed away half of the jetty, 'And they never built it back. I've seen five ton of Mullaway sitting on that jetty, all caught in where those reeds are.'

The background is filled with chatter and laughter. Locals move freely from group to group, catching up on news, planning for the coming weekend.

Rob's empty glass stands on the bar for perhaps a minute before it's wordlessly replaced with a full one, payment taken silently from his change on the counter.

He smiles, 'A good pub's about feeling at home. To be successful in this game you have to have a good relationship between that side of the bar and this side of the bar. We've had our share of pretty ordinary ones but we've had a couple of beauties too. They have to have special skills for a small town like this with daily regulars but with a lot of regular visitors as well from Adelaide and out of town. Everyone thinks this is their own place and it's a juggling act. Thank god these people know how to do it.'

Postscript: John Kingsford Constable, known to all as OJ, passed away on Friday 12 February. His popularity in the town demanded that his wishes for no service were overridden, and as many as COVID would allow packed the bowls club two weeks later in tribute.

His son Darren explained that his dad used to be known as 'JC' and gladly accepted any religious affiliations. But years ago he was playing darts and chalking his regular initials on the scoreboard when a blow-in with the same letters told him he should use something else. It was confusing.

Not an issue at all – he rubbed it off and replaced it with 'OJ'. And when they asked what that meant he looked at the upstart: 'So you never forget, I'm the Original Jesus.' It stuck.

His mates made sure a plaque was stuck on the bar at the spot where OJ drank and when you drop by, you'll likely find a full beer beside it, in tribute to a real original.

WRECKS AND REPROBATES

I'm in the front bar of the Goolwa Hotel and the bloke next to me with eyes that close from the bottom up when he smiles, what my merchant seaman grandfather used to call a 'seafaring beard', hands as wide as a decent T-bone and short fingers as thick as some people's forearms and dressed in the blue polo with 'Goolwa Masts and Welding' on the chest asks me what angle I'm looking for at this pub.

I tell him it's probably going to be built around reprobate rivermen and wrecks and he just points to himself, laughs and says, 'Two birds.'

I've been told by a full hand of people along this trip, including a boatie mate back in Sydney, that when I get to Goolwa, the bloke to chase up is Randall, and two minutes after meeting him in the front bar of the Goolwa Hotel I'm already understanding why. He works on, plays on and all but lives on the river and might just have brackish water in his veins:

'I can't imagine not living near the water. Why would you do that? I could never live away from the river. I really respect people who don't and I one hundred per cent support their decision not to,' he explains with a nascent air of tolerance before revealing altruism is playing no part, 'because if they wisened up and moved here it'd be too bloody crowded.'

Randell, his suffering wife and three sons made this place just that little more crowded about twenty-five years back when they migrated from Victor Harbour because his main ship chandlery business was in Goolwa and 'I was driving to work with the sun in my eyes and then driving home in the afternoon with the sun still in my bloody eyes so I thought, jack this so we moved here.'

Goolwa Masts and Welding is one of several business that keep him busy and when the water calls and the breeze is whispering his name, there's his staff of Rotten Ronnie 'who can find any rot in any boat', Long John 'who's just under seven-foot tall', and Big Al 'who can put any man in the shade' who're able to keep the place ticking over like the bilge pump in a leaky boat.

His sons became musicians and Randall reckons that makes for a pretty good life but it's a poor business decision: 'A musician is a bloke with $5000 worth of equipment which he crams into a $500 car and drives 50 miles to work all night for $5.'

He's on the water twice, usually three times a week, sometimes it's just alone for pleasure but mostly it's with other craft and usually there's a challenge involved.

'We do three types of sailing. Friday nights just around the cans in the pond and the Saturday or Sunday races are destination things to Narrung or Milang, and there's always a party at the other end.'

No-one ever doesn't stay the night. Firstly it'd be dangerous but more importantly it'd be unsociable and for this bloke who'd been racing sailing boats for over fifty years, 'as you get older you enjoy the banter more'.

Then there's 'the important stuff'. Every fortnight during the season, the vintage boat club races and Randall heads out on his 1933 timber yacht with his game face on.

'You win the vintage and you get bragging rights for two full weeks and around this town, that's valuable!' I ask him if he's ever had a win and been quiet about it and he looks at me like I've told him a dog ate his sails.

Steve looks over from behind the bar and asks incredulously, 'Why don't you just ask him if he's ever been quiet about anything?' And then suggests Randall tells me about 'the cruise and the overseas trip you took your wife on.'

'My wife'd had a tough year at work so I promised her a cruise and an overseas trip and she was really looking forward to it and sorted her passport out and everything. So I took her to Kangaroo Island and we lived out the back of the ute for a week. Paradise. Then we got back on the Friday in time for the yacht races and then the next morning we sailed up the river to Tailem Bend and back to Narrung. When we were leaving there we got flattened by 45 knots of wind, bent right over so she had to lower the sails so we could get back upright but we got home and that was the cruise and the overseas trip. Was great. Just a pity I couldn't get any duty free!'

He's resigned to never being considered a local. 'If you come here from out of town, you're not considered a local unless your grandfather helped build the barrages and your father worked on the old ferry, but if you come from Victor Harbour, that's still not enough and you're never going to be accepted.'

'Why are they treated differently?'

'It's all because of the '57 grand final when Victor Harbour played Goolwa, and Victor Harbour kicked a goal after the final siren to win the match and they reckon the umpire was paid off.'

Seems an age to hold a grudge and later, when I'm safely out of range, I do some checking. Victor Harbour sure did win the pennant in 1957 but their GF opponents were Encounter Bay. The only time Victor Harbour's ever been recorded as winning a game with a kick after the final siren was Mark Davis's effort in 1986 but that was against Langhorne Creek and the only time Goolwa's been involved was in 1980 when their Ian Milne booted a big one to beat Yankalilla 85–81.

Later, after Randall's headed off, John and Kelvin take the same seats at the bar. Kelvin's been in Goolwa all his life and was bussed to primary school over in Victor Harbour when he was a ticka. And Randall was one of his classmates.

Kelvin remembers Randall as a pretty brash kid even back then, but he especially recalls the school bus driver:

'He was really short, not much taller than us primary kids and his legs weren't long enough to get to the pedals. So he tied blocks of wood to the bottom of his boots and that way his feet reached the pedals but his left arm was still too short to reach over to the joey box, (the low range gear shifter that was to the left of the main gear lever.) So one of the kids used to have to stand beside the driver in the well at the front door and when the driver with the blocks of wood tied to his shoes would press in the clutch, the kid

would have to change gears. Ten-year-olds double shuffling through gear boxes with no synchromesh. Every trip was an adventure.'

And no, Kelvin hasn't got a clue how the bloke drove home empty.

I tell 'em about Randall's theory of why, as an immigrant from Victor Harbour, he'll never be a local and both laugh. Steve behind the bar laughs.

John starts telling stories about footy in the district – about how it's serious but not too serious – and how training sessions are all ball work, no need for conditioning. He tells of how the brother of 'Turtle' (whose son is 'Yabbie') was a great centre half-back and was courted by Port Adelaide 'and when he fronted for a trial in late January they asked him what sort of pre-season training he'd been doing.'

'How do ya mean?'

'Well have you been running, doing sprints, any weights work in the gym?'

'Nah, never been in a gym.'

'Well you look in decent nick.'

'Yeah well I row the boat down the Coorong every morning and set the traps and then I walk through the sand dunes and set about 50 rabbit traps and then row back in the arvo and clear the lines and get the rabbits and row 'em all back to our place. The scout looked at his clipboard. "Pre-season training ... tick."'

But no. These blokes know football, especially the local comp and that one's just a myth – just maybe, some locals invented this in retribution for the endless current of fortnightly immigrants bragging about the exploits of a little red boat.

RIVER MURRAY.

AN ORDINARY DAILY
AT ONE O'CLOCK.
CHOICE   HORSES
ENGLISH   GUNS and
ALES   DOGS
ON DRAUGHT.   for SPORTSMEN.
By Yours Respectfully. Jno Varcoe.
WINES SPIRITS & CORDIALS
GOOD   STOCK
STABLES.   YARDS.
HORSES & GIGS ON HIRE.

The reason I'm interested in any current wrecks is because this town's history isn't just connected with shipwrecks, this pub is actually built around one.

Around the time that Goolwa was being gazetted as a government town in 1853, the three masted barque *Mozambique* was leaving Cork, Ireland, with a load of coal for the settlement at the Swan River. The weather was rubbish but after 155 days it arrived safely at what today is Fremantle.

There it was repaired and the following August 4th took on twenty-four passengers and headed east. More foul weather eventually forced the captain to run the ship ashore a bit to the south of the Murray mouth. He managed to do this without loss of a single life of the forty-six people on board.

Meanwhile over in Goolwa, a bloke named John Varcoe was busy in the later stages of constructing the eponymous Goolwa Hotel, for which he'd been granted a licence back in December 1853. Varcoe heard about the *Mozambique*'s demise and ordered his workers to stop building the pub and get down to the Coorong to help the rescue effort. Eventually all the ship's survivors were carried to Goolwa where Varcoe fed them and put them up.

The captain of the barque then returned to the wreck and oversaw salvage operations. In appreciation of his efforts, John Varcoe was presented with cedar tables and chairs from the barque plus some other stuff. But most colourfully, the captain presented the publican with the ship's figurehead, a wide-eye, armless, raven-haired, pursed-lipped, young woman in maroon top and a matching set of earrings and necklace. (If you're going to do a face-plant in a beach on the other side of the world, it's always good to wear nice clothes!)

She was originally mounted over the stables at the rear of the hotel but then in 1913 was moved upfront to the parapet, sustained for decades by a 10/– (that's ten shillings, kids!) annuity for her upkeep from a grateful *Mozambique* passenger. (Imagine offering to pay maintenance of the bust of a dead woman you've never been married to! Different times!)

For seventy-five years, battered by every extreme of weather, probably except snow, she adorned the roof of the pub, keeping her blue eyes on the changing face of what is now Cadell Street. Then, after a much-needed makeover in 1988 by local experts Norm and Wyn Paech, she was moved inside to the more genteel and befitting position high on the wall of the pub's back bar. A body double took her mantle outside.

The rescued cedar tables and chairs are a feature display just off the throbbing bistro area at the back of the pub which is more a licensed museum, but there's a far more basic remnant of the *Mozambique* than these mere ornamentations.

The ship's timbers and masts were also salvaged from the Coorong's sands and the main spar and 20-metre mast were retrieved right on schedule to reinforce the pub's main floor. Steve the barman tells me they'd love to extricate the spars but no-one can work out how to do it without damaging the wood or collapsing the pub.

In 1857 John Varcoe added the second storey to the Goolwa Hotel. Now, in the wash-up of the *Mozambique*'s grounding either an intact staircase was retrieved or a load of cedar planks was salvaged. Whatever happened, when the pub grew up, the staircase was constructed from the bones of the ship. And it's still there today – looking stunning and creaking less than my knees when I give it a climb.

As I'm checking it out Michael, brother of behind-the-bar Steve and son of the owners comes by with an information sheet on the pub. And he explains the conundrum of the stairs.

'Because they are out of code, the owners are permitted to use them but we're not allowed to have guests upstairs, but because they are all heritage listed, we're not permitted to modify or alter them at all.'

And that's why there's no longer any accommodation upstairs – no access to the balcony which bathes in the morning sun.

The Adelaide *Register* of Monday 28 August 1854 carried a story titled, 'The Stranding on the Mozambique' in column six of page 2. It detailed the ship being 'driven on shore on the sea-beach outside the Coorong,' one week previously. It detailed the discovery of the survivors, quoting a bloke named James Law:

'I had been to the Salt Creek in my boat, with flour, sugar, and tea, for Mr. Bradford, whose station I was at last Monday week. When I had made about 30 miles on my way back, I went on shore, and having pitched my tent for the night and lighted a fire, I heard some one "cooeying." This was

This regatta was spread over two days and covered both sailing and 'pulling' (oared) races and one event was described as, 'nearly three hours (of) beautiful sailing, and with many illustrations of fine seamanship.'

Once the sails were furled and the sheets knotted:

'(a) large party of gentlemen, promoters of the sports, partook of a sumptuous dinner,' with good wine, at Varcoe's Goolwa Hotel, on which occasion every loyal, local, and complimentary sentiment was received with due honour; and that evening, as well as the day, will live long in the recollections of all present.

In his hospitality toward the *Mozambique*'s survivors and their subsequent gifts to him, and in his sponsorship of the settlement's regatta, John Varcoe had cemented his pub's connection to the river and the people working and playing on it.

Varcoe continued to reinforce the connection whilst no doubt enjoying himself more than a tad. In subsequent years reports from the regatta mentioned him regularly:

The boats were steered by Messrs. Varcoe, of Goolwa; Tripp, Port Elliot; and Bobinson, Encounter Bay; and who were severally dressed in a peculiar uniform corresponding in appearance with the dress worn by their respective crews.

....

The sailing boats took their places as follows:
Victory-Steered by the owner, Mr. Hughes.
Wasp-Mr. Cooke, dressed in the lull uniform of the
Yacht Club.
Sylph-Mr. B. Varcoe.

...

... all seemed satisfied with the day's enjoyment. A considerable number left immediately for their several homes, while the remainder remained to close the festivities of the day with a dinner at the Goolwa Hote'.

last Monday night. I went towards the place and the first person I met was the captain of the vessel, who said they had been wrecked and had nothing to eat. He said there were four females and some children with them, and he would be greatly obliged if I could render them any help. I had only 40 lbs. of flour, which I gave him, and told him that I was going to the Elbow [the Goolwa], and would take the females and children with me if he had any men to assist in rowing the boat.'

In the next column on the very same page was a longer article, still about matters marine, but in a very different tone. It was news of an event which would become an annual affair and which was the first in a tradition which Randall and his mates continue to enjoy. It was headed, 'Goolwa Regatta' and began:

Thursday last was a high gala day at the Goolwa, it being the first anniversary of the launch of the Eureka, the first cargo vessel provided for the Murray traffic. A number of the enterprising settlers in that district had for some time previous determined upon celebrating an event so intimately connected with the navigation of the Murray, and after mature deliberation it was determined to do so by a regatta.

'That,' the 'larrikin of the lake' told me sucking on the long-neck before he'd left 'is the sort of thing I think I could enjoy!'

A few years back Randall's wife applied for a job at the local day care centre and they asked her if she had qualifications and experience working with children. The qualifications weren't a problem – she had the diplomas and certificates. And experience with working with children? She wondered why the interviewer would have any doubt, asking in return, 'haven't you met my husband?'

But this bloke has a serious side and for him the welfare of this town (despite him being resigned to never being considered a local), and water ain't for joking about.

'From the turn of the century this town had a drought and lost two and half metres of water, just a trickle between us and the island but we still managed to get a dozen boats out on the water to race because we were too effing dumb to chuck it in!'

The community had stickers reading, 'Goolwa Needs Water Now' made and they were more common around here than Conargo Pub stickers on country utes. While the water was low, working bees were organised to 'clean all the rubbish off the bed, all the old bottles and gas containers and all sorts of rubbish and glass, and wrecks', but just as the lake's level finally began to rise, the GFC hit.

'The town was in the doldrums for eight years and so we had new stickers made that said 'Goolwa, better than ever' because the water was back and the beaches and swimming areas were all clear of underwater rubbish.'

I tell him that this pretty much sorts out the 'riverman' angle for my yarn about this place, so what about the 'wreck' perspective? What about his 'two birds'?

He finishes off the dregs of this beer. 'My inexorable decline into wreckage is a work in progress.'. And with that, he's off to what he claims is the 'job from hell' and what I take to be just another myth of the Murray!

I rise early the next morning and I head over the bridge to Hindmarsh Island, east past the new swanky marina estates with a jetty for every dwelling, and then an abrupt right, and a few minutes later I'm bracing against the wind coming into my face from the south-west.

Between me and the ocean is firstly a narrow waterway and then the tip of a long sandy finger of land stretching back to my right. A couple of 4WDs are parked on the far beach adjacent a dredge in the middle of the narrow opening and at the end of a line of buoys.

This is the very mouth of the Murray – where any molecules that have survived from Cowomblat Flat up from Benambra and those that've joined the flow along the way will be set free into the briny.

For whatever political and environment reasons, the river's flow now demands the barge be out at the mouth working non-stop to keep it open.

It's not quite dawn and the colours change quickly in the gathering light. My drone battles the gales coming in from the Bight and a pair of terns check it's no bird of prey.

A row of 'shacks' lines the foreshore of the inlet, each one of them a private residence apart from the still sleeping cafe at the parking area.

I'm at the end of this trip and there's not a pub in sight. But I guess just like Ava Gardner and her mythical quote, that's not really the end of the world.

SUPPORTERS

Projects such as this require the support, inspiration, encouragement and the faith of many people. These are (hopefully) most of the folks who've sustained me during the journey. I thank you all.

Shayna Millar
Peter Thoeming
Leah Thomas
Pauline Ladhams
Ravu Truscott
Jeff Byron
Mark Bacon
Myles Baden-Powell
Steve Fiume
Liam Deppeler
Rory Gaynor
Tammy Walters
Renne Hawkett
Alex Baden-Powell
Richard Hulme
Tracey Hulme
Jennifer Connor
Colleen Wright
Bruce Wright
Pauline Archer
Bryan Buchanan
Melissa Johnston
T & S Travalos
Neil Lewis
Fagan Fulton
Peter Knight
Rose Grieve
Bruce Thompson
Chuck & Margaret Hahn
Jillian Wilkins
Phil Marr
A, H, L & B Gray

Tony & Janice Cousins
Adam Lockhart
McArthur Wheeler
Tony Durkin
Sarah T Hamilton
Karen Anderson
Jim Beck
Brenda Milner
Bec Croft
Carla Constance
Mark Sewell
Matt Blair
Jim Davidson
George Kirsh
Tim Lynch
Crooked Mick
Fiona Schultz
Simon Brown
Ben Reusch
Stewie McLean
Stephen Joyce
Denise Perry
Bob Baker
Stuart Paxton
Christi Van Andel
Phil Coysh
Brad Schultz
Wendy Akselsen
Darrin Akselsen
Tanya Gerrie
Justin Rowe
Anita Donlon

Trevor Bagley
Sandra Moon
Tracey Woodhouse
Murray Williams
Alan Macdonald
Rod Woodruff
Ash Walker
Geoff Barnett
Gregory S Moore
Norma Heeley
Diane Noble
Uncle D Meningie
Michael Roche
Dean Duncan
Thea Askew
Tony Smith
Megan Smith
Jeanette Smith
Shane Wilson
Karl Wilson
Geoff Green
Bernie Pramberg
Filthy Phil, Morgan
Brett Wallis
Luke James
Billy Nissen
Graham Akehurst
Tim Stevenson
Arlene Gippert
Jeffrey Byron
Sue Wade
Andrew Varley

Les Broadhurst
Cathy Bowman
Nancy Shearer
Colin Brooker
Deni Griffiths
Mick Lawler
Mark Ford
Sharon Quagliotto
Alan Quagliotto
Stuart Woodbury
Sally Bryant
Peieta Mills
Stuart Glasson
Mel Eaton
Greg Rose
Peter Tasker
Rory Whelan
Robert Bruce
Carl Schmid
Craig Wissell
Nigel Allen
Graham McCullouch
Joe Lannan
Michael Fischer
Liz Hardy
Kieran Volpe
Julie Springler
Andrew Rawsthorne
Lynn Wilson
Colleen Sommer
and especially:
Natalie Whelan

CAPTIONS

Conventions:

Due to the Office of the Bleeding Obvious being closed, where the subject of an image is a no-brainer, like a shot of a punt in a chapter about a punt, no caption is provided. Where more than one image appears on a page, the captions begin top left and continue clockwise unless otherwise stated.

p. 2   'Beachy' host at the ex-'Bogan' Mannum Hotel with customer Di.

p. 9   The bar at the Merbein Hotel.

p. 11   Tooleybuc – bridge and pub.

p. 15   bottom right: Johnno, host at Benambra; Chris, the walking man.

p. 18   Court House Hotel, Corryong, original double-storey section at rear.

p. 20   'Old Grumblebum'; Hume; Welcome fire; 'Sheepdog'.

p. 25   Fanciful Headstone; Towong Racecourse grandstand.

p. 26   Burnt out ranges in the distance behind the Biggara Bridge over the Murray.

p. 27   Lush dairy fields at the foot of burnt hills beside the Upper Murray Road.

p. 28   Noel and Brett at the bar of the Tooma Inn.

p. 34   Tooma views/publicans Kris and Trevor.

p. 35   With the lower Alps as a backdrop, Charlotte gently pushes her cattle along the road north of the Tooma Inn.

p. 42   Betty Walton; Betty at the pianola; Morning brew on the Murray banks; Betty's store.

p. 45   Phil Coysh.

p. 46   Peter Sutherland.

p. 50   The Walwa Hotel.

p. 52   Echidna in the burn zone; 'Lankey' Peter getting some camel love, Lankey's Creek turns out to farewell its WWI soldiers (Image: State Library Victoria); The ruins of the shanty.

p. 56   Rex mowing the road.

p. 58   The old Jingellic Bridge; Beaver's Bridge; Rex Beaver in the sunshine.

p. 62   The ex-Dora Dora Hotel; the Murray at Talgarno, Alf at the old bar (Image: Di Bennett); Clipping from this place's heyday.

p. 66   The punt high and dry during the millennial drought; Amanda with her flock.

p. 74   The Bethanga Bridge, only bridge in two Australian states.

p. 75   Misty morning on the back road to Bethanga; Bethanga Hotel.

p. 76   Max Mitchell, Bethanga.

p. 80   Garry training the staff.

p. 91   The blowhole at the Court House Hotel.

p. 92   Wahgunyah's Mick.

p. 96   Deano and Shirl (right).

p. 104   The Monday Arvo Cockies' Club; Candles without his hand on a beer; Rolly.

p. 112   Bottom: The Yarrawonga Weir – lowest lock-less weir on the Murray.

p. 114   Jess at the 'Finger'.

p. 121   Archie, Ralph and Mongrel, Cobram.

p. 127   Raymond Jones.

p. 132   Looking upstream, Murray on the right with the Edward branching to the left.

p. 133   The fence of cleavage, just out from Mathoura.

p. 137   The Henry Hopwood obelisk; Upper Murray flag; Portside of the Star Hotel.

p. 138   A Hopwood banknote; Hopwood's ferry; bottom centre: Larry Foley's Hotel in George Street, Sydney.

p. 141   Looking down the Campaspe to its confluence with the Murray. Not much's changed in 100 years.

p. 148   Bintang and his accomplice in the Torrumbarry bar.

p. 150   Top: Bones; Max gets a stroke.

p. 160   The bridge and the Royal (Bridge) Hotel; Raffle dunnies; Julie the boss.

p. 161   The Barham Hotel corner when the murder went down; bottom left: A side-wheeler at the wharf.

p. 165   Barham's genuine Bills horse-trough.

p. 166   Suzie in the Hall of Death; Slippery serves another over the burl; Colin works the froth of another.

p. 172   Wall drawings and messages, Mariner caravan (image by Charlie Urwin), Mariboat (image by David Vincent).

First published in 2021 by New Holland Publishers
Sydney • Auckland

Level 1, 178 Fox Valley Road, Wahroonga, NSW 2076, Australia
5/39 Woodside Ave, Northcote, Auckland 0627, New Zealand

newhollandpublishers.com

A record of this book is held at the National Library of
Australia.

ISBN 9781760792077

Group Managing Director: Fiona Schultz
Project Editor: Liz Hardy
Designer: Andrew Davies
Production Director: Arlene Gippert
Printed in China

10 9 8 7 6 5 4 3 2 1

Keep up with New Holland Publishers:
f   NewHollandPublishers
◎   @newhollandpublishers